201
Inspirational
Stories
of the
Eucharist

Compiled by
Sister Patricia Proctor, OSC

Foreword by
Father John Vaughn, OFM

Inspirational Stories Edited by
Anne Marie Lillis

Poor Clare Illustrations by
Sister Eileen Lillis, OSC

A Called by Joy Book

Franciscan Monastery of Saint Clare
Spokane, Washington

www.calledbyjoy.com

ISBN 0-9728447-1-6

Library of Congress Control Number: 2004110069

First Printing September 2004
Second Printing March 2005

Cover by Mike Cox
www.alphaadvertising.com

Dedication

We lovingly dedicate these pages
to our beloved
Pope John Paul II,
who continues to inspire us
with his love of God
and selfless giving
to the people of God.

With Prayerful Thanks

This book is made possible because I live in the best community of sisters in the whole world. At present there are six of us (well, yes we could do with a few young vocations) but in the meantime the six of us who work together, pray together, play together and support each other's projects totally are graced by God in this wonderful vocation. No job is ever undertaken without full community support and backing. My name may be on the cover—but it's only for show—because Sister Mary Rita Dolan and Sister Rita Louise McLean and Sister Jane Wade and Sister Marcia Kay La Cour and Sister Colleen Byrne should easily be included there as well. As I write this three of the sisters are out weeding, planting and watering the garden, one is answering correspondence and another is doing other office work after taking a break from picking raspberries all morning (that's our abbess, Sister Mary Rita). In a small community one hand off the plow makes a difference but my sisters are so behind this book—that they have sweetly (okay, they sometimes think I should take a break and go pull a few weeds) but for the other 98% part besides those few weeds I didn't pull they have made the time available for me to put this book together. Thank you sisters—you truly are *sisters* in every sense of the word!

But I can't say it has been *only* a community project, because the Lord has lovingly roped in a whole other net load of laborers for the harvesting as well.

First I must sincerely thank each and every author who contributed their story. You are the book! Your living witness stories make real the very present love of our God in the Eucharist. Thank You!

Secondly, I must totally thank Anne Marie Lillis for her wonderful job of editing each story. I think you have done an excellent job in retaining the message, and heart of each story and yet helped in those places where grammar, spelling and a bit of tender loving care was needed; you provided just the right touch. As everyone knows who reads my daily Peace Cards—although I love to write—grammar, punctuation and convoluted sentences seem to abound!

Thirdly, this book would absolutely not even be close to the gem it is without our community friend and star of the book, Dale Duncan. Dale didn't do the writing and he didn't do the editing—but he took those hundreds of bits and pieces and made the book. His book designing is equal to none. But he did more than that! He read the stories over and over and over—proofing the proofs—so that you the reader would be able to do just that. Read!

No, I'm not finished with my thanks yet. In fact I am just working up to it! My right hand friend and help mate is Barb Ries. She typed and typed and she typed and typed and yes she typed some more! Whew! The wonderful section of Communion Prayers and Novena is available for you only because of Barb's dedicated fingers. The booklet we had to work from was printed in 1953 and though I have been praying faithfully from it since the time I entered in 1981—it was a bit tattered, a bit gray and very, very small print! In fact eighty-three pages of very small print. I am surprised Barb is still talking to me after that project! Thanks Barb!

Oh! But I have other thanks from Barb's corner of the room, because Barb's daughter Kristina was also roped in to make this book happen. Dale, Barb and Kristina spent (I am not even going to guess) how many hours, going over the proofing—one reading aloud, the other marking up the pages. Whew! Who ever thought how many hands go into making one book happen?

Is there more? Of course there is! In our federation of Poor Clares we have one priest, companion and friend who has stood by us for many years, Father Nicholas Lohlkamp, OFM. Father is a moral theologian, author, teacher and outstanding friar and for many years had graciously accepted the appointment from Rome to be the Spiritual Assistant for our Bentivoglio Federation of Poor Clares here in the United States. Father Nick actually bit the bullet and looked over this book and gave advice on stories that needed to be tweaked a bit or in a few cases actually removed because the theology was a bit unclear or not relevant to the theme. His help was immeasurable! In the end I did have a few stories that he did not have a chance to check over—but hopefully following his suggestions over the others—they are fine. Padre Pio will have to be the backup for those as we rush this manuscript to press!

Then I have to thank all my friends at Park Press who have helped us below, above and beyond the call of duty in printing this book. Going the extra mile is just a common occurrence for them. Kathy Czech who is my main contact with this Catholic family business that does a big job when it comes to book printing. They are excellent par none.

I know there are many more friends who have and are entering into this wonderful adventure with us of promoting the Eucharist. I ask God to bless each of you and reward you abundantly for your goodness in spreading this Gospel message.

I close with just one final thanks and that is to the wonderful people at Saint Anthony Messenger Press who have agreed to take on the full distribution of this book for us. They have been wonderful to work with in the past and we are looking forward to many years of working together in the future.

With grateful thanks,
I ask God to bless you with All Peace and All Good!

Sister Patricia Proctor, OSC

Table of Contents

Stories by Poor Clare Nuns

Appendices

Foreword

I am one of those people who have had the great privilege of assisting at the Mass of Pope John Paul II, and of watching him distribute holy Communion. His reverent actions are a silent sermon. You know that he believes deeply and lovingly in the real presence of Jesus in the Eucharist.

One time the pope came to our international college in Rome, and began his visit by going to the college church. We were all on our knees, waiting for him to rise. Minute after minute he knelt, deeply absorbed in prayer. It was adoring prayer, and prayer for all the needs of the Church and the world. After a good ten minutes he rose, refreshed once again after a long day of work, and continued his visit with energy. I came to realize the source of his strength: the Blessed Sacrament.

The Blessed Sacrament is the greatest treasure of the Church. It tells us who we are, what we should become, and what it is: the body of Christ. It is the goal of all who work for unity among Christians, and it is the way to achieve that unity. Devotion to the Blessed Sacrament is a personal encounter with Christ, whether this is during Mass or at eucharistic adoration.

Sometimes we get the impression that our current culture in the United States is one of "if you don't like it, don't do it" or "it's good if it makes you feel good." I don't think this truly represents committed Catholics, especially younger adults. I think this group in particular is bringing us back to valuing the most precious gift we have: the Blessed Sacrament.

The stories you will read in this book are samples of the living faith of *ordinary* Catholic Christians. Their experiences are a witness to the presence of Jesus in His Church and in the Eucharist. It is the same Lord who is with us in several different and real ways. May these stories help your faith grow as they have helped mine.

Sister Patricia Proctor, a cloistered Poor Clare nun, is especially qualified to edit these stories. St. Clare, the foundress of the Poor Clares, had a special devotion to the holy Eucharist, which her daughters have continued in their monasteries throughout the world for eight centuries. Their cloistered life is spent with the Blessed Sacrament as its center. Like Clare herself, although they are not seen, their life and devotion to the Eucharist is a powerful sermon and witness to the presence of Jesus in His Church—of which the holy Eucharist is the great sign, the Blessed Sacrament.

Father John Vaughn, OFM
Ex-Minister General

Preface

In the past few months, great energy and enthusiasm have emerged from this Poor Clare Community because of this book! As the stories began to flow into the monastery, we grew more and more convinced that Our Lord in the Eucharist wanted these simple testimonies of His love and presence among us to be shared.

Today, the lives of young and old are filled with a great need for understanding and help. The cry of the poor can truly be heard, and it is with this cry echoing in our hearts that this Community of Poor Clare Sisters encouraged and, in prayer, supported Sister Patricia to work on this book.

The truth of Jesus' presence among us must be shared. It must be made known that there is a heart beating in love that's waiting to ease the burdens, pain, and loneliness felt by so many.

As these stories relate, many people have had the experience of this loving God strengthening and guiding their lives through His eucharistic presence. It has been a great desire of all the sisters in this monastery to work and pray for the increase of faith and knowledge of Jesus living among us in the Eucharist. It is before this Jesus that all the petitions and needs of the people are placed, and it is through Him that help and answers come.

For all of you who read these pages, we have asked this loving God to fill your heart with peace, and your steps with strength to continue walking the way to eternal glory!

Sister Mary Rita Dolan, OSC, Abbess
Monastery of Saint Clare
Spokane, Washington

Introduction

When I learned that the dear sisters of St. Clare Monastery in Spokane, Washington, were planning a publication entitled *201 Inspirational Stories of the Eucharist*, I wrote to Sister Patricia Proctor offering a story of the Eucharist from my life. I did not expect the honor of writing the "Introduction" to this wonderful work. Very happily I accepted to do so.

In 1973, I received an appointment which was requested by the Poor Clare Nuns of Perpetual Adoration. It was to guide them in writing their new constitutions. After definitive approval by the Holy See, these constitutions foster contemplative life centered around the Blessed Sacrament. They are the way of life in dozens of Poor Clare monasteries worldwide including Europe, India, and the USA. Mother Angelica and the nuns at Our Lady of the Angels Monastery in Hanceville, Alabama, also follow these constitutions as Poor Clare Nuns. Jesus in the Blessed Sacrament is honored and loved by these daughters of the Church.

In a retreat conference, by way of teaching what a treasure we have in the sacrament of the Eucharist, I relate the following anecdote.

One weekday morning two people went into church where Mass was just beginning. One person was there to attend Mass before beginning her day of raising the children and tending the home. The other fellow came in to get out of the rain. He had a comfortable bench near the door and could see everything that was going on. When they left the church that morning, each was asked the same question: "What happened in there?"

The man said, "Well, I got out of the rain and sat on a comfortable bench where I could watch everything. A man in a colorful robe was standing up in front near a table where there were candles and flowers. He spoke to the people and read from a book. At one time he offered the people present a small piece of bread and a drink of wine, and when it was over, he let the people go. That's what happened, I was there."

The woman was asked the same question, "What happened in there?"

She said, "I was present at the most sacred action that can take place here on earth. There were only a few of us present, but we gathered around the Lord, and He brought us mystically to the foot of the cross. There, He offered Himself in sacrifice for the salvation of the world. In the glory of the Resurrection, He breathed on us the forgiveness of sins, and gave us the gift of divine life in the Spirit."

She continued, "Under the form of bread and wine, the priest sacramentally offered us communion with God, and we received the body and blood, soul and divinity of Our Lord, Jesus Christ. He shared the word with us about God's love for the world, and when the priest dismissed us he said, 'I love you.' Then he said that we were to share that good news with everyone we met. That's what happened, I was there."

Why did these two people have a different story when each was asked the same question? The difference is not that one is telling the truth and the other is not. Both are telling the truth as they saw it. The first person saw only with his bodily eyes, that was all there was to see. The second person related what she perceived through the eyes of faith.

Faith makes all the difference in the world. It enables us to see beyond the visible, to see the mystery of God. This faith is necessary for eternal salvation, and God offers everyone this free gift. The gift of faith, though, benefits only those who accept it and commit themselves to live by it.

This anecdote is a teaching. The hundreds of stories in this book will let us enter the real life experience of those whose lives have been blessed through devotion to Jesus in the Blessed Sacrament.

Sister Patricia told me that the work of this book was placed into the lovely hands of our Blessed Mother, and placed under the care of St. Pio, a Capuchin confrere. In 1958, as a young Capuchin priest of five years, I visited the Capuchin Monastery in San Giovanni Rotondo, Italy, where I served morning Mass celebrated by Padre Pio*.

It is hoped that the stories related in this book will invite each reader to explore the great wonders and gifts that are found in the Mass and in devotion to the Eucharist.

Father Jogues Constance, OFM Cap
Capuchin Retreat
Washington, Michigan

*See Father Jogues' story of Mass celebrated with Padre Pio on page 106.

A Word to the Wise:

by Nick Lohkamp, OFM

To all those who read *201 inspirational stories of the Eucharist:*

Remember that you are reading *stories*. You are not reading a theological treatise. The holy Eucharist is a sacrament, a mystery. We can talk about the Eucharist in theological terms, abstract terms, or we can share our experiences of the Eucharist in very personal terms.

What we have in this book is a number of stories, not a theological work. These stories seek to describe the experiences of ordinary people. These stories touched the hearts, the emotions, the lives of these people. They are trying to share with us these moving experiences in their own words.

Most people have not had the opportunity of studying the theology of the holy Eucharist, so they do not have the language, the terms, the words to describe their experiences in theological language.

A theologian could find many little inaccurate expressions. A theologian might disagree with the words and phrases that are used to described these personal experiences, and the emotions that accompany these experiences.

What we have here are the simple accounts of experiences that people have had of events with the holy Eucharist. We should read the following accounts gently and patiently with that in mind.

A Visit With a Friend

The day is long, the headaches many;
I look for peace, but can't find any.
Amid relentless rush and noise,
life seems devoid of all its joys.

I long for comfort, someone kind,
whose love might ease my troubled mind;
but in this world of constant hurry,
each person has his own deep worry.

There is a place where I can go,
Someone to hear my tale of woe;
One who always has the time
to share the load, to ease the mind!

I open the door and go inside,
where peace and quiet still abide.
Treading softly down the aisle,
I greet Him with a tired smile.

"How good it feels to be with you!
Please help me, tell me what to do!"
At first, this is my fervent plea;
but silence soon descends on me.

It stills my heart, the turmoil ends—
no words are needed between two friends.
At peace with Him, and He with me,
I know I'm where I ought to be.

With Him I'm sure to find the way
to cope with living day by day.
And when I leave, our visit through,
He'll say, "I'm always here for you."

I know that next week I'll return,
to talk and listen, to think and learn;
to find life's meaning and true reward
before our eucharistic Lord.

Gloria J. Pinsker   *Horsham, Pennsylvania*

Special Moments of Memory

All of us are touched by memories, especially memories of our child-hood. I grew up on an apple farm on the Methow River in North Central Washington State. My fondest memories are of my family and the two parishes we attended, served by the same pastor. St. Genevieve's Parish church was up-valley about sixteen miles where I served Mass in the little church. I remember vividly Sister Elaine sitting with me on the front steps of the church teaching the Latin responses for Mass. Twenty-three miles down-valley on the Columbia River was Sacred Heart Parish in Brewster where I also served Mass. The church there too in those days was very small, just a few Catholic families.

My mother played the pump organ with a small group of four or five who were the choir. My father, who was not Catholic at the time, always drove us to church and always attended Mass. One of the strongest memories I have was that of one Sunday morning when our family followed the usual ritual after Mass of going to the local *drug store* to buy the Sunday paper. There were six of us kids in the car with Mom and Dad. My sister and I got into a squabble in the back seat about who would read the comics first. Actually the argument got so heated that we tore the comics in half. My mother turned around and firmly reminded us: "Didn't you kids just go to Communion?" We put the paper down and no one dared say anything more for the rest of the trip home.

My first Mass in Sacred Heart Parish (in the school gym—the parish church was much too small) was a moment I will never forget as well. Just a few weeks ago I returned to the parish to celebrate confirmation/first Eucharist. There were 150 first Communions with probably about 600 present for Mass. Again, we celebrated, not in the parish church, but in the community center…the church was much too small. How wonderfully Eucharist calls us together as a family of faith. And how wonderful the memories.

Jesus at the Last Supper took the bread and wine and said this was His body and blood. He told the disciples: "Do this in memory of me." Indeed we remember this moment as Jesus expressed in such a powerful and wonderful way His love for humanity, for each one of us. We continue to remember those moments of Eucharist as we are nourished by the word, the bread of life, and the community gathered around the altar. These special moments of memory will always be ones for which I am profoundly grateful.

The Most Reverend William S. Skylstad, D.D.   *Spokane, Washington*

As Long as I Am Able

My mother was 88 years old and somewhat sickly, yet she attended Mass every Sunday. She lived with my sister Joan, and every week Joan and I took turns getting her to Mass on time. Annunciation BVM (Blessed Virgin Mary) was her parish for 50 years, and she loved going there.

One Sunday after she had been ill, I told her she didn't have to go to church each week because the eucharistic minister would come to her with Communion.

She answered, "Eileen dear, when your father died, I promised myself that I would pray for him when the priest raised the Host at the consecration. I ask Jesus to hold your father in His arms at Communion time, and I want to continue this at Mass as long as I am able."

My mother died in 1998 and I have tried to follow her example. When the priest elevates the Host during the consecration, I ask Jesus to hold my parents in His arms, and I will continue to do this "as long as I am able." Thank you, Lord, for the gift of the Eucharist.

Eileen M. Glenn   *Havertown, Pennsylvania*

(Excerpts from the encyclical Ecclesia de Eucharistia *by Pope John Paul II. Full text of the encyclical can be found in "Appendix A")*

The Church draws her life from the Eucharist.

Put on the Mind of Christ

Even when our human senses fail us, it is our faith, backed by the word of God, that helps us look beyond the external appearances, and know that Jesus is there in the most humble act of humility and love.

Let us pray for those who do not receive Jesus in holy Communion. Let us all be eucharistic disciples. We do that by trying as best we can to see Christ reflected in others. Let us truly put on the mind of Christ and be Christ to others.

Father John V. Ahern   *Liverpool, New York*

I Always Want to Be With You

One day I was very miserable. Everything seemed to be going wrong. I felt that everyone was against me, and that they were blaming me for things I didn't do. I felt like nobody loved me, nobody appreciated me, that I was just nothing, a nobody. The day seemed dark and cold.

Feeling very downhearted, miserable, and hopeless, I went to morning Mass before I went to work. Where else could I go? Where else could I find a friend, if not in the Lord Himself?

I was a little bit late for Mass, so I sat in the back of the church. When I knelt down, I saw the people in front of me, all praying devoutly. Surely they were all good, holy, nice, and popular people who were loved by family and friends. I knew they all loved the Lord, and the Lord loved them all. As these thoughts swirled in my head, I felt even more hopeless, forlorn, and alone.

If ordinary people didn't love me, I wondered how the Lord, who is adored and loved by almost everyone, could love me. How could He love me, a sinner, a nobody in people's eyes?

Feeling sad and miserable, I went to Communion. While walking towards the priest, I prayed sadly, "Lord, You love all these good people, do you love me too? Me too?"

When I went back to my seat, I heard Him say in my heart, so gently, patient and loving, "See, this is proof that I love you. When two people love each other they want to be together always. Remember when you were first married and when you hugged your husband, you wanted to melt in him so you both would be one person, not two? My love is much, much greater. I love you so much that I always want to be with you. So, I make myself become this little bread for you to eat. Your body will digest it, and every cell of your body will absorb it. Then I will be in you, and you in me. We will be one, and we shall always be together."

Could there be a more perfect union in this world? I became very still, feeling full of awe and wonder. I didn't even dare to think. I just knelt down and prayed, "Thank you Lord, thank you. I love you, too. Help me to love you, and love everyone for you."

I went to work with joy in my heart. Everything seemed bright and peaceful, and my heart was singing. It doesn't matter anymore if nobody loves, appreciates, or knows me. The Lord, the king of heaven, Jesus my Savior, loves me. He loves me so much that He wants to be with me all the time. He makes Himself become food, so He can be united with me. That's so wonderful and beyond my understanding, but I know it's all that matters. I can go on doing my duties as well as I can, and be nice to every one, no matter what they think of me, for Him.

Margaretha M. Ryantini   *Jakarta, Indonesia*

In a variety of ways she (Church) joyfully experiences the constant fulfilment of the promise: "Lo, I am with you always, to the close of the age" (Mt 28:20), but in the Holy Eucharist, through the changing of bread and wine into the body and blood of the Lord, she rejoices in this presence with unique intensity.

I Could Never Quite Believe

Growing up Catholic and attending Catholic schools for twelve years taught me a lot. What it wasn't able to convince me of though, was the real presence of Jesus Christ in the Eucharist. I could never quite believe it. How could that little wafer of bread and the watered-down wine be truly the body and blood of Christ? Granted, they were nice symbols and a nice part of the Mass, but it wasn't God. It took a four-day retreat called a "Cursillo" to change my mind and to open my eyes to the intensity and reality of the Eucharist.

Going into this *Cursillo* retreat (Cursillo is the Spanish word for "a short course in Christianity") I had no goals about my perception of the Eucharist. There was no intense request or need in my heart to understand it.

Each day of the retreat we had Mass. It was on the second day that something happened. We were all holding hands around the altar and the priest said the words, "On the night He was betrayed, He broke the bread…"

Suddenly, it was like someone had flipped a switch. All at once I had a clear understanding of the *realness* of this part of the Mass. Jesus Christ was really and truly present.

I could not stop crying as I stood there with these other women. Without a doubt, I now knew I was in the presence of the true body and blood of Christ. Soon others felt it too, and some began crying as well.

Since that weekend, I have been to many celebrations of the Eucharist where I have received this same gift. It doesn't happen every time, but sometimes it does happen to the point of being overwhelming. The feeling usually begins at the consecration (special blessing of the bread and wine) and the intensity builds as I walk toward the altar to receive the Eucharist. I can only describe it as a feeling of being in the presence of God and a feeling of great humility. Sometimes the person giving me Communion notices the tears in my eyes as I receive, and I think that they might wonder what's wrong with me. There is nothing wrong. In fact, everything is right!

Michelle S. Anderson   *Purcellville, Virginia*

The Martyrs of Zacualpa

Without a doubt, the most powerful Eucharist I ever participated in was in a chapel in Zacualpa, Quiche, Guatemala.

In the 1970s and 1980s, during the civil war in Guatemala, the Guatemalan military tortured and killed thousands of catechists and church workers because of their defense of the poor and their support for human rights.

In 1981, the military took possession of the church buildings of Zacualpa. They chose a storage room behind the church to bring the catechists from the church, and there they interrogated and tortured them as their bodies were strung up on ropes. The torture was so brutal that the blood of the victims stained the walls of the room, and twenty-three years later, the stains remain. The people living near the church still remember hearing the screams of the victims. Afterwards the soldiers deposited their corpses in the garden next to the church.

Recently the bodies of the victims have been exhumed and given a respectful burial in the local cemetery. When I first visited the site in 1990, the friars had turned the building into a chapel, leaving the stains of blood and the hooks in the roof as witness of these brave martyrs. Then, the friars invited us to join them in a Mass. Celebrating the Eucharist in that chapel was a powerful reminder that the sacrifice of thousands of catechists was intimately connected with the sacrifice on the cross that Jesus had made for us.

Jesus continues to be tortured today, but the hope of the Resurrection is evident in each of the family members who know that their loved ones have not died in vain.

We concluded the Eucharist with the reading of the names of those who had died, and with the song, "Be Not Afraid."

Father Ed Dunn, OFM   *Cabo San Lucas, Baja California Sur, Mexico*

Sacrament of Joy

When I was in high school, my spiritual director suggested frequent visits to the Blessed Sacrament. He said that even if I did not say prayers or talk to Our Lord, I could simply stare at the tabernacle and sit silently. This has been a significant reason for my great devotion to the Eucharist, which I like to refer to as the sacrament of joy!

In time, my wife and children have joined me in visits to the Eucharist. As members of St. Mary's Parish in Spokane Valley, we are privileged to have the Blessed Sacrament chapel open twenty-four hours a day.

When our daughters were still in school, we would drop in and visit Our Lord at least for a brief moment. My daughters later would stop at the chapel on their own. When our youngest daughter experienced life threatening consequences following brain surgery a few years ago, our two other daughters and some friends immediately visited the Blessed Sacrament chapel and prayed intensely, then drove all night to be with us at the hospital in Seattle. Thanks to God, prayers were answered and she made a marvelous recovery.

I believe Our Lord will bestow special blessings on anyone who takes even the briefest moment to say "Hi" to Him in the Blessed Sacrament. We are certain He has been extra generous to our family because of these visits to the Eucharist.

Deacon Gonzalo "Chalo" Martinez   *Spokane Valley, Washington*

Increased a Hundredfold

As a result of a phenomenal experience about ten years ago, my devotion to Our Lord in the Blessed Sacrament increased a hundredfold.

My husband and I were at a Marian Conference in Spokane, Washington. It was a beautiful evening in May. They were having a living rosary procession outside on the Gonzaga University campus. As we were going up an incline my husband and I noticed a couple of women looking at the sun and then went on. We thought they were just looking at the sunset as the sun was going down. When we got on top of the small hill, we saw a Host in the sun, with colors of red-orange and yellow going away from the upper part of the Host. We could look at the sun with our eyes. No sunglasses or anything. It was like looking at a picture, no glare whatsoever. I asked my husband if he saw what I saw and he said yes.

The next year the same thing happened again, only this time the colors were more pronounced and the Host was beating like a heart.

I have always had a deep devotion to eucharistic adoration, but after this, it became a very strong, urgent desire to promote eucharistic adoration.

As a result of our experiences, another lady and I started First Friday eucharistic adoration before Our Lord in the monstrance, in a tiny mission church. This church had only nine to twelve catholic families, but we were not discouraged. We were able to have adoration from 8:00 a.m. till 5:00 p.m. every First Friday. We continued with it for five to six years until we had to leave that small community.

We moved to a small town of 250–300 people, and for the last two and a half years, every First Friday has had adoration of Our Lord in the monstrance from 2:00 p.m. until 7:30 p.m. The people are beginning to appreciate and love their quiet time before the Lord. My great desire is to have people come before the Lord, to know Him, to love Him, and to serve Him so that they can live happy lives and in turn lead others to Our Lord in the Blessed Sacrament.

Tom & Lillian Byrne   *Denton, Montana*

The Second Vatican Council rightly proclaimed that the Eucharistic sacrifice is "the source and summit of the Christian life".

Involved in the New Age

As a young child I loved going to Mass. I remember feeling very excited when the priest raised the Eucharist up high as the bells rang, because I knew in my heart that Jesus was present. In fact, I loved the Mass so much that I would often gather all the statues in the house and play church using a round cracker and grape juice in a wine goblet for the body and blood of Christ.

My childlike and simple faith was truly a precious gift from God. Yet as I grew, my life became more complicated, and by the time I went to college, I had left the Catholic Church. In my 20s I began to consult a psychic channeler who was also the reverend of a New Age church. What had begun as mere curiosity became an ever-increasing preoccupation.

I started taking classes on divination, psychic healing and other New Age practices that were actually occult rituals and forms of witchcraft. At the time I had no idea how dangerous these activities were or could become.

In 1988 I became engaged. Ironically, my fiancé and I were working at Catholic Charities at the time. Even though I wasn't practicing the faith, I decided that I wanted to get married in the Catholic Church with a Mass. We made arrangements to be married in the same parish that I had attended as a child, the place where I had received all of my previous sacraments. We went through Engaged Encounter and pre-Cana instructions, and even went to confession before the ceremony. However, I don't remember mentioning anything to anyone about my involvement in the New Age church during my preparation for marriage.

My wedding day arrived, and as I was walking down the aisle towards the altar, I was seized with an overpowering mixture of emotions. It was a combination of relief and restlessness so profound that I openly and uncontrollably wept the entire way down the aisle. To this day, that is all I can remember of the ceremony, except that at the consecration I finally began to calm down and get control of myself.

Throughout the early years of my marriage, I tried to go back to Mass many times. When I did, I experienced the same breakdown and sobbing just before the consecration. The power of the emotion was so great that I would literally run out of the church before receiving Christ. This went on for several years, during which time I was becoming more deeply entangled in the New Age church. Remarkably, as I was spending countless hours practicing the occult, I still professed a belief in Jesus and prayed to Him often.

During those years I experienced infertility, and at the age of twenty-nine was told that I would probably never conceive a child. Then, after seven years of marriage, three operations, a devastating miscarriage and lots of prayers, I became pregnant in 1995. Even with this miracle of miracles happening in my life, I was poised to begin classes to become a leader in the New Age church. Thanks be to God, He had another plan.

One day, as I was sitting in an occult class, I was filled with an overwhelming urge to return to the Catholic Church for good. This revelation shocked and disturbed me. I felt unsure and afraid of the incredible force of the conviction within me. I also recall that I experienced an intense spiritual pulling that was plucking me out of the life I was living and pushing me toward the Catholic life I once knew. There was no confusion about the message my heart received. My soul and the soul of my unborn child were in jeopardy and I was to return to the Catholic Church once and for all.

That Sunday I went to Mass and once again began to weep. I was eight months pregnant and felt so utterly alone and confused that I didn't care who saw me crying. Then I noticed a small boy about four years old crossing the aisle toward me. As I was trying to compose myself, he extended his little hand and offered me a tissue. My heart melted. I looked into his eyes and realized that he was about the same age as the little one I lost. In that moment, a blanket of calm came over me such that I cannot describe, and I knew then that I had finally found my way back home.

Today I am an almost daily communicant. Since that Sunday in early 1996, the Lord and His Blessed Mother have brought me on an incredible journey of mercy, forgiveness, healing and love. My daughter, Mary Grace, is seven years old now and will be making her first holy Communion in the spring. My husband, who has his own story to tell, remarked recently how much he loves going to Mass. My little family is truly a living testament to the power of Jesus in the Eucharist and His burning love and desire to bring us back home to meet Him. As the Venerable Edel Quinn once said, "Our faith tells us that He is in the Eucharist; let us seek Him there. If we knew we could find Him anywhere on earth, we would do our utmost to go there."

Anne M. Costa   *Baldwinsville, New York*

Comfort and Peace

I left work today feeling like I had worked hard but accomplished little. It was one of those days where there was one interruption after another; one stressful event after another, and I just couldn't run fast enough to do all that needed to be done. We all have those days.

When I left work, I drove directly to church. I couldn't wait to sit in quiet in front of the blessed Eucharist. I told Jesus about my uneventful day, and asked Him for patience and understanding. I sat there for an hour in prayer, and felt stillness, peace, and comfort surround me. It was a safe place, and I was totally relaxed. The Eucharist works wonders, and I know tomorrow will be a better day. Thank you, Jesus, for listening.

Debi Jean Hill   *Lansing, Michigan*

For the most holy Eucharist contains the Church's entire spiritual wealth: Christ himself, our passover and living bread.

Find Time Before the Lord

I am a Catholic deacon who has been in ministry full time for 28 years. From the time I was a boy, I have had a love for the Eucharist, and have always been aware of the real presence of the body of Christ at each Mass.

As a child, I was taught that after I received the Eucharist I should sit and speak to my Lord, and He would dialogue with me. Throughout my life as a boy, through my adolescent years, and into my adulthood, I have consistently found time to sit in front of the tabernacle or a monstrance to adore the Lord's presence. I have never been disappointed or found the experience unrewarding. The Lord has always dialogued with me.

Deacon Francis Potts, MTS, NACC   *Portland, Oregon*

Her Reward Will Be Great

The fifteen minute drive to the chapel, and the drive back home on a cold evening in mid-January, may constitute somewhat of a sacrifice on my part to visit Jesus in the Blessed Sacrament; however, that was nothing compared to what I witnessed today.

As I prayed in silence before the Real Presence, I heard car doors slamming and the pounding of children's feet running up and down the handicap ramp that leads into the chapel. Within moments, four very rambunctious, cotton-top boys, all under the age of six, burst in with their older sister. Behind them was their delicate-looking mother holding an infant of about two months.

Each boy genuflected on both knees, making the sign of the cross in the hurried, haphazard fashion of young males who would rather be chasing bugs, and then took their place on an available kneeler.

They all fell into prayer with hands folded reverently in front of their faces. I could tell they had done this before. When Mom seemed satisfied that all her troops were in line, she began breast feeding the fussy infant, or at least attempting to. First the youngest toddler fell off his kneeler, setting off the lights on his sneakers in a wild flashing frenzy. Then the oldest boy socked his sister when she invaded his space. Not to worry! Mom cleared her throat authoritatively, and harmony reigned over potential bedlam. So much for her delicate appearance—this woman was in complete control!

Within ten minutes it was all over. The infant emerged from the coverlet of modesty draped over the mother's shoulder; the youngest toddler's shoes stopped flashing; the oldest boy made peace with his sister; and at Mom's cue, they all rose from their knees, bowed in hodgepodge directions, and trooped out of the chapel, smiling broadly and waving to all the old ladies who remained behind.

In that moment, I truly felt the Lord's pleasure. I sensed it as acutely as I felt the cold air rushing in the chapel door when the family exited. It was not unlike the time when the widow came into the temple and deposited her mite. To some, it might not seem like much of an offering, but Jesus knew what it had cost her.

Today, I am certain God knew what it cost that young mother of six to come for a chapel visit, and I am equally certain that, like the widow, her reward will be great.

Bonnie Taylor Barry   *Sunset, Louisiana*

Christ Comes to the Poor

In the past several months, both *America* magazine and "Origins", the official news service of the USCCB (United States Conference of Catholic Bishops), have published articles describing the mind of the Church in eliciting a profession of faith at the time of Communion.

The minister holds the particle or the chalice before the communicant and says, "The body of Christ" or "The blood of Christ." This elicits an act of faith on the part of the elements, and also in the community gathered by the Holy Spirit and prayed over in the epiclesis (calling down upon). That prayer of the presider invokes the descent of the Holy Spirit, not only to be the catalysis of the transformation from bread and wine into the body and blood of Christ, but also for the ongoing transformation into the body of Christ that is the Church assembled.

This year, after listening to and preaching on the Gospel of Luke and the many references to ministry to the poor, I am more and more taken with this emphasis. The presence of Jesus in the poor, the marginated, the alien, and the downtrodden is a special focus for me, and I have initiated a ministry to Hispanics in our area.

When I see someone in the Communion procession who I know is deeply involved with the poor at any level, be that family, friends, community, or social organization, I can hardly get the words, "The body of Christ" out of my mouth. I become overwhelmed with the awareness that this is Christ in this minister to the poor who is standing in front of me, and I have to fight back tears. Sometimes it is more intense than at other times, but it happens more and more frequently; this terrible but profound awareness of Jesus revealing Himself to me through these ministers to the poor. I want to get down on my knees and bow my head because the divine presence shining through that person is so strong. I thank God repeatedly for this humbling and ennobling experience of His presence.

Father Robert H. Blondell   *Macomb TWP, Missouri*

Again in His Grace

I was in the Air Force in the early 1950s, and before my duties began, daily Mass had been a joy for me to attend. It started my days with a strong purpose, and I positively did not allow anything to disrupt this practice. The anticipation of receiving the holy Eucharist was so joyful that it made me tremble.

Needless to say, temptation was abound when I was called to duty with the Air Force. I fell by the wayside in my practices despite trying hard to evade worldly pleasures.

My guardian angel was at my side, I'm sure, when I became friendly with the chaplain's group in our medical field. They were a wonderful, caring group of people who took part in wholesome activities, and made sure I was included in their fun times. Through comparing myself to them, I clearly saw all that I was doing wrong, and began to truly regret my actions.

The following year I was discharged, and returned home to the parish I had attended as a young child. One morning at Mass, I looked at the crucifix and my entire past flashed in front of my mind's eye. Oh, what great sadness and aching sorrow I felt knowing I had offended Jesus Christ. I resolved that I would never allow myself to be tempted again, and made a vow to Jesus that I would remain loyal to Him.

As I approached holy Communion and stood before the priest to receive the sacred Eucharist that morning, I saw Jesus standing there with His precious body and blood, offering them to me. Me, a sinner to the *nth* degree! Oh, what extreme happiness I felt knowing that all the sins from my past were forgiven and forgotten, and knowing I was once again in His graces and love.

That happened in 1954, and it is now 2004. I still feel His love and presence in my heart. Many times at the elevation of His body and blood during the Mass, my mind goes back to that very memorable day when I was reaffirmed as His child. At 73 years old, I am still His child and always will be.

Helen Hvasta   *St. Augustine, Florida*

Through his own flesh, now made living and life-giving by the Holy Spirit, he offers life to men.

A Guide for Life

I graduated from Immaculate Conception of the Virgin Mary Elementary School in 1957. The school and parish have been located in the South Bronx in New York City for over 150 years and are staffed by the Sisters of Christian Charity.

One of the rules of Immaculate Conception School that I am grateful for is that the entire student body was required to attend the 8 a.m. Mass every day. Sometimes when I tell people this, they are shocked that a school would require that of young children. I tell them that this experience was the foundation that my life was built upon, and that this early training taught me to put Jesus first, to lift Him high, and allow Him to be in control.

Receiving the Eucharist was the high point of my day when I was a young student. I remember carrying my breakfast to school in a tin lunch box every day, because at that time in Church history, we had to fast beginning at midnight if we were going to receive Communion in the morning.

The Mass fascinated me as a child. We were fortunate enough to have a priest in our parish who could offer Mass in both the Eastern and Latin rites, and today I am thankful for having the opportunity to know and appreciate both Catholic Masses.

At the end of eighth grade, as we were preparing to graduate, everyone in my class got autograph books so our parents, teachers and classmates could write good wishes to us for our future. I still have my book, and one entry written by my eighth-grade teacher has been my guide for life. That wise teacher wrote, "Stay close to Jesus in the Blessed Sacrament and your life will be a great success." I have never forgotten those words.

My life has been a great success, not based on anything remarkable that I have accomplished, but because of the power of God's grace in my life. I know God is always with me and even during seemingly painful times of my life, everything has always worked out well in the end.

Beginning the day in the presence of Almighty God and His divine Son in the most Blessed Sacrament as a child had a lasting affect on my life. By God's grace, I have remained close to what I was taught in elementary school. Now, one of the greatest joys I have is when I bring holy Communion to about four or five people who are not healthy enough to attend Mass on Sundays. These home visits are a great honor for me. Receiving the Eucharist is the greatest joy these people have, and it brings me incredible happiness to have the privilege of bringing Jesus to them.

Jesus is, and always has been, the center of my life. The Eucharist is my strength and consolation. My life has been a great success filled with graces and blessings beyond measure because of Him. Jesus is real, and in Him I believe!

Barbara A. Higgins   *New York, New York*

A Chance to Serve

In 1965, while attending St. Stanislaus Kostka Catholic School, I wanted to participate in the Mass as a lector and altar server with my fellow classmates. The idea was quickly dismissed given the fact that I had a congenital birth defect, cerebral palsy, spastic diaplegia. The thought of this happening was a mute point given the mind set of the times.

In 1985, we were assigned a new pastor. One Sunday after Mass, he approached me about becoming a lector. I quickly accepted his offer. Shortly after that, he asked me if I was interested in training to become a eucharistic minister. Clearly, I was taken aback, but most enthusiastically agreed to participate in the training.

I completed the training and became a eucharistic minister, and can still remember the first time I participated in this ministry at Mass. It was the happiest day of my life. Twenty years later my childhood desire to be a servant of the Lord became a reality. This is a true example of things in life happening not in our time, but in God's time.

Since that time, I have assisted aged and ill priests with their Communion calls to people in numerous parishes. I also have had the honor and blessing of bringing the holy Eucharist to nursing homes and hospitals. Each Sunday, I serve as the eucharistic minister at holy Mass. I then travel to an assisted living facility, which is operated by Lutheran Ministries. There are about 25 Catholic residents living there at any given time. We pray together and prepare for reception of the holy Eucharist.

I am truly gifted by God to have the distinct honor of bringing Jesus Christ to this Catholic community. I must admit it is refreshing to see how they anxiously await their Lord in the Eucharist. This ministry has afforded me the opportunity to bring Our Lord and Savior to fellow Catholics at various phases of their life, from old age to illness, and then in their time of preparation to meet their Creator.

In one instance, I met a woman named Nancy who came to the facility after her husband passed away. She told me her husband had forbidden her to practice her Catholic faith, and how she longed to participate in it again. I quickly arranged for her to prepare and participate in the sacrament of reconciliation, and then the sacrament of the holy Eucharist. Nancy faithfully received the Eucharist each week until she became severely ill, at which time she passed away.

I believe that Jesus Christ in the holy Eucharist works wonders at this Lutheran facility. The holy rosary is prayed there on a regular basis, and there is a Blessed Mother altar in the meditation room, as well as on each floor, and in a grotto in the garden. The administrators, staff and the facility volunteers are most accepting of our Catholic beliefs. Undeniably, I have been called by name to this special ministry. It is a blessing and most special gift from the Father.

Edward M. Butler   *Minersville, Pennsylvania*

Consequently the gaze of the Church is constantly turned to her Lord, present in the Sacrament of the Altar, in which she discovers the full manifestation of his boundless love.

Completely Healed

I remember celebrating a healing Mass in Spokane, Washington, a number of years ago, and present was a man by the name of Carlos. Carlos is an artist, and his right hand was bandaged. He'd had an accident and about sliced off his finger. As the small group of people gathered around the altar during the consecration time, Carlos began to remove the bandages, and behold! His finger was completely healed.

Father Dan Wetzler   *Harrison, Idaho*

My Father's Friend

I come from a family of nine children. In an effort to give each of us special time alone with him, my father would invite only one of us at a time to accompany him when he went somewhere. My favorite place to go with my father was to church for adoration of the Blessed Sacrament.

Some of my earliest memories are of being in the half-darkened church of my childhood watching my father pray the rosary using his fingers to keep his place. Since my father had a tendency to lose things, he had figured out that barring any major accident, he would never lose his fingers, so he always had a handy rosary with him.

As we entered the church, my father would point to the monstrance on the altar and tell me that we had come to talk with our friend, Jesus. Then we would kneel in silence and pray the rosary. My mind wandered, and sometimes I fell asleep. When it was time to go, Dad would wake me and remind me to say good-bye to Jesus before we left the church.

When we came into the church for Mass, my father would point to the altar light and whisper in my ear that the light told us Jesus was at home in the tabernacle. I don't think there was ever a moment of doubt in my heart or mind that Jesus was truly present in the Eucharist because of the loving way my father worshipped the Blessed Sacrament.

When I was about six or seven years old, I had my first encounter with someone who wasn't Catholic. My friend Missy from school told me that she was Methodist. I realized then that there were many churches in our town that weren't Catholic. I asked my dad what made all the churches different and he told me, "Jesus loves every church that believes in Him, and He visits them often. But Jesus lives in our church, body and soul, in the Blessed Sacrament in the tabernacle." To this day, every time I enter a Catholic Church for the first time, I search for the altar light that tells me Jesus is home.

Maggie Scheck-Geene   *Bedford, Indiana*

Totally Surrounded by Angels

In the 1990s, a year or two after God called me to become Catholic, I was confirmed at St. Thomas More Church. One day, I asked God to show me what actually happens during the consecration. Instantly I saw that when the Father sends the Holy Spirit down at the moment of consecration, the Spirit comes down very quickly, totally surrounded by angels as though they were forming a column, and the Spirit comes down through the center. Even though I have wanted to see this again, I only saw it happen that one time.

The Eucharist has been very important to me ever since I first became Catholic. Shortly after I converted to Catholicism, I joined a ministry to bring holy Communion to the sick and dying. To this day I continue to serve God and His people through this ministry. I feel this is my calling and it has been a wonderful blessing to me.

Karen Y. Williams   *Mead, Washington*

Centered in My Faith

In the spring of '97, I was recovering from cancer surgery and had not been able to attend Mass for some weeks. On Palm Sunday, even though I was extremely weak, I forced myself to get to Mass. When I received Communion, I was overwhelmed by the power of that experience. Tears of joy and relief welled up in my eyes! I often think of that experience. It keeps me centered in my faith in the Eucharist.

Deacon Ken Dunlap   *Spokane, Washington*

Holy Hour for a Stranger

On July 27, 2002, at 2:40 a.m., I was traveling on Glenwood Avenue in Raleigh, North Carolina, to offer a holy hour at the Holy Family Perpetual Adoration Chapel at Our Lady of Lourdes Church. I had been a weekly 3:00 a.m. adorer since 1996. However, this was not my usual day.

I was sleepless that night thinking about my teenage son who was far away competing in an athletic event. I decided get up and drive to the adoration chapel and make a special 3:00 a.m. holy hour that night. As it turned out, the holy hour was not offered for my son, but for complete strangers.

As I drove, I was startled to see a mass of flashing blue lights encircling a service station convenience store on my route. My stomach pitted and I felt ill. Several years earlier, a manager who had been very kind to my children and me was shot and killed in the wee hours of the morning at that same store. I thought of him and began to pray feverishly.

Only imagining what might have happened, I prayed for all whose lives would be changed by what had occurred. I prayed for any soul that may have suffered an act of violence. I prayed for those who may have been physically injured, and the silent victims who would suffer. I prayed for the innocent family members of both the victim and the perpetrator, and I prayed for the law enforcement personnel, asking for their protection.

When I arrived before Our Lord at the adoration chapel, I continued my prayers. I wrote down my vague petitions on the prayer request cards provided. Adorers sign the cards when they offer up prayers for the petitions requested on them. I continued to pray as I left the chapel.

Later that morning, I heard on the news that a sales clerk at the store had been shot in the stomach. The incident had occurred only moments before I passed by. It sounded as though he was expected to survive.

I continued to pray for the stranger over the next several days. When I attended my regular holy hour, I looked up the prayer card that I had started and was moved by the number of entries from those who had prayed for my intentions. I started a new card for the clerk, thanking God for his life and asking for his continued recovery. A week later many more adorers had prayed for this total stranger!

Driving to my holy hour a few months later, my heart was lifted by a "Welcome Back" sign adorned with balloons that had been placed in front of the convenience store to greet the clerk as he returned to work.

He never knew that within minutes of his terrifying ordeal, total strangers were talking to God about him. The family members, the police officers, and even those who committed the crime never knew that faithful souls were offering prayer on their behalf before Our Lord. They never knew of the praise and thanksgiving offered up for them by the adorers. Total strangers were praying before the Lord for them 24-7, and they never knew. What a magnificent grace!

All who prayed for them are even greater blessed, for they are graced with the trust that, in their own dark hours, brothers and sisters in faith will be offering up prayers for them. Now how awesome is that?

Lynn Oeser   *Durham, North Carolina*

The Upper Room was where this most holy Sacrament was instituted. It is there that Christ took bread, broke it and gave it to his disciples, saying: "Take this, all of you, and eat it: this is my body which will be given up for you."

Eucharistic Distraction

This is a story of my days before entering the seminary as a late voca-tion. During this time of discernment I was dating a girl, but we were sort of staying apart at this particular time. I had gotten very involved in my parish at St. Catherine of Siena in Pittsburgh, and had been instrumental in reinstituting First Friday adoration. The adoration would begin after the morning Mass on Friday, and continue until the next morning Mass on Saturday. It went very well except that we had a hard time with people signing up for the night time hours, so I would sign up for any that were empty. My girlfriend had a lot of trouble dealing with my increasing in-volvement in the parish, so we were in an off time, sort of broken-up, but not absolutely.

This one particular First Friday in the spring of 1993, I was in the church for the 1:00 a.m. to 2:00 a.m. adoration time. At about 1:45 a.m., I heard a lot of noise and disruption. As I turned around to look, I was surprised to see it was my girlfriend, Carrie. She was very loud and sat in the pew behind me, which was very unusual for her. Then she said, "Come with me, I have to talk to you, I am very upset." I said, "Okay, but you have to wait ten minutes until the next person comes, so that Jesus in the Blessed Sacrament is not left alone."

This made her even more upset and she began screaming that I did not care about her, didn't love her, etc. for almost eight minutes. All during this time she would not look me in the eye at all, and every time I moved towards her to comfort her, she moved away from me. It was very weird. There were only a few minutes before the next adorer was to arrive but Carrie was so upset she left. Two minutes later the next person arrived early, so I left quickly and got in my car to drive home, which was about half a mile.

She lived about six miles away. When I got home I called her immedi-ately. I knew she could not possibly have had time to get there, but I wanted to leave a message for when she did. To my great surprise, she answered the phone! She sounded groggy, like she had been asleep. I asked her if she was okay, and she said, "Of course I am, why?" I said, "You just left the church and were crying and yelling that you needed my help." She replied with astonishment, "I don't know what you are talking about; I have been in bed for hours. The girls I went out with wanted to go home early, so I have been home since ten o'clock."

Perplexed, I reflected back on the events in the church and how she had failed to allow me to comfort her by holding her which she usually loved. I thought about how she would not even look at me. I tried to figure out how she could have driven six miles in such a short time through normal city neighborhoods. Since then I have often wondered if this was a visit from Satan trying to pull me away from the Eucharist.

Father Anthony Gargotta   *Natrona Heights, Pennsylvania*

The Blessed Mother or an Angel

Our first child was a son who weighed 9 lbs., 13½ oz. and was born on August 30, 1956 in LaCrosse, Wisconsin. After four days of labor, I was rushed into surgery to have a C-Section and the specialist that was called in said neither my baby nor I would live past noon on that fifth day. He was wrong. However, one week after getting out of the hospital, I developed a blood clot in my left lung, along with pneumonia, and ended up back in St. Francis Catholic Hospital for seven weeks.

Each morning during my hospital stay I heard the little bell that the server who accompanied the priest would ring as they approached the room of the person receiving the holy sacrament. He never brought me the Eucharist, which I desired so much. I was young and naive and had no idea as to how I could arrange to receive Our Lord daily.

After several weeks my condition was still not improving. Then one day a beautiful young nun in a white habit came in and asked my room-mate if she was finished on the bedpan. My roommate said she was finished, so while the nun was taking the bedpan from under her, the nun looked at me and said, "Why are you not receiving the holy sacrament?"

I told her that I would like to, but that I didn't know how to arrange it. She told me to tell the mother superior the next time she came in to see me that I wanted to receive holy Communion and she would arrange it. I told the nun that I thought I should go to confession first, and she said the mother superior could also arrange for a priest to come and hear my confession. Then she left.

Before and after this encounter with the nun in white, I never saw another nun dressed in a white habit at that hospital. I had been there for the birth of our three daughters and had many visits to the hospital for family members, yet the only nuns I ever saw at the hospital were in management positions and always wore black habits.

The mother superior rarely came to see me when I was recovering from my illness, but she showed up shortly after I had talked with the nun in white. I asked her if she would arrange for me to go to confession and receive holy Communion, which she said she would do. Then I asked her who the beautiful nun in a white habit was that I had seen the day before. The mother superior told me there were no nuns dressed like that in this ward.

Shortly after receiving the Eucharist daily, I began to improve. I know it was Our Blessed Mother or an angel who visited me that day, giving me direction when I needed it most. After all, who else would have known that my roommate was on a bedpan when they entered the room for the first time, and that I was not receiving Communion when no one else in the hospital knew, including the mother superior? I am very grateful to Our Lord and Our Blessed Mother for their love and direction in my life.

Coreen V. Marson   *Catoosa, Oklahoma*

"Take this, all of you and drink from it: this is the cup of my blood, the blood of the new and everlasting covenant. It will be shed for you and for all, so that sins may be forgiven."

My Tears for Jesus

When I was a child, my life was not mine. I had no control over what was being done to my body or to my tender mind. It was my stepfather's house and he believed that everything in it belonged to him, including me. He was an abusive stepfather, but no matter what he did to me, I refused to show him my emotions. The only thing I could withhold from him was the satisfaction of knowing how much he had hurt me, inside and out.

Above all, I would never let my stepfather see me cry. No matter what he was doing to me, or how much control he had taken over me, I found that if I concentrated hard enough on not crying, I could retreat inside myself and mentally make him disappear.

It got so I would hate to cry in front of any other people too. My tears were my personal prize because I could hide inside of them. If anything did bring me to tears, I would hold them back until I could run away and be by myself to cry. This prevented anyone from seeing that they had gotten control of me.

By the time I reached adulthood, I had perfected the defense mechanism of never crying. It was something in which I took great pride: I was in control. Crying in front of others would make me feel weak, as though I was allowing someone else to take part of my soul from me, and I was not going to let that happen ever again. I was going to control my own life and no one else could get through to my vulnerabilities.

Sometimes people are impressed by others who are very self possessed, but God is neither impressed nor amused by it. This is not what a child of His should be doing. And so, He reclaimed my tears for Him.

Today, every time I come to God in deep prayer, my tears fall before Him. This happens most particularly in church. Even though I have tried to fight this embarrassing phenomenon, when I pray in church, the tears inevitably flow. I was at first so distressed by my tears in church that I would walk out during Mass. But I couldn't stay away from the Mass, which gives me life, so I tried not praying. I found that it was impossible for me not to pray in church. Then I tried praying that I would not cry in church, only to find myself crying harder.

My love for God overcame my pride. I gave my tears to God by continuing to come to Him in prayer, and I know He gave me those prayerful tears as a precious gift. Through them I know that, no matter what, God will always be the one who is really in control. It gives me great peace to know that even when everything seems out of control, God is always there for me.

Maybe, like Paul, God put a thorn in my side to keep me from becoming too full of pride. I continue to have the gift of tears in church and realize that others might look at me and think all kinds of things about my tears. Church is one of my absolute favorite places to pray. It is my Father's home. It is where Christ has invited me to come and break bread with Him. It is also a gathering of all my brothers and sisters in Christ. And it is where I know that if my own solitary voice is not strong enough that day to carry my spoken prayers, my prayers can rest on the prayers of my brothers and sisters.

Rosemarie Podowski   *Memphis, Tennesse*

Whatever May Happen

A number of years ago, the Lord gave me a second chance with my life. One of the promises I made to Him was that I would go to daily Mass. One day, a family obligation prevented me from going to Mass. Needless to say, I was very disappointed. Receiving Our Lord each day is like a vitamin to me; it is what gets me through my day. So, I was quite disappointed and felt kind of sluggish throughout the day.

The next day I went to Mass and was still not quite over the fact that I did not go to Mass and receive Our Lord the day before. As I did the day before, I expressed my sorrow in my prayers.

Mass went on, and the time came to go up for Communion. I was beside myself with happiness. The joy I felt was indescribable. I stood before the priest, and said, "Amen." Then he placed Our Lord on my tongue. As I walked away, I realized that something was not right. I felt the Host in my mouth and realized that the priest had placed two Hosts on my tongue! Needless to say, my prayer of thanksgiving was tearful. I was not able to receive the day before, so this was Our Lord's way of making it up to me.

This particular incident happened one other time, in a similar situation. I still go to daily Mass, but now I know that if a serious reason comes up to prevent me from going, Our Lord will come through for me in whatever way is His will for me.

Carol Ann Matz   *Hazelton, Pennsylvania*

The Most Important Part of My Day

I am a cradle Catholic who went to Catholic schools for fourteen years. I was married in the Catholic Church thirty-seven years ago to a non-practicing Jewish man. There were a few periods in my life when I stopped going to Mass, and didn't receive the sacraments on a regular basis.

In 2001, I returned to Mass and the sacraments after having been away for several years. At that time, I promised the Lord, and myself, that I would not allow myself to get off track again.

Since I am retired, I was able to begin attending daily Mass upon my return to the faith. I have found that when I go to Mass in the morning, I don't care what happens in my life for the rest of the day, because I know I'll have the strength to handle it. Mass is now the most important part of my day. It gives everything in life meaning.

The pastor of my parish has eucharistic adoration available five days a week from 8:30 a.m. until 1:00 p.m., and during the evening five nights a week. I began going, and discovered that being in the presence of the Lord in adoration is a very special and important time for me.

Remember my Jewish husband that I mentioned earlier? After I went back to Mass and the sacraments in 2001, he told me that he had seen changes in me. As time went on, he began to attend Sunday Mass with me, and surprised me when he decided to attend RCIA classes. We went to the classes together because he wanted me to go with him, and I wanted to do this if it would make it easier for him. On Holy Saturday, April 19th, 2003, he became a Catholic.

My husband's conversion was a wonderful gift, and it was all the Lord's doing. There was a time in our married life that he did not even believe in God. Once he retired, he told me he had started to become more spiritual, but did not attend any church or synagogue until he joined me in the Catholic Church.

I used to be a worrier, but since returning to Mass, the sacraments, and adoration, I am more at peace. I have come to realize that it is far more beneficial to just pray about the situation, and then try to forget it. If one needs peace and serenity, there is no better place to find it than in the presence of the Lord. I always leave adoration with peace in my heart, knowing that I have just spent my time in a most valuable way.

Since I have returned to our faith, I have been filled to the brim with joy, peace, happiness and tranquility. All of these gifts are from the Lord. I have seen changes in myself, which I know is the Lord's work, and I am extremely grateful for His blessings. The Lord truly makes a profound difference in our lives if we allow Him to!

Rita D. Moore   *Pembroke Pines, Florida*

"They devoted themselves to the Apostles' teaching and fellowship, to the breaking of bread and the prayers."

Jesus' Healing Love

When I was about five or six years of age, my family moved into my grandfather's huge Spanish house. We lived with him for a few years until the house my dad was having built was finished. My grandfather's house had many rooms; some of which were used for storing rice, wood, and other crops produced from the lands he owned. These storage rooms were dark, and some were isolated.

Among my grandfather's household was a family whom he adopted, and who eventually took care of things for him. One of the members of this adopted family was a teenager who willfully took advantage of those dark rooms by bringing me to them. Each time he brought me to one of those rooms, he sexually molested me. He assured me that it was normal, and that I didn't have to be afraid. He was also able to convince me that it had to remain a secret.

Because the house was large and we were a big household altogether, it was not easy to determine what activities each person was involved in. If not for my mother who saw me looking for him one day, as he had summoned me again, I would have continued going to him.

I went to kindergarten in a Catholic school that was right beside our church. I was so attracted to the Blessed Sacrament that after school, I would visit Jesus there. I would talk to him for about an hour, and many times I just sat there enjoying Jesus' presence and the peace that came with it. Soon I brought my classmates with me, six-year-old children just like me, and they prayed devotedly also.

I frequently went to Mass and absolutely loved receiving Jesus through the holy Eucharist. The Host always filled me up in many ways that I could never understand. Each time I received Him, joy overcame me. Peace and satisfaction enveloped me.

When sex education was introduced in school, the realization that I had been sexually abused terrified me. I felt outrageously dirty and manipulated, so I ran to Jesus more frequently.

My mother was not a comfort to me as she was busy raising other children. Because she wasn't happy and I happened to be the oldest one around, she unconsciously took things out on me. She constantly yelled at me, and told me I was stupid and ugly. I rarely experienced love from her, so I continued to run to Jesus for comfort.

In college, I was able to go to daily Mass and receive holy Communion. Each time I ran to Jesus, He completely satisfied me with food that gave me strength, and I was beginning to understand why.

When I became a mother for the first time, I stared at my beautiful baby and cried profusely. I didn't know how to love her. I knew at that instant that I needed to be healed, so I called my mother to tell her the affect she had on my life. She apologized, and we both prayed for healing. My dad, my precious loving dad, prayed for healing for both of us also.

About ten years ago, the Lord manifested to me my need for healing for the sexual abuses done to me when I was a little girl. After my grandfather passed away, his adopted family moved away without leaving us an address, so there was no way for me to find the one who molested me. In my prayer for inner healing, I would visualize him standing or kneeling before Jesus, and Jesus Himself forgiving his sins.

I also visualized my molester standing in front of me, and I would forgive him. I combined the approach on praying for inner healing presented by Father John Hampsch, C.M.F., and that of Father Robert DeGrandis, S.S.J. For a year, I came before the Lord praying for healing.

At that point in my life, I came to understand the Lord's presence in me. I realized deep in my heart that He was truly in me. I heard His voice inside of me, telling me that I was completely healed. My entire being received His healing with great joy and peace. I was finally free!

I could never thank and praise God enough for sheltering me in His inexhaustible love. His healing and grace are, for me, gifts of freedom and inner peace. His word and His body and blood are for me, and His gifts of comfort, joy and strength are too.

I now have five beautiful children whom I love very much. I try to love them the best I can because I want them to experience the love of God just as I have. I am also blessed with a loving husband who not only loves God, but is one who is *in love* with God. My mother and I are now good friends.

Because Jesus made the first move to love me, as He loves all of us, I understand that I don't have to wait for people to love me. Just like Jesus who is in me, I am responsible for making the first move to love.

My family lives in an old neighborhood on one of the islands of Hawaii. As simple as our life is, we consider ourselves rich because of Jesus' love. Just as I once visited Jesus in the Blessed Sacrament with little children who were my age, I now go to daily Mass with my own children. Because I homeschool them I have the freedom to do that, which is truly a blessing. They love going to Mass as much as I do.

With a busy life of raising a big family, I surely need Jesus as much as ever. Do I still run to Him? Always! Receiving His body and blood every day gives me the food and energy I need to live a truly full life.

Easter O. Almuena   *Honolulu, Hawaii*

This Really Happens!

Do you think miracles only happened long ago, or in special places like Lourdes or Fatima? One day *I really* heard the words father says at the consecration, "By the power of the Holy Spirit may this bread and wine become the body and blood of Our Lord Jesus Christ," and I realized that this happened! At the Mass, and every Mass, I am in the presence of a miracle!

Patricia G. Scown   *Butte, Montana*

At every celebration of the Eucharist, we are spiritually brought back to the paschal Triduum: to the events of the evening of Holy Thursday, to the Last Supper and to what followed it.

Protect Us from All Anxiety

Mom was very ill. The mitral valve in her heart had been surgically replaced with a plastic one, but the new device was leaking badly. Dad, my sister, two brothers and I were anxious about her condition and poor prognosis. It did not seem possible that death could be knocking at the door already? Mom was only fifty years old.

I had been ordained a priest for three years and I must have said the prayer a thousand times. But one Saturday morning a line in the prayer we say after the "Our Father" caught my attention more intensely. We pray, "…protect us from all anxiety as we wait with joyful hope."

There was the anchor! There, the comfort! Just before we eat the heavenly meal we are reminded to come to the table, not with anxiety, but with hope. How many times I had walked by that burning bush and never noticed, until I needed the encouragement to face my mother's impending death.

The Mass is filled with such moments of grace, waiting to be discovered, when at last we realize the need. Today, thirty years later, I still pray that line with special attention. I share in the same meal here on earth which my mother enjoys in the kingdom of heaven. Her broken heart has been mended, and mine is no longer anxious. With joyful hope I look forward to sharing that meal with her in glory (but not before I've been told, "Supper's ready! Go wash your hands!").

Father Norman Langenbrunner   *Fairfield, Ohio*

A Profound Union of Spirit

In October of 1979 my father was seriously ill in a hospital in Indiana. Although I wanted very much to be with him and the rest of my family that was gathering around him during his sickness, I was unable to do it. I lived more than 1,500 miles away in Canada. My husband and two small children, a toddler of two and an infant of six months, needed me. On top of that, my business was requiring a lot of attention. A few months earlier, we had gone home and spent two happy weeks during the summer staying close to Dad and the family. But now, knowing it was impossible and impractical did not make it any easier. Each day my mother and sisters would call to let me know how Dad was doing.

Two more months passed. Then, during the first weekend of November, I was at a Family Life Conference in our community. I had a merchandise display there and although I tried to focus on making a good presentation and to listen attentively to the conference speakers throughout the weekend, my heart was miles away with my dad and family. He was not doing well and I knew my mom and my siblings were at Dad's bedside waiting and praying with him. How I longed to be there with him.

The conference ended with a joyous celebration of the Eucharist, filled with prayers for families around the world and in all circumstances of life. Of course, I prayed for Dad and that, if he should die, he would know the full glory of the risen Christ.

The Communion hymn was Suzanne Toolan's "I Am the Bread of Life." As we sang that song, the words seemed to be a crystal message meant just for me. "He who comes to me shall not hunger…and I will raise him up on the last day." I experienced such a profound union of spirit with my dad that it is beyond description.

After Mass we picked up the display and packed up all our goods. I was still in a daze as we bid farewell to the conference participants and made our way home. The minute I stepped into the house I could hear the phone ringing. My heart stopped. It was one of my sisters with the sad news that Dad had died earlier that evening.

It took some time for the reality of Dad's death to sink in. Then, this wave of comfort gently washed over me. I realized it was exactly at the time of Communion and singing that special song that Dad had made his passage into eternity. I was completely assured that although I was not able to be with him in body, we had been together in spirit—God's spirit.

Twenty-five years have passed since that day. Yet at every Communion, when that song is sung, I am back in the special closeness of that moment. The spiritual treasure I was given is a comfort that renews my faith in Jesus, the bread of eternal life.

Jane Beyke Kryzanowski   *Regina, Saskatchewan, Canada*

That Was Really Jesus!

I returned to my Catholic faith in 1994 through the intervention of our dear Blessed Mother, Jesus, and the Holy Spirit, in that order. This story is part of a continuation of the beautiful gifts and graces that have been happening since I returned to Catholicism.

In 1995, my friends Cathy, Mary, Ann, and I made reservations to go to a Marian Conference in Rochester, New York. Once we actually made the reservations, I had a strong urge to go to eucharistic adoration as soon as I arrived at the conference. I couldn't wait to leave!

At last, the day of the conference came and the place was packed as usual. As I made my way up the few stairs to the adoration area, my heart sank. The hall was jammed with people. I slowly inched my way through the crowd to the doorway where eucharistic adoration was being held and looked into the room. It was packed with people standing against the walls and kneeling in the aisles. All but one chair was taken which was right smack in front of the monstrance. I couldn't believe my eyes!

I started praying to Jesus, telling Him I'm on my way, please save the seat for me. Finally I made it to the seat, sat down, blessed myself and started to pray. I looked up at the monstrance and couldn't believe my eyes. Someone had taken the Host out and put in a picture of Jesus, or so I thought.

I have to explain why I thought this. When I had returned to the Catholic Church, I didn't recognize it from when I was young. The Mass was now in English, and the priest faced the congregation. There were no more altar railings and the altars themselves were gone from most churches. The tabernacles were now behind a wall or in a chapel in back of the church.

I noticed that now people went to Sunday Mass in short shorts, mini skirts, and even tank tops. You name it, they wear it. There was no respect or reverence to be found. With this in mind, it was only natural that I thought I was only seeing a picture of Jesus.

I sat there alternating between praying and kibitzing to Jesus. I was saying things like, "How can they do this? Does this never end? Why would they do this?" The whole time I was there, I saw only the *picture* and never the Host.

On the way home, Cathy was driving, I was in the passenger seat, and Mary and Ann sat in the backseat. I asked Cathy, "Did you go to adoration?" She said, "Yes." I asked her what she saw when she looked at the monstrance. She asked what I meant by that and I said, "When you looked at the monstrance, did you see the Host or a picture of Jesus?"

Cathy answered that she had seen the Host. I then proceeded to ask Mary and Ann the same questions and got the same answer from them, "the Host." Then they wanted to know why I was asking. I told them that I never saw the Host, I only saw a picture of Jesus. Then it hit me, "Oh my God! That was really Jesus I was seeing!"

Then I told my friends how I was praying and kibitzing the whole time I was at adoration. Cathy said to me, "Was Jesus laughing?" I said, "Not on the outside, but on the inside, He must have been howling." At that time I didn't know how to *tune in* to these things. I do now and if that was to happen today, I would know immediately that it was a miracle of the Eucharist.

Debbie M. Gerard   *Liverpool, New York*

*"Christ...as high priest of the good things to come...,
entered once for all into the Holy Place, taking not the
blood of goats and calves but his own blood, thus
securing an eternal redemption."*

My Birthday Present from God

In 1995, God gave me a birthday present that I will never forget. My story begins in the early part of 1994, when my family and I lived in Layton, Utah. Bishop Weigand, from our Salt Lake City Diocese, was transferred to Sacramento, California, and we were without a bishop for almost a year.

By the end of the year, everyone was still wondering when we would get a new bishop. Finally, in November, the diocese announced that Bishop George Hugh Niederauer would be assigned to us. In December we were told that he would be ordained on January 25th at the cathedral in Salt Lake City. That day happens to be my birthday.

I remember my wife Carmen saying how much she would love to attend the ordination, and I told her it would be almost impossible for us to get tickets. The diocese had given ten tickets to each parish, and only VIPs would be attending. Besides, I wasn't sure I wanted to spend my birthday at a bishop's ordination. It would be a long celebration, there was going to be a large crowd, and we would have to deal with the traffic and the hassle of driving all the way to Salt Lake City. No, I thought it would be better if we just stayed home and celebrated my birthday there.

I didn't think much about it again, until the day before my birthday, when a friend of ours called to tell my wife that she had one extra ticket for the ordination. She wanted to know if one of us wanted to go with her. My wife called me at work to ask me if I wanted to go, and I told her I didn't, but that she should go. She said she didn't want to leave me alone on my birthday.

At the time, I was working at St. Rose of Lima Church in Layton. My wife persuaded me to ask the secretary of the church if they had any extra tickets. I was doubtful that they did, but told her I would ask anyway.

When I asked the secretary about tickets, I was very surprised when she said she knew of one that might be available. She said she was holding it for a woman who was supposed to pick it up by nine the next morning. If it wasn't picked up, she said I could have it. I thanked her but never expected her to call me back. However, the next day she called and said the ticket was mine. I couldn't believe it!

My wife, our friend Dorothy, and I attended the bishop's ordination in Salt Lake City that night. We arrived early and it was standing room only already. It was a beautiful, spiritual service. As I listened to the music and prayed, I knew that God had planned for me to spend my birthday with Him all along.

As I received holy Communion from the new bishop at his ordination, no one knew it was my birthday except God, my wife, and me. It will be a birthday present I will cherish and never forget. Thank you, God!

Juan Rodriguez   *Avondale, Arizona*

I Can't Do Without It

My Scripture professor once stated, "You can't live the Christian life without the Eucharist!" I have adopted this truism as the foundation of my prayer life.

It is from the Eucharist that I receive Jesus' spirit of care and compassion for the youth at Morning Star Boys' Ranch, who have issues and problems that sometimes seem unresolvable. I know that have I said or done the right thing at the right time through the power of the daily Eucharist. I can't do without it!

Brother Tony Cannon   *Spokane, Washington*

What if This Was Just a Sham?

I grew up in a good Catholic household. We attended Mass every single Sunday, and I would occasionally tag along with my dad for daily Mass on Saturday as well. When I was old enough, I eagerly became an altar boy. I liked being involved in the Mass, and getting one of the best seats in the house. Due to a vocations shortage, I sat in the pew with my family only two times for the first three years I was an altar boy. I really liked being an altar boy, so that was fine with me.

After a couple of years of altar boy service, when I was 12 years old, a funny thing happened. I can still remember it vividly. I was serving the eight-thirty Mass at St. Thomas More, and during the first reading, a poisonous thought entered my mind. What if this whole thing was just a well-orchestrated sham? What if a man named Jesus duped us all nearly two thousand years ago? Was that possible? If that was true, then this whole exercise was hollow and empty, and none of it mattered.

"Oh, God," I prayed, "it can't be true." Then another poisonous thought came. If God truly is who He says He is, then He would have no problem performing some sign for me. As a twelve-year-old, I didn't understand the trap I was falling into.

So I clenched my eyes real tight, and prayed some more. "God, if you're truly real, then give me a sign. Not just some warm fuzzy feeling, something concrete. Something real. Have a dove fly into the church, or have something spontaneously catch on fire. Something out of the ordinary that can't be mistaken for coincidence. If you're truly real, and you really love me individually and not generically, then surely that won't be a problem for you. Do something by the end of Mass. If you do, then I'll never doubt again."

Then I watched and listened intently. Maybe there would be a bright light. Maybe some crazy-haired homeless man would run in from the street and yell, "Hallelujah." Maybe one of the religious statues or the large crucifix behind the altar would wink at me. He works in mysterious ways, you know. I waited and I waited—and none of those things happened.

As Mass ended, and I led the procession out of the church, I was extremely disappointed. The sign hadn't come.

After the church emptied, I strode back to the little table at the front to collect the dirty dishes from Mass. What was I going to do? Now that I had determined that this whole thing was a big scam, what now? Well, I couldn't go to Mass anymore—it was a waste of time. How would I share my scientific findings with my dad? He was blinded by the lie—I would never convince him.

I collected the three empty ciboriums and started towards the back of the church. I just might have to go through the Sunday motions until I grew up and moved out. Yes, that would be my only option.

When I got back to the sacristy, I opened the lids on the ciboriums and my jaw dropped. One of them was full to the brim with the Eucharist.

I spun around and motioned for Deacon John, who swiftly and silently scooped up the full ciborium and shuttled it directly to the tabernacle. He came back scratching his head. "I thought I must have put an empty one in the tabernacle. I know we only had three full ciboriums. But I just checked, and all three in the tabernacle are full too. I don't understand—I must be getting old."

I was too scared to say anything at the time, but I knew what had happened. I had demanded that God show me that He was truly, actually, fully, and substantially here on earth—and He showed me Jesus in the Eucharist. I asked for a sign that He had heard my specific prayer, and that He cared about me individually—and I learned that God does answer our prayers, just not always how or when we expect Him to.

At the moment in which I was the most certain that I was alone, Christ was right in my hand, and I didn't even know it. There were no fireworks and a band. No loud noises at all. Just simple, quiet whispers from an attentive God that transcends all. Would anyone believe me? Probably not, but it doesn't matter. I didn't ask God for a sign for everybody.

Our Lord is still patiently, kindly, and mercifully multiplying loaves two thousand years later. Still feeding His people. What a cool God we have!

Eugene H. Dierks III   *Spokane Valley, Washington*

 To contemplate Christ involves being able to recognize him wherever he manifests himself, in his many forms of presence, but above all in the living sacrament of his body and his blood.

Don't Worry, All is Well

I have just finished my confession and penance. Mass will begin in about twenty minutes. A wonderful thought has just washed over me, like the sweet smell of orange blossoms in early spring. I just realized that right this minute I am as pure and clean as humanly possible. I am now prepared to receive my sweet Jesus in the Eucharist.

If I can keep my thoughts on my loving God, praising and thanking Him until Mass begins, I will be ready to receive Him. I will be as close to perfect as possible. I want to give Him a pure heart because of my great love for Him. Oh yes, I love my God, but there was a time in my life when things were different.

It would be nice to think that being raised by a very holy Catholic mother, and having been educated in a Catholic school for all but two years before I entered the university, would have been the perfect foundation for me to lead a holy, saintly life. I had dreams of entering the convent, of serving God with my whole heart, and somehow I lost my way.

The saddest part of my life was when I was lost from God. I was hiding in the shadows, even though I knew God would always love and forgive me. I didn't go to Mass and forgot to pray because I was too busy. God was not the first priority in my life anymore. I was truly lost. My life was like the rosary beads lost among the socks and old jewelry.

All my struggles and hardships were left for me to solve alone, and I was not happy. I was frightened, lonely, sad, and in a loveless marriage of betrayal. Many times in the middle of the night, I would cry for the comfort of my God, but was not willing to return to the practices of my faith. I felt as if I did not belong.

I made many wrong choices during those difficult times. Church had become a foreign place and I had even forgotten the prayers we said at Mass. I found myself wondering what I would say if I went to confession. " Bless me Father, it has been seventeen years since…" Had it been that long?

It was the grace of God and the death of my saintly mother that brought me back home to begin rebuilding my relationship with God. Within one year I buried my mother, my husband of seventeen years filed for divorce, and I had breast cancer. I was at the bottom of a pit, frightened, alone, abandoned, rejected, and feeling unloved.

Feeling unloved was the key that opened the door to my journey back to God. I had been taught that God would always love and forgive me, but would I be able to forgive myself? Wanting to feel whole again, I started to pray short prayers and listen to Christian music. Through this, God reached into my soul. I knew that I would only be able to survive in this world if I would take the hand that God extended to me.

The following Sunday, I returned to Mass, but was not ready to receive Communion. I chose the evening candlelight Mass because the church would be dim and nobody would see me if I was to cry. During Mass I felt God's presence. I poured out my heart and tears to Him. It was wonderful. The music and light were soft and the priest, in his gentle and kind manner, reminded each of us to trust God, and to love and serve Him in all things.

At each Mass I went to after that, I felt as if God had given the priest the exact words I needed to hear to heal my soul. For months I sat and cried at every Mass I went to. I learned many tricks on how to hide my tears and wipe my nose so I would not draw any attention to myself.

Sometimes, when I tried to sing, the words were so profound that they would get stuck in my throat. I was probably the only one who left church with a cleaner face than when they came in! I would pack a quarter of a box of Kleenex in my pockets and off to church I would go each Sunday evening.

Months passed and I was still a stranger in the church. I did not speak to anyone except when I had to give the sign of peace. I made sure I got there just before Mass started and stayed until everybody was gone so I could sneak out the door and rush to my car without being seen. I was a sight! My eyes were swollen from crying and my nose would have put Rudolf to shame.

God's grace kept me coming to Mass. Each Sunday I grew stronger and fell more in love with my God. He became my resting place. I would imagine God holding me in church whispering, "Don't worry, all is well…I am with you." I was not able to attend Mass during the week because of my job, but I began attending Mass in the morning as well as in the evening on Sundays. Attending Mass twice a day? I couldn't get enough to fill my soul.

I finally found the courage to go to confession, which was not the dreaded fate I had imagined. My confession was a release of the past and a step into the light.

Good things began to happen. I was more at peace at work. I learned to laugh again. I talked to God all day long, and He became my constant companion. The spirit of God filled my soul.

I started to volunteer at church, helping with little things, and began to give words of encouragement to others. Above all, I began to love again. I have taught religious education for two years now, and God always gives me the time, lessons, and insights to share our faith with others. No, I am not perfect. I am just an ordinary, single Catholic parent in love with my Lord. *I am His beloved and He is mine.*

Within a couple of years, my children started to go to Mass with me. I am a great cook, so I would invite them for a home-cooked breakfast if they went with me to church. I even saved my money for a pancake breakfast that the Knights of Columbus sponsored once a month. All of this led to my grandchildren enrolling in religious education classes. During this space of time, I realized I was truly home. I was happy again!

One Sunday, as I was being dragged by my grandson Kyle to Mass, this four-year-old shouted at the top of his lungs, "Hurry-up, Nana. It's party time!" That sure changed the mood in the parking lot at eight-thirty in the morning. I think his comment lightened our steps into church that day. These are precious memories, and perfect words out of the mouth of a child. Yes, Mass is a celebration that you and I have been invited to and we should all shout, "It's party time!"

Yvonne M. Flores   *Tucson, Arizona*

Whenever the Church celebrates the Eucharist, the faithful can in some way relive the experience of the two disciples on the road to Emmaus: "their eyes were opened and they recognized him"

What a Gift I Received

I've had many wonderful and moving experiences surrounding my life as a priest. For eleven years, I was a chaplain at large Midwestern retirement center. We averaged about eighty deaths each year, and one of my great privileges was to bring Communion to those wonderful elderly people as they neared completion of their journey on earth.

The story I want to tell is about one Mass I offered at my mom's apartment on the occasion of my fifty-first birthday. It was February 1, 1985. As my mom aged into her late seventies, she was unable to get out to the parish Mass every Sunday. Winter weather was always a factor, as well as her struggles with arthritis. So, when possible on Sundays or special occasions, I would offer the Eucharist and have Mass at her Cincinnati apartment.

My sister, Sister Marianne, S.C., always joined us on those occasions. At the time, there was nothing unique or outstanding about that particular day, other than it was my birthday. We took our customary places at my mom's dining room table, with the chalice, wine, and Hosts all in place. My mom was on my right and my sister was on my left. As we always did, we prayed for my dad. He had died suddenly of a massive heart attack back in 1968 after playing a most enjoyable round of golf on a sunny Saturday morning. As any son would hope, I wished I could have been there with him, to hold him in my arms and pray with him at his death. I knew he had not suffered, though, and that he quietly went home to the Lord.

As we celebrated the Eucharist, my mom, sister, and I exchanged the kiss of peace with each other. We prayed the "Our Father" with our hands joined. Then I offered the consecrated bread and wine to my mom and sister. It was a quiet celebration of thanks to the Lord for many of His gifts, but especially for the gift of life, and for the grace to be gathered for this special occasion. I did not know the real significance of the Mass at that moment.

We went out to eat that afternoon, had a nice day, and returned to Mom's apartment to visit for a while before I left to return to my friary and Marianne to her convent. Before we left, my sister took her camera and snapped an informal photo of me with my arms around my mom. We both had a wonderful smile.

The following evening, on Monday, I called as I usually did to see how Mom was doing. She was fine.

However, on the next day, Tuesday morning around 10 a.m., I was on my way to receive the new postulants into our novitiate nearby when my sister called. One of the apartment neighbors had called her to say my mom's newspaper was still outside her door. It was never there that late in the morning. She might be sick. So, I asked another priest to sub for me at the reception ceremony and rushed to my mother's apartment as soon as I could.

She had the safety chain on her door, and as I cracked it open, I could see her sitting on the couch, almost upright. I broke the chain to get in, and then knew for certain what I had suspected. Mom had died. I called my sister who came right over. After taking some private time to sit with Mom and grieve, we called the police and did all the things one has to do in beginning the process for planning a funeral.

As I reflected some days later, everything we had done on that Sunday came back to my mind. My heart was flooded with gratitude to God for the privilege I'd had, but did not realize at the time. I had been blessed in offering my mom's last Mass on this earth. Without knowing it at the time, we had prayed for my dad, who would be waiting for her to join him just two days later. I had taken my mother's hand in mine and wished her the peace of Christ.

I had the privilege of placing the sacred host into Mom's hand just hours before she died. She held in her hand Jesus, whom she would soon see face to face. It was her last holy Communion, her *Viaticum,* which is a word that means "food for the journey." When I put it in her hand I said, "Mom, the body of Christ," and her response was "Amen," which means, "Yes, I believe." I had prayed, "May this body and blood bring us and you, Mom, to eternal life." Without knowing it, the good Lord was giving me the chance of a lifetime to prepare my mom for death and eternal life with God.

What is startling about this whole incident is that I should not have even been in Cincinnati at that precise time in the first place. I really should have been, and would have been, in California. I had just begun my special assignment that would take me out of my province for a period of six months as visitator general for the Santa Barbara Province of Franciscans. I was not scheduled for my first break to return to Cincinnati until Holy Week and Easter, sometime in early April.

Unexpectedly, there was a break in my schedule of visiting the California friars, and I had decided to go home for a few days to celebrate my birthday. Actually, without knowing it at the time, I went home to prepare my mom for her journey into eternal life by giving her the body and blood of Jesus, her Lord and Savior.

The last photo of my mom and myself has a special place in my room. It is a reminder of how good God was, and how blessed my sister and I were on that Sunday morning, February 1, 1985, as we sat around the table, giving the *bread of life* to my mom.

Father Jim VanVurst, OFM　　　　　　　　　　　　　*Cincinnati, Ohio*

If Every Catholic Realized

I am 46 years old and live in the suburbs of the city of Montreal in Quebec, Canada. I love going to Mass everyday, and receiving the body and blood of Jesus in holy Communion.

The Eucharist became even more precious to me after I heard the pastor of my home parish of St. Luke's preach at a first Communion Mass. During his homily, Father Roger Martineau said, "When you eat meat, vegetables, fish, eggs, etc. they become you, your flesh. When you eat (receive) Jesus in holy Communion, you become part of Him. This may not be scientifically proven, but cell by cell, with each holy Eucharist you receive in faith, you change into Him until one day you are truly Jesus in your behaviour, in your words, in your life."

I was deeply touched by his words, which were actually directed to the children. On introspection, I recognize the change in myself after years of receiving Jesus. I am changed in the way I react to things, the way I reach out to people, and in the way I resolve matters. Jesus is always my first recourse, my first responder. He is my strength, joy, and role model. Christ is my friend and compassionate listener.

I don't even want to imagine the person I would be without Jesus in my life, without receiving Him every day in holy Communion. I feel so privileged and blessed to be Catholic and to live in a city that still has daily Mass. Best of all, I am blessed to be able to spend most of my day in God's house working as a parish secretary. I am just a few dozen feet away from the tabernacle when I am at work. What more could I ask for? God is so good to me!

Another thing I have experienced by receiving the Eucharist daily is the bond of love that is created among the congregation. Often we don't even know each other's names, but by seeing each other there regularly, we notice the absence of a person who regularly sits in a particular pew, or that someone is looking sick or distressed. Then we automatically send up a prayer for that person, whether we know them or not. Yes, the holy Eucharist creates a bond of love among the people of God, just like Jesus promised.

I feel blessed to have freedom of religion, freedom to read my Bible, and to be able to go to church and participate in the celebration of the holy Eucharist. I am blessed to be able to receive Jesus everyday. If every Catholic realized how powerful and healing the holy Eucharist really is, they would stampede to the church to attend every Mass and receive the body and blood of Jesus. May I live to see that day. Maranatha, come Lord Jesus!

Effie D. Cordeiro   *Beaconsfield, Quebec, Canada*

 I have been able to celebrate Holy Mass in chapels built along mountain paths, on lakeshores and seacoasts; I have celebrated it on altars built in stadiums and in city squares…This varied scenario of celebrations of the Eucharist has given me a powerful experience of its universal and, so to speak, cosmic character.

Real Presence in the Eucharist

by Jeffrey D. VonLehmen

How is Jesus present in the Eucharist? Most of us, at one time or another, find ourselves either asking that question or trying to explain the mystery for someone else. Catholics believe that the body and blood of Jesus is present in consecrated bread and wine. We do not say the Eucharist is *like* the body and blood of Jesus, but that it *is* the body and blood of Jesus. In the Gospels Jesus says, "This is my body" and "This is my blood." That is strong language; it is language which Christians have sought to understand for many centuries.

Perhaps we struggle to understand in the good sense of *struggle*. After all, in the Eucharist we proclaim the mystery of our faith. It is a mystery! But unlike murder mysteries, such as the Sherlock Holmes tales, where the author deliberately obscures some of the facts to lead the reader astray, the mystery of the Kingdom of God and the Eucharist is meant to be obvious. It is meant to reveal and not to obscure, although it cannot be reduced to human logic. As a parish priest who has struggled to deepen my own understanding of this mystery, I contend that what is most obvious sometimes is most overlooked.

I invite you to look at the obvious—*our ordinary human experiences*—to help make sense of Eucharist and Real Presence. Why does it make sense for Catholics to believe in what has traditionally been called *transubstantiation* (the changing of the whole substance of the bread and wine into the body and blood of Christ)? Why is it important to say that the Eucharist is a concrete encounter of the *community* with Jesus and not just a spiritual thing between an individual and God? In our own human experience we can discover why real presence and the body-and-blood presence of Christ are important to us and to God.

Flesh-and-blood relationships

We often think of spiritual as invisible. But who wants an invisible relationship with a loved one?

Consider this example. A father leaves work early on a weekday, drives five hours to another city to be present at his son's college basketball game and then drives home the same night. The father arrives home about 5 a.m., catches an hour of sleep, then goes to work.

He does this often. Perhaps it would be enough to tell his son over the phone that he is thinking about him and cheering and praying for him. But think how much more it means to the child that his father is not just there in spirit—he is there in flesh. He is providing a *real presence* for his son. What a big difference!

A flesh-and-blood relationship can make a difference. Consider the true story of a baby who lost both parents in a fire. The child became so traumatized that he clung to himself, arms crossed over his chest, as stiff as a board. When rescuers took the child to the hospital he was placed in a crib just outside the nurses' station. Whenever the nurses and nurse's aides walked by, they would speak softly to the baby and gently caress him.

Over a period of time, the baby began to respond. First a finger loosened, then a hand, than an arm, then a leg, until the baby was completely relaxed and finally recovered from the shock. The body-and-blood relationship with the nurses gradually brought about the child's wellness. Again, what a difference the *real presence* of these nurses made to the child. There's no substitute for a real flesh-and-blood relationship.

When we love someone we want a concrete relationship. If a mother will stay at the bedside of her comatose daughter day and night until her daughter comes out of the coma, is not God going to be with the world, day and night, until it comes out of its comatose state? The loving Spirit of God always seeks a concrete body-and-blood relationship with us. Isn't that what we celebrate in the Incarnation at Christmas, in the death and resurrection of Jesus on Good Friday and Easter? The Spirit dwells in us so we might experience God, who wants a real relationship with us.

Like the little baby in the nurses' station, we need a body-and-blood relationship with God in Christ. Yet where do we learn about body-and-blood relationships? We can only begin to understand the body and blood of Jesus when we understand true love in relationships involving friends, family and marriage.

Sacrifice and life

Think in terms of word associations. When I say "green" someone might think of grass. When I say "blue," one might think of sky. In our culture, when someone says "blood," we more than likely think of something terrible, of violence or loss of life. When we hear about body and blood as sacrifice, as in the sacrifice of the Mass, we think somebody or something has been killed. But in the ancient Hebrew mentality, if an animal was sacrificed to God, the people did not think that the animal was killed to appease an angry God. Instead, they thought of blood as the presence of life. Sacrifice was not so much giving up their best lamb or the first and best part of their crop. Sacrifice meant communion of life.

This brings to mind the wonderful image of an infant in the mother's womb. The infant is being nourished through the umbilical cord by the body and blood of the mother. It's not a violent act—the baby is receiving life. The mother's body is making all kinds of changes and sacrifices for the infant in her womb. But the mother is not thinking, *Oh, my body is making all kinds of sacrifices for the infant in my womb.* Instead, the mother is very conscious of the communion she has with her infant, the communion of life. This relationship is truly a body-and-blood relationship.

The bond between us and God, our loving parent, is just as strong and concrete. God wants a body-and-blood relationship with us. And as God's infants, we need that relationship.

This concrete relationship is made possible in Christ. God so loved the world that God sent his only son. It is interesting in Sebastian Moore's book, *The Fire and the Rose Are One,* that Christ's sacrifice in becoming one like us in the Incarnation and in his passion on the cross establishes a communion of life; a real presence in which our greatest desire is assured: "The one I most desire does in fact desire me." The Eucharist is the continuous concrete encounter of a people with God in the incarnation and passion of Christ. In a loving communion between the mother and infant, that strong body-and-blood presence assures the child that the one the child most desires does in fact desire him or her. In the body-and-blood presence of Christ, we are assured the One we most desire does in fact desire us.

The bread and wine are not simply like the body and blood of Christ; they *are* the body-and-blood presence of Christ. This is because our relationship is that concrete, that real, that wonderful! Jesus is God revealing God's self to us. Neither we nor God want an invisible relationship—we want the real thing!

We can increase our understanding of God's presence during the Eucharistic Prayer and Communion by thinking about being in the womb of God where we are fed concretely through the umbilical cord of the Holy Spirit. During this part of the Mass, the priest says, "This is my body which will be given up for you." Then he says, "This is my blood, the blood of the new and everlasting covenant." Through these words of life, love and communion, we encounter the person of Christ!

Demonstrating the importance of this sacrament, a Catholic visionary once said, "If I had a choice between a vision and the Eucharist, I would choose the Eucharist."

Real reverence comes first

There is no doubt that a body-and-blood relationship exists between a mother and her child. But they don't think of each other as body and blood. They think about the human relationship between them, whether or not it is mutually loving. It's the same way in the eucharistic celebration. We have a body-and-blood relationship with God in Christ. In this encounter, we no longer get stuck on the elements of bread and wine, body and blood. This is because we experience persons instead of things, relationships instead of magic. Real reverence has to be for the person of Christ and for all people for whom he died—the two are inseparable. That is why people are called the *body of Christ.*

There was an unpleasant incident a few years ago regarding whether proper respect had been shown toward the Eucharist at a special youth Mass. Someone noticed that the Precious Blood remained on the credence table after Mass. The Precious Blood sat there during a lengthy youth function following Mass which involved clapping, shouting, and a lot of carrying on. When the function was ended, a eucharistic minister took care of the consecrated wine. What had happened was an unfortunate oversight.

The eucharistic ministers were unable to see that the chalices were still on the credence table after Mass, There was no deliberate disrespect or neglect. Some people, however, felt it their duty to write the bishop about the pastor's neglect. They made no bones about attacking the pastor, accusing him and his staff of sacrilege. They never went to the pastor first to talk about it. They ripped him in front of the bishop and probably everyone else they knew. I firmly believe that real sacrilege, the real irreverence was being done by those people in their actions and attitude toward the pastor. Granted, we must treat the consecrated elements with respect. Real reverence, however, includes how we treat one another preceding and following the Eucharist.

We cannot have reverence for the body and blood of Christ—the person of Christ—if we knock down those for whom he died out of love. For this reason, people are the Body of Christ. Scripture always says it so well; "'Truly I tell you, just as you did not do it to one of the least of these, you did not do it to me'" (Mt 25:45). "Those who say, 'I love God,' and hate their brothers or sisters, are liars…" (1 Jn 4:20). In speaking of the condemnation of the unjust steward, Matthew's Gospel says, "So my heavenly Father will also do to every one of you, if you do not forgive your brother or sister from your heart" (Mt 18:35).

It is simple: We must have reverence for one another. Can a man say he loves his wife if he abuses their children? Are not the children part of her? We cannot abuse one another, cannot help but want a community of compassion, mercy, peace and justice, if we recognize that we all come from the same womb of God, the love of God poured out into our hearts through the outpouring of the Spirit; signed and sealed in the body-and-blood relationship we have in Christ.

Both new and old

Since the Second Vatican Council, the Church has made it a priority to *update and develop* Catholic faith, not simply preserve it. *Gaudium et Spes* says that theologians, whether lay or cleric, "enjoy the freedom to inquire, to think, and humbly and courageously reveal their minds on the matters in which they are expert" (#62). Theologians have developed contemporary models for understanding Christ's real presence in the Eucharist. For example, theologians like Bernard Cooke, Joseph Powers, Piet Schoonenberg and Edward Schillebeekcx have set forth the Interpersonal Encounter Model, which emphasizes Christ's presence in the people gathered to celebrate the Eucharist.

Although this model uses new terms like *transfinalization* and *transignification,* it still adheres to the ontological change or transubstantiation of bread and wine into body and blood of Christ. In simpler language, the bread and wine really do become the body and blood of Christ. Pope Paul VI's encyclical *Mysterium Fidei* allows for these new formulas as long as they hold that Christ is really present in the eucharistic species: "As a result of transubstantiation, the species of bread and wine undoubtedly take on a new significance and a new finality, for they are no longer ordinary bread and wine but instead a sign of something sacred and a sign of spiritual food; but they take on this new signification, this new finality, precisely because they contain a new 'reality' which we can rightly call ontological."

The *Catechism of the Catholic Church* affirms this approach: "At the heart of the eucharistic celebration are the bread and wine that, by the words of Christ and the invocation of the Holy Spirit, become Christ's body and blood" (#1333).

Truly the Eucharist is a real, interpersonal encounter between God and the worshiping community precisely because Christ is body-and-blood present. Our human experiences of love and relationships tell us that any lover seeks concrete union with the beloved. Although there may be new formulas to describe the real presence, the love expressed in the Eucharist is as old as Christmas. It is like the love between a mother and her infant in the womb. It is the love of God in Christ for his prenatal people not yet fully born in to the reign of God: "...the bread that I will give for the life of the world is my flesh....Very truly, I tell you, unless you eat the flesh of the Son of Man and drink his blood, you have no life in you....Those who eat my flesh and drink my blood abide in me, and I in them" (Jn 6:51–56).

Used with permission from Jeffrey D. VonLehmen.

[This article first published in *Catholic Update C0996* published by St. Anthony Messenger Press]

He's So Close to Me

In March of 1987, I had two nephews who were dying of San Filipo–Type A disease. This genetic disease generally kills children in their early teens.

I had a Mass celebrated for the older of the boys on his 13th birthday. After receiving holy Communion, I knelt and prayed, "Lord, please heal Zachy." Instantly, as though a radio had been turned on, I heard a masculine voice say, "But he's so close to me, would you take that away from him?" The Lord had replied in audible voice, something I could never have imagined would happen in this life.

Stunned, I replied, "No, I wouldn't. But what about Cody?" Cody was my other ill nephew. This time there was no answer. I knew then that my nephew would not live long in this world, but had the assurance of Jesus Himself that he would live eternally with Him in the next. Who could really ask for more? Both boys died within a few years.

Sister Briege McKenna, a healer, has written that during the celebration of the Eucharist is the best time to ask for healing. I believe that is true.

Ann Sabocik   *Terre Haute, Indiana*

You Too Must Forgive

When my daughter was ten years old, her friend's father molested her. After three years of nightmares, Melissa finally told me what had happened when she stayed over night at her friend Amber's house. The girl's father was then brought up on charges involving four children, and spent one year in jail.

For a long time I felt responsible for what happened to my daughter. When I had given Melissa permission to sleep there, the Holy Spirit repeatedly brought into my mind a question as to whether or not this was a safe place for my daughter. Unfortunately, I did not listen to my motherly intuition. I visited with this man in his home and had reached the conclusion that I was probably being overly protective. The main reason I let Melissa spend the night there was because Amber had no other friends and desperately needed one.

As time went by, I prayed that I could forgive this man that had made his mark on by daughter's life forever. I prayed that this would not happen to any other child. Just when I thought I had forgiven him, something would happen to bring back all the hurt, and again I would be on my knees asking God to help me forgive him. The process of forgiveness was never ending, and I found that I could not forgive myself. Then God healed me.

Each time I received the Eucharist I could hear in my thoughts, "Look beyond the bread. Look beyond the wine to find the Father." I did not want to do this because I knew I would have to relive the hurt again. But, I heard it every time I received the Eucharist, so I faced the pain again.

As I sat in church during my holy hour one day, I closed my eyes and tears streamed down my face. In my thoughts was the voice of God, the Father, telling me, "I gave in friendship the most precious gift I had to give. I gave my son. He turned to me and asked me to forgive them. You gave in friendship the most precious gift you had to give. You gave your daughter. Now you too must forgive."

I still pray for the man who molested my daughter, and now I know that I have forgiven myself, and I have forgiven him.

Annette M. Wurdeman   *Columbus, Nebraska*

 Because even when it is celebrated on the humble altar of a country church, the Eucharist is always in some way celebrated on the altar of the world.

Worth the Wait

My experience of the Eucharist is somewhat different from the experiences of many Catholics, for I am a convert, raised in the Episcopal Church.

As I was growing up, we celebrated Communion every other Sunday, alternating weeks with Morning Prayer. I was too young to understand that when the Anglican Church broke away from the Mother Church, their priests no longer had valid holy orders and could not consecrate the Host. Therefore, to this day, the elements of bread and wine are not transubstantially changed during their Communion celebration. They remain ordinary bread and wine.

As a child, I knew something was missing in the way that I knew and worshipped God. I wanted more of the presence of God in my life. Then, at fourteen, I attended an international evangelistic crusade with a friend and was overwhelmed by the experience. These people knew God in a personal way, and I wanted to also.

Confronted by my own sinfulness, I experienced a genuine repentance and conversion. After a few months, finding little of the new life and joy I had found in Christ in the Episcopal Church of my childhood, I joined the Baptist Church.

The next twenty-five years were a spiritual roller coaster. I married, had children, and enjoyed being a schoolteacher. Sometimes, particularly during times of genuine adversity, God was very close and very real to me. At other times, He seemed distant and I found it hard to pray or even attend worship services.

One of the hardest aspects of being Protestant was participating in the Lord's Supper. Protestant churches do not completely ignore the Lord's command to, "Do this in remembrance of me." However, something deep inside me cried out, telling me that this ritual, held four times a year with grape juice and tiny crackers, fell short of what God intended it to be. I remembered the solemnity and beautiful prayers of the Episcopal Church, yet also recalled the emptiness that I had experienced there.

Twenty years into my marriage, my husband, who was a reluctant churchgoer at best, began to take our fourteen year old daughter to an Episcopal church across town. Soon the whole family was going. I found the return to liturgical worship surprisingly easy, and for five years we were relatively happy worshipping as a family and singing in the choir. Then things began to go sour.

My husband was deeply hurt by a power struggle between the priest and some other groups within the church. At the same time, a friend invited me to sing at a Catholic church on the opposite side of town. Singing at church had become very important to me over the years. I was learning to cantor and opportunities to do that were available at Blessed Sacrament Catholic Church.

I had never thought very much about Catholicism prior to this. Somehow, while I was in the Baptist Church, I had been spared the anti-Catholic rhetoric that is sometimes present in Baptist circles. Also, during the five years I was in the Episcopal Church, the priest taught and preached a lot of church history. He often intended to put the Catholic Church in a negative light, as he was an ex-Catholic himself. However, truth is truth, and what I heard in his teachings was the long unbroken chain of apostolic succession and tradition within the Catholic Church.

At first the Catholic service seemed very familiar to me. I had no intention of converting, but felt comfortable with the status quo. I began cantering at the Catholic church on Saturday night and attending the Episcopal church with my family on Sunday morning. Soon, the fact that I could not receive the Eucharist became a real trial.

Communion at the Episcopal Church is open to all baptized Christians. I wondered what made these Catholics so exclusive and resented being excluded from receiving Communion. Yet, at the same time, part of me knew that there was something special, something different happening during Communion at the Catholic Church.

Then one day, in an instant, all that I had learned about Church history during the five years I had been back in the Episcopal Church as an adult crystallized. Suddenly I realized that the Protestant Church, which I was a member of, had arisen from King Henry VIII in an act of rebellion against the pope who refused to give him a divorce. Of course I knew there were other issues involved, but that was the central one. I knew that the Episcopal Church was not God's perfect will for His people.

That night I began to study the Catholic Church and her teachings in earnest. I read a good deal about transubstantiation and the real presence of Christ in the Eucharist. All the ideas were very new and strange to me, and I found that by the time I understood them, at least as much as I am capable of understanding them, I already believed them. It was apparent to me that my heart had understood this before my mind did. Then the long wait to receive the Eucharist began.

By June I felt ready to join the Church, having studied the books that were used in the RCIA classes pretty thoroughly. Father Bittner at Blessed Sacrament Catholic Church wanted me to wait until the Easter Vigil to be received into the Church. Since this is a rather small parish and I was the only candidate interested in RCIA that year, the priest suggested that I join a class at another parish. He thought that being in a group with others traveling a similar path to mine would be helpful.

I joined a class at St. Stephen the Martyr Parish, where I also occasionally cantored. Unfortunately, I was impatient as the class considered issues that I had already settled in my own heart and mind. I asked Father Bittner again to receive me before Christmas. His response surprised me. He told me that he would confirm me between Christmas and Lent and assigned me the task of finding a week when the readings were appropriately focused on the Holy Spirit.

God had other plans. I became ill and spent weeks in bed with mononucleosis. When I recovered from that, I spent two more weeks in bed with diverticulitis. What should have been a miserable time was transformed by God's grace into a special time of blessing. Flat on my back, I prayed the rosary many times, a prayer that I was unacquainted with only a year earlier.

When I was well enough to attend Mass, I was filled with a mixture of joy at being there and sadness that I could not receive the Eucharist. My confirmation sponsor assured me frequently that it would be worth the wait and that the Easter Vigil would be a very special time. He was right. When I finally received my Lord; body, blood, soul, and divinity, I knew that I had found what was lacking during all my roller coaster years in the Protestant Church. It was the graces that come to us through the Eucharist.

In the sacraments of the Catholic Church, particularly reconciliation and the Eucharist, I had found the fullness of all that Christ has promised His disciples and all believers. Through the re-presentation of Christ's suffering, death, and resurrection, I die to sin and rise to a new life in Him.

For me, the journey to the Eucharist was a long one. However, as I look back, I realize that at every stage of the journey, God was there, directing my steps. And as my confirmation sponsor had promised, it was worth the wait.

Catharine D. Beaudrie   *Gardendale, Alabama*

Weep No More

In our parish there was a young married lady that I will call Laurie (not her real name). She came to Mass every week and reverently received holy Communion. It seemed there was always a sort of sadness about her. She would receive Communion and then remain after Mass, weeping openly in front of our statue of the Sacred Heart of Jesus.

I asked around to see if anyone knew what made her so sad. I was told that she wanted children very much, but was unable to conceive. Some time went by and others began praying for her. Finally, I think that Jesus could not stand any more weeping after Communion. The parish rejoiced when they learned that she was expecting. She now has two beautiful children. She was like the woman in Scripture that kept pestering the judge to decide in her favor.

As a parish deacon, the highlight of my week is being able to raise the Precious Blood at the conclusion of the consecration. This is the same blood that saved all of us. The blood of Jesus, who heard the weeping of one of His humble servants after she received Him in holy Communion.

Deacon Anthony R. DiMaggio, SFO   *Chowcilla, California*

Life-Changing Summer

Up until a couple of years ago, I was not into my faith much. I went to Mass, but for the most part, it was because I was obligated to. I participated in the youth group, but that was mainly to get out of the house, away from my parents. All of that was about to change.

My father is in the Air Force, so in the summer of 2002, I was able to get a summer job at the base chapel. At first it was like any other summer job I had before. But since there was not a lot for me to do, I found myself going to the daily Mass at noon. Initially I went so my supervisor would not see me sitting around doing nothing.

Soon I found myself actually looking forward to going to daily Mass, and it wasn't so I could get out of doing my work. I truly wanted to hear the reading and father's homily every day. My knowledge of what the Catholic Church teaches grew quickly, especially our belief that Jesus is truly present in the Eucharist. I had known this before but had never really believed it.

Now I always look forward to going to Mass to receive Jesus in the Blessed Sacrament. Through doing this I continue to grow even closer to God. I now believe, and have for a while, that God is calling me to the religious life. I attribute this to the fact that I attended daily Mass during that life-changing summer. Since then I have graduated from high school and am in the process of discerning what part of the religious life God is calling me.

Jorge O. Soto-Pedraza   *Kadena Air Base, Japan*

"What shall I render to the Lord for all his bounty to me? I will lift up the cup of salvation and call on the name of the Lord" (Ps 116:12–13).

Only One Week to Live

Yes, God loved the world so much that He gave His only Son so that everyone who believes in Him may not be lost but may have eternal life (John 3:16).

In my late teenage years I turned away from God and lived a life totally self-centered. The sinfulness of the world, I am ashamed to say, attracted me more than the purity of Christ. This state continued for many more years as my obvious lack of virtues increased.

Later, through several circumstances in my life, friends pulled me back to church where I unwillingly sat at the Sunday Mass, fighting off the negative emotions that were always present.

The years passed by and my spiritual struggle intensified. My breakthrough, however, came in June of 1982 when my mother-in-law was dying of cancer. It was at the same time that Pope John Paul II was to visit Scotland.

My mother-in-law was facing her own struggle at the time, and was fighting for her life. She was a nonbeliever, and although a very compassionate, kind and loving person, her belief did not go beyond this world. I loved her dearly and could not bear the thought of her dying in this state, so I made a pact with God.

At the time, the doctors had given her only one week to live and, as a family, we prayed fervently for her. It was at a holy hour that both her life and mine were transformed. I knelt before the Blessed Sacrament and pleaded with God in the Eucharist for her life and salvation. I was desperate and could not accept the fact that Mum was going to die without knowing she had a saviour. In that desperation, I offered God my life in return for hers.

Little did I realize at the time the enormity of what I had done. God took His opportunity, and not only did He dramatically transform my own life, but He liberated and touched Mums life too. It was amazing! The doctors could hardly believe that a woman so close to death could recover and walk out of the hospital to live and breathe the goodness of Our Lord.

The time ahead for her was blessed. She was able to share her life more fully with Dad (my father-in-law) as they took advantage of an opportunity to go away for a quiet holiday. This was something they had never been able to do very often before due to family commitments. They went everywhere together, and their love blossomed as if in a new beginning. Mum lived a full year, and died in a state of grace at St. Columbus Hospice, Edinburgh, where she recited Our Lord's prayer daily with the nuns.

It was at this time that I, too, experienced the great love of God, as my own marriage was strengthened and I felt our love increasing. My life took on a new meaning as I experienced the grace of God. It was a grace that had always been there but which I had been blind to. At the holy hour, God opened my eyes to His love and I experienced what I can only describe as a soothing, profound peace in my being that I cannot put into words. I had certainly never felt this kind of peace before. This deep peace developed, and with it a greater fervour for prayer, and a deep repentance for my sinful state.

The full impact of the Gospel hit my life, and my understanding of Christ's coming on earth cemented itself into a deeper relationship with Our Lord and Saviour. God's love and generosity can never be outdone, and shortly after my holy hour experience, my whole family was converted. God touched their hearts and entered into their lives, and the graces continue to this day.

When I look back over my life, I realize that only God could have done what He did with our lives. God, in His mercy, transformed us and continues to transform us into the people He wants us to be. May He always be glorified in our lives, and may we never take the credit for anything we have done, for salvation in Christ is a free gift from God, to all.

Maria V. Bartlett   *Kinross, Tayside, Scotland*

In many places, adoration of the Blessed Sacrament *is also an important daily practice and becomes an inexhaustible source of holiness.*

I Became a Pastor

One Sunday morning during Mass, after I had been pastor of St. Monica-St. George Parish in Cincinnati, Ohio, for about a year and half, I found myself looking out at the congregation, and something clicked within me. I felt a profound sense of connection with the people I saw.

I had been there long enough to get to know a good number of people. I knew many of their stories, their struggles and their joys. I knew that one woman I saw had just suffered a miscarriage and was grieving the loss of her child. Another woman had just told me that she was pregnant. I saw a couple that I was preparing for marriage, and I knew of their hopes and dreams.

As I looked into the congregation, I saw the family of a man whose funeral I had celebrated the past week. I saw the family of a woman who was in the hospital suffering from cancer. I saw a woman whose husband was struggling with alcoholism. There was a woman whose confession I had heard, amidst many tears.

There were many, too, that I did not recognize or know their stories. But I knew that each of them had a unique story too. And I knew that each one came to this celebration of the Eucharist with hopes and dreams and prayers in their hearts.

As luck (or grace) would have it, at Communion we sang David Haas's "Song of the Body of Christ," that has the refrain, "We come to share our story; We come to break the bread; We come to know our rising from the dead." It was perfect.

I had a profound sense of the privileged role I had as pastor of these people. I had a profound sense of connection to the people and their stories. And I knew that we had come to a wonderful place together to experience hope. Though I had the title for a year and half, I think became a *Pastor* on that day.

Father Jeffrey Scheeler, OFM   *Cincinnati, Ohio*

God Loves Toto Too

Toto is my beautiful male Birman cat. He is very handsome and has creamy colored fur with blue points. His colored points are on his ears and across his face like a mask, and each leg has a ring of color above the paw. His tail is like a long plume, floating in the air as he struts and walks around our home.

One hot summer day here in Texas, my furry companion and friend became ill and lost his appetite. I thought he was under the weather from the heat, but that one day turned into a few more days that Toto wouldn't eat. He would look at the bowl of food and hunch down to try to eat, but would end up looking very sad and walking away.

Within days, my helpless kitten became dehydrated and laid limp across the floor. I rushed him to the veterinarian and she started him on a saline IV before examining him. She was perplexed and wasn't sure about what could be bothering my seven-month-old Toto.

The doctor decided to give him a couple of shots to increase his appetite. One was a B_{12} vitamin shot and the other was a hormone. She told me to take him home and to cuddle and love him, and said that by tomorrow he should be eating again. She also cautioned me that Toto wouldn't eat until the next day because that's how long the shot would take to get into his system.

I was worried about Toto and wanted to pray for him, so I went to the adoration chapel where Jesus is always present in the Eucharist. I set my kitten in his carrier right outside the chapel door and heard him cry as I walked away and closed the chapel door.

Inside the chapel, I praised God for all the blessings He gives me everyday and told Him how much I love Him. Then I told Jesus about my sick Toto and asked Him to heal my kitten. While I was praying, I could still hear Toto whining in his carrier outside the door.

When I left the chapel I had a peaceful heart knowing God was at work. Then, as soon as Toto and I arrived home, he ran straight to his food bowl and started to eat! At that moment I was so happy that I knelt down and praised God for His divine help when I needed it. He truly does watch over us and listens to our prayers. I know God loves me, and He loves my little Toto too!

Annie-Alex Nathenson   *Austin, Texas*

A Gift from Jesus to Me

I am unable to attend Mass each week due to a stroke and a broken hip. But because of the kindness of eucharistic ministers, I am able to share in the body and blood of my Lord.

This is a vital part of my life, and each time I partake, I realize once again that His love and caring is for this 86-year-old too. I feel so humble, richly blessed, and renewed when I receive Our Lord.

I realize this is a commitment for the eucharistic ministers. They take time out of their day to bring the Eucharist to me, and never make me feel rushed. They don't just arrive and try to give it to me in a hurry and then rush off. Rather, they come prepared to share the Eucharist with me in a sacred and blessed way.

I do so miss church and feel the Eucharist is a gift from Jesus to me. He is here and He loves me!

A. Ruth Talbott   *Springfield, Missouri*

"The Lord Jesus on the night he was betrayed" (1 Cor 11:23) instituted the Eucharistic Sacrifice of his body and his blood.

All the Love

At a recent Mass, after twenty years of administering holy Communion, I looked down into the ciborium and saw all the love that created the universe. I saw all the love that suffered and died that we might have eternal life, and all the love that is willing to take the form of bread just to come into real contact with us. I began to tremble.

Deacon Jim Fuller   *Granbury, Texas*

A Stolen Purse

As part of a sabbatical experience, I was fortunate enough to be able to fly to Mexico City for five days in October of 1982. On Sunday morning, I walked from my hotel with several other visitors to the Metropolitan Cathedral for Mass. In spite of having been warned to never set our purses down in a public place, when the priest came down the aisles for the sprinkling rite at the beginning of Mass, I was so delighted to actually know the Spanish song they were singing that I set my purse down on the bench behind me.

Only a few seconds later I realized what I had done, but by that time my purse was gone. Several people in our group helped me look for it, but eventually it became clear that it was gone forever.

I returned to my pew and sat down to listen to the readings. The first reading was over, and the very first words I heard were: "El Senor es mi Pastor; nada me pede faltar." They were the words of the Good Shepherd Psalm: The Lord is my shepherd; there is nothing I shall want.

All of a sudden, there was absolute calm in my heart and soul. I was unusually at peace with the realization that I had never before been without anything I needed, and that God would not permit me to need anything now. With these comforting words, I was able to enter fully into the remainder of the celebration. I received my shepherd in the Eucharist, and was grateful for the instant freedom from worry that I had experienced.

After the Mass, fellow visitors shared some of their *pesos* with me so I was able to buy a few souvenirs for friends and family. The overwhelming sense of peace has continued since the day my purse was stolen. In losing my purse and its contents, I also lost my worries and gained a wonderful experience of complete dependence on the Lord and others for all I needed.

I was able to get a visa from the U.S. Consulate the next day so I could fly back to Texas, and the airline verified that I had purchased a round-trip ticket, so it all ended well. The peace in my heart goes on.

Sister Mary Lalemant Pelikan, RSM　　　　　　　　　　　　*Lubbock, Texas*

Jesus and Me

Sometimes, as I sit before Jesus in the tabernacle, I cannot think of what to say to Him that He would want to hear. I always ask for mercy for souls, and pray for my friends. I think about how little I say, but realize that just the fact that I am here before Jesus must please Him. Surely He loves me by giving me the grace to be there spending time with Him. Thank you, Jesus!

Carol A. DeGeorge　　　　　　　　　　　　　　　*Centreville, Virginia*

The Eucharist is indelibly marked by the event of the Lord's passion and death, of which it is not only a reminder but the sacramental re-presentation.

With God's People

"O sublime humility, O humble sublimity, that the infinite God would strip Himself of glory to us in the form of a simple piece of bread and a sip of wine!" Over and over again while I was stationed in the Indian missions in the Southwest, this spoke clearly to me, especially on a couple of Christmases.

The village of Vamori had an early Christmas Mass. It was a poor little church with plaster falling off the walls, and the wooden floor being enjoyed by termites. The people had *decorated* the church. Next to the side wall in the sanctuary, sitting on a pile of dirt, were the chipped and broken figures of Jesus, Mary and Joseph. One of the Indians played a violin, from which one of the strings had broken and was not replaced.

As I was celebrating the Mass, I couldn't help but say to the infant Jesus, "Welcome, Lord! You must feel right at home in such surroundings!" And, you know what? So did I!

Father Maurus Kelly, OFM   *Santa Barbara, California*

A Loving and Gentle God

I am a cradle Catholic and have felt drawn to the Lord since I was a small child. I believe receiving the Lord in the Eucharist is an ongoing, timeless experience. My Eucharist story dates back to the 1980s.

After hearing that I was pregnant with my fourth child, I was not happy with the news. I already had three healthy children and thought my *baby* days were over. However, I accepted the Lord's will, and began to plan for the new addition to my family. When I miscarried in my first trimester, I was filled with guilt and anxiety. I blamed myself, and viewed the miscarriage as punishment for not being accepting of a new life.

About three months later I became severely depressed. I cried, slept poorly, and felt like a heavy gray cloud was enveloping me. I felt helpless and cried out to God to help me get over this. He surrounded me with love and support from my husband and friends, and I sought counseling.

On the feast of the Immaculate Conception, I attended Mass feeling very unworthy and guilty (depression will do this to you). When it was time for Communion I convinced myself that I was *too bad* to receive the Eucharist.

As I was kneeling, I heard the priest read the Communion antiphon. "Come to me, all who labor and are heavy laden, and I will give you rest." I thought the message must be meant for me, so I joined the line of communicants and made my way to the front of the church. I was still feeling down, but was hopeful.

I received the Lord and was walking back to my seat when I was suddenly filled with peace and joy. My depression lifted, and I could scarcely believe my good fortune. As I knelt and prayed, I remember thinking, "It really is you, Lord!" I was finally experiencing in my heart what I had known in my head since I was a young child, and it has remained with me ever since. I learned firsthand that the Lord is especially close to the broken hearted and needy.

My depression returned a short time after that, but it never overwhelmed me again. I was able to cope as the Lord healed me gently and slowly. Through this trial I forged a closer relationship with Him and felt a new appreciation for His words, " I will never leave you, nor forsake you." What a loving and gentle God we have, so full of love and grace.

"Suzanne"   *Honolulu, HI*

The Church has received the Eucharist from Christ her Lord not as one gift—however precious—among so many others, but as the gift par excellence, for it is the gift of himself, of his person in his sacred humanity, as well as the gift of his saving work.

Sharing the Eucharist

At every Mass, as I gaze on the consecrated Eucharist on the altar of sacrifice, I am drawn to the warmth of the entire body of Christ. The celebrant and the people of God, united together, encircle and proclaim the presence of our Savior.

As I listen to the instructions of our Lord, "Do this in remembrance of Me," I stand in expectant faith, knowing that the presence of Jesus will empower us to continue His mission to follow His words, actions and deeds.

When the celebrant elevates the body of our living God, I know that our saving Lord has once again come to my side. I continue to recall that I am indeed not worthy to stand in the presence of Our Lord. With gratitude and reverence, therefore, I proceed to the foot of the sanctuary and humbly share with my sisters and brothers, the mystical body of Christ.

Deacon Edward G. Beckendorf　　　　　　　　　*Mohegan Lake, New York*

My Conversion Story

I am fifty-six years old and was received into the Catholic Church five years ago after years of being a *lukewarm* Anglican. For the previous five years I hadn't attended church at all and really missed it. I had been looking for the right spiritual path since I was nineteen, and still had not found it. Once I found the Catholic Church, I knew it was right for me. I was fortunate enough to go to Medugorje and Lourdes soon after my reception and have experienced three different Catholic parishes.

My conversion story began in 1996 when I rented a house across the road from a Catholic church. At the time I thought, in a vague sort of way, that I would visit it someday to see what went on there. About a year later my daughter, who was fourteen at the time, stopped going to school and got in with a bad crowd. It was a terrible time and I never knew where she was or who she was with. It was much worse than it sounds here.

I knew I had to go to church and pray seriously. I couldn't go back to the Church of England, so I thought I would give the Catholic church across the road a try. I was so nervous that I almost didn't go in, but I knew that if I didn't go then, I never would. I told the greeter that I hadn't been there before. She was very nice and said I could go up for a blessing, which I didn't do. As a newcomer, I thought everyone would be looking at me, but nobody did. I stood up and sat down with everyone else.

That day I knew I had found my spiritual home. I went to see the priest and he said that even though it was only October, it was too late for me to start RCIA that year. I had to wait a whole year to begin my lessons.

Shortly after this first Mass, I went on a trip to Cologne Christmas Market in Germany, and went to Mass in the cathedral. I understand German reasonably well and as the bishop celebrated the Mass, I was very excited that I understood most of the homily.

During this Mass, I was overcome at how I was surrounded by ordinary German people taking a break from their Christmas shopping, and here I was, a very new prospective Catholic from England in this wonderful German cathedral, and yet we were all united in the Mass. In fact, I have tears in my eyes writing this, remembering how this confirmed to me that I had to become a Catholic. I have never regretted that decision.

To this day, what I treasure most about Mass is the wonderful feeling of unity among all Catholics. When we say the creed, I feel united to all my Catholic brothers and sisters throughout the world. I love the thought that Catholics everywhere are experiencing the same Mass in their own language, and that the readings are universal.

I often find myself in quiet tears during the Eucharistic Prayer and particularly love Eucharistic Prayer number three where it says, "Father, hear the prayers of the family you have gathered here before you. In your mercy and love unite all your children, wherever they may be." At this point I think of all the Catholics I have met, whether on pilgrimage, online, or in the parish.

Eucharistic Prayer number three also means a lot to me because I have never had earthly brothers or sisters and am thrilled to be part of the Catholic family. Thomas Merton expressed this much better than me in his journal where he wrote of being in a church in Cuba, and when the children stood up and said the creed in Spanish, he was completely carried away by it.

I am in the choir and love expressing my feelings in song, a legacy from my Anglican days, which is a part of God's plan I suppose. Here in the United Kingdom there is much criticism in the media of the Catholic Church, but in the three parishes I have been a member of, the attendance is great. People sometimes say you can be Christian without attending church, but I don't think it is that easy. I feel truly blessed to be part of the Catholic Church.

Sue J. Hodson   *Stamford, Lincolnshire, United Kingdom*

I Will Refresh You

As Jesus' earthly sojourn was drawing to a close, He made us a solemn promise: I will not leave you orphaned; I will come back to you (John 14:18).

This promise is fulfilled every time we offer Mass, especially when we receive holy Communion. On that day you are in me and I in you (John 14:20). He is with us to forgive our faults and failures, to help us shoulder our daily tasks, to fulfill us with His love, peace and joy.

Jesus invites us to offer Mass with Him and says to us: Come to me, all you who are weary and find life burdensome, and I will refresh you (Matt 11:28).

The Mass is the most sublime prayer we can offer since Jesus is offering Himself with us to praise and thank the Father, to implore His healing and forgiveness, and to present our petitions and needs.

Msgr. David E. Rosage   *Spokane, Washington*

When the Church celebrates the Eucharist, the memorial of her Lord's death and resurrection, this central event of salvation becomes really present and "the work of our redemption is carried out".

Sister Gilbertus and Our Lord

Many years ago, when I was young and living in a beautiful neighborhood in the city of Brooklyn, I would frequently visit our parish church. There I would spend time speaking and listening to Jesus, who is ever present in the Blessed Sacrament.

My prayer time was enhanced by the beautiful white sanctuary, the black onyx crucifix, and the mosaic of adoring angels. Often roses were placed above the tabernacle, and I later learned that they were sent to Father Solanus Casey from his parishioners in Chicago. The saintly priest would carefully arrange them above the tabernacle, which was beneath the crucifix. The church was always a special place, and Jesus was certainly there.

There was a beautiful Dominican nun in the parish that not many of the other students knew, but who I came to know well. During my many visits with Our Lord, I would visit her as she cleaned the church. She was crippled and hunched over, and yet was always able to keep Our Lord's sanctuary fresh and beautiful.

Shortly after her death, I was disturbed at night when I thought about this special nun. I thought about her holiness and hard work, and remembered how she would climb about the altar keeping it sparkling clean. I recalled how she would even take the stepladder from the altar table and use it to reach the top of the tabernacle. She also used it to reach the huge crucifix, and to keep the beautiful mosaic of the angels gleaming.

I finally picked a day to visit Sister Gilbertus at her place of rest in the Dominican cemetery, and now I visit it frequently. She is my friend in heaven who is praying to our eucharistic Lord, keeping His heavenly home beautiful while inviting me to come pray with her. Indeed, Sister Gilbertus knew Our Lord, and she passed her faith and devotion to me, placing her humble and holy influence deep in my heart. As I follow her bidding, I come before Jesus and adore Him. He, in turn, grants us many graces and blessings that we need in our own lives.

On Sundays after Mass, I always stop before Our Lord in the tabernacle. When I am there, I often remember Sister Gilbertus and the many nuns, teachers, and neighbors I have known throughout the years who have gone to be with Jesus. I think of all those who passed their love of Our Lord on to me before they departed this life.

May Jesus in the Blessed Sacrament of the altar be ever adored, praised, worshipped, and loved in all the tabernacles of the world, in time and eternity, by all peoples and all nations. May Our Lord of all nations grant peace and friendship to the world, uniting all nations as one family in His holy name.

Robert J. Reddington   *North Bellmore, New York*

My Mass with Padre Pio

In the summer of 1958, I completed studies in canon law at the Urban University in Rome. After that, with another American Capuchin, Father Reynold Rynda, I went to San Giovanni Rotondo in Italy to visit Father Dominic Meyer, who was a secretary at the time to our confrere, Padre Pio. The Padre received bags of mail from around the world daily and was loved by many people. Father Dominic arranged that both of us should serve Mass for Padre Pio. It was Sunday morning, June 29, 1958, ten years before Padre Pio's death.

I clearly remember the experience of that day. The Mass, which was before the Second Vatican Council, was in Latin, and Padre Pio celebrated facing forward, where a large crucifix hung. His Mass that day, without a homily, lasted one hour. There were some periods of what might be described as raptures, when Padre Pio, with eyes open, seemed to be witnessing the events of the Upper Room and of Calvary. At the lavabo of the Mass, or the hand washing ceremony, I poured water over the sacred stigmata. In the sacristy I kissed his hand.

As a priest myself, I have been offering Mass every day for fifty years. The experience of that Mass of Padre Pio still inspires me with devotion and reverence.

Father Jogues Constance, OFM Cap   *Washington, Michigan*

My Doubt Left Me

I am a cradle Catholic, but not an acting Catholic since I was small. My wife was searching for a true faith and to make a long story short, became Catholic five years ago. When my wife and children came into the Church, I came back as well.

My wife likes to research whatever she is interested in, so of course she researched the Catholic faith very intensely. To her there was no doubt that at the consecration the Host becomes the true body and the wine the true blood of Our Lord Jesus Christ. I knew this also in my head, but found myself with some doubt. I kept wondering, how could Jesus be here in this sacrament and everywhere else at the same time?

We became Eucharist ministers but I had a dilemma. How could I be a devoted Eucharist minister with some doubt still about the Eucharist? One Sunday at a Mass, in which I was asked to serve as a eucharistic minister, I prayed very hard about this. I asked Jesus to show me how He could be here in the Eucharist and all over the world.

While I was up in the sanctuary to serve, I watched as the priest consecrated the Host. I saw the face of Jesus in the Host as the priest held it over the wine. I saw a beautiful light come from the wine and consumed the Host and then the profile of Jesus appeared on the Host. I stared at it, not believing what I was seeing! A very peaceful feeling came over me as, all of a sudden, I understood that Jesus was here with us. I was so excited I couldn't wait to tell my wife after Mass!

My doubt left me and I became closer to Jesus then ever before!

Lawrence L. Chlebik   *McAlester, Oklahoma*

What more could Jesus have done for us? Truly, in the Eucharist, he shows us a love which goes "to the end" (cf. Jn 13:1), a love which knows no measure.

Accept the Faith as Your Own

I grew up in a Catholic family deep in South Louisiana, where Catholicism is a way of life. I practiced my faith with my family, but was riding on their coattails. I had not truly embraced the faith as my own. Because of that, it was relatively easy for a young man I met at college to draw me away from the Church. He took me to his evangelical church, but rarely. For the most part, we did not attend church at all. This was very hurtful to my family and created deep divisions between us.

My trips home from college became few and far between in order to avoid conflicts with my parents. I became engaged to marry the man who drew me away from my church and family, and we planned to marry about a year after we graduated college. Thankfully, God had other plans for me.

After graduation, I returned to my home town to look for a job and to prepare for my marriage. I attended a number of evangelical churches in the area, but none of them seemed to have the right mix of dynamic pastor and welcoming community. I could not find a church home.

I found a job about three months after graduation, and began working for the state in the local welfare office. There I met a man who fascinated me. He was funny, bright and a devout Catholic. Soon I felt the need to end my engagement to the evangelical guy because I was having feelings for my coworker. This was in October of 1980.

Being a good little evangelical convert, I invited my new boyfriend to come to church with me. He flatly refused, but invited me to attend Mass with him. Partly to please my parents, and partly as a bargaining tool to get him to my church, I agreed. That Sunday we surprised my parents by attending Mass with them at my childhood parish.

When the priest elevated the Host during the consecration, suddenly I knew that I was home for good. I realized why I had not found happiness in any evangelical church. I had been searching for the true presence of Jesus in the Eucharist, and at last I had found Him. I was filled with joy, a joy that has never left me. I married the wonderful Catholic man who brought me back to Mass on August 29, 1981. We have three wonderful sons, and the oldest and his lovely wife are now expecting their first child. Never again will a man come between me and the Eucharist.

I now work as assistant youth coordinator in my parish, and hope to show the youth of my parish that they must accept their faith as their own so that someone will not steal it from them when they move away from home.

Celeste Robichaux   *Thibodaux, Louisiana*

Navy Chaplain in Peace and War

There is not a holy Mass that I have celebrated since my ordination on May 26, 1973, in which the reality of the real presence of Christ has not profoundly moved me. To make Christ present to others: this is my call, my life.

As a Navy chaplain since June 17, 1984, I have celebrated holy Mass in the field: my altar has been a rock, a stretcher, piled ammunition boxes and even food boxes covered with a simple linen and corporal. The real presence of Christ was felt there, for those Marines, whether in training or real war environment. Christ was there!

I have celebrated holy Mass aboard ships: in the chapel, a classroom, in the fo'c's'le, on deck, on the ledge of a missile launcher (this last one raised some eyebrows until I told the sailors, "You may have to fire these, *let's pray for peace*"). They did fire them, two days after I left the ship. The real presence of Christ was important to them in a time of war.

I have celebrated holy Mass under the sea: aboard a submarine, and in the confines of the deep, the real presence of Christ was brought to His people.

I have celebrated holy Mass in the field: during Operation Desert Storm and during war as the chaplain for Fleet Hospital Eight in Rota, Spain, where we cared for hundreds of wounded Marines, soldiers, sailors, airmen and women and civilians from the battlefields of Iraq and Afghanistan. The real presence of Christ was there for His children.

In all of these places, God's Son, Our Lord and Savior, Jesus Christ, was made present, to bring renewed faith, hope, love and healing, to trusting and faithful men and women, in peace time and in war.

The real presence of Christ, what an awesome gift, a daily blessing! And I have the honor to make present at the altar, this wonderful gift of His body and blood, soul and divinity. As I bring this gift into the world, I think of one thing. Every time you or I receive this real presence in the Eucharist we hear Christ say, "Behold, I make all things new."

No matter what is going on in our lives, one thing is for sure, the real presence of Christ is the gift of the holy Eucharist. "Behold, I am with you always, even to the end of time."…"Behold the Lamb of God, who takes away the sins of the world, happy are they called to His supper." "…I am not worthy…I shall be healed."

Father Anthony M. Trapani   *Bremerton, Washington*

The Furnace Was Fixed

In January of 2004 a heavy snowfall hit Surrey, British Columbia, and its surrounding areas. This part of Canada is known for its mild winters, so this was unusual weather for those of us who live there.

The power in our home went out early that morning because of the snowstorm, and the house was cold when we woke up. The furnace had stopped working during the blackout, and when the power was restored, it still wouldn't work.

We turned on the fireplace in the family room, but it did not give off enough heat to warm the whole house. We knew it would be very expensive to leave it on all the time, so my husband tried everything he could to fix the furnace himself. Knowing the high cost of hiring a repairman, we didn't want to call a professional to repair it if we didn't have to. My husband wasn't successful, so we finally decided to hire someone to come and fix our furnace for us.

After we made that decision, we were worried that we wouldn't be able to get anyone to fix it right away because the weather was so bad. Plus, we were still concerned about the high cost of repairs.

It was almost time for the daily Mass on television, which I watch when I can't get to church. My husband joined me in watching it, and during the consecration, as the priest raised the holy Eucharist, my husband and I heard the motor of the furnace turn back on. It made a sound like it was running okay.

We quickly looked at each other but didn't say a word since the Mass was still going on. As Mass ended, our home was starting to warm up, but parts of the house remained a bit cold. We found out that the furnace fan, which pushes the warm air out of the vents, was not working.

I believed that God had fixed the furnace, but my husband was not completely convinced. He thought that since the fan was not working, God did not really fix the problem. I checked the vents again, and there was still no warm air coming out. I prayed to Jesus, telling Him that I believed He had fixed the furnace, and asked Him if He would do something about the fan so my husband would believe too.

That night, as I was preparing for bed, I felt warm air blowing on my feet. It was coming out of one of the vents! I immediately told my husband that Jesus had completely fixed the furnace. It was humbling to experience firsthand how God takes care of our needs, no matter how big or small they are.

Louise Molina   *Surrey, British Columbia, Canada*

Jesus did not simply state that what he was giving them to eat and drink was his body and his blood; he also expressed its sacrificial meaning *and made sacramentally present his sacrifice which would soon be offered on the Cross for the salvation of all.*

Catholic Magic

It was Thanksgiving, 1996. My family came from Spartanburg to our home in Camden for the Thanksgiving holiday. After dinner, the conversation turned to my niece, Jennifer, whose friend had just returned from Medjugorie. Her friend had purchased a small plastic statue of the Blessed Virgin and *supposedly* her cape had turned blue after visiting the holy site.

I winced and told Jennifer that it sounded like magic to me, and that it called attention to Mary, not to Jesus. I explained that these so-called apparitions of Mary were not really her at all, and that Mary would be horrified if she thought people on earth were kneeling before *visions* of her and praying to her as if she were God.

As I continued my explanation, my brother Steve, who was standing a few feet away from me, said in a very loud, exasperated and angry tone, "Well, she is the Mother of God!" When he said that, I was physically knocked backward by an invisible hand. I stumbled to keep from falling and tried to regain my composure. I mumbled something about her only being a human being and then went away dazed.

As I busied myself with other things, I thought to myself, "Yes, Jesus is God and Mary is His mother. So, she is the Mother of God!" I had never heard this description of her before, or if I had, I didn't remember hearing it.

"It is a pretty impressive thing, to be the Mother of God. I'm the religious one in the family. How did my brother know that Mary was the Mother of God and I didn't?" I thought to myself. "He rarely goes to church. He was raised Baptist just as I was. In recent years he had begun attending the Episcopal Church of the Advent. He must have heard that expression there or in his travels."

Then I reasoned to myself, "Yes, she is the Mother of God because Jesus is God and she is His mother, the Mother of God!" I couldn't stop saying it. I was thrilled with this new revelation but, as a Baptist, I didn't know what to do with it.

Then, Christmas of 1996 came and I received a Christmas card from my friend, Linda Catherine, from Memphis, Tennessee. We had been friends since the early 1980s when we both lived in Clarksville, Tennessee. I opened Linda's card and was surprised to see a *Catholic* picture of the Madonna and the Christ child surrounded by the angels who were holding censors. I laughed to myself that Linda had sent me a Catholic Christmas card and probably had not even realized it. I opened it and began to read with horror that she and her husband Bob had become Roman Catholics. I felt so ill that I fell to my knees.

"What on earth is she thinking? Bob, too? How could this happen?" I tried to think of an explanation. Then I remembered that her dad had recently died and I also remembered that those Catholics actually think it is acceptable to practice necromancy (praying to the dead). I thought, "Linda must be seeking to contact her dad; that is why she has become Catholic."

Christmas came and went. I dreaded getting that telephone call from my friend because I knew she would want to talk about the Catholic Church. I frankly did not know what I was going to say to her. I felt angry. Then, the dreaded call came in January of 1997. Linda began to tell me about the wonderful Roman Catholic faith and about the pope and his desire for ecumenism (a new word to me).

I for one had no intention of being one with the Roman Catholics. After all, I was close to believing the teaching of those who say that the pope is the Antichrist and that those symbols across his pointy hat are the symbol of the Antichrist—666. I tried to be tolerant and listen but was quite disturbed. We ended with an argument about baby baptism.

After that conversation, I decided that the only thing to do was to obtain the book that they (the Roman Catholics) use to teach their own people, and then use their own words to convince Linda that she should abandon this nonsense and come back to the true faith. I went to the Catholic shop in Columbia in search of the "Catechism of the Catholic Church."

When I walked through the doorway of the Catholic shop, I cringed. The sight of all the idols and rosaries and the crucifixes made my skin crawl. There were things called brown scapulars, green scapulars, and holy medals, St. Michael the Archangel chaplets, and holy water fonts.

As I looked around, I thought to myself, "It is a good thing I don't want to become Catholic. Who could learn all this stuff? It would take a lifetime to become familiar with all their paraphernalia."

I purchased the big brown adult catechism and drove home. I began reading it. I could not put it down. I read it from cover to cover. I was fascinated with the intellectual nature of this book that I had expected to be filled with witchcraft. I could not deny the doctrine that was presented there and by the time I had finished the book, I knew that I was on the road to Rome.

Initially, the Lord in the blessed Eucharist changed me by *indulging* my wonderment of His Real Presence and allowing me to sit with Him for hours on end. Then, as you would expect, He started changing my heart and my mind. He began to free my eternal soul from a frightful state of pride and narrow-mindedness, as well as a multitude of other sins that I tried to recount to the patient priest at my first confession.

Before my conversion, I had clung to my understanding of the philosophy of evangelical Christianity. I believed it was not so much about *sin* as about being *born again*. This error had kept me from a repentant heart and it took the miracle of the Lord in the Blessed Sacrament to release me from its cold grasp.

"Well, she is the Mother of God," has so changed my perspective of God that I am now almost afraid to say how in fear I am of not doing justice to the work of God in me.

And so, my story ends; but really, it has only just begun.

Constance F. Harness   *Dillon, South Carolina*

"The Mass is at the same time, and inseparably, the sacrificial memorial in which the sacrifice of the Cross is perpetuated and the sacred banquet of communion with the Lord's body and blood".

Write Before the Lord

My daughter, Chasity, was doing a presentation at Powers Catholic High School. This was part of the selection process to be one of six representatives from Powers to Washington, D. C. for the Close-up Program. Chasity chose for her topic "Prayer in the Public School."

Well needless to say, she didn't get it. The judges and the educators from her school told her that the topic was too controversial. They explained that she needed to pick some other topic that had to do with current issues at hand.

Her heart was crushed. She was a sophomore and the judges told her to try out again during her junior year. I told Chas, "Don't worry, you are going to make it next year!"

But my daughter didn't want to do it again. I told her to pick a topic of current events and then we would go to Holy Redeemer Chapel where they have perpetual eucharistic adoration. "You can write your speech before the Lord!"

In the chapel, Chasity spread out over the last two pews and proceeded to write her speech. I sat up in the front pew praying.

This time for her topic she chose the "Brady Bill" or as it sometimes called, "The Gunnery Bill." We stayed in the chapel for at least four hours. Then she told me she was ready to go home.

On the way home I told her, "Not to worry, you will be picked! Just mark my words and wait and see." She was somewhat skeptical and wanted to know how I knew this. I said, "I know it because Jesus helped you to write your speech and I know you will be a success."

We also prayed to Our Blessed Mother Mary and invoked the Holy Spirit for divine wisdom.

Guess what! She was selected as a winner! Chasity was so excited and now truly a believer of what can happen when one seeks the aid of Our Dear Lord in the most Blessed Sacrament.

Lou Therese Anthony   *Flint, Michigan*

Fifth Luminous Mystery of the Rosary

The fifth and final mystery of light takes us to Jesus' last supper, where He shares His very self with His disciples in the form of bread and wine. It is truly an expression of God's saving presence, God's kingdom of love among us in the form of a banquet. This holy meal unites us in love with God and with one another so that we become the one body of Christ.

This mystery of the Eucharist truly reveals God's amazing care for us. The God revealed here is not a strict judge or lawgiver, but a loving servant ready to hand over His entire self to nurture us, to forgive, heal and unite us, and bring us to fullness of life. He leaves His disciples with a memorial, a sacrament of love by which His saving presence stays with us in a wonderful way until the end of time.

Let's reflect on St. Luke's words describing the event. He writes that Jesus "took the bread, broke it and gave it to them saying: 'This is my body, which will be given up for you; do this in memory of me.'" (Luke 22:19) When Jesus says, "Do this in memory of me," He is not saying simply that we should repeat this liturgical ritual, although He certainly is asking us to do that, and do it meaningfully. He also wants us to repeat the gesture in all its profundity, that is, to imitate what He has done for the community. In other words, we too are being asked to hand over our bodies, in love and service to the community.

Perhaps you and I should ask ourselves: How profoundly do we really celebrate the Eucharist? How well do we imitate, in His memory, what Jesus did at the Last Supper, not to mention the following day?

Father Jack Wintz, OFM   *Cincinnati, Ohio*

My Little Son's Request

I was raised and educated in a Catholic family, but was not very good at practicing my faith. Despite my wife's constant prayers, about ten years had passed since my last confession and Communion.

It was a Sunday afternoon, and I was at church with my family. In one more week, my two boys were going to receive their first Communion. As always, I didn't pay much attention at Mass that day.

When we reached Communion time, people began standing up to go to receive the Eucharist, and I suddenly felt something in my lap. It was my older son. He embraced me and said into my ear, "Dad, I want you to receive Communion with me on my first Communion day." At the time I didn't know that my wife was praying once again that I would receive Communion with my family.

I was moved by what my son had said, and told him that, yes, I would go to Communion next week. Three days later I entered a church, looking for a priest. I could not find one, so I started to walk around the church, and went towards the office next to it. A priest appeared and said to me, "You are looking for something. Come on in."

I went inside and told him that I wanted to confess my sins. He invited me into his private office where I confessed my sins to him. When I finished, he said the words of the prodigal son, and I started to cry.

The next Sunday I received Communion with my two boys, my wife, and daughter. The moment the holy Eucharist touched my tongue, I was struck with happiness, and tears started to come out of my eyes. I could not stop crying. I was very happy! It was a very joyful experience.

Since that day, I have changed. I am always trying to increase my faith and practice my religion. I'm not where I would like to be, and know I need to strengthen my faith in God, but believe I'm on the right track.

Jorge L. Camacho   *Queretaro, Mexico*

The Church constantly draws her life from the redeeming sacrifice; she approaches it not only through faith-filled remembrance, but also through a real contact, since this sacrifice is made present ever anew, *sacramentally perpetuated, in every community which offers it at the hands of the consecrated minister.*

Healing for Povo and Me

Several years ago I was living in West Virginia with two Franciscan sisters who were hermits. I had gone to visit them from Western Canada to discern whether I wanted to live with them, and had taken my two cats, Povo and Chiara, who were named after St. Francis and St. Clare.

After I decided to stay and live with them, I had to return to Canada for about a month to sort out my affairs. I left the cats with a friend in West Virginia, and on the evening of the 4th of July, Chiara, who had been born wild and was always skittish, became terrified of the fireworks. She ripped the screen out of my friend's door, thus escaping into the night.

Povo followed her, just because that is what he always did. Chiara never returned, but Povo was found six weeks later. While he was lost, Povo had tried to get his flea collar off and had gotten his arm stuck in it, severing muscles under his armpit. Also, pieces of the collar had disintegrated into his neck.

My friend, who bred large dogs and was used to doctoring animals, said she was sure the vet would have told her to euthanize Povo, so she kept him home and doctored him herself. He improved considerably, but for a full year afterwards he still had an open wound under his armpit that was about two to three inches in diameter.

I took my injured cat to the vet several times and they tried several antibiotics, and even surgery, but nothing healed his wound. I decided I needed to consider euthanasia because I felt he was in a lot of pain, and as much as I loved him, it was selfish to keep him in such a suffering state.

About this time, I was going through changes of my own, and for unrelated reasons was not eating or sleeping properly. For several years I had been suffering with what was later diagnosed as post-polio syndrome, and had symptoms similar to fibromyalgia. I was extremely tired most of the time and unable to work, and experienced frequent bouts of muscle pain and weakness. My sleep and food deprivation probably added to my already weakened state.

By then, I was living alone in my own hermitage, down the road from the other two sisters. We usually only saw each other at our daily evening prayer in the chapel which was midway between our hermitages.

One day, I slipped into something I can only describe as an altered state of consciousness during prayer, and began seeing everything with great clarity. As I told the sisters later, if they had been there, they would have thought I was crazy. This trancelike state continued for an hour or so. Then, while sitting on the sofa looking at a picture of Jesus on my wall, I felt an inner conviction that I was healed.

At that moment it was as though a powerful energy, or light, went through my whole body. I felt like I was vibrating with that energy. Then I felt like I was being directed to go before the Blessed Sacrament in the chapel and pray.

Our chapel was a lovely, simple straw-bale constructed one, just down the *holler* we lived in, on our little dirt road. As I walked there, Povo followed me. He had never done this before because it was close to where the other two sisters lived, and it was their cat's territory.

When we got to the chapel, he wanted to go in and I let him—something I never would have done in a more rational state, as I didn't feel it was appropriate for our animals to be in the chapel. As I prostrated myself before the Blessed Sacrament in the empty chapel, I gave thanks for my healing. Then I felt or heard within myself, a voice saying to me, "Look at your cat, he has been healed."

I could never even begin to describe the feelings of hope, joy, and fear that I felt. I wanted it to be true because of how much I loved that cat. However, I was afraid it wasn't true, that I really was just hallucinating, so I couldn't look at my cat. It took me about 24 hours to have the nerve to look at him.

When I finally did look at my cat, I saw that the gaping wound was completely healed, with no scabs, just pink skin. That is how it has remained until this day! He never did grow his fur back in that area and vets have said they are amazed he can walk since his muscles had been severed. Today he is fine, fat, and happy. Well, except when he gets into a jealous fit over one of my other cats. He is twelve years old and is living back in Canada with me.

Until now, I have only shared this story with a small handful of people, and that was after I trusted that they would treat it with the respect it deserves. I was healed, and have been back working as a social worker in a local hospital for the past few years. The miracle for me was not just my own healing, it was that God loved me enough to heal my cat.

I no longer worry whether or not others believe my story. I know it happened, and I believe it was God's way of showing me how very, very much I (as we all are) am enfolded in His wonderful love.

Anna Jopling   *Okanagan Falls, British Columbia, Canada*

He Is Still the Same

I had been away from the Catholic Church for 27 years. It was my fault, not the Church's. When I finally returned, things had changed, and Vatican II had turned my world upside down.

When I went to the altar to receive the Eucharist for the first time in years, Jesus was placed on my tongue, and tears ran down my cheeks. I realized then that the Eucharist was the same now as when I received it long ago at my first Communion. To this day, receiving the Eucharist still brings tears to my eyes.

Molly N. O'Connell   *Mason, Ohio*

The Church constantly draws her life from the redeeming sacrifice; she approaches it not only through faith-filled remembrance, but also through a real contact, since this sacrifice is made present ever anew, sacramentally perpetuated, in every community which offers it at the hands of the consecrated minister.

What a Privilege

One Christmas I remember graphically was when I was living in a trailer, ministering to the Indians who were working in the cotton fields of Southern Arizona. I had celebrated a midnight Mass at one camp where they had a Christmas tree decorated with cotton balls, right off the plants.

Now at this camp, at about two o'clock in the morning, I was to celebrate this second Mass. The only place the people could find for us to gather was under an open shed containing bales of cotton. This became the altar. Dogs took the place of the ox and the ass.

The people brought candles, and the little children were all excited. St. Francis had celebrated the first representation of Christmas at Greccio, under similar circumstances. Again, as Jesus responded to the words of consecration, I couldn't help but greet Him with, "Welcome Lord! I know you are happy to be with these simple people. So am I, what a privilege you give me! Thank you, Lord! Happy Birthday!"

Father Maurus Kelly, OFM   *Santa Barbara, California*

My Return

I was born and raised Catholic by very devout parents, and was the oldest of nine children—two girls and seven boys. We lived in Spain throughout my high school years and that is when I met an enlisted Air Force man whom I fell in love with.

My boyfriend and I wanted to get married while I was still in school, but my father insisted I finish high school, which I did. However, the day after I graduated we were married, and after I got married, I stopped going to church. Shortly after my wedding, my parents moved back to the United States, and so did my husband and I.

Years later, when I had three children and was pregnant with my fourth, my husband left me. At that time my parents were living in Turkey. When they returned to live near us in California, the children and I started going back to church.

Every Sunday at Mass, when it came time for Communion, I started to cry. Even though I could receive the Eucharist, I didn't because I felt it wasn't right for me to. Then came the final divorce, and after that, a quick second marriage. During all of this, my children and I continued going to church.

Finally, I met my soul mate. At the time we met, he was separated from his wife and was in the process of getting a divorce. We were just friends giving each other support during difficult times until after his divorce when our relationship quickly changed. We have now been married 30 years.

Ten years ago I decided to return fully to the Catholic Church after going to a mission at my mother's church. The priest told me that my children would not be considered illegitimate, so I proceeded to get the required paper work done so we could officially be part of the Catholic Church again.

Within two years I was able to go to Mass and receive my lord Jesus Christ in His full glory in the Eucharist. I felt like I had finally come home, and cried tears of relief and joy. My life was given back to me after years of sadness. God is good. May His children never have to face the time when they lose His love and compassion. God bless everyone!

Donna K. Hill   *Goldsboro, North Carolina*

"The sacrifice of Christ and the sacrifice of the Eucharist are one single sacrifice*".[14] St. John Chrysostom put it well: "We always offer the same Lamb, not one today and another tomorrow, but always the same one. For this reason the sacrifice is always only one...Even now we offer that victim who was once offered and who will never be consumed".*

Giving Us Life and Healing

I do believe that God's love for us is poured out in the sacrament of the Eucharist where Christ is truly present for us, giving us life and healing. I also believe that as a priest, daily Mass is a unique channel of communication with God. With this mental framework, let me share with you an incident that took place five years ago.

I work in the Diocese of Diphu, Assam. While working in one of the parishes at Diphu, one day I had a sick call from one of the remote villages of the parish. It was during the rainy season, when we have an onslaught of malaria in this region. Malaria is one of the killer diseases here, and every year several people die from it.

Although it was in the evening, and knowing well the three hours of journey ahead, I hurried to the village with the Blessed Sacrament. The driver of our parish vehicle did not want to go, saying that the road was risky due to wild elephants and poor road conditions. He insisted that we go the next day. However, I decided to go right away.

We reached the village around nine p.m. The sick person was a girl of thirteen years. At the request of the villagers, I administered the last sacrament. Thinking that the child would die, the villagers had already dug the grave for her. Seeing the condition of her, my mind was saying that the child would live if we took her to the hospital. I proposed this idea but was met with stiff resistance. However, after my continued insistence, they agreed to send the child with me.

We started the journey with a few relatives of the child to the presbytery, and then to the hospital. On our way, the heavy rain made the road condition very difficult. The vehicle got stuck in the middle of the jungle for four hours. We tried our best to pull it out of the ditch, but in the meantime the condition of the child became very serious. I requested the people in the vehicle to pray for the child, and it was one of those desperate moments in my life when I sought the intervention of the Lord in a powerful way.

By the time we reached the hospital it was already morning. After admitting the child, I went to the presbytery and offered Mass. My intention was for the sick child I brought to the hospital. I desperately asked the

Lord in the Eucharist to shower His blessings on her. Soon after the Mass, the hospital sisters informed me that the child was responding to the medicines. What good news! The next day, Mass was again offered for her. God really worked, and the child was able to walk home after two weeks.

This experience was one important incident in my life where Jesus truly showed me the power of the Eucharist. For a priest, the most important asset is that he is able to celebrate Mass, and that he is able to offer the same sacrifice that Jesus offered. May the power of the eucharistic Lord be glorified at every moment.

Father Tom Mangattuthazhe   *Diphu, Assam, India*

Healing for Miriam

My siblings and I were raised by two devoted, and very loving parents. They completely dedicated themselves to their family. However, through life's journey, they carried a heavy cross.

At the age of ten years old, my younger sister Rita fell into a deep depression, causing terrible worry for my parents, my older brother and myself. We were eventually told that she had schizophrenic tendencies, and much later we learned that she suffered from paranoid schizophrenia. At the same time, in 1975, my youngest sister Miriam was born. She grew up in an atmosphere of distress and anxiety, which surrounded Rita's illness.

This went on for years, so that by the time Miriam was a teenager, she had been deeply affected by all that had happened in the family. She declared herself vegetarian and stopped eating dairy products, meat and chicken. She would eat fish with vegetables but barely enough to survive on, no matter how much she was coaxed to eat more.

Miriam grew thinner and paler. Her food intake became less and less. Her monthly cycle had stopped and she was becoming, if not already, anorexic. She knew within herself that things were not right, so every day on her way home from school, she would stop at the local church, which was only a short distance from where we lived. She told me that she would walk up to the altar and kiss the tabernacle where she would cry before the Lord and plead with Him to heal her.

Everything was falling apart at the seams. My parents were very worried about Miriam and her teachers asked for a special meeting with them to discuss their worries. Mother came home from the meeting crying, not knowing what to do or how to bear a second serious illness in the family.

Some days later, Mother went to her regular daily Mass and the priest told the congregation that in a few moments Jesus would be present among them in the holy Eucharist. He told them that anything they asked of Jesus that day would be answered. They should just believe. With all her heart, Mother prayed that Miriam would return to good health, and she put her full trust in the Lord. When she returned from Mass, she recounted the words of the priest and this gave her hope.

That very same afternoon, Miriam returned from school with a new light in her eyes. She excitedly said, "Guess what happened at school today?" Mother stood there not knowing what to answer or what to expect. Miriam went on to say that a dietician had come to explain how necessary it was to eat well and to drink lots of milk, especially during the teenage years. She had taken time to talk privately with Miriam about her diet.

From that day forward, Miriam became serious about eating a good balanced diet, and as a result, her eating habits improved over time. Today, thank God, she is completely well and a healthy mother of four beautiful children. We give praise and thanks to Jesus in the holy Eucharist, bread from heaven, food for our souls, the bread of life.

Brid M. Gemayel   *Cornet Chahwan, El Matn, Lebanon*

 The Mass makes present the sacrifice of the Cross; it does not add to that sacrifice nor does it multiply it.

My Eucharistic Miracle

My eucharistic miracle took place in the Woman's Center Chapel where there is a daily Mass and twenty-four-hour exposition of the Blessed Sacrament. It is a very small chapel that holds only about thirty people. Often after Mass, the priest asks if anyone would like to go to confession, and he stays if he is needed.

One day I had a very heavy heart and prayed to God for help. I also asked St. Pio to help me make a good confession if the priest offered to hear them that night. I went to Mass, and afterwards was happy when he invited us to go to confession. I knew my prayers had been answered.

I went to confession as a *sick* person, and came out healthy. It was one of the greatest confessions I ever had, which I attribute to the intercession of St. Pio.

By the time I was done speaking with the priest, all the lights in the chapel had been turned off except for those over the exposed Blessed Sacrament. Only one other person was in the quiet chapel with me. I knelt about two feet from the Blessed Sacrament, closed my eyes, and started praising God. I thanked Him for forgiving my sins, and for the awesome sacrament of reconciliation.

Suddenly I noticed a beautiful scent. It smelled like I was standing in a field of many different flowers. The strong smell forced me to open my eyes and investigate where it was coming from. I looked all around, in back of me, and behind the little altar, and found absolutely nothing. Not one single flower. I looked further, thinking that perhaps I missed something. Still I found no source for the overwhelming, beautiful smell of flowers.

Then I realized what was happening. I moved closer to the Blessed Sacrament and there it was. The smell was coming out of the Eucharist! My heart fainted in the joy and honor of experiencing this miracle. I bowed and stayed there for very long time until the smell went away.

I knew the Lord had granted me a physical sign of His presence, and along with it, His forgiveness. Although I felt totally unworthy of this gift,

I was ecstatic. This experience filled my heart with joy and peace for a long time. My everyday problems, aches, pains, and disappointments are still with me, but they are not as important anymore. I am able to keep smiling right through my difficulties.

Halina A. Makowski   *Chicago, Illinois*

God is Waiting

I was married in the Catholic Church when I was nineteen. A lovely daughter was born to us, but the marriage did not last, and after several years ended in divorce. Because of the divorce I was no longer able to participate in the body and blood of Christ. I felt very lost and unworthy. I did not feel like even going to Mass. It was a hard and lonely period.

After a time I married again but it was ten more years before I felt ready to pursue the difficult process of obtaining an annulment and returning to being a *whole* Catholic. It took three years of meeting with Sister Raphael, OSB, and the priest, filling out papers, going over everything and waiting, waiting, waiting before it was finally granted.

Then the annulment came through! My husband and I had our marriage blessed in the Catholic Church the eve before our daughter's wedding. The next day, during the wedding Mass, for the first time after so many years I was able to fully participate in the body and blood of Christ. It was a moment I shall never forget.

As the priest came up to me and placed the body of Christ on my tongue it was as if I had no bones in my body. My body radiated totally from my head to my feet, tears filled my eyes, and I quivered uncontrollably. In that awesome moment, I felt God saying to me, "Welcome home, my child!"

I am now fifty-eight years old and that moment will never escape me. Not even if I live to be ninety! All I can say to anyone who may be reading this, no matter if you feel you are unworthy, please, stop what you are doing and go talk to a priest or a religious or somebody and get the ball rolling to come back to the fullness of your faith. Let nothing stop you from knowing the experience of God that I am experiencing. God is waiting to say to all, "Welcome home my child, I've missed you!"

Kathy Meyer   *St. Marys, Pennsylvania*

God's Love Touched Me

My 78-year-old mother had not been well for a couple of years, and yet she helped care for her older sister until her sister's dying day in August 1996. When we found out my mother had cancer, she was not given much time to live.

I have a 46-year-old sister who lived with Mom and Dad; she is developmentally disabled and unable to live on her own. In reaction to all this stress in the family, she had a severe asthma attack. She never had this problem before, and was admitted to the hospital where she received care and was discharged a few days later. Two weeks after that, Mom was admitted to the hospital and the doctors told her the cancer had spread to her liver. It was too far along to treat so she signed up with hospice so she could die at home.

One Sunday when I went to Mass with my three children, there was a visiting priest there whom I had never seen before. All through Mass I was distracted, almost to the point of annoyance, because the priest looked so much like my sister who had just been in the hospital. I even leaned over to my kids and asked if they thought he looked like her. They didn't see a resemblance and thought I had lost it for sure!

I couldn't stop thinking of my sister. At the beginning of Communion, I looked up to the altar, and could feel God's love touch me. Everything around me was quiet, and everything had faded away except a beautiful, soft light around the altar. I felt filled with joy, love, and God's bountiful love. God gave me everything I needed in that brief moment. I can't really explain the depth of that feeling of love. It was over soon, but I knew I had been given a wonderful gift.

I wanted to speak with the visiting priest as we left the church, but we saw some friends and talked for a few minutes. I was hoping I hadn't missed my chance to talk with the priest, when I saw him walking up the aisle right towards us. To my amazement, he looked nothing like my sister. At that moment I believed even more that Jesus had been speaking to me personally that morning. Through this experience, He assured me that He is always with me. I had these troubles in my life and He was telling me to trust in Him and accept His love.

My mom died January 1, 1997. My sister and dad continued to live together until 2003 when she moved into an apartment. She is learning to be independent and is progressing quite well. The Lord has placed many people in her life to help her. My family still misses Mom but we are comforted by our trust that God holds our simple, small lives in the palm of His hand, and that we are His children. We trust and love Him.

It is now 2004 and I can still feel the love of that experience as if it were yesterday. I want it to happen again, although I understand that I don't need it to because God's love is everlasting and I will always have it. He had tapped me on the shoulder to remind me that He is always with me, and I wouldn't have to go through the rough times alone. I don't have the best memory, but I will never forget this. Just recalling this gift helps me feel loved in the difficult times of my life, and makes the good times much sweeter.

Teresa M. Bechtel   *Lakewood, Colorado*

"Taking part in the Eucharistic Sacrifice, which is the source and summit of the whole Christian life, they offer the divine victim to God, and offer themselves along with it".

The Real Presence: Jesus' Gift to the Church

by John Bookser Feister

Ask Catholics about the real presence of Jesus in the Eucharist and you're likely to hear a variety of personal experiences. Once I was in a faith-sharing group with a man who was known as one of the "pillars of the parish." He was always available for parish committees, helped with the festival, occasionally led the rosary during prayer services and was very devoted to his family. He told our group about his *feeling* the real presence of Christ during quiet moments of prayer one Sunday after he had gone to Communion.

On that Sunday, he had visualized the body and blood of Jesus, consumed in the form of bread and wine, breaking down into smaller and smaller pieces, all the way down to the tiniest element, being carried to every part of his own body by his beating heart. He felt literally "nourished by Jesus" throughout.

He also felt deeply connected to those around him, he said. He felt the Eucharist, the presence of Jesus, at the very center of his being and at that point, he felt connected to that same central point in everyone else who had just received Communion. He experienced, in a mysterious way, the real presence of Jesus, an experience of both transcendence with God and of communion with the body of Christ, the Church, indeed the whole world. His experience points to an authentically Catholic understanding of the Eucharist.

Recent years have seen a growing concern about Catholics' understanding of the real presence of Jesus in the Eucharist. Some surveys show that a number of practicing Catholics are not clear about the doctrine of real presence. Some think of consecrated bread and wine as only symbols of Jesus' presence rather than a genuine change of bread and wine into the body and blood of Christ, the long-standing Catholic understanding. In 1999 a large group of U.S. bishops petitioned their fellow bishops to join them in addressing the problem. They termed confusion about the real presence to be a "grave" situation.

The first result of the bishops' efforts is a 2001 pastoral statement, *The Real Presence of Jesus Christ in the Sacrament of the Eucharist: Basic Questions and Answers*, published by the U.S. Conference of Catholic Bishops. That document, which was introduced to the bishops' conference as a resource for pastors and religious educators, presented 15 questions and answers, some of which are, by the bishops' own admission, a bit technical. There was nothing new in the document; it was merely a presentation of existing Catholic teaching. There was a plea from some of the bishops for easy-to-understand resources that would explain real presence for everyone. We'll take a look at the principal themes of the bishops' questions and answers, including some of the renewed insights about real presence expressed at Vatican II.

Why do we even need the Eucharist?

The Eucharist is, for Catholics, both a meal and a sacrifice. The Lord gave us the Eucharist at the Last Supper because he wanted us to share in the life of the Trinity, the loving communion of the Father, the Son and the Holy Spirit. We become united to God at our baptism, and receive a further outpouring of the Holy Spirit at our confirmation. In the Eucharist we are nourished spiritually, brought closer to God, again and again: "By eating the body and drinking the blood of Christ in the Eucharist we become united to the person of Christ through his humanity," write the bishops. They remind us of the words of Jesus in John's Gospel: "Whoever eats my flesh and drinks my blood remains in me and I in him" (Jn 6:56).

This meal of fellowship and unity, though, also is understood as a sacrifice. Why is that? Because Jesus died for our sins. Human sin was so great that we could never share fully in the life of God. Jesus came to reunite us. The bishops write, "Through His death and resurrection, He conquered sin and death and reconciled us to God. The Eucharist is the memorial of this sacrifice. The Church gathers to remember and to re-present the sacrifice of Christ in which we share through the action of the priest and the power of the Holy Spirit. Through the celebration of the Eucharist, we are joined to Christ's sacrifice and receive its inexhaustible benefits."

At the Eucharist, we re-present the outpouring of Christ's life so that our life can be restored. This gift of life is happening in eternity, always. We remember this in a special way when we sing the Holy, Holy, Holy at Mass, recalling the words of Isaiah 6:3, the hymn of the angels before God. We sing our praise before the "lamb of God," slain to take away the sin of the world, all that separates us from God (see Jn 1:29).

Why does Communion still look like bread and wine?

This perhaps is the greatest stumbling block for belief in the real presence. We are not the first generation of Christians to ask the question. Each generation has found the answer through the eyes of faith.

The Church teaches that the transformation into the Body and Blood of Christ is taking place "below the surface"—that is, in the "substance" of the bread and wine. What can be seen, tasted, touched and smelled is indeed the same as the bread and wine. But there has been a real change that requires faith to accept.

Medieval theologians, following the inspired genius St. Thomas Aquinas, talked of this transformation using the word *transubstantiation*, a technical theological term of that era. The recent *Catechism of the Catholic Church* discusses this term in Section 1376. In brief, we Catholics believe that, at their deepest reality, but not in physical characteristics, the bread and wine become the body and blood of Christ when they are consecrated at Eucharist.

After consecration, they are no longer bread and wine: They are the body and blood of Jesus. "As St. Thomas Aquinas observed, Christ is not quoted as saying, *'This bread* is my body,' but *'This is my body.'*"

Once the bread and wine become the body and blood of Christ, they remain so "as long as the appearances of bread and wine remain" (see also the *Catechism, #1377*). They never revert back to bread and wine, because a real and permanent change has taken place. That is why we reserve the Blessed Sacrament, as we will see below.

Christ is fully present in every fragment of the consecrated host and fully present in every drop of consecrated Precious Blood. So a person receiving only the consecrate bread or wine receives Christ fully. Yet it is preferable, a more complete sign of the heavenly banquet, to receive the sacrament under both forms rather than only under one.

If it's real presence, why symbols?

It is particularly fitting that Christ should come to us in the Eucharist, write the bishops, for "Jesus Christ gives himself to us in a form that employs the symbolism inherent in eating bread and drinking wine. Furthermore, being present under the appearance of bread and wine, Christ gives himself to us in a form that is appropriate for human eating and drinking. Also, this kind of presence corresponds to the virtue of faith, for the presence of the body and blood of Christ cannot be detected or discerned by any way other than faith."

The bishops here are reminding us that, even though real—not merely symbolic—change has taken place, there is still tremendous symbolism at work. All sacraments use symbols, because symbols help us to understand the deepest connections between things. Here are two of my favorite examples: Just as food nourishes us, God nourishes us. Or again, just as grain of wheat must die to become bread, so, too must we. The symbolism of the Eucharist is a deep and nearly inexhaustible topic. It in no way diminishes the fact that a real, substantial change has taken place. In the bishops' words, "God uses…the symbolism inherent in the eating of bread and the drinking of wine at the natural level to illuminate the meaning of what is being accomplished in the Eucharist through Jesus Christ."

Why the tabernacle?

As we saw above, the body and blood of Christ, once consecrated, do not revert back to bread and wine. Although it all could be consumed at Eucharist, the Church, from early times, has found good reason to preserve that which was not consumed during the community's celebration of Eucharist. First of all, the Blessed Sacrament is reserved to be administered as "food for the journey" (Viaticum) for the dying. It is also used for the sick of the community and for those who were, for some good reason, unable to be present for the community celebration.

Another pastoral practice arose as the faithful, centuries ago, began to see the value of being in the presence of the sacramental body and blood. Exposition of the Blessed Sacrament allows an opportunity to adore God, whether in eucharistic exposition or Benediction, or in eucharistic processions. The body of Christ in the form of bread in the tabernacle provides an excellent opportunity for private prayer. "Many holy people well known to American Catholics, such as St. John Neumann, St. Elizabeth Ann Seton, St. Katharine Drexel, and Blessed Damien of Molokai, practiced great personal devotion to Christ present in the Blessed Sacrament," write the bishops.

The presence of the Blessed Sacrament is cause for the greatest reverence, write the bishops, both during and after the celebration of the Eucharist. Canon Law states that the tabernacle in Church is to be in a place "distinguished, conspicuous, beautifully decorated, and suitable for prayer."

"According to the tradition of the Latin Church, one should genuflect in the presence of the tabernacle containing the reserved sacrament," write the bishops. They also instruct that greetings and conversations are best reserved for the vestibule, not the main portion of the church: "It is not appropriate to speak in loud or boisterous tones in the body of the church (that is, the nave) because of the presence of Christ in the tabernacle."

Fasting before receiving Communion, in accordance with Church law, is another form of reverence for the sacrament.

What if someone receives who doesn't believe?

Even though the body and blood of Christ are really present in the Eucharist, faith plays a strong role in how we respond to (or accept) that presence. It is commonly asked whether or not a nonbeliever has received the body and blood of Christ if he or she receives Communion. The answer is yes, in the sense that what the nonbeliever has consumed is really Christ. But a lack of belief prevents someone from receiving the spiritual benefit of the Eucharist, "communion with Christ."

A related question arises about a person receiving Communion while in a state of mortal sin. Once again, the disposition of the recipient cannot change the fact that Jesus is truly present in the elements of the Eucharist. "The question here is thus not primarily about the nature of the Real Presence, but about how sin affects the relationship between an individual and the Lord," write the bishops. "Before one steps forward to receive the body and blood of Christ in holy Communion, one needs to be in a right relationship with the Lord and his Mystical Body, the Church—that is, in a state of grace, free of all mortal sin. While sin damages, and can even destroy, that relationship, the sacrament of penance can restore it."

How else is Jesus really present to us?

The Church teaches that Christ is present to us in other ways at the Eucharist besides in the Blessed Sacrament. He is present in the priest, the assembly gathered to worship, in the holy Scriptures.

It is indeed a mystery that God became flesh in Jesus, and that Jesus becomes present to us in sacrament and Scripture. *Mystery*, our bishops remind us, refers not to a puzzling reality, but rather, to "aspects of God's plan of salvation for humanity, which has already begun but will be completed only with the end of time."

"St. Paul explained that the mysteries of God may challenge our human understanding or may even seem to be foolishness, but their meaning is revealed to the people of God through Jesus Christ and the Holy Spirit (cf. 1 Cor 1:18–25, 2:6–10; Rom 16:25–27; Rev 10:7). The Eucharist is a mystery because it participates in the mystery of Jesus Christ and God's plan to save humanity through Christ."

Used with permission from John Bookser Feister.

[This article first published in *Catholic Update C0901* published by St. Anthony Messenger Press]

I Heard a Lovely Voice

There was a small, quiet chapel at our church, Christ the King, in Richland, Washington. We didn't have adoration of the Blessed Sacrament, but it didn't matter to me whether the Blessed Sacrament was exposed or in the tabernacle. I'd go into the chapel after morning Mass, when it was usually deserted, and give God my voice, singing hymns to Him in praise and thanksgiving.

One day I had been reading the messages from Medjugorje, and one of them stuck in my mind. Our Blessed Mother had said, "I am wherever my Son is. He waits in every tabernacle, and I am there beside Him."

I didn't know if this was a true message because I didn't know if the messages from Medjugorje were true, but they were uplifting and helpful to me in many ways. They did not hurt my faith.

One morning, I woke up with terrible laryngitis. The only sound I could make was a raspy whisper. After Mass, I went into the chapel and sat down. I whispered toward the tabernacle, "Sorry, Lord, I can't sing to you today. I can't even talk!" Then, I felt a presence swoosh right next to me, and immediately a warm softness swept across my throat. I heard in my mind a lovely feminine, laughing voice say, "There, now you can sing to my Son!"

My laryngitis was gone. I could talk and sing normally. This experience was a tremendous gift that reassured me of Our Lord's presence, along with our Blessed Mother.

Madeleine D. Fisher   *Carlsbad, New Mexico*

The Eucharistic Sacrifice makes present not only the mystery of the Saviour's passion and death, but also the mystery of the resurrection which crowned his sacrifice.

Faith Makes the Difference

When we are privileged to celebrate Eucharist almost every day, we sometimes *take it for granted*; we forget the grace and power of Jesus in the Eucharist.

Way back in 1970, not too long after Vatican II, I was teaching moral and spiritual theology at our house of theology in Centerville, Ohio (outside of Dayton, Ohio). We were beginning to implement a whole new approach to the teaching of theology to our students who were preparing to become Franciscan priests. The new method was far different from learning the material from textbooks, lectures, and then giving it back on tests. It focused on the person of the student, and emphasized four aspects: the theological content, the ministerial aspect, the spiritual life of the student, and the integration of all this in the person and life of the student.

In the fall of 1970 the faculty was in retreat, preparing for a new year. One task was to prepare a syllabus for the courses we were to teach. I was trying to come up with a syllabus for a course on moral issues in the area of sexuality and was having a very difficult time. I could not even get started. I struggled and struggled, and could not even begin. I was caught up in the fact that there was a great difference between the official teaching of the Vatican and the teaching of the vast majority of theologians on the issues I was to treat in this moral course. I needed to address the meaning of human sexuality, marital infidelity, homosexual genital behavior, masturbation, etc. and was torn. Somehow I found it impossible to reconcile these differences. I thought I was losing my faith.

Then two things happened. First, one of my brother teachers asked me what was holding me up. I explained my conflict, and he simply said, "Remember, Nick, there is a tremendous difference between faith and theology." That reminder helped me a great deal.

The second thing happened the next morning as we were celebrating Mass. Nine of us were concelebrating the Eucharist. As the principal celebrant was saying the words of institution: "This is my body…This is the cup of my blood," I was overwhelmed with feelings of humble awe. I was stunned, and found myself saying to Jesus, "O Jesus, I do believe that you are here. You are really here under the sign of bread and wine. There is no doubt, no confusion, you are really and truly here: truly and fully God, and truly and fully man. Dear Jesus, I may have all kinds of questions and doubts about many moral questions. But, one thing is true and clear and certain. One thing is at the very foundation of my whole life and teaching. You are here under the sign of bread and wine. You are always with us, even as we struggle to find the truth in other areas of our lives."

With that, I felt I was on the solid ground of faith. Theological controversies will come and go, but Jesus in the Eucharist is with me, and He will not leave me adrift.

Father Nick Lohkamp, OFM

Canton, Ohio

The Warmth Was His Love!

I clearly remember the day Christ revealed Himself to me in the Eucharist. It was Lent of 1990 and I had been battling metastasis breast cancer. After my diagnosis, I had gone through a modified radical mastectomy, and had completed two rounds of *big guns* chemotherapy. The realization that I needed God had driven me back into his arms, and I was in the process of rediscovering the Church of my birth.

It was a brisk, almost cold, Florida day and I had decided to go to Mass that morning as a gift to my Lord, to have *break fast* with Him. When I arrived, people were already gathered, but there was no Mass. Instead, the monstrance was on the altar with the Blessed Sacrament in it, and I found myself at my first eucharistic adoration.

I entered the church and sat about midway to the altar. As I was getting ready to kneel down and pray, I faced the Eucharist and felt warmth wash over my face. My first thought was, "Whoa, guess it was colder outside than I thought!" Then, when I bowed my head, the warmth moved to the top of my head. I could distinctly feel it because I had no hair to insulate. This surprised me, so I looked up and again I felt warmth wash over my face.

Experimenting, I turned my face to the right. The warmth moved to the part of my face that was facing the Eucharist. I turned to the left and the same thing happened. All of a sudden a profound realization came over me. It was Christ! The warmth was His love radiating from His presence in the Eucharist! I dropped to my knees in complete awe and prayed with my entire heart.

An hour had gone by in what seemed like mere moments, and suddenly they were taking Him away. My heart cried out in silence. The loss was tangible. I wanted to stay with Him, and my heart ached as they walked away with Our Lord.

Never again have I experienced His presence in the Eucharist so profoundly, and seldom have I prayed with the intensity I managed that day in His presence. I strongly feel that if we all believed in the real presence of Our Lord in the Eucharist, the church would be full around the clock with people who would not want to leave.

I wish I could say that every time the Host is consecrated at Mass I am fully aware of His presence. What a gift that would be. In reality, I have to often rely on the memory of what occurred all those years ago at my first eucharistic adoration to remind me that He is truly there in the Eucharist. I also need to have faith to believe that what I experienced that day was real.

That cold Florida morning was one of the defining moments of my life, an event that changed how I look at my world and my God. I know without a doubt that He is a God of mercy and love, and He is present to His people in the Eucharist.

Kathleen M. Ellertson   *Moore, Oklahoma*

St. Ambrose reminded the newly-initiated that the Eucharist applies the event of the resurrection to their lives: "Today Christ is yours, yet each day he rises again for you"

My Dad's Faithfulness

It was the summer of 1954, on a bright and sunny Sunday morning. My father brought me outside to see our new sandbox, complete with new sand, shovels, buckets, and even a canopy. I was entranced in my own world of imagination when my father told me it was time for us to go to church. I told him I wanted to keep playing, and he looked at me and said, "I can't believe you don't have one hour to come with me and thank God for all He has given you." He backed out of the driveway and went to church alone.

Dad came home and wouldn't say one word to me. I called his name a few times before he finally listened to my apology. He forgave me, but I felt sad that it would be a whole week before I could go to church to thank God for my blessings. Until I was able to get to church, the sandbox was a reminder of how a friend should treat a friend.

That fall, I started first grade at St. Peter's Catholic School. Dad took me to Mass sometimes, but he usually just dropped me off, and I went alone. By the time the sisters prepared us to receive our first Communion, I was hungry to have God come to me through the Eucharist. I remember the anticipation of that day, and the moment I received Jesus for the first time. I wanted to stay in church with Him, and didn't want to have a party. I just wanted to be with Jesus.

Somewhere during this time I began noticing that the other students weren't sitting alone when they went to Mass on Sunday. They were with their families, all praying together. Occasionally my mom went with me, but I was usually very lonesome for my family at church.

I began to pray for my father to go to church with me. Every week I asked him if he would go with me, and he would hand me the envelope with his offering for the church and say, "This is my job, and your job is to go to Mass." He was persistent at not going with me, no matter how often I asked.

One day, Dad and I talked about God, "I want you to understand," he said, "I'm not mad at God. It's that Church! It's not God, it's that Church."

Then he told me the story of when he and my mother were married. My mother wasn't permitted to get married at the main altar because she was not Catholic. His bride was hurt, and that hurt him very much. He had a hard time forgiving the Church for that.

My father went to church on Christmas, Easter, special occasions, and every now and then when he felt good. As I got older, my mom and sister started going to Mass regularly.

For years I prayed at every Eucharist with all of my heart, "Please, dear God, bring my father back to church with me, please!" During those years, I grew up, graduated from college, and was married. I had my first teaching job, and began raising three sons, one of whom was very sick for a while.

On Palm Sunday, 1984, I went to my parent's home for the weekend. Mom and I attended a Fire Conference at the University of Detroit while I was visiting them. As always, I prayed for my father to return to the Church.

After Communion, I was given a spiritual picture of Dad and my children returning to their seats after receiving the Eucharist in the balcony of a church. The picture moved me, but I thought I was just dreaming about what I had been longing and praying for.

Memorial Day weekend at Black Lake was always the waited for holiday in my family. As we were getting ready for Mass, my husband Jim came into our room asking, "What's up with your dad?" I asked him, "What do you mean? What's up with my dad?" He said, "He's all dressed up in a suit, like he's getting ready for Mass."

My mother heard my husband, and rushed into our room. "Shhh. Oh, you don't know yet, Zen has been going to Mass faithfully every Sunday since Easter." We looked at her in shock and asked what had happened that made him change his mind about going to Mass.

She said she didn't know; he woke up on Easter Sunday and said, "I am going to Mass." She said he had been going ever since, and asked us not to say anything about it around him.

It was pretty quiet in the car on the way to Mass. When we arrived, the church was overflowing with people. There were only a few seats left together, and they were in the balcony. My dad and sons took them, while my husband and I found single seats on the main floor of the church.

This was a very different Mass experience for all of us. My boys were at Mass with their grandfather, and I wasn't close to them. There they were in this tiny balcony, high above me. Would they stay put? Would busy little Nicholas get too close to the edge and fall over? Oh! I was a mess!

Concentrating on Jesus at this Mass was very hard. After returning from Communion, I looked up to see if the boys were staying away from the edge of the balcony. What I saw was the picture God had shown me on Palm Sunday. It was my father in the balcony, receiving Communion with my children.

It hit me that God had answered my prayers and had brought my dad back to celebrate Mass with me. What a joyful day that was!

For the next twenty years, my father went to Mass every Sunday, only missing once or twice when church was cancelled due to snowstorms. My family was blessed being with my dad at Mass, giving thanks to the Father for giving us His son Jesus.

In June of 2003, my dad broke his back. He did not like medicine, had very limited vision due to cataracts, was deaf, and refused much of what the doctors recommended. I was very concerned for him.

On July 20, 2003, I was at a Teen Life Mass praying for my sick father. I prayed for him throughout the Mass, especially during the consecration. I asked God to allow him to receive all the beautiful gifts that He had for him.

The youth sang so beautifully that night, I thought I was hearing angels. I wept through the whole Mass, and when people asked me what was wrong, I said I didn't know what was making me cry. I couldn't understand why I was weeping.

Little did I know that during that time, God was taking my dad home, and I really was hearing angels! They were carrying Dad to be with Him forever in the Father's mansion that Jesus had prepared.

Monday morning, my son and I were packed and ready to travel to my dad's house, which was a six-hour drive. It would be Nick's first visit with his grandfather since he had returned from the Navy. Dad was very proud of him, and was eager to see him. We called to let Dad know we were on our way, and he did not answer.

At the prayer service for Dad, Father Jerry told us he had seen a spiritual picture of my dad bringing my mom to meet him, and telling him how great heaven was. Dad said he could see and hear now, and that he was without pain.

This was a great confirmation of God's love, and of His restoration of us through Jesus. I thank God that He answered my prayers for my dad during the Eucharist. He is now receiving all the gifts God had for him!

Cynthia A. Bertagnoli   *L'Anse, Michigan*

His Protective Love

On Oct. 1, 2003, I moved my Catholic bookstore from one area of Edmonton to another. The area wasn't the best, but it was right across the street from a Catholic church, and I felt it was where God wanted me to be. I was certain that this was going to be a wonderful location.

However, during the first eight weeks that I was there, my store was broken into three times and robbed once. A friend wisely suggested that we start offering Mass every month for the safety and protection of the store.

The last robbery took place on November 27th and the first Mass was celebrated the very next day. The second Mass was Dec. 19, 2003 and the third was on January 23, 2004. Since the Masses started I have had no problems at all, and I believe I owe it all to the power of the Eucharist.

Janet P. MacLellan   *Demonton, Alberta, Canada*

St. Cyril of Alexandria also makes clear that sharing in the sacred mysteries "is a true confession and a remembrance that the Lord died and returned to life for us and on our behalf".

Running out of Sacramental Grace

I am a cradle Catholic, raised by devout Catholic parents. After attending parochial schools from kindergarten through high school, I knew my catechism well. Unfortunately though, when I was a college student, I started to wander from the Catholic Church and began a journey along the evangelical route.

I married my non-Catholic husband in the Church, but 18 years after our marriage, I decided to leave our Catholic faith forever. My decision was made with the hope that my marriage would be stronger if we attended a nondenominational church together, since my husband did not wish to become a Catholic.

In the various protestant churches we attended throughout the years, the Communion service was merely a symbolic remembrance of the Last Supper. At those moments, my mind would always take me back to the day of my first holy Communion when I, along with 99 fellow second graders from St. Anthony's Grammar School, received the Eucharist for the very first time. I would recall the solemnity of the sacrament of the holy Eucharist.

Eventually, my dear prayerful brother gave me a gentle reminder. He said, "Susan, you are running out of sacramental grace." Suddenly I realized that something was truly missing from my life.

Not long after that, I felt led to visit a nearby church close to where we were living at the time. That church was St. Anthony's Catholic Church but it was not the church of my childhood. I felt that St. Anthony, who had always been my dearest and favorite saint, had helped me find my way home to the Catholic Church.

During Lent I began to attend Mass on Sundays. At Communion I would kneel and pray with great sadness, quietly crying because I was unable to receive this life-giving sacrament. Every weekend I faithfully returned to Mass and wept at the loss of the Eucharist in my life.

Again, God spoke gently to me through my brother Peter. He told me that all I needed to do was go to confession and I could receive Communion again. So, on Palm Sunday, I asked one of the parish priests to hear my confession. "Bless me, Father, for I have sinned. It has been over eighteen years since my last confession..." I experienced incredible healing and restoring power as the priest gave me absolution and then welcomed me home.

As I left the church that day, I felt as though I floated home on a cloud. Taking the phone book, I found a local parish with an evening Mass which I attended that very evening. Receiving Jesus in the Eucharist that night was a moving and emotional experience. I wept once again, but this time they were tears of joy!

Since returning to the Church and the sacraments, I have known a profound peace and my soul is continually refreshed. Often after receiving the Blessed Sacrament, I am overcome with tears. My children ask me if I am all right, and I just nod and smile. I love my Lord Jesus, who is with us in the holy Eucharist, body and blood, soul and divinity.

If you have been away from the Church and the sacraments, come home. Open arms are waiting to welcome you and Jesus is waiting patiently for you in the Eucharist. Receive Jesus often and with utmost awe, reverence and thanksgiving. How blessed we are as Catholics to have Our Lord come to us in holy Communion, strengthening us with His life-giving grace!

Susanna M. Stewart   *Colorado Springs, Colorado*

Receiving the Eucharist Saved My Life

I have been Catholic my whole life. I went to a Catholic school for twelve years, always believed in God, and went to church. However, as the years went by and life got busier with kids and work, I knew God was there, but He wasn't a very important part of my life.

Then, a few years ago I got very sick with chronic fatigue syndrome and fibromyalgia. Due to this, I lost my job and income, and became very depressed. I wanted to kill myself even though I knew suicide was wrong. The only thing that stopped me from taking my life was the love I have for my children.

During this time, a neighbor kept inviting me to come to her Bible study class and I finally went. That proved to be a turning point in my life as I decided then to welcome God back into my life. It had been a while since I had been to church and I decided to go that very next Sunday.

Throughout the Mass, and especially when I received Communion, I could not believe the feeling of peace within me. It truly felt like God was with me and that He was looking out for me. I felt as if His arm was around my shoulders, and it felt that way for several weeks. A short time later, my disability was approved and I started to receive my checks.

Since that time I have joined our church chorus with my younger daughter, and Mass means more to me now than it ever did before. Through praying and singing to God, I can actually feel Him being a part of my life. I love going to church and look forward to Sunday Mass, cherishing the peaceful feeling I get when I receive the Blessed Sacrament. I am very close to God and believe that going to Mass and receiving the Eucharist saved my life. For this I am eternally grateful.

Shirley J. Bobek   *Fombell, Pennsylvania*

This sets forth once more the perennially valid teaching of the Council of Trent: "the consecration of the bread and wine effects the change of the whole substance of the bread into the substance of the body of Christ our Lord, and of the whole substance of the wine into the substance of his blood. And the holy Catholic Church has fittingly and properly called this change transubstantiation".

For the Rest of My Life

When I first entered the monastery of the Franciscans, I remember that first night and how I thought with joy, "Gee, I'm going to live with Jesus in the same house for the rest of my life!" And, except for brief times in the hospital, so it was.

After Vatican II, we were allowed to stay with our family and close friends during our vacations. Although I found everyone very kind and the visits pleasant, I was always glad to return to my monastery because I had some loneliness in my heart from missing Jesus' eucharistic presence.

Father Campion Lally, OFM   *Kiryu, Gumma, Japan*

A Committed Catholic

I was born a Catholic, raised a Catholic and went to Catholic schools from elementary through high school. I taught in Catholic schools, married a Catholic and raised my children Catholic. Most of my friends were Catholic, although that has changed over the years as my horizons broadened.

From the cradle (I guess that's where the phrase *cradle Catholic* emerged), I have been attending church and Mass and received all the sacraments I could receive. You might say that I have gone to Mass a gazillion times. It would take an extreme situation for me not to be present at Mass on Sundays. It is as much a part of my life as getting dressed or eating. It is ingrained into my very psyche and would affect me deeply if I could not be a Catholic, go to Mass and practice my faith. I have a friend who occasionally says to me, "Are you still a Catholic?" I think I looked at him in complete shock the first time he said that. I would never think of being anything else but Catholic! It would be denying a part of who I am.

I have to admit there was a short period of time in my younger days, when my children were small, that I didn't feel like it, and didn't want to go to Mass. I had a lot of excuses: I was too tired, too lazy, too busy, and so I tried staying home. Needless to say, it did not make me feel any better. I didn't feel right. I felt so guilty that after a few short weeks of not attending Mass, I decided that staying home was not for me and I started going back to church.

When Sister Patricia wrote that she was going to write another book, I really wanted to be a part of this book, especially since my story was in the *101 Stories of the Rosary*. I wondered how I could get a story into the book when I didn't have any special stories to tell in regards to the Eucharist. Well, Sister Patricia suggested that we ask Padre Pio for help. "St. Pio is in charge of this," she said, "So if you need some help thinking of something that has happened to you through the holy sacrifice of the Mass— talk to him!" I had already been praying to Padre Pio anyway, so the next time I attended church, I asked Padre Pio to help me figure out what was special about Mass for me. Well, low and behold, an inspiration did come!

Mine is a very ordinary story much like many Catholics in the rest of the world. The holy sacrifice of the Mass and the Eucharist is a very special time for me with God. Often before going to Mass I am overwhelmed and stressed out by all that life throws my way. At times, it is all I can do to function on a day-to-day, minute-to-minute basis. As I enter the peaceful environment of the church and sit in the pew, I begin to feel as if I was getting a massage of the mind and spirit, which makes my body and soul more relaxed. My cares and stresses begin to melt away as I offer them up to God and let Him be in charge. I get a new perspective of the life situations that my family and I have. I know that it will be all looked at, providing I have faith and ask for guidance along life's journey. As I listen to the readings and the homily, some special part will stand out, which fits with the problems in my life.

These words help me and inspire me to do things better. Life has not always been kind, but I know from experience that God is kind and loving. I am never alone. All I need is to ask for assistance and to trust. He doesn't always solve the problems the way I would have imagined, or in the length of time that I think it should take, but a solution has always come. We live in a drive-through, fast-paced society and the Eucharist helps to put on the brakes in my life and to rest in the presence of God.

Mariella G. LeBeau   *Guelph, Ontario, Canada*

The Most Humble Love

To me the Eucharist is the most humble love of Jesus Christ, the ultimate love as He gives us Himself in bread and wine. It is the ultimate act of elevating the other, the beloved, us. It is the reality of the Passover come alive as we are freed from sin and led to the promised land of heaven. He, our God, becomes man, stepping in place of the lamb of the Passover meal. We have this Passover meal feasting on our God, Jesus unblemished.

The Eucharist is our God loving us so much that He places us in control of Him. He allows us to choose to adore and love Him, to be nourished by Him in the food, or to ignore and disrespect Him. It is our God bowing to us, wanting to be with us so badly that He allows Himself to be in this food, under our control, for our benefit. It is the ultimate marriage consummation, our God giving Himself totally to us as the groom, and we receiving Him as His bride.

When we participate in the adoration of the Blessed Sacrament, we are fulfilling what Jesus asked the apostles to do in the garden; to watch and pray, and to keep our focus on Him and what he was about to do. There He was about to give His life, as I have stated, in place of the Passover lamb, in which this whole action becomes our Mass.

Jesus asked the apostles to stay focused and pray with Him before He gave Himself totally on the cross. In adoration, it is a moment of time frozen from Mass, before we consume the Lamb of God, before we consummate our marriage with Him. It is like gazing intently upon a loved one before entering into the full act of love, in awe of each other. We come before Him in awe of Him, and He is in awe of us, wanting to give Himself fully to us. Eucharistic adoration is the intimate time we spend with our groom, to know the depths of Him as we prepare to become one with Him.

Father Anthony Gargotta   *Natrona Heights, Pennsylvania*

Jesus Cares and Jesus Knows

Several years ago I attended a healing Mass in Boston, Massachusetts. My son, who was fifteen years old at the time and an A student, had an emotional breakdown and I was there to pray for his healing.

Until then, I couldn't understand why Jesus wasn't healing him. I had been praying with my entire heart and was now asking God why He was turning a deaf ear to my prayers. Only I knew this question that was in my heart.

The priest, Father Lazanski, celebrated Mass, and then the healing service began. The congregation stayed in their pews and waited for the priest to come to them, giving everyone his healing prayers and blessings. I was at the back of the church and watched as he came up the aisle blessing adults and children as he went by, stopping at times for individual attention.

The priest finally came to me and put his hand on my shoulder. Then he clearly said in my ear, "God did not turn a deaf ear to your prayers." I gasped because I knew that Jesus was the only one who had known that was in my heart. I continued to pray day after day, and eventually my son was healed. The moral of my story is, don't give up because Jesus never will. Jesus cares and Jesus knows.

Jeanette M. De Rosa   *Revere, Massachusets*

 Truly the Eucharist is a mysterium fidei, *a mystery which surpasses our understanding and can only be received in faith, as is often brought out in the catechesis of the Church Fathers regarding this divine sacrament:* "Do not see—St. Cyril of Jerusalem exhorts—in the bread and wine merely natural elements, because the Lord has expressly said that they are his body and his blood: faith assures you of this, though your senses suggest otherwise".

From Sola Scriptura to Eucharistia

As a Lutheran, I thought I knew Jesus Christ because I was familiar with the word. Martin Luther's rallying cry had been *Sola Scriptura*, and Scripture was the primary focus at the Lutheran churches we attended. The Liturgy of the Word consisted of Scripture readings and a homily. Three Sundays out of four, that was the Lutheran service.

It's what happened every fourth Sunday, however, that eventually led me into the Catholic Church, for on the first Sunday of every month, we had a Communion service.

Approaching the Lord's table for the first time, as a Lutheran, I recall the strange mixture of both excitement and nervousness in being able to receive what I felt was Christ's body and blood.

I approached the Communion rail and knelt while waiting for the pastor to approach. First, he broke a piece of wheat bread from a loaf he held in his hands and said the words, "The body of Christ." I responded, "Amen," and took the bread in my hands and consumed it. The young associate pastor followed him with a tray of thimble-sized plastic cups filled with wine. With the words, "The blood of Christ," I again said, "Amen," and drank from one. I found the taste of the wine strong. It lingered with me even as I found my place back in the pew. While I was unable to vocalize it, something was different. I felt more spiritually mature, and felt as if I was now a full member of the community that made up St. Andrew's Lutheran Church.

Communion, as it was termed in the Lutheran church, was a significant part of the Lutheran service for me. I longed to receive Communion as often as I could. However, since Communion services were held only once a month, if we skipped church on Sunday, it could easily be months before we would again receive Christ in the form of bread and wine.

It would be fifteen years before I would have a true understanding of the Eucharist. That came about through my experiences living in a mixed marriage with my Catholic wife.

For the first five years of our marriage, we did the mixed marriage thing, often attending both the Lutheran and Catholic Church on any given Sunday. I was struck, at first, by how similar the two services were. Often times the Scripture readings were exactly the same. However, as time went on, I was struck by the one big difference.

In the Catholic Church, the Liturgy of the Word is followed by the liturgy of the Eucharist at each and every Mass. As I remarked earlier, this was not so in the Lutheran churches I attended. What became clear to me is that there was a different emphasis.

In the early 1990s, when the Lutheran Church softened its position on abortion, I knew I could no longer remain Lutheran. I had been threatened by abortion in the womb. To support abortion would be against my own existence. I suddenly realized that being Lutheran meant more than sitting in the pew each Sunday. It meant believing everything the Lutheran Church teaches and believes.

That began my spiritual journey. The epiphany came, in of all places, before the eucharistic Christ, exposed in a monstrance at perpetual eucharistic adoration.

Out of convenience, I had started attending the Catholic Church with my wife. In September of 1994, Bishop Harry Flynn instituted perpetual eucharistic adoration at the parish. As a lazy prayer, not fully realizing what eucharistic adoration was, I signed up for an hour each week. I figured that the practice would give me some discipline in my prayer life.

The first time I went to adoration, I don't remember genuflecting or even kneeling, but Jesus was slowly working on me. It didn't take long for me to ask, "Who is this that I'm praying before?" Once I realized the answer to that question, there was nothing that could hold me back from entering the Church.

I liken it to Christ's appearance to the disciples on the road to Emmaus. Like them, I thought I knew Christ because I was familiar with His word. Yet, in the story, when Jesus uses the Old Testament to reveal Himself, the disciples still do not see Him. It is not until they reach Emmaus, and He breaks bread with them that He is revealed. Once He is revealed, nothing can hold them back. They return to Jerusalem, running to tell the others of their encounter with the risen Lord.

Lutherans believe that the bread and wine remain along with Christ's body and blood. Catholics, however, believe that an actual change takes place. At the consecration, the bread and wine no longer remain. This is why a Catholic is able to do something that a Lutheran would never do: adore Jesus Christ in the Blessed Sacrament.

Once Christ was revealed to me, body, blood, soul and divinity, my conversion was imminent. I had been going through a "Fundamentals of Catholicism" class at a nearby parish, and approached my pastor. "I cannot wait until Easter to come into the Church," I told our priest. "I believe everything that the Catholic Church teaches and believes. To wait feels like I am somehow denying Christ."

"Pick a date," he told me.

On March 19, 1995, I was confirmed into the Catholic Church, and for the first time accompanied my wife to the eucharistic table of Our Lord. Now, nine years later, I continue to keep my weekly appointment with Christ, not only through the Mass, but also through the means by which I came to first know Him, in perpetual eucharistic adoration.

Tim A. Drake   *St. Cloud, Minnesota*

Note: Tim Drake serves as staff writer with the *National Catholic Register*. He resides with his wife and five children in St. Cloud, Minnesota. An author of several books, one of his most popular is *There We Stood, Here We Stand: Eleven Lutherans Rediscover Their Catholic Roots.*

"Every theological explanation which seeks some understanding of this mystery, in order to be in accord with Catholic faith, must firmly maintain that in objective reality, independently of our mind, the bread and wine have ceased to exist after the consecration, so that the adorable body and blood of the Lord Jesus from that moment on are really before us under the sacramental species of bread and wine".

Nothing He Could Do

When I was pastor of Saints Simon and Jude Parish in Huntington Beach, California, I received a phone call from a woman whose husband was dying of cancer. He was in the front room of their home in a hospital bed. She had called the local parish, but when the priest came, he discovered that they had been married outside the Church and that the husband was non-Catholic. There was, he said, nothing he could do. She asked if I would come. I told her I could come the next morning, and asked her to have her adult children present.

After some basic catechesis, I baptized the husband, confirmed him, gave him his first Eucharist (which was also *Viaticum*), married them, absolved him, and anointed him. We celebrated every sacrament except Holy Orders. There was not a dry eye in the room as his wife, children and I prayed around his bed. He died later that week and was buried from our parish church. Such is the grace of God.

Father Laurence P. Dolan, OFM　　　　　　　　　　*Scottsdale, Arizona*

He Is Truly Present to Us

The latter part of 1997 was very difficult for me. I was thirty years old at the time, and at first I couldn't understand why God was allowing me to go through such a trying time.

My husband Tony has kidney stones quite often, and passes at least one a year. This time he had a stone that was nine millimeters, and it was stuck. The doctors had to insert a tube for a few months until they could schedule a procedure that would hopefully break it into smaller pieces, allowing him to pass it. This resulted in a serious kidney infection that he was hospitalized for.

At the same time, my thirty-six-year-old brother Robert, who had been very sick for years due to complications from AIDS, was hospitalized. Thankfully, Robert was transferred to the same hospital as Tony, which was a five minute drive from my job. My brother and husband were in rooms just a few doors away from each other, which made it easy for me to visit both of them after work.

After a few days, Robert was released from the hospital. Shortly after that I got a call from my husband, who was very distraught. He said his mother had a heart attack while she was visiting him in his hospital room. I rushed to the hospital, and went back and forth between their rooms reassuring each of them of the other's condition. All the while I was praying that everyone would be okay. Finally, everyone was back home, and I hoped things would settle down. That wasn't to be the case.

Once again I got a phone call at work. This time it was my mother. She told me that Robert had to be rushed back to the hospital in the middle of the night because he was having difficulty breathing. They had transferred him to the same hospital, and she asked if I could please go there to be with them after work. Then she told me she didn't think my brother would be coming home this time.

When I arrived, my mom, dad and aunt were there. All of them were exhausted because they had not slept since the day before. I sent them home, reassuring them that I would stay with Robert for as long as he wanted me there.

At first Robert tried to put on a brave face, and attempted to send me home. However, I could see the fear in his eyes as he started getting tremors in his legs that he couldn't control. I sat and rubbed his legs until the shaking stopped, and told him that I would stay all night if he wanted me to. He lay there silently, so I told him to just think about it and he could decide later.

Prior to my husband's most recent kidney stone, for which I had stayed with him for about thirty-six hours in the emergency room, and then longer as he had a tube inserted, I never would have thought to offer to stay all night in the hospital. However, I realized at this point that God had been preparing me to be there for my brother.

A few hours later, after more tremors and Robert's temperature spiking several times, I asked him once again if he wanted me to stay all night with him. This time I received a silent nod, so I phoned my husband to let him know I wasn't coming home that night. After getting something to eat in the cafeteria, I settled in a chair next to Robert's bed.

That night was the most intimate experience of my life. Not much was said vocally except for when Robert expressed his wishes that if he died, he didn't want to be resuscitated. Volumes were spoken in silence between us that night. When his temperature spiked, I dabbed a cool cloth over his face. I rubbed his legs when his tremors started, and stroked his hair like our mother did to comfort us when we were children. He asked me to hold his hand, and I did.

All my life I had heard how we're supposed to be as Christ to one another, but it never really hit home until that night. He was the image of Christ for me in his suffering, just as I was to him in my comforting him. We were the image of Christ for each other in our being present to one another in love. At that moment, even though I've always believed in and loved Our Lord in the Eucharist, His true presence in the Blessed Sacrament, and in His life, death and resurrection took on a new meaning for me.

The next morning when my parents arrived to relieve me, I asked Robert if he wanted me to call Father Gary so he could receive the last rites. Previously, I had worked with Father Gary at the chancery office, and he had given me his card to give to Robert.

Robert nodded yes, telling me to call the priest. At that, tears streamed down my mother's face. You see, Robert, being gay, had been away from the Church for about twenty years.

Thankfully, Father Gary was at work when I called. He rushed to the hospital so Robert could receive the sacraments of reconciliation, Communion, and anointing of the sick. Just a couple of hours later, Robert was placed on a ventilator and was sedated. At that point he wouldn't have been able to vocalize his wishes, say his confession, or receive the Eucharist.

A few days later the doctors were starting to push us to have the ventilator removed. Fears of him dying by suffocation worried us all. My parents and his partner told him it was okay to go home, and, as a tear ran down his cheek, he slipped away. Again, Jesus was present in Robert's death.

The following Sunday at Mass, when I went to Communion, I did so on my knees with tears streaming down my face. I finally realized in my heart how intimately He gives Himself to me, and how He is truly present to all of us in the Eucharist.

Carolyn D. Susin   *Martinez, California*

Jesus Changed My Heart

One day, I went to Mass with my sister-in-law, Carol, and her four-year-old son, Henri. As we got out of the car, Henri wanted to bring a toy with him to Mass. His Mom didn't allow him to do so, so he decided to pout all through the Mass. He sat on the floor, not budging to stand or kneel or anything.

At Communion time we asked him to come with us to receive a blessing from the priest. He refused to do that, too. As we got up to go, he noticed he was going to be alone in the pew, and followed us. After we both received Communion and he got a blessing from the priest, he went up to his Mom and declared, "Mommy, Jesus changed my heart!"

Then, he was back to his normal, fun loving self, and we both hugged him. What a lesson that was for us, and for those around us who heard him. Through the mouth of babes! The gift of the Eucharist is truly a healing gift.

Madeleine R. Porter   *Cumberland, Rhode Island*

The saving efficacy of the sacrifice is fully realized when the Lord's body and blood are received in communion.

In Communion With Christ

To receive Communion is not only to be in-communion with Christ, but also with His body, the Church. To be in-communion means to be in a relationship of love and compassion with everyone in the Church, especially with the members of our family, friends and neighbors—even our enemies. Receiving Communion and not being in-communion with everyone in the body of Christ is tearing the body asunder and making our sacramental reception a liturgical farce.

Father Noel Wall, OFM   *Lemont, Illinois*

The Pope Blesses Newlyweds

I opened the door to the church hall and looked inside. My first thought was "Ooh, tall blonde guy, never seen him before." I had prayed for many years for my future spouse, and after too many bad blind dates, I was ready to meet Mr. Right. We both showed up to a book study at church and no one else was there, not even the priest who was teaching the class. Something prompted me to ask this man to join me for a cup of coffee; it must have been the Holy Spirit.

Although we didn't know it, from that very day, we began the journey of a sacramental marriage. It started with me inviting him to join me on my Friday night dates with Jesus, when I would go to adoration for an hour. This time alone with Jesus was very special. It was a quiet time to pray, meditate, and adore Our Lord. The best part was that Jesus didn't even get jealous when I brought along another guy on my date with Him.

By spending time in silent adoration with Jesus, we strived to keep Christ at the center of our relationship. We also attended numerous church functions like book studies, apologetic classes, and eventually helped with the Lifeteen Youth Group. This time of ministry was a wonderful way for our relationship to grow and be nourished by the grace of God.

After dating for over a year, we got engaged and started planning our wedding. We decided that the wedding was a sacrament we wanted to celebrate, not only with our family and friends, but with all the people we worked with in ministries at our church. We had the Lifeteen band play at our nuptial Mass, and as I walked down the aisle with my dad, I was singing, "Shout to the Lord."

It was a wonderful wedding celebration. I'll always remember how special it was for us being close to the altar, sharing in the Eucharist for the first time as a newly married couple. We witnessed to many people through this holy celebration, and walked out of the Mass singing, "Testify to Love." That is what we intended to do with our marriage.

We decided that it was more important to have a wonderful wedding celebration with all of our friends than to plan a fancy honeymoon right after the wedding. While our family was in town, we wanted to spend time with them. However, after our family left, we did sneak off for an overnight stay in the mountains.

Shortly after our wedding, I read an article in a Catholic magazine about Pope John Paul II blessing newlywed couples during his Wednesday audiences. We read that the pope meets and greets newlyweds that come to Rome within the first six months of their marriage. I thought, what an unbelievable experience that would be, so I asked my husband if this was something he would like to do. That was when I found out that my husband had dreamed for years of going to Rome to study architecture. We prayed for God to provide us a way to get this special blessing if it was His will.

A few weeks later, while we were sitting at the airport, the flight we were on was over-booked, and anyone willing to give up their seat would receive a travel voucher for $200. That was the initial financing of our trip to Rome. With numerous internet searches and the vouchers, we eventually found tickets we could afford. Then we spoke to a wonderful priest who told us of a special place to stay, a retreat house just to the west of St. Peter's Basilica.

Off we went for the honeymoon of a lifetime! We thoroughly enjoyed the beautiful sites of Rome, Italy. We celebrated the sacrament of the Eucharist in several churches, and in several different languages, and finally recognized the true universality of the Church.

On Wednesday morning, we got up and dressed in our wedding attire, and were on our way to the Vatican. The taxi driver dropped us off at a flower shop, a short way from St. Peter's. I tied a few roses together and pinned a rose to my husband's lapel. We walked the rest of the way to St. Peter's square and enjoyed the beautiful November morning.

We felt our excitement build as we looked forward to meeting the holy father. For the next several hours, my heart pounded with the anticipation of meeting such an awe-inspiring man. As we waited in line, we were instructed to stand, not kneel, and bow and kiss his ring. We were told the pope may say a few words to us, we were to listen, and then move along. Okay. It was our turn.

My husband bowed and kissed his ring, and guided the pope's hand to mine. I kissed his ring and looked into the most beautiful blue eyes I have ever seen. He said to us in English, "May God bless you!" as he made the sign of the cross over us. I said to him "I love you, Papa," and he squeezed my hand. We were ushered off. This all took place in less than thirty seconds.

When we walked away my husband turned to me and said, "That was awesome, imagine if every Catholic got that excited when meeting Christ in the Eucharist at Mass?"

Kristin Sommer   *Peachtree City, Georgia*

The Eucharistic Sacrifice is intrinsically directed to the inward union of the faithful with Christ through communion; we receive the very One who offered himself for us, we receive his body which he gave up for us on the Cross and his blood which he "poured out for many for the forgiveness of sins" (Mt 26:28).

One Bread, One Body

A few years ago, a college student attended Mass for the first time with a new Catholic friend and wrote of the experience: "We attended an ordinary Sunday morning Mass in a local parish church. We arrived late, so we had to sit in the front pew. We arrived in time for the Gospel and the homily, but I confess that I do not remember either of them. What I do remember was the Eucharistic Prayer. We were kneeling because God was there. God was as real as my own breath that I could feel on my hands. I was afraid to raise my head to even look toward the altar."

Jesus Christ offered Himself in the holy Eucharist to be shared so that we, in turn, learn to break with others, heal the wounds of division, and ultimately be transformed into a reconciled community and a united people of God.

Let me suggest three ways we can bring about a deeper reflection on the real presence of Jesus in the holy Eucharist in relation to our daily lives. Namely, they are: one bread, one body, and one people.

One bread: Our Lord has blest and broken one bread to be shared among us so that we become one with Him and through Him, with our brothers and sisters in the whole world. "The one who eats my flesh and drinks my blood abides in me and I in him."

One body: The Eucharist makes us, who are members of the Church, one body of Christ. St. Paul aptly expressed it: "Because the loaf of bread is one, we, many though we are, become one body, for we all partake of the one loaf." The Eucharist, through the Spirit, transforms us into a communion and a community. This communion empowers us to forgive each other and be reconciled with each other, it empowers us to work for unity, solidarity, and sharing what we have and what we are to one another.

One people: If unity and sharing constitute the essence of the Eucharist for all of us Christians, then we ourselves become the living sign of what we received. St. Augustine pointed out: "The bread which you see on the altar, consecrated by the word of God, is the body of Christ. The chalice, or what it holds, consecrated by the word of God, is the blood of Christ. If you have received worthily, then you are what you have received."

"The bread that I will give is my flesh for the life of the world." It was with good reason that Jesus was born in Bethlehem, for "Bethlehem" means the "House of Bread." Jesus, the living bread, was always moved to compassion at the sight of people who, according to Him, are like sheep without a shepherd, and are starved for food that nourishes both the body and spirit unto eternal life.

Today, so many hungers of the human family cry out for attention. There is the hunger for peace and understanding, the hunger for justice and freedom, the hunger for truth and love, and the hunger for God, Jesus, and the Holy Spirit. And most obviously is the hunger for material bread, simply because not too many as yet are truly imbued with the self-sacrificing spirit of Christ, as to be able to give themselves to be broken and be shared with the teeming millions who have less or nothing in life.

All around the globe are people who struggle for survival. So we ask, are we here celebrating the richness and fullness of the few, or abject poverty of the many?

Our eucharistic celebration will be a sign of contradiction and inconsistency if we do not see the meaning and intimate relationship between the Eucharist and our lives and relationships as brothers and sisters in Christ. We need to see this relationship as we partake in His one body broken for all of us so that we become truly one people under our one heavenly Father.

May Jesus inspire us towards our earnest desire to belong to one another and become one people of God.

Msgr. John Z. Vargas   *Tampa, Florida*

Are You Really There?

My wife and I struggled with our Catholic faith after reading nearly every book and listening to every tape we could find on Christianity. We were confused because most of our resources were Protestant, and they contradicted what we knew, or thought we knew, about the Catholic Church. We felt that our faith in Jesus had grown strong and deep over our few years of searching to learn more about Christianity, but our trust in the Catholic Church had waned to barely a thread.

Many things we read and were told by people outside of the Catholic Church during those years had us absolutely befuddled. We became convinced that praying to Mary, and asking for the intercession of saints was wrong. The idea of going to confession seemed suspicious. And, with two small children in our house, subscribing to something like Natural Family Planning seemed nothing short of preposterous. We prayed about our dwindling faith in Catholicism as best as we could.

Until that time, I had never been to eucharistic adoration. I had heard the term, but didn't understand the practice itself. One night when my confusion over the Church was at it's worst, I moved on an impulse and went to our parish chapel. It was the first Friday of the month, when our parish is blessed to have overnight adoration.

It was late at night, and inside the chapel it was quiet and still. About a half a dozen people sat or kneeled in prayer before Our Lord in the monstrance upon the altar. I took a seat in a pew and stared at the Blessed Sacrament. Only one prayer came to mind, and I said it over and over. "Are you really there?" I prayed. "Are you really there?" I went home that night feeling peaceful, but still not satisfied.

One of our neighbors was a recent convert to Catholicism and loaned us a copy of *Rome Sweet Home* by Scott and Kimberly Hahn. In perhaps one of the greatest stories of conversion ever told, the Hahn's not only explain how they came into the fullness of the Catholic Church, but also provide striking evidence to defend so many of the teachings my wife and I had started to doubt. One of the most critical points was their explanation of John 6:53 which reads, "In all truth I tell you, if you do not eat the flesh of the Son of Man and drink His blood, you have no life in you."

I suddenly understood that the truth had been in front of me the entire time, and I had not seen it. I was struck with the realization that Jesus is truly present in the Eucharist, and that this belief is at the core of what the Catholic Church teaches. I also realized that if I believed this truth when so many of the books I had been reading didn't teach it, then logically I must also believe other teachings of the Catholic Church as well. I knew then that I couldn't be a cafeteria Catholic, believing only what I chose to believe. I couldn't believe solely in the Eucharist, while simultaneously denying the other tenants of the Church.

As I read *Rome Sweet Home*, I cried. An intense peace came over me and every doubt about the Catholic Church was removed. When I went to adoration for that first time and prayed, "Are you really there?" Jesus heard me, and He answered with a resounding, "Yes."

After reading that book, everything changed for my wife and me. We started praying the rosary, studying early Church history, and went to adoration every chance we could. In June of that year, we went to the Eucharistic Congress in Atlanta, Georgia. With nearly 20,000 Catholics in attendance, I felt truly at home among my brothers and sisters in faith.

The morning of the conference we arrived late and had to rush our oldest son to the children's track before rushing down to the main rooms to listen to the speakers. As we quickly navigated through the crowd of people, we heard hushed whispers coming down the hall. "Jesus is coming. Here comes Jesus. Jesus is coming."

All around us, people dropped to their knees wherever they stood. And then we saw Him, Jesus, shining in His monstrance at the end of the hall, being carried in a procession to a special chapel made ready for Him that day.

My wife and I fell to our knees as well, and as Our Lord went by I could barely lift my eyes to Him. In my heart I heard my prayer from just a few months ago, "Are you really there?" As Jesus passed me that day, He answered once more. "Here I am." He has stayed there ever since.

Gregory L. Willits   *Conyers, Georgia*

We are reminded of his words: "As the living Father sent me, and I live because of the Father, so he who eats me will live because of me" (Jn 6:57).

I Know Where You Are

In my ministry at a large Midwestern retirement and nursing facility, I was also on-call for one of the nearby hospitals when emergencies came in. One Sunday evening in August, just after suppertime, I received a call to come to Southview Hospital as soon as possible. A man named George, about fifty-five years of age, had just arrived by emergency squad. He was DOA (dead on arrival).

George had been at his company's employee picnic that afternoon. It was late afternoon when the heart attack came. His family had not been with him because of other commitments.

His wife had just been notified by the emergency room coordinator, but was not told anything other than her husband had been brought in with a heart attack. Then I had been called. They wanted to make sure the wife and family made it safely to the hospital, and at the same time have me there to meet them and break the news to them.

I arrived at the hospital within minutes of the call, went to the cubicle where the body was, and offered the prayer of the dead for George. I decided to wait by the emergency room entrance so that when I spotted the wife and family arriving, I would be able to approach them in the parking lot to tell them the news. There is never a good time to break such sudden and tragic news, but I thought it would be better if they knew as soon as possible and be prepared for what they would see. True, such news would dash their hopes, but it would at least ease some of the shock when they entered the emergency room cubicle to see their dead husband and father's body.

George's family, his wife, Alma, and his three adult daughters, arrived shortly afterwards. As I approached them, even before I could say anything, they began to realize my presence. They knew my coming to meet them meant their loved one had died. I informed them that he had apparently died on the way to the hospital. I offered my condolences and assured them that I would go with them to support them and offer once again the prayers of the Church.

Naturally, there were lots of tears and sobs as we made our way into the emergency area of the hospital. We went into a small waiting room to allow the family a few minutes to gather themselves and to allow George's sudden death to sink into their hearts. A sympathetic physician came in to confirm George's death. He explained to them that the heart attack had been massive and that there was simply nothing anyone could have done. After the oldest daughter made a couple of phone calls to tell the news to other family members, it was time for them to go into the cubicle to see George's body.

Understandably, their first sight of George's body brought about more tears and sobbing. As often happens in such difficult circumstances, they talked to George as though he was alive. They told him how much they loved him and how dear he was to them. A little while later, I offered the Prayers of the Dead. I prayed, "Loving and merciful God, we entrust our brother, George, to your mercy. You loved him greatly in this life; now that he is freed from all its cares, give him happiness and peace forever."

These prayers of the Church are wonderful because what they do, even in a moment of tragedy such as this, is to remind those present that while they see a body with their eyes, their hearts remind them that their dear husband and father is alive and in God's hands. I asked Alma what had happened earlier that day. She said it had been an ordinary Sunday and as usual, she and George had gone to the 11:00 a.m. Mass at their parish. A couple of hours later, George left for his company's picnic.

As I imagined Alma and George at Mass just hours before, I said, "Alma, do you remember what happened at Mass this morning?" She looked at me curiously. I continued, "You and George went to Communion. And just before Communion, the priest held up the Host for all to see and said, 'This is the body and blood of Jesus. May His body and blood bring us all to everlasting life.'" I went on and said, "And as George took the sacred Host in his hand, the priest said, 'The Body of Christ.' George once again made an act of faith as he had so often done and said, 'Amen' (I believe).

"Remember what Jesus said?" I continued, "'Whoever eats my flesh and drinks my blood will never die, but will have life everlasting.'" Those words touched Alma very deeply and at that tragic moment she understood them in a way she had never done in her life.

Then Alma did something that was a real proclamation of her faith. She looked at her husband, placed her right hand affectionately on her husband's chest, and with a voice that was filled with faith she said loudly and clearly, "George, I know where you are! I know where you are!" Her heartfelt faith would not lessen her sorrow, nor did it end her tears. But her heart had just proclaimed her absolute conviction of what she and her daughters believed.

In the midst of sorrow and tears, Alma knew that her husband of thirty-four years was, at that very moment, with God. They would not be separated forever. It was what Jesus promised Alma and her husband earlier that morning at Mass. "George, Alma, I am the living bread. If anyone eats this bread he shall live forever." (Jn 6:51)

As Alma and her daughters made their way home from the hospital that sorrowful evening, Alma knew where her husband was with more certainty than if she held a printed map in her hand.

Father Jim VanVurst, OFM   *Cincinnati, Ohio*

The Bread of Life

Every Saturday night after Mass, my husband and I take the Eucharist to the Catholic residents at Prescott Country View Nursing Home. For the last two years we have only had one communicant, Margaret Higgins, who celebrated her 101st birthday on January 4, 2004.

Margaret is quite a remarkable lady for more reasons than her age. She bore eleven children, nine that lived. It is by her own choice that she lives in the nursing home rather than take turns living with some of her children, but nevertheless they still take care of her. She is probably one of the most visited nursing home residents. One of her daughters makes sure her room is always cheerfully decorated for the current season or holiday. She is always fashionably dressed, and her hair is neatly cut and styled. She gladly tells us who brought her the new sweater or necklace she is wearing.

Though she is very hard of hearing, her mind is alert, and her memory is incredible. She makes it a point to watch Mass on television on Sunday mornings, and will tell us if she missed it the week before. She always tells us how much she appreciates us bringing her the Eucharist.

One Saturday night about six weeks before her 101st birthday, we arrived to find Margaret in bed instead of up in her wheelchair waiting for us. Three or four nurses aides were flitting carefully and quietly in and out of her room, and one hurried in from the hallway to whisper to us that Margaret had talked of nothing but going home to God and her husband for the last two days. She refused to eat, and would not get out of bed. She appeared gaunt and pale, and her voice was raspy. She said she was tired and did not feel well. When asked if she wanted to receive the Eucharist, however, she said, "Yes." We prayed the "Our Father" with her and gave her the body of Christ, and quickly and quietly left for home. As we left, my husband said he thought we had given her "food for the journey home."

All week I expected a call from the nursing home, or from her son, telling me Margaret had gone home to heaven, but the call did not come. Before Mass the next Saturday, I called her son. He said that as far as he knew, his mother was all right. We arrived after Mass to find her up and dressed, sitting in her wheelchair waiting for us. The aides told us she began to get better the following day after we had brought her the Eucharist. In my mind, it turned out we gave her "the bread of life" instead of "food for the journey home."

MaryBarbara McKay   *Pleasanton, Kansas*

The Eucharist is a true banquet, *in which Christ offers himself as our nourishment.*

Jesus Is Really There

I have seen Our Lord in the Host on several occasions. To set the scene, I have been a spiritual child of Padre Pio's for many years. I also have a great devotion to Our Lord's Sacred Heart and His precious wounds.

One time I was lying in the hospital awaiting open heart surgery. Our priest brought me Communion, and as he was holding up the Host, first of all, Padre Pio appeared. I gasped and then immediately saw our sorrowful Lord appear. When I received the Host, I felt at peace. I made it through the operation and thought a lot about what had happened.

I am a eucharistic minister in a large Catholic hospital. Periodically, when I am offering the Host to patients, our sorrowful Lord will appear in the Host as I am offering it. I believe this is a sign that Our Lord is giving them a special blessing. Some have seen it but most do not. Afterwards, I notice specks of red in my pyx when I put the Host back in the tabernacle.

I always have a relic of Padre Pio and a relic of the true cross in my pocket when I am ministering to others. This is a very humbling experience. I know what I have seen; there is no doubt in my mind. Jesus is really there.

Barbara Barlow   *Reynoldsburg, Ohio*

Outpouring of Love

Many years ago I was on retreat and got up in the middle of the night to pray. It was three o'clock in the morning, and I went quietly into the still chapel to sit in simple contemplation before the Eucharist in the tabernacle. It was very peaceful. The only light was from the vigil candles, and the red candle close to the altar that signaled the presence of Jesus in the Eucharist. I sat in awe, simply breathing in the nearness of God. It was a very healing time, and I needed much healing, as this was a difficult time in my life.

When I was very still, the Lord overshadowed me in a tremendously powerful way. He gave me a *vision* which continues to change how I live, and provides fire for my love of the Eucharist. Whether the vision was with the eyes of my body or the *eyes* of my soul, or both, doesn't really matter. Such things are unimportant when God draws us near and writes on our hearts.

In my vision, I saw the tabernacle open, and out of the tabernacle came an incredibly bright red flowing river. It was the blood of Our Lord. Surprisingly, this river of blood was far from being frightening. It was amazing, exhilarating, and almost intoxicating. It was very alive and full of light, and was covering everything. It flowed with a wonderful current.

The light from this river covered my hands, which were open in prayer. Quickly, I was completely drawn into the flow of the river, this holy living river of life-giving blood. It was warm, and full of light and life. In the midst of it, I felt such love that I really thought it was too much for me to contain, and that perhaps I might be taken up to heaven. It was intense and yet so very gentle. Such are the turnings of God in the soul, and words pale so much before the experience.

I saw this river flow, not only out of the room, but out of the building, out of the city, and throughout the world. I was carried with it, and the Lord brought me to many places that night. He showed me places in the world where there was much suffering, and showed me the faithful hearts of people calling out to Him. By this time I was overcome with tears. He explained to my heart that all of us are indeed one in this holy river of His blood. It is poured out for us every hour of every day.

He told me there were no real barriers between people anymore, that His blood was bathing all human souls, and uniting all human hearts. He said many people were refusing to let the light of His love soak into them and heal them. He told me to travel through His heart to needy souls throughout the world, and in the presence of my prayer in this mystery of the Eucharist, to truly join Him in healing the darkness that continues to oppress humanity.

Jesus also told me that I could travel through this holy river to who-ever was alive in His heart, that in the holy Eucharist we were really one. Not in some theoretical sense, but in a very real incarnational way. He told me that part of the real presence in the Eucharist was His presence, mak-ing us really present to each other. He told me the love that is our heritage has no bounds and no limits to its power, just as His blood cannot be contained in a tabernacle, and that His light is more powerful than our eyes can ever imagine.

We *traveled* for what seemed like hours, perhaps all night long, although it was likely that the true passage of time was not great. I went to China and comforted a young child dying of an infectious illness, and was in Africa with someone being tortured. He took me to Central and South America where I walked with modern saints persecuted for their faith. Then it was to India and the streets of Calcutta where I shared precious water with the thirsty. After that, I traveled back to the United States, into an inner city where a child hovered in fear with the threatening sounds of the night.

The river kept flowing. I witnessed the birth of a child, and the joy of the parents in the gift of new life. I was in a nursing home as a very ancient man died, surrounded by those who kept vigil in love. I continued travel-ing, and everywhere the river flowed, Jesus spoke to me simply, with the silence of hearts that know each other in a shared glance. He was showing me how the true bread of the Eucharist feeds us all and changes us to become His loving presence in the world.

Gradually the vision faded and all that was left was the quiet of the chapel. The tabernacle door was again closed, and all was very still. I was changed forever by the *vision* of that holy night.

We need to remember that the Eucharist is alive and passionately pow-erful. As wonderful and awe-inspiring as it is, the Real Presence isn't simply the great mystery of Jesus present to us in bread and wine, becom-ing truly one with us in a sacrament that is beyond the grasp of human wisdom and intellect. Through this mystery of the Eucharist, we are taken, blessed, broken, and given to each other as Jesus is given to us. Through this mystery we are drawn into the living river of His holy blood. It contin-ues to flow in light and love throughout the world, to heal and make whole all who let the river in.

The depth and profoundness of the Eucharist is powerful and life-changing. I wonder sometimes if we really see it as so. Often we feel overwhelmed by tragedy and sorrow in the world, or in our personal corner of it. Much of this suffering and evil causes unnecessary pain. We tend to feel very small in the midst of the greatness of the problems facing the world, and our lives.

If we come to know with our whole beings that we are all part of this glorious river, and have even a small appreciation of the strength of this current, and the great passion of love contained in it, we will not be so afraid or feel as overwhelmed. We would know we are not helpless. We would indeed rest in the great light of love that is held so powerfully in the gift of the Eucharist. We would come to the table with confidence and hunger, certain of His mercy, compassion, and healing.

This gift was given to me many years ago. I have had many challenges and troubled times since then, and sometimes this journey has been very costly. I have moments of discouragement, and struggle like everyone else. But all the garbage, and some of it is very heavy, is washed away in a powerful stream of light that flows out of the tabernacle of each of our hearts by His holy blessing.

In this wine and in this bread we are all truly fed exactly what we need to weather the storm of another day's journey home. Not only are we given enough for ourselves, but we are given plenty for many others to whom Jesus sends us. That is the miracle of His blood, which is still poured out for us. God bless us, everyone. See you along the way, in the current of His love!

Maria de la Luz Lozano, M.D.   *Ohmsted Falls, Ohio*

When for the first time Jesus spoke of this food, his listeners were astonished and bewildered, which forced the Master to emphasize the objective truth of his words: "Truly, truly, I say to you, unless you eat the flesh of the Son of Man and drink his blood, you have no life within you" (Jn 6:53).

How Do I Do That?

Reflecting immediately after Communion with the Lord God is to me a most sacred moment. When I am in this sacred presence, sometimes my desire for special friends is that they be lifted free from their troubles and inertia of faith. When this desire happened recently, the powerful and challenging word came to me, as an inner voice. It said to me, "Bring them to the Eucharist." Now, this left me wondering all the more, "And how I am to do that?"

Father Roch A. Coogan, OFM   *Belleair Bluffs, Florida*

Not in Outer Space

Through God's amazing grace, and through the faith and love my husband shared with me, I joined the Catholic Church a year and a half after our marriage. A year later, I found myself struggling through early menopause and the agony of depression.

One afternoon, while recuperating from surgery, I lay down on the bed to rest. I wanted so badly to just leave this world and go up to heaven to talk things over with God. Before I knew it, I fell asleep and had the most spectacular dream of my life.

In my dream, I found myself driving up a mountain road. At the top, I got out of the car and surveyed the magnificent scene below. It was a picture-perfect day with sunshine, blue sky, and a mighty flowing river traversing the emerald green valley.

All of a sudden, my spirit left my body and I found myself floating upward, like a feather. My eyes spotted a car driving on the road alongside the river, and it surprised me to see my husband and myself in that car. Then, a brilliant flash of light flared in the sky. It was like a giant firecracker exploding, sending a shower of golden stars down upon the earth. I marveled at the exquisite beauty of it all.

Although I didn't hear anything, I understood that it was time for me to return to earth. I didn't want to go back, but as my spirit reentered my body, the slight jerk awakened me.

I pondered this dream occasionally over a period of ten years, wondering what it all meant. During that time my father died, and my mother came to live with my husband and me. The stress from my mother's failing health, and having to nurse her through a difficult surgery and healing, threw me back into depression.

My parish priest referred me to Father Vincent Beuzer, S.J. After listening to my story he anointed me, and then counseled both my husband and myself. He also offered a healing Mass for me, and we received Jesus in Communion. For two weeks following this anointing and Mass, my husband and I shared an extraordinary conversion experience. Bathed in God's holy light, we viewed creation with enhanced vision.

Soon we were led to Father Beuzer's sister who shared with us her involvement with adoration of the Blessed Sacrament. Through her guidance, we started an adoration program in our parish. We maintained this program for a number of years, until we moved from the parish.

One evening, while praying before the Blessed Sacrament, I thought about the dream I'd had years earlier. Because I still wondered about the purpose of this dream, I asked the Lord why I had dreamt it. Once again I didn't hear anything, but the understanding flashed into my mind almost immediately. "My child, you were looking for me in outer space and you needed to learn that I am right here with you on earth."

"Grateful Soul"   *Spokane, Washington*

In the Eucharist, everything speaks of confident waiting "in joyful hope for the coming of our Saviour, Jesus Christ".

The Eucharist Kept Me Alive

My parents taught me very little about religion, God and the Church. In fact, I was usually sent to Mass alone, if I went at all. My religious education was almost exclusively through my teachers at school, and in my religion class.

One Sunday when I was sixteen, I received the holy sacraments of confession and Communion after not having received them in a long time. That same afternoon, I went for a ride with my cousin on his motorbike and we were in a bad accident.

My cousin was driving the motorbike at nearly 100 kmh (65 miles per hour) when we crashed into a car whose driver didn't see a stop sign. He had come from the right through a crossing with poor visibility.

My cousin died immediately, and the driver of the car died just minutes later. It is a miracle that I am alive. I only had to stay in the hospital for three weeks, and had a plaster cast on my knee for three weeks more. I am sure that the Lord in me through the holy Eucharist was the reason I survived this deadly crash.

Heinrich Mueller   *Donau, Austria*

No Longer Fighting

This is a story of the healing power of the Eucharist that took place during my seminary days.

Before I entered the seminary, I often cared for my younger cousins. I loved Paul, one of my cousins, very much but we always seemed to find something to fight about. Often we would be at odds with each other for months at a time.

During October of 1977, we were once again at the point of not talking. This time it seemed to be final. I did not like this, but all we would do is fight and we were both very hurt from each other. One Sunday afternoon I had some free time from the seminary and was with Paul's sister. She said, "Why don't we go down to the Burning Bush?" This was a place that had perpetual adoration. As we were going she said, "Let's go see if Paul wants to go, I know he has never been there and he wants to see it." I said, "I don't want to stop at his house and fight with him anymore." But I gave in. It was a cold atmosphere when we met, but he agreed to go with us on the condition that we would go in different cars because he had heard I liked to spend an hour at least there.

We went in and after about twenty minutes, he was ready to leave. So, I walked out of the chapel with him. All of a sudden he reached out and hugged me, something that was very hard for him to do even when we were at peace! Since that time we have never had a disagreement or an argument. It has been six years now and we have grown closer together than can be imagined. This was truly the healing power of Christ.

My cousin continued to go to the Burning Bush often. In fact, he even proposed to his wife in front of the Blessed Sacrament! They have a beautiful marriage.

Father Anthony Gargotta   *Natrona Heights, Pennsylvania*

Jammies With Jesus

A year ago I attended a life-changing weekend retreat at my parish in Allen, Texas. The whole experience was deeply touching, but one aspect of the retreat I'll never forget was *jammies with Jesus*.

Throughout the retreat weekend, we were blessed to have a perpetual adoration chapel, which we could freely visit at any time. At one point on Saturday, an announcement was made that a sign-up sheet was available for anyone who wanted to spend time in adoration during the late night or early morning hours.

By the end of this first retreat day, all of us were drained, exhausted, and ready for a good night's sleep. Somehow, that sheet still filled up, and all through the night my fellow retreatants, and the team hosting the weekend, rose from their much needed sleep to go to the chapel and spend time with Our Lord in the Blessed Sacrament.

Some of us were worried that we might fall asleep in adoration during that cozy, late hour, but we were assured that it would be worse if we didn't have *jammies with Jesus*. So, off I went at my given time to be with the Lord, thoroughly nervous that I would fall asleep on Him, but assured that it would be okay if I did.

Well, that hour came and went with the speed of lightning, and never once did my head even nod. That silent, candle-lit evening in the chapel alone with Jesus, in my jammies, changed my life forever. I not only stayed awake, but was deeply touched by the awareness that I was right there with my Lord and Savior. Just as He had been in the Garden at Gethsemane, now I had my chance to *stay awake for just one hour* with Him.

To this day, my heart is touched and blessed by this one precious hour I spent with Jesus. Now when I go to adoration, I feel the same special presence that I felt during my *jammies with Jesus* time at the retreat.

Recently I was blessed to spend several hours in the adoration chapel while that same retreat was being conducted for a whole new group of women. I noticed a very beautiful and profound thing while I was there.

All through the morning as the retreat was going on, different members of the team presenting the retreat would come into the chapel one by one, and kneel in silent adoration. Then they would get up and return to their activities. It seems that their lives were changed forever by *jammies with Jesus* too, as they recognized that their strength in ministering on this retreat came from spending time before the Blessed Sacrament.

Julie A. Murtha   *Allen, Texas*

This is no metaphorical food: "My flesh is food indeed, and my blood is drink indeed" (Jn 6:55).

Time of Grace

Our nine-year-old son had Down syndrome, and died from complications of diabetes. For many weeks after his death, my greatest sense of grief and loss came after receiving Communion at Mass.

In that special time of grace and closeness to Jesus, I could experience and share the pain of my son's death without having to put on a brave face, or end up trying to comfort my friends and family in their grief.

Since then, I have learned that this particular form of grieving during Communion is not unique to me, and I know others who have experienced it as well.

Kathy L. Lefferson   *St. Petersburg, Florida*

Look No Further

Many years ago I suffered from severe panic attacks that kept me from attending church and any places where there were crowds. Sometimes I was even afraid to go outside my home. Because of this, for one whole month, I did not attend daily or Sunday Masses. In desperation, I had even considered attending a smaller church that was not of my Catholic faith.

One Sunday afternoon, I felt the urge to go to church to make a visit and pray. It wasn't Mass time, so I knew nobody, or maybe just a few people, would be there. My dear mother-in-law went with me since I would not drive by myself.

As I walked into the church, there He was in all His glory on the altar in a beautiful monstrance. Suddenly my heart felt a deep joy and peace.

Our Lord spoke to my heart saying, "I am here, look no further. I will be with you always." That was the beginning of, and eventually, the complete healing of my body and soul.

This took place over thirty-eight years ago, and my ongoing conversion will not end until my beloved Lord calls me home. Our Lord, Jesus Christ, is truly ever present in the Blessed Sacrament.

Pax Bonum

Margaret J. Jackson, SFO   *Lebanon, Indiana*

The Moment of Consecration

I often wondered when the ordinary unleavened bread became "The body of Christ." For a time I thought it was when the priest said, "Let your spirit come upon these gifts so they may become for us, 'The body of Christ.'"

Then while reading a book about the Mass, it stated that the bread becomes the body of Christ when the priest says, "This is my body." Some celebrants roll over that line without inflection or pause, and others put special emphasis on those four words and reflect for a second before continuing.

If we think about this moment of the Mass, we may perceive the priest at this time taking on the presence of Christ. As he prays those words, "This is my body," the bread truly becomes the Lord's body. I think how little we understand that we are in the presence of the greatest act of love that ever existed.

God so generously gives Himself to us to nourish our spirits, to feed our hearts, and to draw us into a oneness with Him that will last for all eternity.

Through the Eucharist, God makes us eucharistic people, to be Eucharist to others. His body and Precious Blood challenges us to seek Him in a deeper way each time we receive Him.

Deacon Bob Thomson   *Edgewater, New Jersey*

The Sacrament of the Eucharist: What Has Happened to My Devotions?

by Thomas Richstatter, O.F.M.

What happened to Benediction, kneeling for Communion, and silence in church? I have been going to Mass and receiving holy Communion for nearly fifty years. As I look back over that half-century I see that many of the devotions and signs of reverence for the Eucharist that were so dear to me in my younger days I no longer practice! What has happened to my devotion to the most holy Sacrament of the Eucharist?

I have spoken about the Eucharist to many parish groups across the country. And as I listen to the questions and comments of people at these talks, I pick up their concern regarding the changes in Eucharistic devotion. Many have experienced changes in their own devotion or witnessed it in others, and they sometimes worry that something important has been lost.

I hope that describing the change in my Eucharistic devotion will help many other Catholics to understand and appreciate their own Eucharistic devotion and to see the reasons for some of the changes in the devotional practices of their parishes. I'll admit here at the beginning that I am more than just a little scared to talk about my Eucharistic devotion. I have been a priest for over 25 years and this is certainly not the first time I have talked or written about the Eucharist. Yet it is always difficult to talk openly about something so intimate and so important to me personally—and to you personally.

My devotion to the Eucharist is not something merely external, something that *I do*; it is something that *I am*. It lies at the very heart of my identity: how I see myself as a Christian, as a Catholic priest, as an American.

Changes in devotion to the Eucharist affect me—as they affect you— much more deeply than many others changes in my life. To say "I no longer kneel down when I receive holy Communion" touches me in a deeper place than to say "I no longer put salt on my mashed potatoes," although both of these changes in my external behavior are the result of changes in understanding and inner conviction. To explain the changes in external behavior I must talk about the inner changes in belief and understanding.

I have come to believe that in order to understand the Sacrament of the Eucharist adequately, my understanding and my piety must include three images: Good Friday, Holy Thursday and Easter Sunday.

Good Friday: The holy sacrifice of the Mass

Good Friday was the main image that shaped my Eucharistic devotion when I was a child. When I entered our parish church the first thing I saw was a larger-than-life crucifix. Being at Mass was like kneeling at the foot of the cross on Calvary. My silent reverence at Mass reflected the reverence of Mary and John at the death of Jesus.

I learned about the Mass and the sacraments from a little book called the Baltimore Catechism, which most Catholics my age remember. I remember question 357: "What is the Mass?" I memorized the answer: "The Mass is the sacrifice of the New Law in which Christ, through the ministry of the priest, offers Himself to God in an unbloody manner under the appearances of bread and wine." Even though I did not understand the full meaning of some of these words, the mention of "sacrifice," "priest," "offering," "blood" brought to my mind the image of Good Friday and permanently associated the Eucharist with Jesus dying on the cross.

I never thought much about the "meal" aspect of the Mass (the Holy Thursday image) when I was a child. I remember that very few people received holy Communion at weekday Masses, and on Sundays in my parish holy Communion seemed to be reserved for special groups who went to Communion once a month (the Holy Name society on one Sunday and The Altar Society on another). But because Good Friday was the dominant (and nearly exclusive) image out of which I understood the Mass, the number of people going to Communion was not an issue.

My devotion to the Sacrament was shaped by the image of kneeling at the foot of the cross, gazing at the sacrifice of Jesus, and expressing gratitude for so great a love and sorrow for sins which caused so great a suffering. The image of Good Friday remains an essential element of my understanding of the Eucharist; but while it is essential, it is not enough.

Holy Thursday: Eucharist as sacred banquet

When I was in grade school, I was one of those "strange" children who went to holy Communion each morning (and ate breakfast from a little paper bag during first period). If "Good Friday" was the dominant image in my understanding of the Sacrament of the Eucharist, the image of Holy Thursday and the Lord's Supper was never absent. I remember as an altar server kneeling for hours (it seemed like hours) and staring at the picture of the Last Supper carved on the front of the altar at St. Anthony's in Wichita. But it was only during the 1950s and 60s when more and more people began to receive holy Communion during Mass that the image of Holy Thursday gradually began to play a larger role in my understanding of the Eucharist.

During the 70s the parish with which I celebrated began to use a host for the Eucharist that looked and tasted more like real bread. People began to receive Communion in their hands and to drink from the cup. Mass began to look more like a meal. Altars began to look like tables. The prayers of the Mass and the songs we sang spoke openly about eating and drinking, about meals, suppers and banquets. All of these things caused the image of Holy Thursday to be added to the image of Good Friday in helping me to understand the Sacrament of the Eucharist. My devotion began to take on a more joyful tone. We began to speak of "celebrating" the Eucharist. To the image of "kneeling at the foot of the cross" I added the image of "sitting with Jesus and the disciples at the Last Supper, listening to his words, sharing the bread and cup."

Not all Catholics experienced this same journey and some hold on to an understanding in which Good Friday is the dominant image. I think of the woman who asked me after an explanation of the "new Mass:" "Father, why are we singing all those happy songs while Jesus is dying on the cross?"

Easter Sunday: Union with the Risen Lord

If the addition of the Holy Thursday image to Good Friday enriched my understanding of the Eucharist, the addition of the Easter Sunday image has helped me even more. When St. Paul experienced the Risen Lord at his conversion, he experienced a Christ who was so identified with us that to persecute the Christians was to persecute Christ.

Not just once, but three times the experience is described in the Acts of the Apostles. In Chapter Nine we see Saul (not yet "St. Paul") terrorizing the followers of Jesus when suddenly, one day on the road to Damascus, Saul "Fell to the ground and heard a voice saying to him, 'Saul, Saul, why are you persecuting me?' He said, 'Who are you, sir?' The reply came, 'I am Jesus, whom you are persecuting'" (Acts 9:4–5).

Later Paul himself retells the incident: "I fell to the ground and heard a voice saying to me, 'Saul, Saul, why are you persecuting me?' I replied, 'Who are you, sir?' And he said to me, 'I am Jesus the Nazorean whom you are persecuting'" (Acts 22:7–8). Paul tells the story again in Chapter 26: "I am Jesus whom you are persecuting" (26:15). The experience revealed to Paul that Christ cannot be separated from his members. The Risen Lord is so united to the Christian that what we do to one another, we do to Christ.

This was the very point that was at issue in Paul's first letter to the Corinthians, Chapter 11, the earliest written account we have of the Last Supper. When Paul writes to the Corinthians in about the year 50 A.D., he has some concerns about their "eucharistic devotion."

"In giving this instruction, I do not praise the fact that your meetings are doing more harm than good. First of all, I hear that when you meet as a church there are divisions among you, and to a degree I believe it....When you meet in one place, then, it is not to eat the Lord's supper, for in eating, each one goes ahead with his own supper, and one goes hungry while another gets drunk. Do you not have houses in which you can eat and drink? Or do you show contempt for the church of God and make those who have nothing feel ashamed?" (1 Cor 11:17–22)

Paul reproaches the Corinthians for celebrating the Eucharist without recognizing the Body of Christ—the poor who go hungry while the rich get drunk. His criticism of their Eucharistic devotion is not directed toward some liturgical rule, toward the songs they were singing, or the vestments they were wearing or not wearing, or whether they received Communion standing up or kneeling down—or any of the issues that might disturb some Catholics today—the issue was much more important. They were trying to remember Christ without remembering his Body, which includes the poor and the "unacceptable." They wanted to celebrate the "head" without the "body"—a risen and glorified "sacramental" Christ separated from his actual Body now. Paul's experience at his conversion had convinced him that the Risen Lord is so identified with the disciples that the two cannot be separated.

St. Paul tells the Corinthians that they must examine themselves as to which body they are celebrating. The Christ they are proclaiming is the Risen Christ, glorified in his members, inseparably united with the poor and suffering. This is the Body they must see in the Eucharist if they are to celebrate worthily, for all who eat and drink without discerning this Body, eat and drink judgment on themselves (see 1 Cor 11:29).

Paul reminds us of an awesome responsibility. Coming forward at Mass to receive holy Communion is a promise that we will treat each person who receives the bread and drinks the cup as a member of our own body! It is no longer "us and them" but "us." Sharing the meal is a promise that we will treat all men and women as Christ would treat them, indeed as we would treat Christ himself.

This is an enormous responsibility—one which I do not think about enough—and yet one which has greatly influenced the changes in my Eucharistic devotion. It is easy to lose sight of this relation: Risen Christ

- Mystical Body - Eucharistic Presence. The Eucharist is not merely a celebration of Real Presence, but a celebration of Real Presence which brings about unity and reconciliation in the whole Body. As the early Christians sang at Eucharist: As many grapes are brought together and crushed to make the wine—as many grains of wheat are ground into flour to make the one bread—so we, although many, become one Body when we eat the one Bread.

Balancing Good Friday, Holy Thursday and Easter Sunday

Balancing the images of Good Friday, Holy Thursday and Easter Sunday (sacrifice, banquet, unity of creation) is not an easy task. Sometimes I feel like a juggler at the circus trying to keep three objects in the air at once. I am no good at juggling three objects. Yet, I think the Church is asking us to keep all three of these ideas balanced in our minds—just as the opening paragraph of the Second Vatican Council's treatment of Eucharist very carefully balances the three:

"At the Last Supper (Holy Thursday), on the night when he was betrayed, our Savior instituted the Eucharistic sacrifice of his Body and Blood. He did this in order to perpetuate the sacrifice of the cross (Good Friday) throughout the centuries until he should come again and in this way to entrust to his beloved Bride, the Church, a memorial of his death and resurrection (Easter Sunday)" *(Constitution on the Liturgy #42)*.

Jesus, Church, Eucharist: Sacrament of the invisible God

The changes of the past twenty years have led me to broaden somewhat my understanding of a sacrament. Besides the traditional seven sacraments which I learned as a child, I now hear people speak of Jesus and Church as sacraments. I believe what they are saying is this: The invisible God, whose wonder and love are beyond even our imagination, wished to become visible and close to us. God wanted to let us in on God's secret plan for creation. The God who lives in unapproachable light, the source of life and goodness (Eucharistic Prayer IV), spoke the word of creation and the word took flesh and dwelt among us in Jesus of Nazareth. "In him we see our God made visible and so are caught up in love of the God we can not see" (Preface for the Mass of Christmas).

In times past, God revealed this plan, this mysterious sacrament, in bits and pieces through the prophets. But in the fullness of time, in these last days, God has revealed the mystery fully in Jesus (see Hebrews 1:1–2). In Jesus we see God's desire that all things be reconciled and come together in unity. Jesus is God's love made visible, so much so that seeing Jesus is seeing the Father (John 14:9).

While everything that Jesus said and did can be seen as a sacrament of God's mysterious plan, the sacrament we call the Eucharist focuses especially on the paschal mystery of Jesus' passion, death and resurrection. At the Eucharist, however, when we hear the Holy Thursday words "do this in memory of me," we are told to do not only what Jesus did at the Last Supper but also what Jesus did throughout his entire life: to heal, to teach, to comfort, to be an ambassador of reconciliation (see 2 Cor 5:16-21).

We, the Body of Christ, are certainly expected to be part of this sacrament. And this stretches my idea of sacrament. I had always been taught that sacraments are visible signs and instruments of God's invisible grace—channels of God's saving love to the world. I now see that, along with Jesus, we who form the Church are instruments of grace; we are the ordinary way God graces today's world. As Jesus is the sacrament of the invisible we who are baptized into Christ become the sacrament which is Church. Indeed, Vatican II speaks of Jesus' "body, the Church, as the universal sacrament of salvation" (*The Dogmatic Constitution on the Church,* #48).

It is at the liturgy and particularly at the Eucharist when the full reality of Christ becomes visible. This means that not only does the Body and Blood of Christ become present under the appearances of bread and wine. But the Body of Christ, the Church, also becomes visible for all to see. The liturgy "is the outstanding means whereby the faithful may express in their lives and manifest to others the mystery of Christ and the real nature of the true Church" (*Constitution on the Liturgy,* #2). The

Eucharist is not only one of the seven sacraments, it is in a sense *the* sacrament—for it contains all that we are, all that the Church is, all that Jesus is and says of God.

What has happened to my Eucharistic devotion?

One way of answering this question is to say that formerly my devotion stopped short: it went only "halfway." My devotion was focused on the first transformation: The transformation of the bread and wine into the Body and Blood Christ. I had forgotten the warning of St. Paul and did not recognize the second transformation: the transformation of the Christians into Christ. This second transformation is the purpose of the first: Christ becomes really present in the Eucharist so that we may really become his Body. This is precisely what Eucharistic Prayer III is saying when it pleads, "Grant that we, who are nourished by his body and blood, may be filled with his Holy Spirit, *and become one body*, one spirit of Christ."

I think the second transformation is especially hard for American Catholics. Our American culture places a high value on the individual, on independence and freedom from obligations to one another. I hear people saying, "I have to own a gun because no one is going to protect me but me. The police can't even protect themselves. I work hard for my money. I am not going to let the government take my money and waste it on welfare." If a culture is infected with racism or sexism, the Christians who are formed by that culture will find it difficult to express devotion to a Eucharist which proclaims that there is no longer "Jew nor Greek, there is neither slave nor free person, there is not male and female; for you are all one in Christ Jesus" (Gal 3:28).

In baptism I renounced "Satan," I renounced racism and sexism and exaggerated individualism and I was born into Christ Jesus. Each time I approach the Eucharist I renew that baptismal promise. As I come to the church for Eucharist, I dip my hand in the baptismal water and renew those baptismal vows. Each time I get up and go to holy Communion I give a sign to the community that I am committed to all that the Eucharist stands for —I am committed to "do this" in memory of Jesus—to live as He lived, to live no longer for myself but for his Body.

I can't stop halfway: I can't celebrate the transubstantiation of the bread and wine without celebrating Christ's presence in my brothers and sisters. Some Christians still separate the two. I am reminded of the man who once asked me: "Father, why do I have to shake hands with all those people before holy Communion? I don't know those people; and the ones I know, I don't even like."

Where did the beauty go?

I remember with nostalgia the magnificence of Solemn High Mass during Forty Hours devotion. I remember the weariness in my little altar boy arms trying to light the dozens of candles on the altars, the smell of the incense, the glitter of the spotlights on the gold threads in the priests' vestments. I remember the monstrance with its jewels which I imagined to be diamonds and rubies and emeralds. The memory is vivid; as a child this was the most glorious thing I had ever seen; the most beautiful room; the most elegant movement; the richest attire. Where did it all go?

If Forty Hours and Solemn Benediction were the high points of the liturgical year then, what is the high point now? The Easter Vigil perhaps? There we experience nervous catechumens sitting around a fire, hearing the stories of creation and salvation—water splashing, wet feet slipping on tile floors, clothes being changed rapidly with the whir of hair dryers in the background, the smell of the oil of Confirmation, breaking bread and sharing a cup for the first time with these new members of the parish. Where did the beauty go? Where is the grandeur? What has happened to my devotion?

I can only say that I am getting a new perspective. I see a new beauty and a new grandeur. It takes a different eye to see my God in the faces of my sisters and brothers with whom I share the broken bread. But there is true beauty there, and I find that beauty can still move me to tears of joy and devotion. Today I judge whether a liturgy is "good" or "bad" not by the number of candles that are lit, nor by the cost of the vestments, nor by whether or not I like the singing.

Today a "good" liturgy is one which transforms me and my fellow parishioners in such a way that men and women of today's society will see the full implication of the Sacrament of the Eucharist. And they will say of us as they said of the first Christians, "See how they love one another! There is no one poor among them!"

Used with permission from Thomas Richstatter.

[This article first published in *Catholic Update C0992* published by St. Anthony Messenger Press]

Kissed by God

Sometimes my husband and I go to a beautiful old church in downtown Ottawa for Mass. There, confessions are heard for as long as necessary, and you kneel to receive Communion, which we both enjoy.

Since St. Patrick's is in the heart of the city, it is usually crowded with various employees of government departments, visitors to the city, and regular parishioners. We always sit close to the front.

One day, when there was an especially long line for Communion, we were blessed to witness a beautiful young woman and her husband carrying their baby in a carrier. When they arrived at the front of the church, they seemed alone at the altar. The man put the beautiful gift from God that was asleep in the carrier on the altar railing. The parents then knelt on either side of the babe.

The wise old monsignor who was serving Communion approached this wonderful site, took the Host, and gently brushed the sleeping baby's lips with it. Then he gave the Host to the mom, and then the dad.

I felt a sense of time standing still at this sight. It deeply moved me, and I'm sure it touched many others who had the privilege of witnessing it. This was one of those pure moments of grace that seldom happens.

We are very blessed to have our faith and the joyful moments that are offered through it. God is good!

Claudette Winchester   *Ottawa, Ontario, Canada*

Through our communion in his body and blood, Christ also grants us his Spirit. St. Ephrem writes: "He called the bread his living body and he filled it with himself and his Spirit…He who eats it with faith, eats Fire and Spirit…Take and eat this, all of you, and eat with it the Holy Spirit. For it is truly my body and whoever eats it will have eternal life".

My Faith's Journey

In high school, I met a cute girl with a dark-haired ponytail. She stole my heart. One night when I came to call, her mom met me at the door and told me, "The family is saying the rosary and you'll have to wait till we finish." As an Anglican, I listened intently to the repetition of prayers. This happened a few more times and I began to ask questions.

Soon her father asked me if I would like to go to Benediction on Sunday night at seven o'clock. I went and was amazed at what I saw in the dimly lit Stella Maris Church. It was a revelation to experience the mystery of the Eucharist on display and the reverence shown during this event.

Years passed, I joined the military and went away, returning on occasion. Often I would think of the Catholic Church and it's beautiful prayers. I would reflect how special I felt in that environment. On one visit home, I met Claudette again. We chatted and went our separate ways, but corresponded regularly. After a time, I asked her father for her hand in marriage, and he agreed.

My experience with the Catholic faith had planted a seed in me, and I started the process to become Catholic with a military chaplain. We set a marriage date and were married in October of 1958. On my wedding day I received holy Communion for the first time. How vividly I remember that special moment.

We had four children and under the guidance of Claudette, our family practiced the faith she had grown to love. I was always grateful for this formation process that helped me to grow deeper in my faith. Naturally, the eucharistic celebration became important to me, and I began to attend Mass daily. There was no doubt the Holy Spirit was influencing me during this period. I prayed for an opportunity to be more involved within the Church, but being naturally shy, I never pursued it. I talked but never started "walking the talk."

However, during this period, things started to happen. I started taking theology courses at the local university, I discovered the Third Order Franciscans, I went on my first retreat, and I was introduced to soup kitchens and prison ministry. Finally, one day, a priest asked if I would consider becoming a deacon.

I had to discern about it for quite awhile. Even though I had been a Catholic for several years by now and was quite comfortable with our faith, I was humbled and never felt worthy. I discussed this at great length with my wife, and we finally decided to begin the four-year formation after going through the screening process.

At the time we both were working, and often found the process difficult. We enjoyed the other couples and the instructors very much though, and our faith deepened. We both agreed that this was what we wanted to do. In 1995, I was ordained and retired from my regular work to devote full time to the ministry of service.

Daily Mass, the Eucharist, and rosary are all essential to my faith journey. They sustain both of us to meet the challenges we are faced with daily. I thank God for the gift of a strong Catholic family who introduced me to the Eucharist in the Catholic Church.

When I preach at a parish or hospital eucharistic celebration, and when I preside at the exposition of the Blessed Sacrament and Benediction, I celebrate the presence of Jesus in the Eucharist. But, I remind myself that as Christians we are what we eat, and through the Eucharist we become Jesus for those we serve. In the words of Mother Teresa, "We do it with Jesus, to Jesus and for Jesus." We are eucharistic people!

As I reflect back to my first introduction to Benediction, my first Eucharist on my wedding day, and the gentle way that Jesus has nurtured me along my faith journey, I know that I have been blessed.

Deacon Lee Winchester   *Ottawa, Ontario, Canada*

A New Desire

One of the joys of spring is the birth of nature. Nature invites us to new beginnings, and so it was in the spring of 1951, in the heart of a little girl on a parochial school playground.

Many things in life require a *breaking-in* period. We have new shoes, new cars, and new jobs. I now had a new desire for a deeper union with Jesus in the holy Eucharist. It manifested itself like a magnet pulling me to go and make visits with Him. When I would go into our church, I would tiptoe up as close as I could and then whisper, "I love You." Sometimes, I would tell Him about what was transpiring in my life. Jesus taught me in my childlike faith that the Eucharist is not a thing, but a person. It is Jesus Himself.

The little girl grew into an adult with a hunger for this solitude of kneeling before Him daily. During my quiet hour with Jesus, I simply imagine that I climb up on His lap and take all of the concerns that people have placed in my heart, and put them into His heart. Then I simply tell Him that I love Him, and thank Him for taking care of all these concerns.

When distractions arise or I become restless, I know that my very effort of being present to Him fills Him with inexpressible joy. I hear Him say in the Scripture, "Taste and see how good the Lord is." As I look up at Him, my response is, "You are absolutely delicious."

As Brother Lawrence taught, "God's will comes to us in the present moment." He uses ordinary things, and ordinary people to lure us into this divine love affair. To be in love with Jesus is the epitome of happiness. Just as fire transforms everything to itself, so too, does Jesus in the holy Eucharist transform everything to good in the fire of His divine love.

Mary L. Schuster   *Joliet, Indiana*

 And in the Roman Missal *the celebrant prays: "grant that we who are nourished by his body and blood may be filled with his Holy Spirit, and become one body, one spirit in Christ". Thus by the gift of his body and blood Christ increases within us the gift of his Spirit, already poured out in Baptism and bestowed as a "seal" in the sacrament of Confirmation.*

Story of the Lard Light

…A primary source of trouble was the sisters' desire for a chapel and religious services. Since a convent without a chapel is an anomaly, nothing was more natural than that the sisters should plan to have one at St. Colettas as soon as possible. Small as the house was, Mother Antonia designated one of the rooms as an oratory and immediately set about securing the altar and other requisites for the offering of the holy sacrifice. The sisters already had four beautiful imported vestments, the gift of Father Heiss. They confidently expected that occasionally the pastor would offer Mass for them; they also hoped that the Blessed Sacrament would be reserved in the chapel.

Unfortunately for the sisters, Father Jansen did not at all approve of these hopes and procedures…he made no move to yield to the sisters' request for further religious services in their convent chapel.

In the hope of overcoming Father Jansens obduracy, the sisters had recourse to the only weapon at their disposal, prayer. Some of them spent entire nights on their knees before the empty tabernacle entreating their Divine Spouse that He would deign to take up His sacramental presence in their midst. Before the feast of St. Joseph, 1865, the sisters united with their superior in a novena in honor of the saint, fervently begging him to use his intercessory power with his Foster Son. If ever in the life of the congregation there was an answer to prayer bordering on the miraculous, it was the response that followed this outpouring of petitions to St. Joseph.

To add to the trials of this first year at Jefferson, Mother Antonia was at times seriously ill, and, from all appearances, very near death. Several days before March 19 of this year, she was suffering from one of these attacks of illness. What was the surprise of the infirmarian-portress, Sister Michaela Nepper, when on Sunday morning, the feast of St. Patrick, Father Jansen, greatly agitated rapped at the convent door before proceeding to the parish church for Mass. She was still more startled at his distraught questions: How is Mother Antonia? Is she still living? Wondering what could have caused his perturbation, Sister Michaela answered, Yes, she is living, but she is very ill. Father Jansen responded, Tell her I shall visit her after services.

When he came to the sick-room later, he demanded of Mother Antonia, Where were you last night? In reply to her statement that she had been nowhere but in bed, he insisted again, Tell me honestly, where were you between eleven and twelve oclock, and what did you do during that time? To this, Mother Antonia answered simply, Throughout the entire evening I was heartsick and so much oppressed that I could not sleep. I prayed earnestly to St. Joseph that he would plead with God to touch the heart of your reverence; that He would move you to give us the Blessed Sacrament. Then, suddenly, I must have gone to sleep; I don't know what happened thereafter.

It was now Mother Antonia's turn to wonder and to be startled at the priest's incoherent and almost vehement outburst; You shall have it, but hereafter leave me alone. You came to me last night. I saw you in my room and you threatened me. Never disturb me again at such a time. On St. Joseph Day I shall read Mass in your chapel and we shall have everything as solemn as possible. I shall leave the Blessed Sacrament exposed all day so that you may have adoration. Prepare things meanwhile. Suddenly and strangely the answer had come to the sister's persevering prayer.

The cause of Father Jansens change of heart is matter for conjecture. Was there some kind of mental telepathy, or was Mother Antonia, like her patron saint of old, favored for a moment with the miracle of bilocation? Or had only a vivid dream aroused the priest? It does not matter now. Only the confirmed skeptic can refuse to see God's direct intervention in the incident. Father Jansen's housekeeper later told the sisters that she had heard him spring from his bed, talk excitedly aloud, and for a long time walk back and forth in his room much disturbed. The next morning he said to her, I fear that Mother Antonia is dead and that her spirit came to me last night. Father Heiss, when questioned on the matter, always evaded an answer. In his historical sketch he contented himself with recognizing the underlying mysteriousness of the affair and with attributing the turn of events to the intercession of St. Joseph. Sister Michaela had only one account to give. Fearing to leave her patient alone during the night, she had remained at her superiors bedside and had noticed that about eleven oclock, Mother Antonia had fallen into a deep sleep which lasted until morning and from which she awoke considerably refreshed.

The last two days of the novena became days of thanksgiving. Mother Antonia's health improved rapidly, and the sisters went about preparing for St. Joseph Day…On the morning of the nineteenth, Father Jansen arrived at the convent long before the expected hour…After the Mass, Father Jansen exposed the Blessed Sacrament in the small combination ostensorium-ciborium he had brought for the purpose, for the community did not yet own a monstrance. Throughout the day, as the sisters, novices, and postulants knelt in adoration before their eucharistic king who had come at last to abide with them, joyous hymns were heard to alternate with fervent prayers of thanksgiving and petition. In the evening, Benediction fittingly and solemnly closed the first St. Joseph Day at Jefferson, a day that will live in the memory of a grateful community until time shall be no more. As Mother Antonia was expressing her appreciation to Father Jansen after the services, he remarked once more, But, Mother Antonia, hereafter, do not every again disturb me at night.

Only as the candles were being extinguished and the fragrance of the burning incense diffused in the night air, did the sacristan and Mother Antonia recall that in the hasty preparation for this event, so eagerly anticipated and so unexpectedly realized, no provision had been made for a sanctuary lamp. Their embarrassment was greatly relieved when Sister Alphonsa Head, then a novice, explained how she had seen the Sisters of Mercy at a Detroit hospital produce a satisfactory night lamp by putting a wick of twisted tissue paper into a deep saucer filled with lard. Mother Antonia agreed that, as poor as such a light would be, to use it would be more appropriate than to leave the Lord without the symbol of His eucharistic presence.

With the novices help, the light was quickly prepared, and Mother Antonia herself carried it to the chapel and placed it upon the altar. Then, in the flow of that flickering light, a memorable scene was enacted, and before that altar a vow was made, the fulfillment of which became the congregations greatest ambition and remains its most cherished privilege. Sisters who had lingered in the chapel for a farewell visit or who had reentered to witness this last act of homage, heard their superior pray audibly in a voice vibrant with emotion: Dear Lord, accept this poor light. It is the best we can give you now, but if you will help us and bless the community, we will one day establish the perpetual adoration of the Blessed Sacrament and build for you as beautiful a chapel as our means will allow.

A new spiritual life had begun for the sisters. They were no longer alone. From that eventful March 19 of 1865 until the actual introduction of the perpetual adoration of the Blessed Sacrament in the congregation, each successive St. Joseph Day was observed with exposition and adoration at the motherhouse; and, throughout the decades, the devotion to the Foster Father of Jesus has grown in the community. The exact date of the origin of the custom is obscured in the shadow of these early days, but catching its spark, as it were, from that first sanctuary lamp at St. Colettas, a memorial lard light burns each March 19 before a statue of St. Joseph, not only in the motherhouse but in every affiliated convent and mission station, no matter how small or how distant it may be.

Excerpts from *A Chapter of Franciscan History.*
Sister M. Mileta Ludwig, FSPA, pages 130–135.

The Franciscan Sisters of Perpetual Adoration did indeed begin adoration before the exposed Blessed Sacrament on Aug.1, 1878. They have continued this constant vigil for over 125 years.

Submitted by Cristeen Custer FSPA   *La Crosse, Wisconsin*

Those who feed on Christ in the Eucharist need not wait until the hereafter to receive eternal life: they already possess it on earth, *as the first-fruits of a future fullness which will embrace man in his totality. For in the Eucharist we also receive the pledge of our bodily resurrection at the end of the world: "He who eats my flesh and drinks my blood has eternal life, and I will raise him up at the last day" (Jn 6:54).*

His Presence is Powerful

I was not born into a Catholic family. In fact, my mother despised the Catholic Church. From the time I was very small, she tried as hard as she could to make me feel the same way, but failed. Sadly, my mother was not a nice person. She was cruel to everyone around her and I'm sure this made me question her stories about the Church. Her negativity towards the Catholic Church had the opposite affect on me than what she had intended.

My family was Anglican, and even as a child, I hated going into an Anglican church. No matter how many people were there, the building felt empty to me. I felt the same emptiness in all churches except the Catholic Church, where I felt God's presence the first time I entered. His presence is so powerful that I can't understand how some people do not feel it.

I knew He was there, present in the Blessed Sacrament, even before I knew the Catholic faith was centered on this belief. I knew it was not the bricks and stones, or the people that gave me this feeling of His presence, but that He was actually there in the tabernacle.

Despite my mother's influence, I believed that only the Catholic Church taught the truth. It was in this Church that I was able to feel the actual presence of God, and where I discovered that, in Our Lady, I had another mother who was not of this world. She was one who cared for me, loved me, and who would help me.

I first came in contact with Catholicism when I saw it portrayed on the screen, in films like *Boys Town* and *Going My Way*. Through watching these movies, I felt drawn to the Church immediately. It was as if a hand had reached out and touched me, and a voice inside me was saying, "You belong here."

I remember a day long ago like it was yesterday. It was when I was only fourteen years old, browsing in a record shop. I recall picking up an extended play album of Mario Lanza, the famous opera singer who died in 1959. The record had "The Lord's Prayer" on it, which I had heard sung in the past and had liked. However, I had never heard Lanza's version of this beautiful song. I asked the lady in the shop if he was a good singer, and she said yes, and played it for me. I bought the record and when I got home, I played the entire recording. I discovered that I had found the most beautiful piece of music I had ever heard, and still feel the same way about it today.

The track was on Charles Gounod's "Ave Maria." When I listened to it, I felt like I was in a huge cathedral with music soaring up into the rafters and right into heaven. I knew the instant I heard it where my destiny lay, and that the voice that had been calling me for so long now sang in my heart. I knew I would become a Catholic, and that it was only in that Church where I would find God.

During the early 1990s, I began taking instructions so I could officially join the Catholic Church. The elderly parish priest had one of his parishioners teach me. The lady's name is Moya, and she is a wonderful person, and a great friend.

During that time, I was battling severe depression and was taking a prescription drug that made my problem worse. I stopped functioning, couldn't concentrate, and was suicidal. I stopped my instructions, and Moya could not understand what had gone wrong. I was not well enough to find the words to explain it to her. Then I moved to a different city, and my mental health continued to get worse despite changes in the amount of medicine I was taking.

Moya, who has always had a great devotion to the Little Flower, kept in touch and continued praying for me. Then, when St. Therese's relics were brought to Australia, Moya went to visit them without telling me. She knelt, placed her hand on the box they were in, and asked St. Therese to help me in any way she could.

A few weeks after that I walked into the doctor's office and told her that if she didn't change me to a drug that I had taken successfully years earlier for depression, I would leave and find a doctor who would. She took a deep breath and agreed. In doing so, she went against the advice of two psychiatrists who felt the newer drug was better, even though I knew it was making me more depressed.

I am convinced that it was Our Lady and St. Therese who gave me the courage to face the doctor and speak to her that way, and that they influenced her to agree to change my medicine.

Once the different medicine kicked in, I began to think a lot about St. Therese and Our Lady. Moya had once sent me a picture of St. Therese, which I had shoved into a drawer, but clearly had not forgotten. I hunted it out and started trying to pray again.

I downloaded a virtual rosary and began saying it regularly. Then I wrote to Moya asking her to get me a picture of Our Lady, and one of Our Lord. I also asked her to send me some rosary beads, and told her I would send her the money for whatever they cost. I needed her to shop for me because I didn't know where to buy them. Then I went to church for the first time in years.

My first action was to go to confession. I asked the priest to help me with my confession, and explained what had been happening in my life. He asked if I'd had doubts about the Catholic faith, and I said yes. He told me I could trust what the Catholic Church teaches because it teaches the truth. He spoke with such authority in his voice that, right there in the confessional, I sent a prayer heavenward thanking Our Lady and St. Therese for bringing this priest to me.

Moya sent me the pictures and rosary beads, and when I rang to thank her, she asked what had happened to me. I explained about the reaction I had to the first medication, and how I had felt St. Therese and Our Lady reaching out to me and calling me home to the Catholic Church. Then I told her how I felt them give me the courage to confront my doctor about changing me to a different drug. That was when she told me she had asked St. Therese to help me when she had visited her relics.

I was finally confirmed into the Church here in Mansfield, and believe that Jesus called me to become Catholic. He used Our Lady and St. Therese to reach out and reel me in, similar to the way He promised the apostles that they would become "fishers of men." I am convinced that the gift of feeling Him in the Eucharist had to come from Jesus.

Grace Tolson   *Mansfield, Victoria, Australia*

And You Shall Be Healed

For years I had suffered from stomach ulcers. Then, one Saturday I attended a healing Mass at a nearby convent, and as the priest held up the Blessed Sacrament during the consecration, I was filled with a strong feeling that the Lord would heal my ulcers.

I responded to the priest's words with a heartfelt, "Lord I am not worthy to receive you, but only say the words and I shall be healed," and went to receive Our Lord in the Eucharist. When I returned to my seat, I had a deep feeling of peace. No fireworks, just deep peace. As the days passed, I began to feel less and less pain.

Several weeks later I needed to see the doctor for another ailment. He examined me, then sent me for tests. He also included a routine test to determine the state of my ulcer, including the level of scar tissue that had built up over the years as the ulcers had healed and reopened.

When I returned to him for the results, he looked at my file, then looked up at me and said, "Didn't you have ulcers?" I said, "Yes," and he responded, "That's funny, the test results say you have no sign of an ulcer, and there is no scar tissue." I had been healed by our merciful and loving Lord in the sacred Eucharist!

Sister James Marie Fitz-Gordon   *Kingston, Jamaica*

This pledge of the future resurrection comes from the fact that the flesh of the Son of Man, given as food, is his body in its glorious state after the resurrection. With the Eucharist we digest, as it were, the "secret" of the resurrection. For this reason St. Ignatius of Antioch rightly defined the Eucharistic Bread as "a medicine of immortality, an antidote to death".

A Beam of Light

I grew up in an Italian-American family in upstate New York. Our family attended St. Michael's Church, the National Shrine of North American Martyrs, and Kateri Tekakwitha Shrine. As I was growing up I went to Mass but didn't understand very much about my faith. In our home, we were told to go to church, so we went and that was it. Since I was young, every time I went into a Catholic church or went to Mass, I got a strange feeling in my heart, but never told anyone about it.

As an adult I moved to Birmingham, Alabama, and started visiting Our Lady of the Angels Chapel in Irondale. Each time I went into the chapel, I had that feeling again, and it was stronger than ever. It reached the point where I could not even drive by the chapel without feeling that tug to my heart.

Soon I met quite a few people that worked and volunteered at Our Lady of the Angels Chapel and EWTN, (Eternal Word Television Network). One day I was invited to join the Lay Missionaries of the Eternal Word founded by Mother Angelica. Each Sunday morning Mother Angelica and several priests from around the world taught me more about Catholicism. I was fascinated by my faith.

I finally asked someone about the tugging feeling in my heart that I experienced each time I went near the chapel. They explained that it was Jesus in the Blessed Sacrament and that He was really there. Learning this made me feel like a window had just opened for me.

Right away I called my Catholic friends from childhood and told them that Jesus is really present in the Eucharist. The majority of them said they knew that already. I asked them why they didn't tell me this when I was growing up, and they told me they thought I knew.

After that, I would often sit in the chapel and just stare at Jesus in the Blessed Sacrament. Sometimes I would question the Real Presence, but that tugging feeling in my heart told me different.

One day I was sitting in the chapel praying for strength because I was going through a very difficult time in my life. I was divorced, had two children to raise by myself, and was not receiving child support. My burdens felt heavy. I sat there and asked Jesus to reveal Himself to me, to show me He was really there and listening to my prayers.

Suddenly I saw a beam of light come towards me and as I looked up at the monstrance I saw Jesus' heart pulsating. It was His human heart just beating and beating, and there was a fire around it. I never felt such peace before in my life. I knew in that instant that He was really there, He loved me, and that He would take care of me. I felt like time stood still, and I couldn't take my eyes off Jesus' heart. It seemed like this went on forever but it was just a few minutes.

I have been truly blessed and have shared my faith and the miracle of Jesus revealing Himself to me with many people. The people I tell all say they feel such a peace about them when I share this story. They can tell the story is true by the peaceful expression on my face when I share it.

My miraculous experience with the Blessed Sacrament has brought many friends of mine back to our Catholic faith. My children are more prayerful and spend more time in front of the Blessed Sacrament since this happened to me. I know without a doubt that Jesus is truly present in the Blessed Sacrament.

Sandra A. Lauriello   *Irondale, Alabama*

Good News!

The Eucharist is the heart of my relationship with God, the Catholic Church and my parish. Humbled to receive the Eucharist, I experience an overwhelming joy when distributing the host to the faithful. What greater privilege exists than to carry the bread of life to those unable to attend liturgy because of age, incarceration, or illness. I often advise them, "Good news! I bring a visitor who will never leave you!"

Deacon Gene Mastrangelo   *North Beach, Maryland*

His Love Held My Heart

Several years ago, God called me to attend a Cursillo weekend retreat, and the decision to go was not easy. In fact, I didn't go the first time He asked. I guess I didn't believe it was really a call from God. When I finally went, it turned out to be a very profound awakening to Christ's love for me.

One particular moment occurred that weekend that still takes my breath away. It happened at a time during the retreat when the ladies at each table were invited to go to the chapel to kneel and pray before Jesus in the Blessed Sacrament. By that time, we had come to know about each other's lives and hearts, and were growing in sisterly love for one another.

Some of the women had tears that began to flow during adoration. As the small pyx with Jesus inside was laid into my hands, I looked down upon this tiny piece of my Lord's body, and began to cry too. I said a few things that I had never allowed myself to say in front of others. As I looked upon Him, a warm power that I cannot explain flowed all around me.

I felt like His love was actually holding my physical heart in His hands. The feeling was so powerful that, as I write, I still sense it strongly. From that time on, I have had more strength, grace, and courage. I am able to follow through with the ministries of home and church life, as well as what I do in the world, in a much more dedicated way.

There is no way to fully explain how a tiny piece of bread that becomes Our Lord can carry that kind of power. I thank Him for giving me His love through the Eucharist as I go through my earthly journey.

Suzanne L. McConnell   *Bloomington, Indiana*

Proclaiming the death of the Lord "until he comes" (1 Cor 11:26) entails that all who take part in the Eucharist be committed to changing their lives and making them in a certain way completely "Eucharistic".

Occupational Hazard

For all of my 37 years as a priest, I have always felt that taking the Eucharist for granted was a bit of an *occupational hazard* of the priesthood. It's so easy to *go through the motions* of daily Mass, to see Mass, Benediction, exposition etc. as just another job to do.

As always, God stepped in at just the right time. Six years ago I was assigned here to St. Tarcissus Parish, a very nice middle class parish on Chicago's far northwest side. In our church we have two statues and a stained glass window of St. Tarcissus, the boy saint who was carrying the holy Eucharist to a sick family member when Roman soldiers stopped him. Unwilling to betray his faith in the Eucharist, he was put to death by the Romans. He was a true martyr to the holy Eucharist. Pictures, statues, etc. of St. Tarcissus always show him with the pyx around his neck for carrying the Eucharist.

He has become for me a constant reminder of the importance, value and beauty of Christ's greatest gift to us, the gift of the holy Eucharist. St. Tarcissus is also the first parish I've been assigned to that has eucharistic adoration. Especially on a frantic, hectic, confusing, busy day, nothing restores serenity and peace for me like some quiet time in front of the Blessed Sacrament, especially praying the Liturgy of the Hours.

As always, God knew best. When I needed a reminder of the unique importance of the body and blood of Jesus Christ in my life, he steered me to St. Tarcissus. The boy saint and his parish have done the rest.

Father Dan McCarthy   *Chicago, Illinois*

Thank You, Jesus

From kindergarten through high school, I attended a school that was run by sisters from Spain. They had a small chapel that was not large enough to hold all the students in our school at one time. Therefore, any-one wanting to go to holy Communion was allowed to leave class for ten minutes every day to go to the chapel. Because we were excused from the monotony of classroom work, and this was another way to socialize with friends, we gladly took advantage of the short break. This was how the holy Eucharist became a fixture in my life.

As I grew up, I experienced many difficulties in my life. Going to church as often as I could always gave me the strength I needed to handle these challenges. When I got married, I had two children who were only a year apart. My husband worked on construction that was three hours away from where we lived, and he was not home much. He would come home on Friday evenings and leave again early the following Monday morning at four o'clock.

As my children reached their preteens, my life became very stressful. I juggled a full time job from eight o'clock in the morning to five o'clock in the evening. My son had a newspaper run, and I went with him as he delivered the newspapers every morning before I went to work. I did not feel it was safe for him to be on the streets alone at that young age.

I had exactly one hour for my lunch break everyday and used it to drive fifteen minutes each way to go home and check on my children. I wanted to make sure they were safe and staying out of trouble. My boss was very strict, and anytime I was late for work, I was reprimanded. I felt extremely pressured to make sure I was on time.

Taking time out for myself was difficult. As a result of my highly stressful life, I needed triple bypass heart surgery at the young age of forty. This was God's way of slowing me down. During this time, I realized that I desperately missed going to Mass and receiving holy Communion. I was on medical leave frequently, so when I was off of work and my kids were in school, I went to Mass. It was at this time in my life when I finally realized the real presence of Jesus in the holy Eucharist.

During the petitions, the priest would ask those present to offer their prayers aloud. They usually asked for prayers for themselves, family members who were sick, or for someone who was traveling, etc. But this time it was different. All of a sudden I heard an older lady speak. Although she looked very frail, weak, and slightly bent, instead of asking prayers for herself or her condition, she said, "Thank you Jesus for your presence in the holy Eucharist."

I was very surprised. I had been caught up with my own problems, and my focus clearly changed upon hearing this simple "Thank you." The rest of the petitions by the congregation were the usual list of needs and personal concerns, but how struck I was by this simple little lady who was only concerned with thanking Jesus.

Throughout my entire life Jesus had always been there with me, and yet I had never said, "Thank You." I had taken His presence for granted. Jesus is no longer just an excuse for me to take a break, or a timeout from everyday problems. I look at the holy Eucharist, and receiving the body of Christ, so differently after hearing this beautiful lady thank Jesus for His real presence.

Every time this lady attended Mass, she continued to say nothing else during the petitions but words thanking Christ. Little does she know how much she helped me figure out a very integral part of my life, which is now to thank Christ who has been with me all along in the holy Eucharist.

Rosario Perlas   *Elk Grove Villiage, Illinios*

"Do you wish to honour the body of Christ? Do not ignore him when he is naked. Do not pay him homage in the temple clad in silk, only then to neglect him outside where he is cold and ill-clad. He who said: 'This is my body' is the same who said: 'You saw me hungry and you gave me no food', and 'Whatever you did to the least of my brothers you did also to me'...What good is it if the Eucharistic table is overloaded with golden chalices when your brother is dying of hunger.

Start by satisfying his hunger and then with what is left you may adorn the altar as well": St. John Chrysostom, In Evangelium S. Matthaei, hom. *50:3–4: PG 58, 508–509; cf. John Paul II, Encyclical Letter* Sollicitudo Rei Socialis *(30 December 1987), 31: AAS 80 (1988), 553–556.*

My Search for a Church

As the third child of eight, I loved to hear the story of my parent's quest for a church. As newlyweds, my father and mother set out to find a church in which to raise a family. After researching several churches and their histories, they decided on the Catholic Church because they believed it was the one true Church that was set up by Christ.

As time went on, our family grew. There came a time when my oldest brother began to question the Church. My brother and father argued terribly, and these arguments would send me running from the house in confusion and fear. I was especially afraid that I would lose my faith as my brother had, so I prayed to Jesus to always keep me faithful.

When I grew up, I fell away from the Catholic Church and began to research other religions of the world. I had long forgotten my prayer to Jesus to keep me safe with Him. As I look back, there must have been many battles my guardian angles had to fight for me, as I put my soul in harms way time after time in my quest for the truth.

Time passed and I finally realized that Christianity was the true religion of God, but now I had to find a church. I went to all of the Protestant churches, but never felt comfortable in them. The people were friendly and welcoming, but something was missing. Something kept me from making a commitment to one of them.

Then, one day, the good Lord took one of His own to Him. It was my neighbor's husband. I knew them casually, but was not friends with them. When the ambulance came, I looked out as all my other curious neighbors had, and was struck by the hopelessness I saw on the woman's face. A thought totally out of character for me said, "Go to her." I went to her and told her I would take her to the hospital where her husband was. Her husband died that night leaving her alone. They had not had any children in their 40 years of marriage.

I accompanied my neighbor to her husband's funeral, and found myself in a Catholic Church. As I looked around taking in the fragrance and beauty of the church, I noticed the Stations of the Cross, and remembered the many times that I had prayed the rosary with my family. The lost memory of the day that I prayed to Jesus and asked Him to keep me close to Him came flooding back to me.

As the priest began the communal prayers and held up the Host, the Lord placed a thought in my heart that was very pure and peaceful. It was so powerful that I still cling to it to this day: "Here is your church." I began weeping, my tears joining the others who were mourning for Anna's loss. But my tears were tears of joy as I realized the amazing grace that was given to me that day. What I was missing in all those other churches was His real presence in the Eucharist. God had heard my prayer as a child, and kept me close. God is faithful though His children may wander.

Anna and I became close friends and attended Mass together for many years. In one of our many conversations, she told me that her husband had told her to trust me. He said this as he was dying.

I believe God when He tells us He will work all things to the good for those who love Him. He took a little girl's prayer, a dying man's love, and a grieving widow, and worked it for good and to His glory.

Maureen A. McNamara   *Tigard, Oregon*

Two C's of Communion

As part of my ministry as deacon, I sometimes serve as chaplain at a local Catholic hospital. There I am usually called to minister to families whose loved one is seriously ill, or who has just died. These pastoral visits are *communion* (small *c*) in that Jesus works through me to reach His people in their time of crisis.

On the other hand, I also serve as a eucharistic minister at another local, public hospital. On these visits I bring *Communion* (large *C*), the visible body of Christ. As I walk into each room, the eyes of the patient are fixed on the small black case around my neck. They know that inside that small case there is a pyx containing Jesus, and their eyes truly light up, not from seeing me, but from seeing Jesus coming to be with them.

Deacon Robert C. Campbell   *East Rockaway, New York*

Jesus Dwelling in Me

Mom was in the intensive care unit at the hospital, and I had gone home to be close to her. I have never been good with sickness, and actually felt a physical aversion to it. The first day Mom was in the hospital, I didn't know how I could possibly visit her twice a day. Her strength was gone and her heart had just about given out. Every moment was sad, so I decided to go to Mass in the mornings, before visiting hours began.

The first day, after receiving Communion, all I could do was cry. My husband was miles away in Pennsylvania with our daughter, and I was alone. I told Jesus everything. After Mass, I felt completely refreshed. I went to the hospital and visited Mom, no longer fearing the hospital and her illness, or its final outcome.

I went to Mass every day, and each day I was better able to deal with the health and family issues that came up. I was even able to check Mom's bedsores for her, something I never could have done before. I know that it was Jesus, dwelling in me from Communion each day, that enabled me to handle whatever needed to be done, with love.

Patricia E. Wolf, SFO   *Hummelstown, Pennsylvania*

You Asked for a Way

A few days before Ascension Thursday in 2003, something happened in my life to cause me to need to go to confession. I was beside myself because there were no confessions being held before Mass on Ascension Thursday. I had a spiritual director, but this was something that I was uncomfortable going to him with. My biggest concern was that I did not feel right receiving Our Lord on Ascension Thursday. That, in addition to my sin, was hurting me the most.

In our town there is a church that has 24-hour adoration. I went there to pray in the hopes that, well, I really don't know what I hoped, but I prayed anyway. I begged Our Lord for forgiveness but knew that it was not enough. So, I prayed that He would understand that if I did not go to confession, I would not be able to receive Him.

I went out of the room to get something to read from a bookshelf that was nearby. At that moment, one of the priests was going into the sacristy. It was evening which was an unusual time for a priest to be there. I said hello and proceeded to go back into the adoration room. I knelt down and was continuing to pray when I heard, "You asked for a way."

I was a little perplexed because there were other people in the room who were silent. With a puzzled look on my face, I basically said, "What?" and was told, "You asked for a way, and that way is outside." Then I realized that I was being directed to the priest in the sacristy.

I was quite a bit uncomfortable and stated that I did not even know the priest and was uncomfortable asking him to hear my confession. I was then told, "You asked, I gave." That was the end of the comments. I wrestled with my conscience, got up, left the chapel and went into the sacristy to ask the priest to hear my confession. He was most gracious and helped me with my problem.

After that, I went back into the adoration room, knelt down, and said my penance along with a great big "Thank you," of which I got a, "Your welcome." I felt a great big peace in my soul.

Carol Ann Matz   *Hazelton, Pennsylvania*

Incorporation into Christ, which is brought about by Baptism, is constantly renewed and consolidated by sharing in the Eucharistic Sacrifice, especially by that full sharing which takes place in sacramental communion.

Gather to Welcome

As the Lenten season calls for their involvement in the liturgy, celebrations with catechumens and candidates who have been through the RCIA process have always been meaningful to me. I especially cherish the times when we met on a weekly basis in preparation for their entry into the Church through the Easter sacraments.

My personal connectedness with their journey through meetings and eucharistic celebrations, as we approached their full immersion into the Church, have been inspirational, especially knowing what they have been through to become Catholic in a world where some give them a bad time for their conversion experience. Their courage and enthusiasm gives the Eucharist even more meaning as we gather to welcome them into the body of Christ.

Father Mel Bucher, OFM   *Oceanside, California*

My Bread of Life

The Mass has always been the focal point in my life. At an early age, I was inspired by the splendor of attending daily Mass through the example of my mother and grandmother, who graciously allowed me to tag along with them.

Our home parish was Holy Trinity, a beautiful structure that reminded me of a cathedral because of its grandeur. Often, I would sneak away from my grandmother's house, which was near the church, for visits to the Blessed Sacrament. Although the building was huge, I always felt at peace when I knelt in the dim church, lit only by the votive lights, and spent time with my Lord.

My first holy Communion day was the most momentous day of my life. My excitement was probably enticed by the prospect of wearing a white dress and veil, and receiving a new prayer book and rosary, yet I can still recall the solemnity of the Mass like it was yesterday. Even now, I still get teary eyed as I hear the hymn: O Lord I am not Worthy That Thou Shoudst Come to Me.

Many burdens during my lifetime have been made lighter through the gift of the Eucharist. I feel a special closeness to Jesus during the moments after I receive holy Communion. That is when I spill out my love, joy, and worries to Him. I sense that He really listens to me, and allows me to walk away trusting that although the problems won't always disappear, I am not alone in bearing them.

My faith is renewed each time I receive holy Eucharist, and that faith instills trust and confidence in Our Lord as I continue walking my life's journey, which hasn't been easy. My husband I have dealt with job injustices and losses, economic problems, and painful family misunderstandings.

One particular crisis happened twenty-one years ago as my family returned home from Saturday evening Mass with two of our friend's children in tow. In the excitement of unloading the car of children and sleeping bags, our ten-year-old son decided that he would help by scooping the three week old baby from his car seat. Before my husband or I realized what was happening, Billy had fallen with baby Gregory. Even though his head had been protected by his winter garb, we could immediately see that Greg had a displaced skull fracture.

The hours that followed where filled with tears, prayers, and anxiety. The next morning after the Sunday Masses were over, Father Phil, our parish priest and close friend, came to the hospital carrying with him the prayers and well wishes of our friends. He blessed Greg as he had done the evening before in the emergency room, and we continued to place our infant son in God's hands.

Greg was scheduled for surgery on Monday morning to repair a depressed skull fracture, but the neurosurgeon wanted a second cat scan done before he did the procedure. That evening, when the doctor received the results of the second cat scan, he came to our hospital room with the wonderful news: the eggshell fracture was no longer depressed, and Greg would not need surgery.

Our parish family and friends rejoiced with us as we gave praise and thanksgiving to Our Lord for interceding for our baby's healing. Today Greg is a junior at Ohio State University and we continue to give thanks for the gift that he is to us.

As I celebrate my golden years, daily Mass continues to be a blessing in my life. I now have the joy of teaching my granddaughter to love Our Lord in the Blessed Sacrament. From the time she was an infant, I have had the pleasure of helping my son and daughter-in-law to care for this lovely child.

Often I take Isabelle to Mass with me. We especially enjoy devotions every Monday during exposition of the Blessed Sacrament. This is a special time for Isabelle, who loves to show her stuffed animals to Jesus. When Isabelle was a babe in arms, she would reach out to the monstrance on the altar and giggle. I know Jesus was making her laugh!

Our journey continues as we face job insecurity and financial stress, but my husband and I continue to find our strength in the beauty of the Mass. We believe in God's promise that through the grain of wheat that becomes bread, and the grape that becomes wine, He will continue to feed us with the body and blood of Jesus Christ through the holy Eucharist. He is always with us, and He will not forsake us.

Jeanne M. McCale   *Vermilion, Ohio*

We can say not only that each of us receives Christ, *but also that* Christ receives each of us. *He enters into friendship with us: "You are my friends" (Jn 15:14).*

If You Are Humble Enough

The first time I was asked to bring Our Lord in holy Communion to anyone, it was to thirty patients at the National Orthopedic Hospital in Alexandria, Virginia. I was the DRE (Director of Religious Education), and a newly ordained permanent deacon at Our Lady of Lourdes Parish, near Reagan National Airport.

Our new pastor, Msgr. Burke, handed me his pyx, which is the small metallic container that we use to carry holy Communion, and then gave me a list of the patients I would be visiting. I asked him what he wanted me to say when they received Our Lord, and he said, "Just go now. They are waiting!" After I had removed the Hosts I needed from the tabernacle and put them in the pyx, I knelt before Our Lord and said, "Please Lord, tell me how you want me to bring you to your people." No response.

All the way to the hospital, I prayed, asking for the proper way to present Our Lord to these patients. Somehow, it just didn't seem like enough to merely hold up the Host, the sacred body of Christ, and just say, "The body of Christ." No response. Going up the elevator, I prayed again, but still got no response.

When I reached the first room, the nurse said, "This woman just came out of surgery and she's just now coming out of the anesthetic." I saw a young woman in her mid-twenties, facing the wall, grimacing in pain. I stood at the foot of her bed. Our eyes met, and I asked her if she wanted to receive Our Lord in holy Communion. She turned toward me and nodded her head, still with an expression of pain. I held up the Host, and then it came to me. "Unite your sufferings with those of Our Lord's on the cross, for your salvation and for the salvation of those you love. Receive the body of Christ."

She received Our Lord, lay back on her pillow, and closed her eyes. I sensed the presence of Jesus taking care of her. Leaving the room, I looked back and saw her resting in the peace of Christ, with a faint smile on her peaceful face. This happened with every single one of the patients at the hospital, even those preparing to leave.

On the way back to Our Lady of Lourdes, I thanked Our Lord for letting me bring Him to those patients. I said, "I did a good job for you today, Lord, didn't I?" What came to me was humbling. It was as if Jesus was saying, "If you are humble enough, and innocent enough, and pure enough, I will let you take me to my people, like that donkey in Jerusalem."

Deacon Joe Benin   *Annandale, Virginia*

Ministry of the Sick

My husband and I are ministers of the sick for St. Joseph's Church in Crescent City, California, and we serve all of De Norte County as well. Our responsibility is to visit the homebound and sick of our parish, as well as patients at Sutter Coast Hospital, our local convalescent hospital. We also go to Addie Meedom House, an assisted care home, to visit the people there. On our visits, we bring the holy Eucharist to those that can receive it, and pray with those who, for different reasons, cannot receive.

Several years ago we visited a couple that lived out of town. The husband was disabled and not able to get to Mass. When we arrived at their home, his wife Annie was not there because she had just been taken to Sutter Coast Hospital. She had been injured when she fell as she was bringing firewood into the house. I assured Mr. Ackerman that my husband and I would go to the hospital and track Annie down, and bring her the holy Eucharist.

We found Annie in the emergency room area of the hospital. I knocked on her hospital room door and entered the room. There she was, lying on a hospital cot. She looked up at me and all she said was, "Thank you Lord for coming to me in my distress." I will never forget that beautiful response.

Annie just celebrated her ninetieth birthday and is now living in Texas near her daughter. Her wonderful husband Ed Ackerman died several years ago. He was a lovely, spiritual man.

As Catholics, we are truly blessed to have the gift of the holy Eucharist. My husband and I continue to bring the Lord Himself to people who cannot go to Him. What an honor this ministry is for us.

Victoria A. Zizzo   *Cresent City, California*

God Opened the Door

It was a dark and stormy night. Everyone has heard that phrase at one time or another, and that is what I was experiencing in my life back in 1994.

As a religious sister, in 1993 I had been commissioned to work at Mary Immaculate Catholic School, which is one of the oldest Catholic schools in Florida. It was founded in 1868 and is on the island of Key West, also nicknamed "paradise of the tropics."

For some time though, I had been experiencing anything but paradise in my life. I believe it all started when I began caring for my dad who had been diagnosed with cancer. After his death, I had to sell my parent's home so my mother could move into a residence for independent living. This was 150 miles from where I was living. During this time I was also facing the prospect of accepting a new position as principal at the school.

I was feeling the enormous responsibilities of being an only child combined with the fact that my personal life was facing major changes as well. The stress of moving to a new place and culture, far from my religious community and my mother, plus difficulties in day to day dealings with the people I lived and worked with started to take a huge toll on me. I was falling into a state of depression.

Even though I could sense something was not quite right, I continued taking little time for my own needs and putting everything and everyone else's needs ahead of my own. I began to feel that God had abandoned me.

The chapel in our Spiritual Renewal Center had a daily Mass at 5:30 p.m. that I liked to attend because the Mass, and especially the Eucharist, was very important to me. I prayed that God would hear my anguish and open a door for me.

On one particular day, the priest saying the Mass was the director of the center and a T.O.R. Franciscan. That day I had been feeling my lowest and was badly in need of spiritual and emotional help. I considered going to the priest for help, but again thought I could handle it all myself. Instead, I prayed for a sign of some kind from God to direct me.

At Mass that day, as I went to receive Our Lord in holy Communion, tears started to flow and I renewed my plea for God's help and direction. As I offered my thanksgiving, I distinctly heard a voice say to me, "Go to him!" Shocked, I turned around to see if I was mistaken by the voice I so clearly heard, but everyone was in silent adoration. After Mass I had the courage to ask the priest for an appointment.

This was the beginning of my healing process. A rough road was ahead of me, but I was eventually freed from my depression. Peace returned to me and my life was changed. I had renewed hope and will always be grateful to this Franciscan priest for his help. God renewed my faith that day with the touch of His voice. He truly does hear our prayers and pleas for help in times of trouble, when life turns into a long, dark and stormy night.

Shortly after this experience, our chapel was turned into a Divine Mercy perpetual adoration chapel. It is open twenty-four hours a day, seven days a week with at least two parish adorers every hour. Above the tabernacle is a large Divine Mercy image of Jesus, so lifelike that His eyes seem to follow you. We have been blessed with a little "paradise" on earth!

Sister Georgene M. Golock, F.D.C. *Key West, Florida*

Indeed, it is because of him that we have life: "He who eats me will live because of me" (Jn 6:57).

My Conversion Story

I first came to hear of God's love at a Billy Graham Outreach tent meeting on September 1, 1955. It was there I gave my life to Jesus.

I grew up under a very loving but strict evangelical family. We went to various churches.

On September 2, 1961, we attended a Pentecostal church (AOG) where I was baptized in water and on September 20, 1961, I was baptized in the Holy Spirit and received the gift of speaking in tongues. I am recording these dates as they were very special milestones in my Christian life.

In my teens, much to my shame now, I rebelled badly and wanted nothing to do with God. Later, I got married and moved from Essex down to Derbyshire. I still had these niggles in the back of my head: I had forgotten God, had God forgotten me as well?

My wife and I began to attend a variety of churches similar to my youth but we never felt at home in any of them, though to be honest, the people on the whole were good and kind. It was while I was working away from home down in Dorset as a computer system's engineer that I came across a church in a school that was truly alive and full of God's love.

Once again I recommitted my life to Jesus and knew I was His child. Later we found another church in Essex where we went for some years. Things were fine, but it wasn't to last. On December 31, 1985 tragedy struck. I was involved in an accident at work. I became a T10 paraplegic.

My case was not taken up in time so we had no compensation, but blessed be God, all our needs were met. Then the difficulties really began.

I have believed and still do believe that God can heal people today, but the church we were attending at that time took the verses of the Bible sadly out of context. Because I was not *healed*, it had to be because there was either "sin in my life" or that "I didn't have enough faith." They said things like, "Sorry, God has not given me a 'word for you,' " and "I had no hope," etc. To my surprise and the complete bewilderment of my fourteen-year-old daughter we were eventually *dropped*.

I say this now to show that there is no bitterness in my heart. I continue to pray for those who acted this way but at the time I did weep at the unloving and apparent uncaring nature being shown to us. I knew that God loved my family and me. It was through this great love of Jesus that I could accept that He was in control. I had lost *the fellowship* and since they had no wheelchair accessibility or warmth in their hearts toward me, I felt abandoned by man, but not by Jesus.

I tried to find somewhere else to worship but it was not easy as many churches were not wheelchair accessible. We found one, locally, that was evangelical and the people were polite, but the next day I had a visit from the pastor who told me in no uncertain terms, "We do not believe God heals today." We felt devastated since we had not said one word about this and had only been to one meeting. I then decided that perhaps I could stay at home and read my Bible, pray and keep my relationship with Jesus on my own. As you will know if you are a Christian, this is nearly impossible.

Around our local shops I used to occasionally run into a nun named Sister Fidelma who later became one of my sponsors with Mary Kimberley! She was charismatic, literally, and the love of Jesus shone out from her face. We had some great times of fellowship in the stalls and wherever and whenever we met.

I should say here that for thirty-odd years I was fiercely anti-Catholic and was taught what verses could be used to counter Catholicism, but God has a marvelous sense of humor.

I had an intense longing to pray somewhere other than my home and Sister Fidelma suggested that as her church was accessible, why not in there? I was mortified. I did enjoy her company and good fellowship, but she was a Catholic!

Months went by and my longing to find a place to pray increased. Finally I asked if I could "but only under the condition that there was to be no preaching at me or any pressure!" She smiled and said to let her know the time and she would make sure the doors were open and I would be on my own.

If you have not had my upbringing you will never understand the problems I had just going into a Catholic church.

The day came and I went with my Bible, holding it tightly and remembering over and over in my head special *anti-Catholic verses* just in case anyone tried to convert me.

It was worse than I thought. The first thing that caught my attention was an idol of Mary. Then I saw an idol of Jesus on the cross. I looked around desperately and found solace at the side of the church where there was a stone pillar with a brass box on top with a candle by it. I positioned myself in front of it so that this pillar blocked my view of these terrible idols!

My first prayer was "Please Lord, do not strike me dead for being in here, I just want to be alone with you and pray." I knew nothing of Catholic beliefs at all except that they worshipped Mary, that the Catholic Church was the *whore* of Rome and the pope was the Antichrist. This did not sit well with me, but I just sat there thinking of all the good things that God had blessed us with.

I am not sure how long I had been praying when this *voice* came so clearly into my head, "My child be still. My child be still and know that I am God." It amazed me. My immediate reaction was "How can you be in a place like this?" I was so shocked I hastily closed my Bible and went straight home.

The next Thursday I went again, once more positioning myself so that I couldn't see the idols. The same thing happened, "My child be still. My child be still and know that I am God."

This time I felt that I should just be still. I waited and as I sat there in my wheelchair praying, I had such a wonderful sense of God's love as peace flooded over my whole being. Silently, I began to worship in tongues and told Jesus how much I loved Him and missed being with others to have fellowship with. About three hours later I left for home.

For about six weeks this happened every Thursday and eventually I meet the priest, Father Alan, and asked if I could just have a chat with him. We arranged to meet two days later.

He had such a love of Jesus, and he never retaliated when I asked about the idols, but just explained the Church's teaching on statutes and that worship belongs to God alone. He was so patient and kind. I told him what had been going on for the past six weeks and when I told him about being still—he asked me where I was when this happened. I showed him.

A huge smile spreads across his face. "Do you know where you were sitting?" he asked.

I said, "Hiding from the statues."

He smiled as I said that, and explained that its called the tabernacle. They believe that Jesus becomes fully present during holy Mass and the remaining *Hosts*, that is, *His real presence,* are reserved there.

This meant absolutely nothing to me, but he seemed very excited. I asked him not to pray with and for me, as I was a Christian and he was a Catholic. With a loving smile he said that Catholics are Christians, I was his brother in Christ, and he would pray for me when I was gone.

I couldn't get out fast enough! I didn't want anyone to see the tears in my eyes because I knew God was both there and in this priest's life and I had been so rude. His loving reply drove deep into me like a sword and rebuked me far more than words could.

When I prayed that night the first thing I asked was that God would forgive my unloving attitude. I then phoned up Father Alan and asked his forgiveness. He said it was not necessary as he understood and any time I wanted to chat about anything to just let him know. He finished by saying, "God bless and keep you, you are in my prayers."

Next day we went to a jumble (rummage) sale and another little nun came up to me (I never found out her name, but still pray for her and thank God for her). She gently put her hand on my shoulder, smiled and said, "God bless you. Do you know that the love of Jesus is in your eyes?" This was getting to be much too much for me. Before I left her she gave me a little paperweight in wood that I later found out had the images of Our Lady of Perpetual Succour on it. I took it simply because I didn't know how to respond to such kindness and obvious love without causing offense.

Some weeks went by. Now I knew that Catholics loved Jesus too but what was new to me was the fact that they honored Mary as being someone very special.

I started going to holy Mass on Sundays. I didn't understand most of it but I knew that Jesus was truly there and that at the consecration when everyone knelt I saw love and worship in the congregation's eyes. To be honest, I just wanted to get out of my wheelchair and prostrate myself at this point of the Mass as it *felt* so holy. I was amazed at how much Scripture was used all through the Mass, in fact it all appeared to be from the Bible, which added to my confusion.

Much later I saw a notice on the bulletin board saying there was going to be an RCIA course and everyone was welcome to come and learn what the Catholic faith really taught. I let Father Alan know I would like to go and he was delighted. It is important here to say that not once did he force his beliefs on me and in fact at times even tried to dissuade me, but always said, "Seek God for yourself what He wants you to do."

To cut a long story short I was taught what the Church really believed and my desire was to receive my blessed Lord's body and blood. I knew this had to wait until I was confirmed and received into the Catholic faith.

Then another mishap occurred...I was due to be received into the Church on Easter 1995; however, another medical problem had flared up so badly it meant I had to have surgery. By the time I recovered, Easter would have come and gone! My longing was so great that I half asked, "Can I not be received into the Church earlier as I can not receive any of the sacraments I have been taught about?" I said it was unfair that I would miss the sacrament of the sick before surgery again and that reconciliation, confirmation and most importantly—to be able to partake in Our Lord's body and blood with my Christian family there.

February 11th there was a special meeting in the church as the relics of Our Lady of Guadalupe were coming. When I went up to be blessed while the others received Communion, Father Alan said, "Would you like to be received into the Church tomorrow?" My smile was a mile wide! "Yes, please!" I said. It is more than I could believe. Father had phoned the bishop to obtain this special permission and thank God it was granted.

I went home and told Marian (I should state here that Marian has been 100 percent supportive and encouraged me in my quest. Truly Proverbs 31 was written about her). She was delighted. I phoned my parents and what shook me was my dad, who has since passed away, may he rest in peace, said, "Yes, he would like to come."

The next day was just full of blessings and great emotion. It was Sunday, February 12, 1995. I was received into the faith that is so precious to me. I remember the loving look from Father Alan as he held the Host up and said, "The body of Christ," and then after he offered me the chalice and said, "The blood of Christ." My reply to both statements was, "Amen," and I humbly and joyfully received the sacrament at last. This is still the center of my Christian life and I truly thank God for it.

To this day my life is central to Our Lord Jesus Christ, especially the privilege to receive Him at holy Mass. I love the sacrament of reconciliation, it is still embarrassing but then Jesus is there always waiting to forgive and restore through His priest.

The pope, who I now honor and believe to be of apostolic succession to St. Peter, was one of the *keys* on my journey when I saw him forgive the man who tried to kill him.

Reading John's Gospel, chapter six, was a really *major key* for me, and reading about an obscure place called Medugorje during my quest affected me greatly for the good. God has used many things to get me this far. Out of His great, unconditional love for me and us all. I am a fellow pilgrim on my way to meet my Blessed Lord and His Blessed Mother.

I have learned that I am part of God's marvelous family and grieve at the disunity there is in His body. I am persuaded that I have something to do for Jesus. Something that I can do (each of us has a unique ministry). Mine is to tell of His marvelous love wherever I am, either physically or mainly now on the IRC (Internet Relay Chat). Please pray for me that God's will may be achieved in my life.

John A. Barton   *Grays, Essex, Great Britian*

The Eucharist thus appears as both the source *and the* summit *of all evangelization, since its goal is the communion of mankind with Christ and in him with the Father and the Holy Spirit.*

My God, You Are Healed!

My mother loved God and the holy family very much. We often went to daily Mass, and on First Saturdays she would take us children for toast and hot chocolate at a restaurant. What a treat that was!

Once she had a very bad sore throat and her regular doctor sent her to a throat specialist. Mom said that when the doctor looked into her throat, he gasped. He said she would have to have surgery, and may even loose the ability to speak. He told her to go home and prepare her family, and to come back the next day.

Mom left the doctor's office and went straight to St. Rose of Lima Church in Carbondale, Pennsylvania. There, my frightened mother spoke to Father Harrity. He blessed her and told her that when she went to Mass the next day she should offer the Eucharist to help her through this difficult time.

After Mass the next day, she went to see the doctor again. When he looked into her throat, he was shocked. He said, "My God, you are healed!" There was no sign of any disease.

My momma has since passed away, and I am convinced that she is in heaven with Dad. I'll bet God has His arm around both of their shoulders as they live with Him in His heavenly home.

Roberta H. Para-Sefchick   *Prompton, Pennsylvania*

Eucharistic communion also confirms the Church in her unity as the body of Christ. St. Paul refers to this unifying power *of participation in the banquet of the Eucharist when he writes to the Corinthians: "The bread which we break, is it not a communion in the body of Christ? Because there is one bread, we who are many are one body, for we all partake of the one bread" (1 Cor 10:16–17).*

My Favorite Place to Pray

Some years ago, before entering the seminary, I frequently visited Sacred Heart Church in Seattle immediately after work. I used to make it to the church just before the doors would be locked up for the evening. There was an elderly sacristan there named Bill Cole who, without ever asking me to leave, would go about his business of turning off the lights and locking the door before he went home, which was typically just a few minutes after I got there. This gave me the chance to stay and pray, sometimes for an hour or longer, and then let myself out when I was through.

My favorite place to pray was in front of the tabernacle, knowing Jesus Christ was inside. I'll always remember the long row of comfortable chairs and a couple of kneelers in the portioned area with a very large crucifix hanging on the wall above the tabernacle. Right off the sanctuary was the beautiful icon of Our Mother of Perpetual Help, whom I never ceased praying to for help.

In the winter months, when it got dark earlier, it was particularly prayerful in that quiet church next to Seattle Center as I prayed with no one else around. The only light in that dark building was from the sanctuary lamp and the many, many votive candles that were lit. Their reflection dimly lit the wall and flickered about. Some evenings it was difficult for me to pull myself away and go home. It was almost mystical; a little foretaste of heaven.

I spent a lot of time in discernment there, talking to God about a vocation to the priesthood, and most importantly, waiting and listening. Do I really have a calling? What was God's will for me? The answer became clearer as time went on.

I came to rely on the power of prayer in the presence of Our Lord in the Blessed Sacrament. I still do. As a priest, I make frequent visits throughout the day to the tabernacle. And more often than not, I pray the Liturgy of the Hours there, too. My devotion to Our Lord in the Blessed Sacrament is as strong as ever.

Father Victor M. Blazovich   *Colville, Washington*

Wisdom and Consolation

As a child and young adult, I had attended daily Mass, Benediction, Forty Hours devotion, and various other devotions. I spent many hours in front of the Blessed Sacrament and Mary. After I finished college and entered the work force, I wasn't as consistent in these practices. I regularly went to confession and Sunday Mass, but didn't take time for visits with Jesus.

My story begins in 1993, on a Wednesday evening following the parish monthly Altar Society meeting. We were standing outside listening to one of the members who had just returned from Medjugorje. After listening to Lisa witness about her experiences in Medjugorje, and to the voices of others in the following years, my faith was ignited once again. I started going to Mass more frequently during the week, and gradually my husband joined me in going to daily Mass.

In 1994, a small group of us approached our pastor and asked if we could have a time slot for a weekly rosary in the Blessed Sacrament chapel. We began in late August and have met every Wednesday evening since. Several months after we started, we again approached our pastor and were given permission to begin adoration for one hour a week, which we still continue. My husband, who was a convert, would come on his own each week and stay for about 45 minutes, silently talking to Jesus.

As time went on, I was drawn more and more to adoration before the Blessed Sacrament. Sometimes I went in the afternoon, and very frequently late at night after everyone was in bed. Looking back, I felt that Jesus was gently preparing me for what was to come.

In November of 1997, two days before Thanksgiving, it happened. On that Tuesday morning, we had received a fresh snowfall, and my husband went out to clean the snow from our daughter's car while she was getting ready for work. Our son had already left the house.

Suddenly I heard a thud and thought my daughter had dropped something in the downstairs bathroom, which was not unusual. A few minutes later she reached the bottom of the stairs and screamed up to me with a piercing urgency. My husband was lying on the floor. I ran downstairs and told her to call 911 and then call our pastor. A policeman arrived within a minute and he and our daughter began CPR immediately.

Although Don rode his bike 15 to 20 miles a day year-round, watched his diet, and had just passed a physical with flying colors two weeks prior, God called this great father, husband and friend home that morning.

It was a tremendous shock and loss to my family, and to many others who knew him. Our priest arrived within minutes of my call and kept watch for my son to get home. When we had called Scott, we told him he needed to return home immediately, and didn't tell him what was wrong. I can only imagine what was going through his mind as he turned the corner and saw the police cars and ambulances in our driveway.

When my son arrived home, the priest went right out and accompanied Scott inside where the four of us stood in disbelief as the paramedics continued to work on Don. At last, they said there was a faint heartbeat, and asked to take him to the hospital. Hope was reborn in the children at that moment, only to be squelched a short time later at the hospital.

Our pastor had lost his mother several months earlier and our family, as well as other parishioners, had attended her out-of-town funeral. We had prayed with him, and for him. He was truly touched that so many people would do that for him. Consequently, he was able to fully empathize with the children as to what was happening in their young lives. He was a great comfort and support to us that morning, and in the days and months to come.

Following my husband's funeral, I continued attending daily Mass and receiving the Eucharist with even more fervor. I spent more and more time before the Blessed Sacrament.

I cannot begin to recant the many graces, blessings, experiences, and gifts I have received from the privilege of that time spent with the Real Presence living in the tabernacle of our church. I can never begin to thank Jesus enough for all the knowledge, wisdom, and consolation He gave me as I sat with Him.

MaryJoan Douglas   *Saginaw, Michigan*

By the Grace of God

Back in 1957, I was preparing for my first Communion with the second grade class at my parish school, Holy Guardian Angels in Reading, Pennsylvania. Sister Felicia, MSC, encouraged us children to pray *ejaculations*, or short prayers of love and adoration to Jesus as we were walking up the aisle to the Communion rail.

Sister gave us examples of these short prayers, and by the grace of God, my mind fastened on this prayer: "I love you, my Jesus, I love you. I adore you above all things with my whole heart and soul. I love you, my Jesus, I love you."

I used the phrase, "By the grace of God," because today, almost fifty years later, I can assure you that this prayer has been on my lips and in my heart on a daily basis, ever since my first Communion year. I thank God for this grace of loving Him so much, and wanting to praise and adore Him.

In my adulthood, visiting Him in the Blessed Sacrament has become more difficult to do because many of the churches in my city are locked during the day. Thankfully, the pastor of St. Paul's Church in Reading, my new parish home, has adoration of Jesus in the Blessed Sacrament from 7:00 a.m. until 7:00 p.m. every weekday. Visiting Him in the Blessed Sacrament is still one of the most important parts of my week, and of my life, and I thank God for this grace. I thank the Lord for all of the many graces in my life.

Teresa M. Pietruch   *Reading, Pennsylvania*

St. John Chrysostom's commentary on these words is profound and perceptive: "For what is the bread? It is the body of Christ. And what do those who receive it become? The Body of Christ—not many bodies but one body.

The Eucharist

By Thomas Bokenkotter

Recently I spent four weeks in Israel digging with some archaeologists who were uncovering the town of Bethsaida. While there I was able to offer Eucharist on a number of occasions for the Catholics present.

One of the most memorable was at Tabgha, a lovely site on the Sea of Galilee where, according to an old Jewish Christian tradition, Jesus multiplied the loaves and the fishes (Mark 6:35-44).

A mosaic in the pavement of a fifth-century church there depicts the loaves and the fishes. Nearby, close to the altar, is a large piece of rock on which Jesus is supposed to have placed the five loaves and two fishes.

I also visited the Upper Room in Jerusalem that is believed to be the traditional site of the Last Supper. A constant stream of pilgrims moves through the room in silence, many of them prayerfully meditating on what they believe happened there the night before Jesus died.

Our eucharistic tradition has its roots in these two events. Jesus' actions at the Last Supper became the basis for our celebration of the Eucharist. Those actions in turn reflect the earlier miracle of the multiplication of the loaves to feed the crowds.

We will take a closer look at the biblical accounts of these events, as well as other essential passages about the Eucharist from the Acts of the Apostles and Paul's writings. In doing so, we will come to a deeper understanding of our own celebration of Eucharist.

Bread Blessed, Broken and Given to All

All four of the Gospels include the story of the multiplication of the loaves and fishes. The similarity between this event and the Last Supper is striking. It indicates the early Christians' belief that the multiplication of the loaves was an anticipation of the Eucharist, which in turn anticipates the messianic banquet.

In the Synoptic Gospel accounts of the multiplication we read that Jesus looked up to heaven, blessed and broke the loaves and gave them to His disciples to give to the crowds (Mark 6:41; Matthew 14:19; Luke 9:16).

These actions—blessing the bread, breaking it and giving it to the disciples—will be repeated by Jesus at the Last Supper, when he will explain the significance of the bread and wine as his body and blood.

In John's Gospel, Jesus doesn't wait until the Last Supper to explain that the bread he gives is himself. In fact, John's most explicit treatment of the real presence of Jesus in the Eucharist doesn't take place at the Last Supper at all. Instead, John uses his account of the miracle of the loaves to give Jesus' extended sermon on the Bread of Life.

In the sixth chapter of John's Gospel, Jesus tells the crowd that he is the living bread come down from heaven. He explains that just as God gave their ancestors manna in the wilderness through Moses, so now he gives them the bread of life.

He goes on to say that the bread he gives for the life of the world "is my flesh." And when some of his listeners object to such an unheard of idea Jesus says, "Very truly I tell you, unless you eat the flesh of the Son of Man and drink his blood you have no life in you" (6:53).

The offense taken by his hearers, many of whom deserted him at this point, stemmed from the plain meaning of his words that excluded any figurative understanding. All attempts to interpret Jesus' words symbolically fail to take in the whole context of the chapter and the practice of the early community.

John's account of this story told in four Gospels makes clear to us the significance of this event in the development of our Eucharistic theology.

'On the Night Before He Died'

Our Eucharist commemorates the Last Supper Jesus celebrated with his disciples. What Jesus said and did that night with the bread and wine forms the basis for the Church's sacrament of the Eucharist. What we know about this gathering comes from two separate traditions.

First we have what is known as the Marcan tradition. This includes primarily Mark's Gospel (hence the name), but is also includes Matthew's Gospel, which follows Mark's interpretation quite closely, with only some slight changes in the wording.

The Lucan tradition includes Luke's Gospel, and his sequel to the Gospel, The Acts of the Apostles. It also includes Paul's account of the Last Supper in his First Letter to the Corinthians.

In spite of some variations, the important thing is that our two independent sources agree that what Jesus did included four things.

He gave thanks over bread and wine. He identified the bread and wine with his body and blood. He gave them the bread to eat and the wine to drink. Finally, he told them that his coming death was for the forgiveness of sins, and he prefigured that death by breaking the bread and pouring out the wine.

According to Mark 14:12–16, Jesus and his disciples gathered for supper in a room that had been prepared for them. His enemies were encircling their gathering, and the passion is clearly at hand. Whether this meal was a Passover meal or not is uncertain from the details in Mark's text.

Mark interprets Jesus' actions in the light of the Old Testament sacrifice traditions. Jesus says of the cup, "This is my blood of the new covenant," a clear allusion to Exodus 24:8.

In that verse Moses takes the blood of the sacrificed oxen and dashes it on the people, saying, "See the blood of the covenant that the Lord has made with you in accordance with all these words."

Mark's Jesus goes on to say "which is poured out for many," a clear allusion to Isaiah's suffering servant: "Therefore I will allot him a portion with the great and he shall divide the spoil with the strong because he poured out himself in death and was numbered with the transgressors, yet he bore the sin of many and made intercession for the transgressors" (Isaiah 53:12).

Luke, like Mark, sets the Eucharist in the framework of a meal. More clearly than Mark, however, his account follows the basic sequence of the Passover meal, which began with drinking a cup of wine. Then a second cup was prepared and the paterfamilias told the story of the Exodus, after which a second cup was drunk.

The meal proper began with the breaking of the bread and after the meal a third cup would be consumed. In Luke, Jesus takes the cup and says, "This cup is the new covenant in my blood." Thus in Luke's reinterpretation of the Passover, Jesus' death becomes the new Exodus—a liberation from sin and the inauguration of a new covenant that constitutes a new people of God.

'I Pass on to You What Was Handed on to Me'

On the basis of these actions, the theology of the Eucharist was developed after Jesus' resurrection. It began with Paul, who taught that the Eucharist was the Lords' Supper (1 Corinthians 11:20), the meal where the new people of God are nourished by spiritual food for their journey. The meal identifies them as the people of the new covenant (1 Corinthians 11:25).

Paul tells them, "For I received from the Lord what I handed on to you, that the Lord Jesus, on the night he was handed over, took bread, and, after he had given thanks, broke it and said, 'This is my body that is for you. Do this in remembrance of me.' In the same way also the cup, after supper, saying, 'This cup is the new covenant in my blood. Do this, as often as you drink it, in remembrance of me.' For as often as you eat this bread and drink the cup, you proclaim the death of the Lord until he comes" (1 Corinthians 11:23–26).

Note here the actions of taking, blessing, breaking and giving the bread. These words have been handed down from that day to this and at each and every Eucharist the priest and people call them to mind once again in the institution narrative of the Eucharist Prayer.

Paul taught that Jesus is truly and really present in the Eucharist. He made this clear when he took the Corinthians to task for their inappropriate behavior at the Eucharist. Some were starting to eat before all were gathered and some went hungry and some even got drunk. Paul told them that by consuming the bread unworthily they were guilty of a serious sin insofar as they were "answerable for the body and blood of the Lord" and were "eating and drinking judgment against themselves" (1 Corinthians 11:27–29). The obvious explanation of these words is that Paul identified the bread and wine with Jesus himself.

According to *The New Jerome Biblical Commentary,* "One cannot argue away the realism of the identity of Christ with the Eucharistic food in Paul's teaching, even if he does not explain how this identity is achieved." Later theologians would develop the explanations and understandings that Paul left unsaid.

Paul also taught that the Eucharist makes present the sacrifice of Christ on Calvary. He told the Corinthians, "As often as you eat this bread and drink this cup you proclaim the death of the Lord until he comes" (1Corinthians 11:26).

In other words, he told them, you make Jesus present in the act of offering himself for us; you are showing forth God's saving love as embodied in his Son's sacrifice.

The Eucharist, then, must be celebrated in the same spirit of love that Jesus showed if it is to be truly a showing forth of God's love. How can it show God's love if you are mean and nasty to your neighbor—getting drunk, gulping down the meal before all are present and so on. In doing so you are "eating the bread and drinking the cup of the Lord unworthily" by not discerning the body of the Lord—not relating lovingly to Christ's body—that is, the members of his body. You are therefore answerable for the body and blood of the Lord.

Finally, Paul brought out the eschatological aspect of the Eucharist, for he held that the proclamation of the Lord's death must continue "until he comes" (1 Corinthians 11:26).

From the very beginning of the Church, the Eucharist formed the center of its life of worship. This is clearly indicated by the Acts of the Apostles. In the second chapter we hear that the 3,000 people baptized by the apostles on Pentecost devoted themselves to "the breaking of the bread," a Lucan term for the Eucharist. To this day, each time we gather for Eucharist, we remember and make present the Lord as Christians have done since Jesus first said, "Do this in remembrance of me."

Used with permission from Thomas Bokenkotter.

[This article first published in *Scripture from Scratch N0697*
published by St. Anthony Messenger Press]

The Joy of Our Lord

I always had a calling to be a Catholic. In high school I would go to Mass with a friend, and longed to receive holy Communion, but not being Catholic, I knew I couldn't. Then, thirty-five years ago, I married my husband who is Catholic, and that's when I finally joined the church. I felt so much peace from receiving the Eucharist.

When my children received their first holy Communion, I was so happy, it was like I was receiving it for the first time too. However, throughout the years my husband was transferred frequently with his job, and we stopped going to Mass. For fifteen years we drifted through life one day at a time. Then, when my husband retired four years ago, we moved back home.

I had an empty feeling even though we had our family and friends around us again. Then, I realized what I missed, and it was St. Mary's Catholic Church. We started going to Mass again and haven't missed it in almost four years now.

The first time I went to Mass, after having been away from it for so long, I cried all the way down the aisle as I went to receive the Eucharist. I felt like I was really coming home. I am now a eucharistic minister, and celebrate the joy of Our Lord with everyone who receives the precious body and blood from me.

Kathy Laird   *Frankfort, Indiana*

For as bread is completely one, though made of up many grains of wheat, and these, albeit unseen, remain nonetheless present, in such a way that their difference is not apparent since they have been made a perfect whole, so too are we mutually joined to one another and together united with Christ".

True Adoration

When I celebrated my first Mass of thanksgiving on the Vigil of Pentecost in 2003, I was, of course, all caught up in the moment of actually presiding at the Eucharist, something I had dreamed, and daydreamed of, over the fourty-seven years of my life. Many times, as I proceeded through five years of studies for the priesthood, I would wake from dreams at night of celebrating Masses, the Liturgy of the Hours, prayer, retreats, daily Mass, ministry opportunities and adoration of the Blessed Sacrament.

On the night of my first Mass, when I prayed the Eucharistic Prayer, and especially during the words of institution, it was as though the whole congregation, and all my new brothers in the priesthood, had been walled off from me. It was like I was in a glass enclosure with the eucharistic presence of Jesus in my hands; first the Host, and then the cup. Each genuflection was a true act of adoration from which I did not want to rise. I will never forget that day.

There was a time when I took the Eucharist for granted, even saying to myself that I could live without daily Mass, and that adoration was superfluous.

I am a delayed vocation to the priesthood. Before I began my formation to become a priest, I served as a music minister and liturgist for twenty-two years. At one point I said to my spiritual director, Father Bob, that my familiarity with the Eucharist (I played and sang for four to five Masses a weekend) was making my reception of Jesus in the Eucharist feel so blasé. He wisely pointed out that it was through my irreverence that I was experiencing these feelings.

He suggested Holy Hours and praying or singing that old hymn text, "O sacrament most holy, O sacrament divine, All praise and all thanksgiving, be every moment thine." I was obedient to his suggestion because I wanted to recapture the sense of awe I had before.

I began to pray the Liturgy of the Hours and to meditate before the Blessed Sacrament, and I always ended prayer with the little prayer, "O sacrament most holy…" I began to have a more profound appreciation of the gift of the Eucharist. As I went through seminary formation for the priesthood, I continued this practice, admittedly sporadically. But the devotion had not only returned but had been established.

Father Donald P. Malin   *Grand Junction, Colorado*

Until Jesus Comes

Mom was a Catholic convert who fell away from our faith and returned to the religion of her childhood. Although she did not practice Catholicism, she raised her children Catholic, as she had promised.

Towards the end of her life, my mother came to live with me. I took care of her for about three years before her death. Late in September of 2001, I knew she would be leaving our earthly life soon, and I promised Mom that I would be there holding her hand until Jesus came to take her hand from mine. I prayed with her, and for her, nightly.

On September 30th, I knew only a short time remained. I fell into my bed late, with my ears, mind, and heart attached to the life in the next room. I prayed to God that she would not die on that particular date because my son had died September 30th, 1973.

That night, I prayed feverishly that when she died, Jesus would come and take the hand I held onto so dearly and tightly. I was almost to the point of telling God that I just couldn't let go of her until He sent Jesus to come get her. He had to be there, and not just in the way He is always with us. I had to know that He was really there, or I could not bear to let her go. "Oh God," I prayed, "I'm sorry about being so bossy. It's just that I know you can do this. So, I ask like a beggar, even if I seem demanding."

The morning of October 1st arrived. I called my sisters and told them that there were only hours left before our mother would leave us to go home with Our Lord. Then I placed a call to my parish priest, Father Tom, which was the fourth or fifth call I had made to him in the past four or five weeks. He did not come to our house when I had called for him those other times. This time, I called and left a message. Very soon he called me back and asked, "How is your mother?" I coldly answered back, "She is dying!" He said he would be there right away.

Father Tom arrived that afternoon shortly after four. My sister Sharon and I were at Mom's bedside, and we listened to the priest's prayers of comfort and forgiveness. We received the Eucharist in our mother's name because she was unable to receive it. Then we thanked Father Tom, and he left. The rest of our family started to arrive, and at five, Mom died quietly and peacefully.

When my family left, I was alone, and sat curled in a corner of the couch. I was tired and did not feel connected to the world around me. Then it hit me fully, with all the force that only God possesses. It was like thunder and lightning in the enormous quiet darkness. I had seen Jesus in my home! It was His very real presence that had come for my mom in her very last hour of life.

I broke into tears of joy and awe. God, in His wisdom and in accordance with His will, knew that I would be calling out for Him in desperation at that particular moment in time. Only God knew why the priest didn't come when I had called for him several other times prior to her death. Only God knew that He would gift me with yet another awesome revelation of His plan in His time.

Janice M. Wagner   *Honey Creek, Iowa*

The worship of the Eucharist outside of the Mass *is of inestimable value for the life of the Church.*

Not for You

It was Easter of 1990 and I was sitting in a pew with my bald head covered with a silky scarf. My military husband had given it to me to assure me that I was still his beautiful girl, even though my long locks of auburn hair were missing, thanks to the ravages of chemotherapy.

My husband was on temporary assigned duty, and I was alone in a strange community. God was with me though, making me feel safe and connected. It had been a good Lent, in fact my best ever. I had fasted and prayed, and said innumerable rosaries. Masses were wonderful celebrations of His love for me, and for all His people. I had become aware of His real presence in the Eucharist only a couple of months before during eucharistic adoration, and so the Mass had come alive for me.

This particular Sunday the Mass was to become even more special. As the priest raised the Host during the consecration, for a split second I saw the living face of the crucified Christ on it. Then I heard interiorly, "Not for you" and the face disappeared.

I was so surprised that I did not know what to do about the experience. I wondered, "Who do I tell that to?" and finally went to the priest who had presided over that particular Mass.

I asked Father Tobin if he had noticed anything different that day at Mass. When he asked me why, I told him my story. As I did, his face became pale and his demeanor quite serious. He told me that he knew why I had heard, "Not for you."

The priest told me that person the miracle had been intended for had come to him earlier that week with the same story about seeing the crucified Christ on the Host. My vision served as a confirmation for both the priest and the other man that the miracle he had witnessed had truly occurred. This was another confirmation to me that, yes, we certainly do have an awesome God!

Kathleen M. Ellertson   *Moore, Oklahoma*

He Will Heal You Too

I received an urgent call from a friend at a nearby hospital. Tony's daughter, Angela, had been in surgery for over six hours. Her first words were, "Bring me Jesus." She repeated this several times as she slipped in and out of a coma.

Her father was unemployed and without insurance. He told his sick daughter to pray and for six days she only got worse. Tony asked friends and prayer groups to pray for Angela. Then her illness became critical. Her eyes rolled back in her head and she was comatose. Tony called the ambulance and finally took her to the hospital. Then he called me to bring her Our Lord in holy Communion.

When I arrived at Fairfax Hospital, I found a sick little girl lying in bed with an intravenous needle in her arm, and a large tube filled with dark brown, almost black fluid, in her stomach. I asked Our Lord to bless Angela and take care of her. Her eyes opened and she looked at me. I asked her if she wanted to receive Our Lord in holy Communion. She nodded her head.

Just then, a nurse stepped in front of me. "Listen Deacon," she said. "I am Catholic and you are not going to put Our Lord in that filthy infected fluid." I said that I was going to give Angela a small piece of the Host on her tongue. The nurse said, "No. You are not going to put the body of Christ in that child's stomach."

I took the Host out of the pyx and asked Angela, "Do you want to receive Jesus?" She said, "Yes." I said just say "Amen" when I finish this prayer. It was the Spiritual Communion by St. Ignatius Loyola. Angela struggled, trying to repeat the prayer after me, but she was very weak and could only repeat every third word or so. When I finished, I said, "Amen." Angela said, "Amen."

I raised the Host and said, "Angela, receive the body of Christ, in the name of the Father, and of the Son, and of the Holy Spirit. May Our Lord Jesus come to you and heal you in mind and heart and body and soul. May He bless and protect you and remain with you now and forever. Amen."

Angela whispered, "Amen." Then she lay back on her pillow and a little smile appeared on her face.

Fifteen minutes after I returned home, the phone rang. It was Tony. "Deacon Joe," he said. "Right after you left, the fluid in the large tube in Angela's stomach turned clear! She called for the nurse and sat up in bed. The doctor removed the tube and she went to every room on the children's ward. She said, "Look how much Jesus loves me! He healed me and He will heal you too, if you ask Him." Tony said that it was her way of thanking Jesus for coming to see her in the hospital and for healing her. She wanted everyone to know how much God loves us, and how He is really present in the Blessed Sacrament!

Deacon Joe Benin   *Annandale, Virginia*

A Long Wait to Become Catholic

I converted to Catholicism many years ago when I was a teenager. My mother was a Catholic and as a child I desired to become one too. However I could not even be baptized because in those days, in the early fifties, the laws of the Church stated very clearly that I needed my father's permission to be baptized. My father was very anti-Catholic and would never give his okay for me to become Catholic. My mother went with me to several different priests and the story was always the same. Without his "Okay" I could not become a Catholic.

When I was ten years old, I went to Mass with a friend who told me it was okay to receive Communion even though I wasn't Catholic. I didn't know any better, so I went up to the altar and received the Eucharist when she did. As I sat back down in the pew, a heavy hand came down on my shoulder and as I looked back, a very stern nun was glaring at me. I thought I would die. By then I knew something was wrong.

She leaned down and whispered to me in a serious voice to never wear gloves to Communion again. It was like the voice of God speaking to me. To this very day I don't know why gloves were forbidden because back then, in the early 1950s, we received Communion only on the tongue. I felt so guilty that I told my mother what I had done and she said she thought God would understand. Even so, I still felt guilty for many years. [The wearing of gloves has never been forbidden as a policy of the Church—Ed.]

I was accepted into the Church when I was married at sixteen years old. It felt wonderful to finally be part of this body of Christ in the Catholic Church. Every time I see the priest hold up the bread and wine and turn them into the body and blood of Christ, I believe that through the Eucharist I can become the heart, hands, eyes, and ears of Christ.

Since the time of my conversion, I have been active in the Church, and have taught religious education for many years. One of my jobs is to prepare the little children, as well as some older people, for their first holy Communion.

Once when I was ill, I received the anointing of the sick and had a vision of a hooded figure. The face was in the shadows, the hood was bright yellow, and a voice called me by my name. It told me that love and forgiveness are all that matters, but first you must forgive yourself. This image will be with me always. I know Christ is with me. Even though I often fail, hopefully through the Eucharist I can become a better person.

Joyce A. Iida   *Sixes, Oregon*

The presence of Christ under the sacred species reserved after Mass—a presence which lasts as long as the species of bread and of wine remain—derives from the celebration of the sacrifice and is directed towards communion, both sacramental and spiritual.

God's Remedy

When I think of the Eucharist, many thoughts and feelings come to me. Allow me to bypass the essential and most important points of what the Eucharist means to me.

There is one facet of the Eucharist that is very special to me. In the Old Testament, God's people were dying of snakebite because of their rebellion. Exodus 21:4–9 gives God's remedy for total healing for everyone. It was gazing at a bronze serpent on a pole. Today we are bitten by our weaknesses and fall into sin and rebellion. We have more than a symbol and sign of the presence of God through a bronze serpent. We have God Himself to gaze at. He is present as our healer in the Eucharist, to be received and adored. He really is.

How sad it is that so many Catholics believe Christ is present in the Eucharist only as a symbol. He is truly present, body, blood, soul, and divinity. As I adore Him and gaze upon Him, I am healed of anger, selfishness, apathy and safe mediocrity. What a relief! What a needed healing, daily!

Father Duane Stenzel, OFM   *Alexandria, Louisiana*

Spiritual and Physical Healing

Years ago my sister Mary Ruth had fallen away from the Catholic Church and joined the Pentecostal Church. On Divine Mercy Sunday in 1999 though, she went with me to Mass to celebrate this, my favorite feast day.

My sister suffers from Crohn's disease, a disease that affects the colon. At about three that afternoon, she became extremely ill while we were in the rest room. I quickly summoned Karen Moses, a nurse of thirty years, who was working at the celebration.

As Karen held Mary Ruth's cold hand, she observed her face and noticed that it was drained of all color. Then she saw that my sister was hemorrhaging severely. She was immediately concerned that Mary Ruth was going into shock. Karen saw the fear in Mary Ruth's face, and also a plea for help in her eyes.

At first the nurse wanted to dial 911 to get her to a hospital and transfused with blood as soon as possible. However, a small voice deep within her was saying the opposite. She was being told to, "Trust in my mercy."

At the time, I was not aware that my sister was in such a life threatening state. She would not allow me into the rest room stall because she did not want me to see what was going on. Karen was the only one who knew what was happening. She asked me and several other women who were in the rest room to pray, and so we did. I remember singing a prayer, "Heal us, Lord. We Come to You on Bended Knees."

In the meantime, Karen was busy making decisions regarding Mary Ruth. At last she yielded to the little voice inside her after making a bargain with Our Lord. She was trying to trust Him as she watched my desperate sister barely holding on to life. She said, "Lord, if her diastolic blood pressure is below 50, I will call the paramedics. If it's above 50, I will do whatever you ask." Mary Ruth's blood pressure was exactly 50. Again, the voice within Karen was urging her to "trust."

Karen prayed with Mary Ruth, along with the other women and me, and we begged our Jesus of mercy to heal her, as He had done for the woman in Scripture who had hemorrhaged. Miraculously, the bleeding slowed enough for Mary Ruth to return to the arena.

A wheelchair was rolled into the rest room for my sister, and she came out of the stall looking fine. She insisted on returning to the arena for the rest of the Mass. The procession was just beginning when we arrived, and Abbot Eugene Hayes elevated the Blessed Sacrament as he walked slowly around the ground floor of the arena.

He stopped directly in front of my sister, holding the holy Eucharist for what seemed like a long time. We later found out that he had never done that during a procession before. Mary Ruth instinctively got out of the wheelchair and on her knees as a gesture of reverence. Since she had been away from the Catholic Church for so many years, she had no way of knowing the significance of what had just happened.

When we were driving home after the services, Mary Ruth and I were very happy, and she was healthy and strong. I asked her why she had insisted on going back to the arena and not to the hospital. She said, "Because this feast day meant so much to you."

I began to get teary-eyed when she said this to me. Not only did Our Lord physically heal Ruthie, but He had stood in front of her as if to say, "Be not afraid for I am with you."

When I arrived home, I called Karen to tell her that Mary Ruth had not only received a physical healing that afternoon, but a deep spiritual healing as well. It also had a lasting affect on me. Since that special day I have been a eucharistic minister to the sick and elderly, and a daily communicant. In addition to that, I hold the 3 p.m. holy hour during our monthly 24-hour eucharistic adoration.

How blessed we are to have our Jesus truly present in the Eucharist, waiting to heal us. And how blessed we are to have Abbot Eugene Hayes, and all of our bishops and priests, who alone can consecrate the bread of life, that we may fully receive and be healed. Oh Jesus of mercy, we trust in you!

Alice Broussard   *La Habra, Califonia*

 It is pleasant to spend time with him, to lie close to his breast like the Beloved Disciple (cf. Jn 13:25) and to feel the infinite love present in his heart.

Hospice Chaplain

I am a hospice chaplain who spends time with many special people in their final chapter of life as we know it. As I reflect on the Eucharist, one person comes to mind. She has shown me how the loving presence of Christ is with us on our journey.

Penny, at forty-five years old, was married with six children, and had a brain tumor. I only knew her for a very short time. At my first visit, she was unconscious. I laid hands on her and prayed with the family. Two days later her husband called me to come right away, as Penny was awake. I went, and brought the Eucharist with me.

When I arrived, Penny was in her hospital bed in the living room, awake and with her family all around. She was unable to talk because of the pressure of the tumor on her brain. I asked her if she wanted me to pray with her, and if she'd like to make a profession of her Catholic faith. I told her that if the answer was "yes" to blink her eyes once, and she did. When she needed to respond to the questions with "I do" she blinked once. Then I asked her if she would like to receive the Eucharist, and again she blinked once. I broke a small piece of Jesus' body and gave it to her. Her eyes began to swell, and filled with tears. Her face glowed with Jesus' loving presence. One hour later she died.

Jesus said in John's Gospel (6:51–58), "I am the living bread that came down from heaven; whoever eats this bread will live forever; and the bread that I will give is my flesh for the life of the world."

Deacon John Ruscheinsky   *Spokane, Washington*

How God Found Time

When I worked a full time job, I never had time (or so I thought) to attend our weekly eucharistic adoration. However, all that changed when

I was diagnosed with an incurable form of cancer. After a year of dealing with work and cancer, it became impossible for me to continue working.

Shortly there after, I decided to sign up for an hour's adoration. When I went, I would sit and pray, and then, just sit and listen, for Our Lord to advise me on what steps to take in this cancer journey. At the end of an hour I would leave the chapel feeling a cloak of peace surrounding me.

I did not worry about the disease or the fact that there was no cure. Instead, I was able to look for things I could do to help others on their cancer journey. I was able to hear Mary and Our Lord tell me what my purpose on earth is.

Most of us go through life never knowing what their specific purpose is. I feel I was put here to help others walk through their cancer journey without great fear. I've met people, in our parish and others, and have talked with them and tried to help them take control of their disease by education, but mostly by faith. Many of these people I had seen for years at Mass but never knew their names. Now I've been able to meet them and reach out to them as personal friends.

I have met the most amazing people and gained so much from them. In the end, this horrible disease has been a blessing. I do not fear death because I know Our Lord and Lady are right here next to me. If I had never gotten this disease, I would still be going off each day to work and never to our parish adoration. On weeks when I'm not well enough to attend, I feel a sense of loss. I know the Lord is still with me, but I miss experiencing His presence in the holy Eucharist.

Jeanne M. Bechtel   *Reading, Pennsylvania*

 If in our time Christians must be distinguished above all by the "art of prayer", how can we not feel a renewed need to spend time in spiritual converse, in silent adoration, in heartfelt love before Christ present in the Most Holy Sacrament? How often, dear brother and sisters, have I experienced this, and drawn from it strength, consolation and support!

He Belonged to God

Each time I receive Jesus, I can feel His love inside me. My life has been full of trauma. The worst time was when I lost my thirteen-year-old son. Like Mary, my heart was broken, but at his funeral Mass, I gave him back to Jesus at the offertory because I knew that he was only on loan to me. He belonged to God.

When I received the Eucharist that day, a beautiful peace came into my soul. I knew he was in a better place. That he was with Jesus. Yes, a part of my heart went with David that day but I know that some day we will be together again.

Now when I receive the Eucharist, I feel two loves, the love of Jesus and the love of my son. They will always both be very precious to me. I have overcome many pains and trials through the Eucharist because when I feel rejected, alone, sad or angry, Jesus always gives me the strength to go on. He has given me the gift to forgive those who have hurt me in life. All I can say is Jesus is my friend, my lover and my all. My heart and soul always feel at peace when He comes to visit.

Lynn Y. Francis   *Providence, Rhode Island*

An Important Event

About ten years ago I was asked to offer holy Mass at a home, during which a girl was to receive holy Communion for the first time. During the service, all two dozen folks present received the Eucharist after the girl and her parents had received. Now, years later, whenever I am where the young lady is, she makes a point of reminding me that I had given holy Communion to her the first time. I know that she is a very dedicated young lady, and that receiving holy Communion is still a very important part of her daily life.

Father George Morbeck   *Republic, Washington*

Amen!

On Thursday, July 8, 1976, my grown son Ray fell from the roof of the place where he worked onto the asphalt parking lot below. "He smashed the back of his skull into a hundred or more pieces," the neurologist told us.

I had worried about my son for years. He had attended Catholic schools in Portland, Boise, and Spokane as a child, and had graduated from Gonzaga Prep in 1965. After that, he went directly into the Army. At that time, Ray rejected the Church saying, "I can't stand all the hypocrites." A couple of years before his accident he was married secretly before a justice of the peace, and didn't let us know for weeks. Then, he and his wife adopted astrology as their religion.

On the third day after Ray's accident, I stood with his wife beside his hospital bed holding a vial of Lourdes water in my hand. The chugging of the respirator was the only sound in that otherwise deathly quiet room where Ray lay in a deep coma.

With the sign of the cross, I marked Ray's body, head, chest, belly, and legs, with the Lourdes water. His wife stood there, wide-eyed and still in shock. At the moment of Ray's accident, her obstetrician had confirmed that she was pregnant with a child they both longed for. She had also grown up in Christ and had rejected Him.

I left Ray's bedside to make a long distance phone call from a pay phone to the Poor Clares in Spokane, begging for their prayers. That was twenty-eight years ago and they are still praying for him.

Ray woke from his coma totally paralyzed except for being able to shake his head, lift his eyebrows, and blink his eyes. He could not speak nor could he swallow. Soon he was transferred to a Catholic hospital that had a rehabilitation program he needed.

Almost a year later, after anxious, heart rending months in which Ray nearly died several times, Ray's wife relinquished her guardianship of him. Later she divorced him for desertion. She carried their daughter to term, in spite of persistent spotting, and was given custody. Ray saw his daughter only twice.

My husband and I brought Ray home to our small family farm in May of 1977. There he stayed in a hospital bed in our living room. Cats slept on Ray's bed, and through the windows at his elbow, he could see the forested ridge to the east. He was paralyzed from his chin down. A surgeon had opened a hole directly into Ray's stomach, and we fed him with a calf syringe, pushing *goop* through that hole. The little bit Ray could speak could not be understood.

I phoned our very large parish in town, asking for someone Ray's age to visit and to bring him Communion. Visitors came from the church, but the pastor refused to allow them to bring Communion.

Controversy raged in our parish for five months. "It would be blasphemy." "Ray's mentally incompetent." "He'll choke on the wafer." "He can't be confessed." Everyone had an opinion on why he shouldn't receive Communion.

The week before Halloween, one of Ray's visitors, a eucharistic minister who knew Ray well, brought Communion to him for the first time.

The visitor stood by Ray's bed. He lifted the Host into Ray's view. "This is the body of Christ," the visitor intoned. "Happy are those who are called to His supper."

"Amen!" Ray shouted, his voice breaking. Then he burst into deep, sobbing tears. He did not choke on the Communion wafer then or anytime after that. He always swallows it.

By Easter, 1978, Ray was able to sit in a wheel chair. On his birthday we took him to Mass at the Cathedral in Portland and he wept through the entire Mass.

Ray's healing has been slow, as it usually is with severe head injuries. Now, almost twenty-eight years later, Ray bathes and dresses himself, fixes his own breakfast, chews and swallows his food, talks so he can be understood, can write his name, and plays games with his computer. Last Christmas at Mass, he was able to stand without help for the Gospel reading. I wish you could see his beautiful smile. There truly is healing in the Eucharist!

Carol Bergener   *Westport, Washington*

What Did I Believe?

I remember very little of my first Communion as a second grader, but often reflect on my first *real* Communion as an adult.

I was a seminarian sent out at Christmas to help at our former parish in Tigard, Oregon. The pastor offered me the use of his car for the day if I would do the Communion service at a distant retirement center. I said yes, and was looking forward to the day of freedom.

At the retirement center everything went well. All the Catholic residents were present and happy to see a friar in his habit. Everyone seemed alert. We did the readings, had a nice lively discussion, prayed the "Our Father," and then I began to distribute the body of Christ. I sat down for the time of thanksgiving, and was planning my escape for the day, when I realized that one of the first ladies to receive a Host was playing with it.

She kept taking it in and out of her mouth, looking at it, putting it back in her mouth, then taking it out. Her mouth was dry and you could see the strings of saliva on the Host. She obviously no longer knew what it was.

I took the Host from her. She smiled. It was wet. What to do with it? I could go back to the church twenty minutes in the wrong direction for my escape, or I could consume it. It had been in her mouth and was wet. Yuck!

Was it just a Host, a piece of bread, or the body of Christ? What did I believe? I had stood in line many times to receive Communion but that day I really received the body of Christ.

Father Ben Innes, OFM   *Oceanside, California*

St. Alphonsus Liguori, who wrote: "Of all devotions, that of adoring Jesus in the Blessed Sacrament is the greatest after the sacraments, the one dearest to God and the one most helpful to us".

The Wedding Feast

When I was visiting my in-laws in Green Bay, Wisconsin, I read in their local newspaper that there was going to be a Marian procession at a shrine in a neighboring town. Before this, I had never heard about this shrine which is run by the Franciscans, or the story behind it.

In the late 1800s, the Blessed Mother appeared to a young woman shortly before Wisconsin's Great Peshtigo Fire. This little known tragedy was the worst fire in American history, which happened at the same time as the Great Chicago Fire of 1871. The fire was blamed on a severe, six-month drought that the town of 2,000 residents suffered through. It killed 1,125 of those people in the two hours it took for the entire town to burn down.

Our Lady requested that a chapel be built in that small logging town, and that the children be taught their catechism. Years later the chapel was built, and when the fire came, flames surrounded the chapel like a ring. Hot ash fell like snowflakes, and the local farmers, their families, and cattle fled from their homes to the chapel for refuge.

In an act of faith, they carried the statue of Our Lady around the perimeter of the chapel grounds while praying the rosary on their knees. At midnight, it rained and the threat was over. The rustic wooden fence that bordered the grounds had been burned on the outside, while the inside remained untouched by the fire. It is still that way today.

I went to the Marian procession and visited the shrine a few more times before we drove back home to Illinois. On the last visit, I brought four of my six children with me. We visited the small chapel that contains crutches and other similar items, as well as messages of healings that have taken place there. While we were there, I noticed many cars filling the large parking lot and discovered that the crowd was arriving for a wedding. Since I hadn't been to Mass that day, I decided to stay for the wedding Mass.

The bride was so beautiful, she looked like a princess. I could tell that the hundreds of people arriving were mostly from the nearby farms. My children and I stood at the back of the large church, which was built close to the little chapel. Since my children suffered from asthma and were tired, I decided to take them to the only vacant pew, which was second from the front, on the groom's side.

Everything was perfect until the priest went to the altar to begin the Liturgy of the Eucharist. He paused, and went back to the pulpit to explain that when he was at the rehearsal the night before, he had neglected to check the number of Hosts for Communion. Now he realized that there were not enough for such a large crowd, which overflowed into the parking lot, and apologized. He said that when the Hosts started to run low during the distribution of Communion, he would put his hand up to alert those in the next pew not to come forward.

Since I was in the second pew, I could clearly see everything that happened as he distributed holy Communion. I was surprised he didn't break the consecrated Hosts, and that he gave everyone an unbroken one.

Row after row came forward for holy Communion. Even the people who were standing in the aisles went forward, and then the people in the vestibule. Finally, the people who were standing outside came forward to receive Communion.

As the last person received the body of Christ, the priest had a big smile on his face. He stood there with his hand ready to bring forth yet another Host, letting us know that there were more left over. Then he silently went back to the altar and continued the holy sacrifice of the Mass.

I remembered this miracle when I visited the Holy Land in the year 2000. We visited the place where Jesus had turned the water into wine at the wedding feast at Cana, and then visited the place where Jesus multiplied the loaves and the fishes. I thought to myself, that is exactly what had happened at the wedding in Wisconsin, and it's still happening today in the celebration of the Eucharist. Jesus Christ is the same yesterday, today, and forever!

Rose Mary Danforth   *Jacksonville, Florida*

Three First Communions

First Communion stories from students of St. Stanislaus Kostka School in Wyandotte, Michigan:

Sharing One: First I felt scared and nervous before I went to Communion. Then after I said, "Amen," I wasn't scared. I was happy because I was thinking now I can always receive Jesus. I though about good and happy things. I thought about my brothers and my mom and dad. I said one "Our Father" and one "Hail Mary" in line. I feel good about Communion. That's all I know.

Molly Annmarie Neimann's own words

Sharing Two: I was very, very happy and crying because of joy. The experience was good, but I didn't like the taste of the wine.

Alexandra Haltinner's own words

Sharing Three: On the day that I made my first holy Communion, I woke up very early—I was full of happiness. I get to have Jesus for the first time. I could not wait.

I keep asking my Mom when do I get to go to Church.

I feel so happy. I was so happy that my family was there to make it so special. I love you, Jesus.

Ryan Guckian's own words

The Eucharist is a priceless treasure: by not only celebrating it but also by praying before it outside of Mass we are enabled to make contact with the very wellspring of grace.

Our God Is Near

Moses asked the people, "What great nation has its god as near as Yahweh, our God, is to us?" (Deuteronomy 4:7)

In four-five years as a priest, I've experience the close presence of God in celebrating Mass with parishioners I knew and loved, with Franciscan brothers and sisters, with retreatants, and with God's people in small chapels and big churches. One setting is especially alive in my heart.

My mother lived to be ninety-nine. From my earliest childhood, I remember her going to Mass every day. The last five years of her life she was blind and could not go, but the parish brought her Communion. I lived in another city, but when I visited her, I would celebrate Mass. Sometimes other family members would be there, and sometimes it was only Mother and me. She could not see but knew all the prayers by heart, even the priest's prayers. For example, she responded to the offering of the bread and wine, and even before I started to wash my hands, I could hear her whisper, "Lord, wash away my iniquities and cleanse me of my sins." A few days before she died during the night, I celebrated Mass with her for the last time.

Father Jeremy Harrington, OFM   *Cincinnati, Ohio*

The Wonder of It

I attended a small, four-room school run by the Glen Riddle Franciscans. In those days, the sisters took care of everything in the church. One of their chores was to take care of the altar and sacristy. A great deal of mystery was associated with the wonderful things in the sacristy, and we considered it a treat to be able *help* sister.

One day, sister asked me to help her, and I was thrilled. In those days girls weren't allowed in the sanctuary, so being able to walk around it and touch the altar was a very special and exciting event.

On this day, after she took care of the flowers, sister began filling the ciborium with Hosts. My eyes were as big as saucers. Then she asked me if I would like to have one. I was aghast. I couldn't believe she was touching the Host. At that young age, I didn't understand why we shouldn't touch it, but was certain something terrible would happen if we did.

Sister saw how frightened I was and made me sit down as she explained in the most beautiful way that this was just bread. She told me that it wouldn't become the body of Christ until the priest said the words of consecration. Then she recited the words of consecration, explaining what they meant with incredible love and deep faith. I can't express the depth of feeling that was imparted to me that day about God's love for me. It was one of the most spiritual moments of my life.

It was after her patient explanation that Communion became *real* to me. I have never lost the sense of wonder and mystery that sister instilled in me that day. Since then, when I hear the words of consecration, it is like Christ is saying them.

For some years now, I have been an extraordinary minister of the Eucharist. The little girl who was afraid to touch an unconsecrated Host is now an old woman who regularly touches the consecrated Host, and still stands in awe at the wonder of it!

Anne Cominskie   *Deptford, New Jersey*

"In the course of the day the faithful should not omit visiting the Blessed Sacrament, which in accordance with liturgical law must be reserved in churches with great reverence in a prominent place. Such visits are a sign of gratitude, an expression of love and an acknowledgment of the Lord's presence": Paul VI, Encyclical Letter Mysterium Fidei *(3 September 1965): AAS 57 (1965), 771.*

The Face of Our Lord

About a year ago, as I was praying the rosary during eucharistic adoration, I looked up at Our Lord and thought I saw His image appear in the Host. Then I decided I was just imagining it, and did not tell anyone.

A few days later, I went back to adoration with my son who was eighteen at the time, and noticed that he kept staring at the Host very intently. After we left, he told me that he had seen the Lord's face in the Host. After that experience, he has never missed a Sunday Mass.

Juan F. Zorrilla   *Miami, Florida*

His Support

On my first trip to Rome, I had the privilege of being at a general audience of Pope John Paul II. As he came down the aisle, he stopped at my seat, held my hand, while he shook the hands of those around us. He used me as his support! I had a wonderful feeling as we stood there.

Later as I reflected on this, I thought, how I should be even more thrilled each time I have the Eucharist in my hands, as I assist at Mass!

Deacon Rich La Rossa   *East Rockaway, New York*

My Little Taste of Heaven

My experience with the power of the holy Eucharist took place over thirty years ago in a small Catholic church in rural Pennsylvania, and yet I can recall it as vividly as if it happened just yesterday.

This particular church was the church of my youth. It held all of the special moments of my life as it was where I had received my first sacraments. All of the parishioners knew one another, and Sunday Mass was a time to gather together and worship. It was during a typical Sunday Mass in which my story begins.

In order to fully share this moment with you, I must backtrack and explain that I was a young girl at the time and in special need of the strength and love only Our Lord can supply. Not long before this Mass, my beloved father had been diagnosed with terminal lung cancer. My mother and I had been struggling to come to terms with the unimaginable thought of losing him, and were wondering how we would carry on without his presence in our lives.

In the days prior to this special Mass, I was particularly drawn to my faith, frequently stopping at our little church on my way home from school each day. There I prayed and had conversations with Jesus and our Blessed Mother. Through these visits, I came to realize that I had to accept that a cure for my father was not likely to occur. I gradually began to ask that my father's passing be as easy as possible for him and for us. After my father died, I found out that my mother's prayers had been identical to mine!

It was following the death of my father that I found myself praying beside my dear mother at holy Mass that Sunday. As I reflect back, it started as a Mass most of us have experienced from time to time where we seem to just *go through the motions*. Prayerful, of course, but there are perhaps hundreds of other things in our daily life to think about. What was soon to happen on that particular Sunday jolted me into the realization of why I was there that day.

After the sermon, Mass suddenly became different for me. I began to feel as though I was starting to wake up from a particularly long nap. I became very focused and intent during the consecration. Next came a feeling of intense happiness that began to overwhelm me. No longer was sadness a part of my life. I was intensely happy and eagerly awaited holy Communion and the opportunity to receive Our Lord in this wonderful sacrament.

I remember looking around at the other parishioners and wondering if anyone else was experiencing the same thing. I wondered how they could contain their joy because I was having some difficulty containing mine!

After receiving holy Communion, my joy was even more intense. I felt as though all of my troubles had been lifted from me and replaced with pure, powerful love. I truly understood for the very first time in my life that I was a child of God.

I like to call the experience my "little taste of heaven" because I imagine that heaven must be a full realization of God's love. Although I wanted the intensity of the feeling to last forever, I realized it wouldn't. By the time Mass was over, it was gone.

In many ways though, the profound peace I experienced that day never left me. I know the incredible power of the holy Eucharist because I experienced it firsthand. I have never had such a powerful experience since then, but am thankful I did get to feel it once and that I have such a wonderful memory to cherish.

Why did this happen to me? I believe this was the way God let me know that my father was with Him, and that everything would be okay for my mother and me. Perhaps it was also meant to happen so that thirty years later I could share this story with you.

Since that time, I no longer fear death and believe it is a passage we go through so we can be with our God for eternity. That "little taste of heaven" awaits us all through the power of the holy Eucharist. It is there for each and every child of God.

Marian K. Peck   *Lebanon, Pennsylvania*

If the Eucharist is the centre and summit of the Church's life, it is likewise the centre and summit of priestly ministry. For this reason, with a heart filled with gratitude to our Lord Jesus Christ, I repeat that the Eucharist "is the principal and central raison d'être of the sacrament of priesthood, which effectively came into being at the moment of the institution of the Eucharist".

Masses Around the World

On December 25, 1990, John Quigley, O.F.M., and I celebrated Mass at the Altar of the Magi, which was fewer than fifteen feet from the Silver Star marking the spot of Jesus' birth. That star is in the grotto under Bethlehem's Basilica of the Nativity. We had previously assisted at the midnight Mass celebrated in St. Catherine Parish, the Latin-rite parish physically attached to that basilica.

Our 3:00 a.m. Mass in English was understood by few of the people devoutly praying in the corridors close to the altar. That didn't matter because everyone understood perfectly what the Church was celebrating in this place and on this date.

Three days earlier, John and I had concelebrated Mass at Jesus' tomb in the Basilica of the Holy Sepulcher in Jerusalem. We were joined by two other friars. That space can hold only four grown men standing shoulder to shoulder. But there we were, celebrating the Paschal Mystery in the tomb of Jesus! I almost pinched myself to verify that this was indeed happening.

For six and a half years I worked at the international headquarters of the Order of Friars Minor in Rome. During those years and in later visits, I assisted at numerous Masses in St. Peter's Basilica and in St. Peter's Square. I concelebrated the Chrism Mass in the basilica at least twice, and a few days before my return to the United States was able to concelebrate the pope's morning Mass in his private chapel.

All these occasions were memorable and reinforced that ours is a worldwide Church. But every other Mass that I have celebrated in my twenty-nine years as a priest (including Masses in China, Japan, Taiwan, Greece and Turkey) has been a linking of a particular group of believers to the worldwide Church through the Eucharist, food for our journey as disciples and a foretaste of the heavenly banquet.

I have always had a special fondness for the prayer that the celebrant says immediately before the sign of peace: Lord Jesus Christ, you said to your apostles: I leave you peace, my peace I give you. Look not on our sins, but on the faith of your Church, and grant us the peace and unity of your kingdom where you live for ever and ever.

In heaven there will be no Eucharist as we know it because we will already be totally and forever in God's presence. But here below, we have great need of the Eucharist as the place where, like the disciples in Emmaus, we recognize the Lord Jesus in a unique way and are strengthened to spread His good news by word and example.

Father Pat McCloskey, OFM   *Cincinnati, Ohio*

When I Have a Need

Whenever I have a need, I always try to ask Jesus for the answer as I am on my way up the aisle to receive the Eucharist. I believe that many healings have been granted to me at that time. After all, to receive the blessed Lord physically must mean that He will *clean up* the home He's going into.

One morning, about ten years ago in Lynwood Parish in Perth, I was walking towards the altar to receive the Eucharist when I said, "Lord, I have two needs today that I want you to heal." Then I told Him what they were.

I was amazed to see that when the priest gave me the sacred Host that morning, he accidentally gave me two of them. I knew then that once again my Lord had heard my prayers.

The sad part of this story is that after Mass I quietly told my friend, the priest, about this. He laughed and said, "You have such simple faith, Kath." I didn't feel that he was paying me a compliment with those words, although I took it to be so. God bless that precious priest.

Kath M. Ryan   *Halls Creek, Western Australia, Australia*

A Little Prayer for a Long Trip

Our church, St. Peter the Fisherman of Mountain Home, Arkansas, has been very blessed to have perpetual eucharistic adoration for over nine years now. Our congregation has volunteers in the adoration chapel twenty-four hours a day, seven days a week. My husband Joe and I have had the same hour since adoration started at our church. We are there from 5:00–6:00 a.m. every Thursday morning.

Eucharistic adoration has always been a wonderful way to start our day. Over the years, when planning any travels, we have always felt our hour at adoration was a good way to start a trip. With that in mind, we planned a trip to Colorado a few years ago to attend our niece Aly's wedding. We would leave after our hour at church.

As usual, we spent our hour of adoration that morning in quiet meditation, spiritual reading and prayer. Just before we left at the end of our hour, we each prayed a simple, short prayer request for a safe journey. We headed west at 6:05 a.m.

Oddly enough, our problems started in the town of Peculiar, Missouri. After refueling, our good old Chevy wouldn't start. We were fortunate to be quickly noticed by an attendant who surmised the problem might be a bad starter. He secured a local company to pick up a new starter and install it for us. After the kindly attendant had left for the day, the car once again wouldn't start. We got a jump from another stranger and got back on the road.

In less than an hour, somewhere near Kansas City, the car started to choke, stutter, and eventually died completely on the side of a road near an exit ramp. Once again we were lucky. We saw a garage nearby where we purchased a new battery. Soon we were on the road again.

While driving on the Kansas Tollway, we thought we heard a slight noise from one of the tires, so we pulled over and checked the tires. No tire problems, but then the car wouldn't start again. Within minutes, a highway patrolman stopped to help.

In the *very small world* department, he asked where we were from in Arkansas, and said he was going to visit his in-laws in Mountain Home soon. Upon our return home we discovered that his in-laws were St. Peters parishioners! The patrolman jump-started the car and followed us to a service station he recommended. The station people stayed late, installed a new alternator, and once again we were on our way.

About an hour west of Topeka, with the sun near to setting ahead of us, Joe innocently commented that thankfully about the only thing that hadn't happened to us, and the car, was a flat tire. It wasn't thirty seconds later that we were startled by the unmistakable, dreaded, loud noise of a rear tire blowing out!

We safely pulled over, changed to the small spare, and drove to a small convenience store that was just closing. Tacked near their pay phone was a business card for a local tire dealer. When we called him we discovered he usually closed early on Thursdays, but had been puttering around his store for no particular reason for the past hour—an hour beyond his usual closing time. He gave us directions to his store and we bought a new replacement tire. Then, we were on the road—again.

Thankfully, we arrived safely in Colorado the next day and on time! The wedding of Aly and Shaun was wonderful and the time spent with family and friends in the beautiful Rockies was awesome. With no further car problems (well, we did have a new starter, alternator, battery and tire...) we took the scenic route home to Arkansas.

The thing that stands out most in our minds about our trip is that, in spite of four potentially very dangerous situations with serious car problems, we traveled with a constant answer to our simple, short prayer, prayed at the end of our eucharistic adoration hour. It was one small, simple prayer that was powerful enough to be answered again and again. Praise, thanks and glory to God!

Diane E. Stefan   *Mountain Home, Arkansas*

 The Second Vatican Council saw in pastoral charity the bond which gives unity to the priest's life and work. This, the Council adds, "flows mainly from the Eucharistic Sacrifice, which is therefore the centre and root of the whole priestly life".

God Is Present

I will be celebrating my forty-fourth anniversary as a priest in June, praise God. The moments that have been most precious for me are those of celebrating the holy sacrifice of the Mass. I have had the privilege to do so in several rites, and it is in the breaking of the bread and the drinking of the Precious Blood that I know for a fact that God is present.

Jesus told St. Faustina that many receive Him as a "dead object," so I make certain that I receive Him in the fullness of His life, with deepest awareness of His wanting to give all graces needed and desired. For the past several months this has been a cry for holiness for all those present, and for priests and religious. They are the leaven, the salt of the earth, which helps all to recognize and know that all baptized are salt of the earth and light of the world. As long as we are all in total union with the Lamb of God who takes away the sins of the world, we may, "Ask and you shall receive." I know I have and do.

Father Richard J. Drabik, MIC   *Stockbridge, Massachusets*

I Knew in That Instant

Another Mass, another Host, and another Sunday of wondering, "Am I the only one who receives Communion, but questions the Real Presence?" Then I felt the guilt. Oh, the guilt. I am one to embrace guilt. I felt guilty about being a good mother, guilty about being a good wife, and guilty about being a good Catholic.

My conversion to the Catholic faith, at the age of twenty-three, was a surprise to only one person—me. An ancestral history of Protestants came to a climatic end with my birth in a Catholic hospital run by the Benedictine sisters. After I was born, a loving priest made the sign of the cross over my mother's bulging tummy and declared, "She will be a wonderful Catholic!"

Attending Sunday morning Mass with a classmate and her family on sleepover weekends was a special event for me. No, I did not like the 5:00 a.m. wake up call, nor the absence of breakfast, nor the stern looks when I asked, "Why do you pray to statues?" However, I loved the peaceful feeling during the Mass, and the unfamiliar language made me feel like I was in the presence of God.

Later on, during my confirmation process to become Catholic, I did not question my Catholic lessons, but did wonder how a piece of man-made bread could become the body and blood of Christ. As a child, when my mother was avoiding an uncomfortable question from me, she would say, "Just because I said so!" I decided that I could accept the Real Presence, just because the priest *said so*.

My guilt about questioning the Real Presence continued at each Sunday Mass, each reception of the Eucharist, and every time I said a special thank you prayer. Then, one day a new friend suggested that I ask God to show me the truth of the Real Presence. Wow! Why didn't I think of that? I knew, though, that if God did not answer my prayer, I would absorb more guilt because I would think I didn't phrase my question to Him correctly.

Little did I know that when I prayed that special prayer the following Sunday, that God would choose that day to reveal Himself to me as the body and blood of Christ in that little round wafer. As it dissolved on my tongue, I knew in that instant that He is truly real in the blessed Eucharist, and that He wants me to receive Him daily, whenever possible. I have been transformed since that Sunday; there is joy, love, and peace in my heart. I'm still working on the *guilt* part of my life, though, because, He *said so!*

Trudy L. Doramus   *Fort Meyers, Florida*

The centrality of the Eucharist in the life and ministry of priests is the basis of its centrality in the pastoral promotion of priestly vocations.

I Didn't Die

A long time ago I got very sick from a mosquito bite. I had high fever, and a headache that was so painful, it seemed like my head was going to explode. All my bones were in pain, and I felt like I had been beaten. Light bothered my eyes, so I had to keep them closed.

I wasn't able to take care of my three children because I was extremely weak, and was bedridden. My husband, Juan, was in charge of the house and the kids, and my mother, Rosa, came every day to help.

After a week, I felt worse and thought my time was over. I thought I was going to die. I said, "Oh God, I can do nothing, so here I am." Then, Sunday came, and I asked my mother to turn the television on so I could listen to the Mass. I still couldn't open my eyes.

From my bed, I listened to the holy Mass attentively. I followed along, listening, praying, and living each part. Then came the consecration, and Communion. I lay on my bed thinking, "Oh, Lord, I can't receive the holy body of my God!" I wished with all my heart and soul to receive my dear Jesus, and I'm in tears just remembering this.

For a moment, with the *eyes of my soul*, I saw Him wearing a white tunic. It was my risen Lord, Himself. He was coming to me smiling, carrying a gold ciborium, and a Host in His holy hands. He came near and gave me the Eucharist.

There are no words to fully describe this experience. I can only add that after that, the fever stopped. I opened my eyes, and woke up the next day. I didn't die! Thank you, Lord, for your great love that makes you stay hidden in the holy Eucharist.

Don't be afraid to trust in the real presence of Our Lord in the Eucharist. Visit, adore, pray, and give thanks to the risen Lord in the tabernacle. He is there like a prisoner, waiting for our love. He is waiting for us, let's not leave Him alone. Jesus, I trust in you.

Nivia Gonzalez   *Arecibo, Puerto Rico*

A Gentle Lesson

When our parish began receiving Communion under both species, the Eucharist and the Precious Blood, it was a new experience for all of us. One day, when we had just started this, I was on my way to receive Communion and noticed that the pastor had an unusual blue and gold chalice with small gems on the side. It was very unique and quite beautiful.

While I was walking up the aisle to receive Communion, the cynical, unbidden thought came to my mind that I didn't think he would ever use that beautiful chalice for us. I was appalled that I would think such a thing, and quickly asked for forgiveness for such a mean thought.

After I had received the sacred Eucharist and was walking to join the line to receive the Precious Blood, I saw the pastor coming down the steps from the altar. He was carrying the beautiful chalice in his hands. It was almost as if he was intercepting me, and I was the first to receive from this beautiful cup. I was so overcome that I almost cried right there. Father couldn't have known what I was thinking, but Our Lord did, and it's an experience I've never forgotten.

Anne Caron   *Hartford, Connecticut*

Who Is Worthy?

We priests offer the holy sacrifice of the Mass as if it were our last Mass on earth. The consecrated bread and wine is immersed in a brilliant shinning light that is reflected from the host of angels, and from the person of our Blessed Mother standing by the altar with the priest. Who is worthy to receive Jesus in the Eucharist? None of us! But Jesus calls us to come to Him, to eat and drink from the cup for the forgiveness of our sins.

Father John V. Ahern   *Liverpool, New York*

I Know Only You Can Heal

A few years ago our parish had eucharistic adoration one Sunday evening a month from six to ten o'clock. I always took the last hour from 9:00 to 10:00 p.m.

It was wintertime and on this particular night, I felt like I was coming down with a cold. As I knelt there praying, I began to feel worse. My throat was hurting, I began to ache all over, and I was very cold. I looked at my watch and it was only 9:45 p.m. All I wanted to do was go home, have a cup of hot tea, take a hot bath and go to bed. I didn't see how I was going to make it until the end of the hour.

Our priest was in the rectory and I was thinking to myself, "Okay father, you can come over early and put Jesus away. I just want to go home." Then I remembered that at a Marian peace conference I had recently attended, the priest told us how he once took a baby that had a severe skin ailment up to the tabernacle, and placed the infant's hand on it. Then the priest prayed and asked Jesus to make her well, and she was healed.

I bowed my head in prayer and then looked at Jesus in the monstrance and said, "I know only you can heal. Please reach your healing hand out, touch my throat, and make me well. Let me be able to spend these last few minutes with you in prayer."

Within just a few seconds my throat quit hurting, I didn't ache anymore, nor was I cold. I was able to spend the remaining time with Jesus in prayer. When I got up the next morning, I had no sign of a cold or sore throat. Thank you good and gentle Jesus for healing me that night!

Beverly A. Lynn   *Caney, Kansas*

The Eucharist thus appears as the culmination of all the sacraments in perfecting our communion with God the Father by identification with his only-begotten Son through the working of the Holy Spirit.

Miracles of the Holy Eucharist

The miracles of the holy Eucharist that take place at every Mass are astounding. The healings that occur include physical, emotional and mental, but the greatest gift of all healings is the realization of God's love for us in the person of Jesus Christ.

We become tabernacles when we receive Jesus in the Eucharist. At the moment we receive Him, life is given to our souls. It's like a nuclear explosion that takes place inside of us.

Father John V. Ahern   *Liverpool, New York*

I Knew I Was Forgiven

About twenty-seven years ago my husband and I were living in the small town of Rockyford, Alberta. My husband befriended the local parish priest, Father Wrigley, who would stop and chat at the post office where Doug was postmaster.

My husband was always somewhat leery of anyone who had anything to do with religion. Surprisingly, he had a good rapport with this priest. He told Father Wrigley that we were married four years ago in the United Church in Lethbridge, and that I had always wished that we had been married in the Catholic Church—the church I had grown up in. Since I had married outside the Church, I was not able to receive holy Communion, and I had a great longing to be able to receive it again.

There were a lot of things in my past that needed to be cleaned up. Father Wrigley was very good in helping me through the sacrament of reconciliation. He told me to read the Bible, especially Psalm 103. When I read verse 12, "As far as the east is from the west, so far has He put our transgressions," it was as if a great weight had been lifted off my shoul-

Vocational Signs

This is a story of my discernment and gaining answers through the Eucharist. The year was 1993 in Pittsburg, Pennsylvania. I was discerning a possible late vocation and so I went to daily Mass and several devotions. One morning, as I attended Mass at St. Anthony Chapel in Pittsburgh, I told the Lord, "OK, if you want me to be a priest, make something strange, very strange happen when I receive you in holy Communion."

When I received, two Hosts were stuck together! One was hanging from the other, not side by side, but hanging! The priest tried to get them apart, but they would not separate and so I received both. Now, I know that Hosts sometimes stick together, but hanging from each other at the very time I had asked for this sign was amazing.

During this same time period I had been instrumental in reinstating the First Friday adoration at my parish of St Catherine. Each time I went to adoration, the number *2900* came to me very clearly. I did not know what it meant, so I decided I should play that number in the lottery. I did but I never hit. Later when I went to find out more information about becoming a priest, I found out that the address of the seminary was 2900 Noblestown Road!

I understood these as special signs of Jesus asking me to be a priest.

Father Anthony Gargotta   *Natrona Heights, Pennsylvania*

Now Is the Time We Pray for You

In August of 2003, my husband was diagnosed with multiple myeloma, a dreadful cancer for which there is no cure. Luckily though, there are treatments for this disease.

Before Dan's diagnosis, I was deeply involved in three church communities in our area. I was active in rosary groups, eucharistic adoration, and as a lector. After his diagnosis, I cut back on my involvement with these ministries. For a short while, I was not active at all, and then I began to realize how much I missed these things. I especially missed eucharistic adoration, so I returned to that ministry first. During my hour of adoration, I always felt the peace of the Eucharist. I went into the hour feeling tired and stressed, and always came out more rested and refreshed than when I had arrived.

After the first line of treatment began to decrease in it's effectiveness for Dan's cancer, we were told that we needed to go to the Mayo Clinic in Rochester, Minnesota. It was decided that Dan needed a stem cell transplant, using his own stem cells. While we were there, we lived in a facility called The Gift of Life Transplant House, three blocks from the Mayo Clinic. We stayed there from December 8th, the feast of the Immaculate Conception, until January 31st, which meant we were away from home for Christmas.

During that time, my prayer life dried up. I tried without success to pray the rosary, and tried to simply sit in God's presence at Mass, but found that any time I tried to pray, there were no words. I was exhausted. My friend comforted me when I told her of my difficulty in praying. She said, "That's all right. Now is the time we pray for you." It meant a lot to me to hear that reassurance.

All of my time was spent taking care of my husband. By the end of the day, I could only mutter a quick prayer of goodnight to God. In the morning, I would try to say a quick hello. I was not able to attend daily Mass, nor was I able to go to the adoration chapel which was only a few short blocks from the Gift of Life Transplant House. I felt like I was stranded in a desert where I was mute, trapped, and unable to communicate with my Lord. These were the most difficult days of my life.

Our God is a God who gives us hope. One of my main desires was to be able to attend Mass on Sundays, and all of the feast days during this sacred time of Advent. I feel blessed to say that I did find a church or a chapel where I could be present for Mass on those days. While I was at Mass though, I was there much more physically than spiritually. However, the Mass and Eucharist did seem to bolster my strength and push me through the trying days and nights we faced.

As caregiver for my husband, I was on call twenty-four hours a day. Because of the chemotherapy and other medications he received, Dan suffered a great deal. My heart shattered the first time he asked me to push him around in a wheelchair because he did not have the energy or the strength to walk to his appointment at the Mayo Clinic.

When we returned home, things didn't change regarding my prayer life or my stress for about a month. The words still weren't there, even though I tried. I'm happy to say that my prayer life is now slowly returning, and Dan is feeling better. We are hopeful that the stem cell transplant is successful, but won't have a true idea for another month.

Today, when I look back at that time from December, 2003, to January, 2004, it is clear to me that it was through eucharistic adoration, and the continued prayers of friends and family, that we were strengthened during that extremely difficult time of our lives. Jesus, through the intercession of the Mother of God, pulled us up by our bootstraps and carried us through those challenging days.

No one could go through what we did, and survive, without God. When I cried out, "My God, why have you forgotten us?" He showed me that He didn't forget us. He carried us and continues to surround us with His love and forgiveness.

Mallory Hoffman   *North Mankoto, Minnesota*

...a distinguished writer of the Byzantine tradition voiced this truth: in the Eucharist "unlike any other sacrament, the mystery [of communion] is so perfect that it brings us to the heights of every good thing: here is the ultimate goal of every human desire, because here we attain God and God joins himself to us in the most perfect union".

A Sacred Moment

Our need for comfort was great as we hurried to our church, the Church of Scotland, for the Watchnight Service on Christmas Eve. It was our first Christmas without our mother, who had died suddenly in March of that year, and our hearts were filled to the breaking point with sorrow that night. To our great dismay, the service had already started and the doors had been closed by the time we arrived. We stood outside the church in stunned, numbed silence. Afraid to enter, we timidly retreated and began our walk home.

In the distance, we could see the lights from the Catholic church. After some debate, the four of us decided we should go in and have a look. I was nineteen years old, and was with my older sister and brother, and my younger brother.

We entered through a side door into the packed vestibule. I remember holding my little brother by the hand as I squeezed past people so we could see further into the church. We had no idea what was happening, but we were inside, and even though we could not see the altar, we were happy to be there.

Eventually, a bell rang out and people began to kneel. Somehow, I was certain that something holy was happening. The pain in my heart lessened, and I knelt on the floor. I knew He was there. My God was there. He saw me, He knew me, and He soothed my sorrow. That sacred moment continues to be precious to my heart.

Sometime later, when the consecration was explained to me, I was overwhelmed to learn that God had chosen that special moment to reveal Himself to me. It was during that most holy and sacred moment of the Mass when the priest said, "This is my body which is given up for you."

Three years later, I left the Church of Scotland to enter the Catholic Church. What love our God has for us! He chose to die for each one of us personally. We are His personal choice, and we each must respond to His individual call for us. We must personally choose the way He has chosen for us so that we may glorify and praise Him every day of our lives.

I thank Our Lord for calling us and ask Him to help us to always respond to His call, no matter what path He is leading us to. I pray, "Thy will be done."

Catherine Sweeney   *Kinross, Scotland*

Now I know

Today is March 27, 2004. We have just finished celebrating a Mass for my Mother's anniversary of death. She died on March 31, 2000. below is an excerpt of Mother's note, verbatim. A copy of this was given to me after Mother's funeral. Mother died talking proudly and happily about her thirteen children according to the nurse who attended to her. Now I know where my Mother received her courage and strength. It was from Jesus! When I was younger, I did not quite understand why Mother spent so much time in the church and at prayer. Now I know! Thank you, Jesus.

1965—Santo Tomas Church in Batangas, Philippines

I was alone in the church at 3:00 p.m. (I join the Cursillo) I was at prayer in front of the Tabernacle. Praying and talking to Jesus. I was telling Him all my hardship—all my disappointments in life. Why did He take my husband from me? I was crying, full of resentment.

Suddenly, there was a glow in the Tabernacle and a loud voice telling me, "Is it not enough I have given you thirteen children?" I was stunned! I could not move. I was dazed, blinded by the glow. After a few minutes, I sat down, trying to analyze the meaning of what I heard. I kept on thinking, "Now I know my children are my wealth."

From that moment on, I did not complain about my hardship. Everyday, before I work, I say thank you Jesus for the thirteen children you have given me.

Maria Perpetua S. Siglos　　　　　*Burnaby, British Columbia, Canada*

Straight for the Altar

One afternoon, I was praying before the Blessed Sacrament in my parish church and saying the Liturgy of the Hours. At that time I was working in the airline industry and actively praying about a vocation to the priesthood. I formed the habit of praying before the Blessed Sacrament in college, and have always tried to have an hour a day there. The Blessed Sacrament and the Mother of God keep me going as a priest now.

As I was thus praying, I looked up to see a small bird fly in through the doors to the church and literally land out-of-sight behind the altar. I couldn't believe my eyes, so I walked up into the sanctuary to see what the attraction was back there, but the bird flew back out (there was nothing at all behind the altar except the bird).

I sat down to continue praying when the bird flew in the church *again* and went *straight for the altar*. It landed out-of-sight behind the altar again, where it stayed until I got up and shooed it away.

I sat down to pray before the Blessed Sacrament again, after first closing the church door so there wouldn't be a repeat performance. The psalm I was praying said this (Psalm 84): "The sparrow herself finds a home, the swallow a nest for her brood. She lays her young by your altars, Lord of Hosts, my king and my God. They are happy who dwell in your house, forever singing your praise."

I remember calling Sister Marcia Kay (an old friend of mine and member of Sister Patricia's community) and asking her what she thought God was trying to tell me. She said, "If that bird can find the altar, why can't you?!"

Now as a priest, I think of the bird, the psalms, sister's remarks, and I think, "Lord, you're not too subtle with me!"

Father Gary Zerr   *Tillamook, Oregon*

St. Teresa of Jesus wrote: "When you do not receive communion and you do not attend Mass, you can make a spiritual communion, which is a most beneficial practice; by it the love of God will be greatly impressed on you".

My Unique Perspective

Priests and lay people are renewed constantly in their eucharistic faith when they witness children for the first time receiving Eucharist. I have been privileged for many years to be a part of the first Communion bond between Jesus and children. Each new experience helps me to relive my first Communion day, and see again the face of innocent faith.

One of my favorite feast days is Corpus Christi. I am privileged to carry the monstrance, or sacred holder of the Host, in procession. The Eucharist is placed in a glass luna at the center of the monstrance. It is then that I have the unique perspective of seeing the faith and adoration of the people as they gaze upon the monstrance that I am carrying. I can see them ever so clearly through my side of the glass luna. It is as if Christ were giving me a privileged view into the hearts of His faithful.

What a rush of joy this is for the celebrant in the procession. There is no question in my mind that at these great moments I am privileged to carry *My Lord and My God.* Apart from holy Mass and my own reception of Communion, these are some of my special times of spiritual renewal in the Eucharist—first Communion days for the children, and the solemn procession of the Eucharist at Corpus Christi. God is Good!

Msgr. James M. Ribble   *Spokane, Washington*

I Was Unhappy with Her Behavior

It was a very hot Sunday morning as I was preparing for a large family birthday celebration. I was depending on our two daughters to help with all the pre-party preparations that we needed to do prior to going to Mass.

Sharon, our thirteen-year-old, was not very cooperative, and on the way to Mass I told her I was unhappy with her behavior. I led our family parade into church, entered the pew, and knelt. Bowing my head, I prayed. I asked the Lord to help heal the unhappy emotional feelings between my daughter and myself. Finishing my prayer, I sat back on the pew, and glanced at my family sitting next to me. That's when I realized Sharon was not sitting with us.

I looked around the horseshoe shaped church, and saw her sitting straight across the church from us. I felt relieved to find her in the congregation, and prayed that Jesus would heal us through His holy Eucharist.

As the ministers of the Eucharist assembled prior to the distribution of Communion, our pastor noticed that one more eucharistic minister was needed. He looked over and motioned for me to help. I was directed to be one of the two distributors on the aisle where Sharon had decided to sit.

As I was distributing the Eucharist to the long line of communicants, I saw the smiling face of Sharon with her hands raised, ready to receive the healing Eucharist from me.

During the last thirty-five years as a catechist, I have told this story many times to my teenage classes. As I look into the sweet, smiling faces of these teenagers, I know they understand the healing power of Jesus in the Eucharist.

Loretta C. Wnetrzak   *Charlotte, North Carolina*

Miracle of Peace

My mother-in-law, Veroniqua, was a very devout Roman Catholic who loved our Blessed Mother. When she was fifty-four years old, my father-in-law, who was only fifty-eight, died suddenly from a massive heart attack.

After the death of her husband, my mother-in-law experienced para-lyzing grief. She was devastated, and wanted to die. She couldn't stop crying and retelling the story of the morning he left for work with a pain in his chest. It got to the point where everyone was getting upset with her behaviour.

One day during my lunch break at work, I went to Mass and offered my Communion with Jesus for her healing and peace. After I returned to my office, she called to tell me that a miracle had happened during her lunch at home. She said she had been crying, and suddenly the *greatest* peace came over her. She felt wonderful and, "Just like that!" she finally accepted Dad's death.

When she called me with the good news, Mom did not know that I had gone to Mass that day for her intentions. Since I was the only one who would listen to her for hours as she struggled with her grief, it was me she called to share this wonderful news with. After she told me about her healing, I told her I had gone to Mass and offered my Communion for her peace during my lunch break that day.

After that, she began to grow more spiritually. She started attending charismatic meetings, and traveled to many, if not all of the shrines of our Blessed Mother throughout the world. We thank God for this miracle of the Eucharist!

Helena Lieskovsky, SFO   *Sherwood Park, Alberta, Canada*

Our Day Begins

Our day begins with morning prayer and the Eucharist. The sacrificial meal of the Lord is, without doubt, the epicenter of my spiritual life. There are many ways to pray. The Liturgy of the Eucharist satisfies my daily need to listen to and speak with our Triune God, and to be nourished by the body and blood, soul and divinity of our brother Jesus the Christ. This is certainly the best way to grow as a member of Christ's mystical body.

Father Clyde Young, OFM   *Cincinnati, Ohio*

Healing and Peace

In the summer of 2001, I was weary and depressed by memories of traumatic events in my childhood that had recently surfaced. Although I was working with an experienced and gifted therapist and taking medication, there were many times when I felt like I was at the end of my strength. Through those months, Sunday Mass was an oasis for me in a desert of pain and despair. One Sunday in particular stands out from the others, and I wrote in my journal of the experience.

As I knelt on the hard, leather kneeler and prayed before Mass on Sunday, August 19, 2001, I heard God speaking to my heart: "You are never alone. I am with you always. I am watching over you, to keep you safe from all harm, to protect you from falling, to empower you to complete your journey toward wholeness and healing."

Then, during the Mass, the psalm response for that Sunday was: "Lord, come to my aid!" and the verse from Psalm 40 declared: "The Lord heard my cry. He drew me out of the pit of destruction…He made firm my steps…Many shall look on in awe and trust in the Lord."

Tears ran down my cheeks as God's message to me was echoed in the psalm for that Sunday. How did it happen that the words of David, written centuries before and chosen for this Sunday in 2001, echoed the message God had given me just moments before Mass began?

Jesus brought healing and peace to me that day. I was cradled in the loving arms of God.

Janet L. Smith   *Haymarket, Virginia*

Every commitment to holiness, every activity aimed at carrying out the Church's mission, every work of pastoral planning, must draw the strength it needs from the Eucharistic mystery and in turn be directed to that mystery as its culmination.

Eucharist Is Life Giving

I am a sister in the Congregation of the Handmaids of the Holy Child Jesus. The only thing I can say about the Eucharist is, "Taste and see, you know that the Lord is good." At first, when I started receiving holy Communion as a new convert, I did not feel any effects in my life. I said, "Our own is better than this," because I converted from the Protestant to the Catholic.

One day they took me to Benediction, and during the time the priest was putting the large Host in the monstrance, I saw somebody carrying me in his hand. As the priest was carrying the Host, he said, "I am the life, the way and the truth, do not doubt, believe." I looked around but I saw no one.

I tried to sing what they were singing, but I didn't know how to sing the "Tantum Ergo" at that time, but that was what they were singing. Since then my attitude to the holy Eucharist has changed. The greatest thing God has done for me is, there is not a day I have not been receiving Communion. I have not stayed in a place where there is no Mass. The most important thing Jesus is doing for me is, everyday is new happiness and inner joy. I don't know how to express. He is really the life giving.

Sister Agnes Nneka Nnodu   *Winnipeg, Manitoba, Canada*

Life Giving and Saving Grace

In the year 2000, I transferred from Pittsburgh, Pennsylvania, where I worked mostly as a preacher and evangelist to Cincinnati, Ohio, to begin a career in teaching. It was a very painful move that coincided with the loss of a network of familiar friendships and ties to the parish communities I had served for four years.

That very same year, my father had a major heart attack, which raised my awareness of mortality and the fear of loss to an all time high. I desperately needed a sense of belonging, a place to feel grounded, balanced, loved and accepted. I missed my old community and I was such an emotional wreck, I had to take a break from preaching.

Those were difficult times, but through them I discovered something wonderful. Jesus called me closer to His presence in the Eucharist than I had ever felt before. Matched to that sense of fear, loneliness, and isolation was an invitation to receive the Eucharist with love and devotion. The sign of peace at Mass, that seemingly hurried hug or handshake and the words, "Peace be with you," became a sign of hope and an invitation to endure and to grow. The Lord saw me through this time of depression and doubt, right into the loving arms of yet another parish of His big Christian family.

That same year, with my whole family gathered around, I celebrated Palm Sunday Mass at my father's hospital bed. He held a little cross made of palms and we placed all of our trust for his recovery in the hands of our Savior Jesus Christ. Today, my father and mother are both alive and as well as can be expected. They live in Uniontown, Pennsylvania, near the St. Anthony Friary. They are both members of the Secular Franciscan Order.

Listening to the Palm Sunday readings with their tremendous emotional highs and lows has come to signify for me the great ups and downs that families experience when facing medical emergencies and other life-changing events. The Mass encompasses both the cross and the Resurrection of Jesus. He feeds us with life giving and saving grace. The Mass continues to be a daily place where I am fed by the Lord with His word, the loving embrace of His body in my brothers and sisters, and the precious gift of His body and blood. I know my life is sustained by the Lord in the Eucharist. I invite anyone who is hungry for meaning and consolation, to seek it in the food which is our Lord.

Father Mark J. Hudak, OFM   *Cincinnati, Ohio*

Who Should I Pray For?

I experienced a miracle of the Eucharist during a Cursillo retreat weekend in October of 2000. At the time of the retreat, I had an array of things going on in my life. I had changed jobs and had taken a position teaching children with autism, which I love, but the first year was quite lively.

Our family had taken in a wonderful foster son who had developmental delays along with the issues that come with moving from six different placements in three years, and my husband Richard was in end-stage renal failure from an inherited kidney disease. We knew the time was coming that he would need dialysis, and judging by test results, that time would be sooner than later. We were ready. He had already had surgery to create a fistula in his arm so that when the time arrived, dialysis could begin without interruption.

Friday afternoon of the retreat came and we went to Mass. I love Mass. As a new Catholic, I'm still enamored by the Mass. It is a tremendous gift, and if the presence of our Savior in the Eucharist can't lift a soul closer to the Lord, then I don't know what can.

I had realized through the retreat presenters that if anything was going to be accomplished in my Christian walk, it would be through prayer and seeking God's face. During the intentions presented before Our Lord at Mass that Friday, I silently asked the Lord who I should pray for. My husband, Richard, came to my mind.

In the Eucharist we have Jesus, we have his redemptive sacrifice, we have his resurrection, we have the gift of the Holy Spirit, we have adoration, obedience and love of the Father. Were we to disregard the Eucharist, how could we overcome our own deficiency?

"Okay, I'll pray for Richard," I told Him. So, I began to pray for my husband silently in my heart. Then the Lord moved me to say Richard's name out loud, and I resisted.

"That's okay Lord. I'll just pray for him myself. It really doesn't matter if I pray silently to myself or say it out loud," I thought.

"You need to say his name out loud."

"But, Lord." I replied.

"Say his name out loud."

"But, you're a big God. You don't need me to say anything. You'll hear, even if I just pray here quietly to myself," I argued.

"Say it out loud." (While I'd like to think that I'm like Mary in her faith and her resounding "yes" to the Lord, obviously, I'm not even close.)

I began to think that if I didn't say something quickly, Father Hanley was going to move on and I would be furious at myself for not speaking up. Father Hanley allowed quite a long pause for intentions, and believe me, I remember well that long pause.

Finally, I resigned and prayed out loud, "For my husband Richard. He's in renal failure. Pray that the Lord provides a donor. We pray to the Lord."

"Okay, I spoke the request out loud. Are you happy now, Lord?"

The doctors, my husband, and I had never even discussed the possibility of a donor. We had only talked about how many patients live and do fine on dialysis, and had started looking at adjustments in lifestyle that would be needed as we began this life saving treatment. We were comforted knowing that dialysis saves lives that would otherwise end much sooner for people with renal failure. We were very grateful that dialysis was an option and were well aware that it was not even an option fifty years ago. So, where did the request for a donor come from?

We continued with Mass and I was mortified. I had never spoken an intention at Mass before and was rather embarrassed. As I walked up to receive holy Communion, Brenda, who had been at my table for the weekend, grabbed my arm and asked, "Was that you? Did you request prayer for your husband?" I told her it had been me, and she responded, "Be sure to talk to me after Mass." I was sure she had an encouraging story to share with me. Maybe she had a family member in renal failure as well and we could exchange notes.

After Mass, Brenda explained that her nephew had been typed and evaluated as a live kidney donor, and had been praying that the Lord would show him who he needed to donate to. This nephew was Erick, Kathy's son. Kathy had also been a team member for the weekend. As I stood outside the chapel that afternoon, I could almost hear the Lord humorously say, "Happy now, Deb?" I was stunned into humility. I had fought the spirits leading me during the intentions, and now it became crystal clear why the Lord continued rather adamantly to prompt me to say my petition out loud.

Another part of the miracle is that Brenda has macular degeneration. Her vision consists of blurred images at a well-lit, close range. Brenda and I had spent time together at the same small group table talking, laughing and praying. When I spoke my intention at Mass, I was directly across from Brenda, but we were about 30 feet away from each other in a dimly lit chapel. She could not see me.

Kathy had been in the kitchen and did not recognize who had spoken the prayer request during Mass, so she asked Brenda if she knew who it was. Brenda knew it had been me, not by sight, but because she knew my voice. The Lord had this plan all along, and in His providence had placed Brenda and myself at the same table so that even though she could not see my face, she knew my voice. The providence of God is amazing!

After a period of medical testing and evaluations for Erick and Richard, we were notified that they were an excellent match. Again, I became very grateful for the Lord's presence and persistence during Mass that afternoon in October. I know that from now on when the Lord says speak, it's probably a good idea to speak. When He says, "Jump," I'll ask, "How high, Lord?" His power and workings are amazing. He directs our lives with purpose and His directions have reasons. We may know that reason now or later, or maybe only God will ever know the reason. We must trust that there is always a reason for how He is guiding our ways.

The day of the transplant arrived. I had never met Erick, and when we did meet, all I could say before he was taken into surgery was, "Thank you." I also realized that all I could say to the Lord was, "Thank you," for

His gift of life to us in the cross and in the Eucharist. There will be no balancing the scales. I can never pay our Lord back for His total sacrifice on the cross. I realized that day that our Savior keeps giving His all to us in the sacrament of the Eucharist so that we can, in turn, have the strength we need to give our all to Him.

It was the day before being discharged from the hospital that we were able to talk to Erick and express our gratitude. In giving his gift of life to Richard, Erick had experienced complications and needed more than the expected time to heal. His recovery was difficult and painful. We told him that there was no way we could ever fully express our appreciation in a way that could equally measure the gift he gave, not just to Richard, but to us as a family. Erick's response was, "God just asks us to pass it on."

We can be a glimpse of the glory of our Lord in the things that we do. Can we pay Him back? Can we balance the scales? No, but we can point the way to the one that is the source of this gift. And that's all He asks.

There is a song by Avalon that I heard when I first came into the church. After our encounter with the Lord in the presence of the holy Eucharist at Mass that day, it has become my heart song. The chorus says:

For as long as I shall live, I will testify to love,
I'll be a witness in the silences when words are not enough.
With every breath I take, I will give thanks to God above,
For as long as I shall live, I will testify to love.

Deb G. Goerger   *Dover, Deleware*

The path itself is long and strewn with obstacles greater than our human resources alone can overcome, yet we have the Eucharist, and in its presence we can hear in the depths of our hearts, as if they were addressed to us, the same words heard by the Prophet Elijah: "Arise and eat, else the journey will be too great for you" (1 Kg 19:7).

I Am with You

Just ten weeks prior to my ordination, at the age of twenty-seven years, I was diagnosed with breast cancer. This resulted in my ordination being moved ahead from May 20, 2000 to March 25, 2000 (the Solemnity of the Annunciation).

I was ordained on a Saturday morning and began chemotherapy on the following Wednesday. Since my diagnosis, and months of chemotherapy and radiotherapy, I have had many opportunities to celebrate the Eucharist. However, no celebration of the Eucharist can compare to the actual Mass celebrated on the day of my ordination. For not only was this the first time I was able to celebrate the Eucharist, it was for me a sacramental moment filled with joy and pain.

Many people attending the Mass said they spent most of the ordination ceremony either in tears or laughing. I suppose they, like me, had come to realize through my very public experience of cancer, how precious and fragile life is. Through the Eucharist, this fragility of life finds its meaning.

I remember a definition of the Eucharist used by the well-known Australian biblical scholar, Father Francis Moloney, SDB. He says, "The Eucharist is a body broken for a broken people." Over the last four years, I have come to see that this definition is so true. Each time I celebrate the Eucharist, be it at our cathedral or with a patient at their sick bed, I realize how, through this sacramental moment, we come into contact with the One who said to His frightened disciples, "Do not be afraid. I am with you." It is He who says to each of us, through the joys and struggles of our lives, "Duc in altum," put out into the deep.

Father David Catterall   *Wollongong, New South Wales, Australia*

"Duc in altum - Put out into the deep" (Lk 5:4): Christ spoke these words to Peter after he and his companions had toiled all night without catching anything. We heard them in the Gospel of this Sunday's liturgy: after preaching to the crowds precisely from Peter's boat, Jesus said to him: "Put out into the deep and let down your nets for a catch" (Lk 5:4). Trusting in Him, Simon and the other apostles cast their nets and caught a great number of fish (cf. Lk 5:5-6).

John Paul II, *Angelus*, Sunday, 4 February 2001

"Master...at your word I will let down the nets" (Lk 5:5). This is how Simon Peter responds to Christ's invitation. He does not hide his disappointment over the unsuccessful labour of a whole night; yet he obeys the Master: he sets aside his own beliefs as a fisherman who knows his job well, and trusts in him. We know what happens next. Seeing the nets full of fish, Peter realizes the distance between him, "a sinful man," and the one he now recognizes as "Lord." He feels *interiorly transformed,* and at the Master's invitation he leaves his nets and follows him. The fisherman of Galilee thus becomes an apostle of Christ, the rock on which Christ will found His Church.

Homily of John Paul II,   Pastoral visit to St. Alphonsus Mary Liguori Parish, Sunday, 4 February 2001

Christ in the Monstrance

The Host in the monstrance invites me to spend time with our ever present Lord. It is an honor to come into this unique form of worship that speaks so much in total silence.

I can feel the holiness, peace, and calm of Jesus consecrated in the Host when I am at adoration, and think the unbelief of Christ in the Eucharist is one of the major apostasies of our time. To say that He is not spiritually there is a lie that tries to plant itself in our minds. His victory over sin, evil and death allows us the privilege to seek His presence in the unleavened bread.

As I approach the altar, I genuflect in reverence and quietly sit as close to the altar as possible. I close my eyes much of the time to feel His holiness, and to block out distractions as I pray for others, the Church, and for special intentions. My conversation is a mental dialog with an old trusted friend who gives me His full attention, and who has mine as I pray.

Sometimes it may take an hour to calm my thoughts to a still plane so Christ can enter in. He is an unseen, radiant light that fills my spirit and delivers peace and calm to my mind, soul, and body. All fear, pain, and worldly cares are expelled during this time. The time as we know it in this world passes quickly when I am with Him, without me being aware of it.

I find myself in contemplation, and completely absorbed into another place of holiness during eucharistic adoration. I feel a gentle but firm pulling of my soul towards the monstrance, as Christ pines to unite with me in spirit. It is hard to finally decide when to leave, as this place is peace without conflict. I end with another genuflection and leave with a new strength, peace, and joy to face the problems of this life. I know I will return again. I invite you to take a few minutes to place yourself before the Blessed Sacrament.

Dennis J. Casnovsky   *Alma, Michigan*

Why Am I So Lucky?

"Through Him, with Him, in Him, in the unity of the Holy Spirit, all glory and honor is yours, almighty Father, forever and ever." This is the beauty and the mystery of the Eucharist—that we are praying through and with Christ, Our Lord. Jesus gives us His very self so that we can become one with our Triune God.

"Do this in memory of me." We enter into the love of God; that blessed exchange of giving and receiving. The Eucharist is such an awesome gift and mystery. It is a tremendous privilege to be a priest and to celebrate the Mass. Sometimes I wonder why I am so lucky.

Father Mike Maybrier   *Coffeyville, Kansas*

Inspired by love, the Church is anxious to hand on to future generations of Christians, without loss, her faith and teaching with regard to the mystery of the Eucharist. There can be no danger of excess in our care for this mystery, for "in this sacrament is recapitulated the whole mystery of our salvation".

I Didn't Want It to End

Several years ago I went through a period where I was suffering a great deal of pain in my stomach. My family doctor referred me to a gastroenterologist who admitted me to the hospital and performed an endoscopy. This is a test that examines the throat and the inside of the stomach. The doctor discovered a severe gastric ulcer, which he showed me on the screen. I was told to come back the following week for more tests, at which time the doctor would decide whether or not I needed surgery.

A couple of days after my endoscopy, my eldest son phoned me to say that a Father Theo Rustia was in town from the Philippines, and would be having a healing Mass at a church near where he lives. He wondered if his father and I would like to go to it with him. My husband and I attended Mass daily, but had never been to a healing Mass before. Given the news that I had just received from the doctor, I jumped at the chance to go.

Father Rustia celebrated the most beautiful Mass we had ever attended. I can honestly say that I had never felt as close to God as I did that night. Even though we were in church for three hours, it seemed more like thirty minutes. I didn't want it to end.

I can't emphasize enough how big a part the Eucharist played in that Mass. In fact, the importance and beauty of the Eucharist was the main theme of the entire Mass. The actual healing part of the service took only about twenty minutes, and the rest of the time was taken up with the Mass, and prayer and adoration to our heavenly Father through the gift of His body and blood.

As we all approached the altar for Communion, we could feel Jesus right there in that church with us. It was wonderful to feel that close to Him! Partaking of the Eucharist took on a whole new meaning for me that night, and it definitely changed my life for the better. That night Father Rustia made everyone see very clearly just how much the Eucharist means, and what a gift it is that Our Lord gave to us so many years ago.

After Communion, we all went up to the foot of the altar for the laying on of hands, and I must admit that I was a little nervous. When Father Rustia got to me, he suddenly stopped, looked at me, and then asked me what was wrong. I told him about my condition, and he laid his hands on my stomach, and prayed over me.

I had a feeling of euphoria that night when I left the church, and a feeling of peace had come over me. I can't even describe the extent to which it affected me. Somehow in my heart, I knew that everything was going to be okay. This priest was truly a man of God, and I definitely felt as though God had given him the power to heal.

When I went back to the hospital a few days later, one of the first tests the doctor did was another endoscopy. During the procedure, I noticed an incredulous look on his face, and he exclaimed, "This is impossible, I can't believe what I am seeing. There is no sign of the ulcer! It has completely disappeared!"

I knew at that moment that it wasn't impossible. God had cured me through His servant, Father Rustia. I was truly blessed, and to this day, there has never been any sign of the ulcer returning.

Since then, I attend Mass and receive Communion every day of the week. I have also been a lector at our church for the past several years. In addition, I am now a member of the Marian Prayer Group, and we meet each weeknight to say the rosary. Through this miraculous healing Mass, my life has changed, and definitely for the better.

This wonderful priest, Father Rustia, comes to Toronto twice a year and holds healing Masses at various churches in the diocese. My husband and I try to attend as many as we can.

Diane E. Comishen   *North York, Ontario, Canda*

In the humble signs of bread and wine, changed into his body and blood, Christ walks beside us as our strength and our food for the journey, and he enables us to become, for everyone, witnesses of hope.

Longing for Home

I was born in a rural community outside of Cleveland, Tennessee. This small town is tucked in the southeast corner of the state, right in the heart of what is known as the Bible Belt. Throughout this region, many different fundamental faiths are practiced and there are very few Catholic communities.

My family belonged to the Church of Christ, which is very different from other faiths because of several strict beliefs and practices that are unique to this religion. As I was growing up, I began to question these beliefs, and these questions ultimately led me to search for and find our Lord and Savior in the Catholic Church.

The church I was raised in preached *hell, fire, and brimstone* and that God is to be feared. We learned that He is not a loving God unless you give up everything and follow Him as the apostles did. The Church of Christ is extremely strict—teaching that the Bible is to be taken literally—a belief that was firmly instilled in me throughout my childhood. I was taught Scripture and had it memorized before I could even read. Once I learned to read, I read the Bible from cover to cover several times. Although I realize that reading the Bible doesn't make a person a scholar, I learned a lot from reading it frequently and am grateful for this practice.

Life in the Church of Christ was intense and the rules were unbendable. For example, instrumental music is not played in the Church of Christ because it is considered a sin, so songs are sung without musical accompaniment. The bread and grape juice served during the celebration of the Lord's Supper every Sunday is a memorial of Christ's passion and not the actual presence of Christ's body and blood. Consumption of alcohol is considered a sin, even though Christ used wine on several occasions.

Playing card games is sinful, even if it is an innocent child's game. Wearing makeup, going to movies, and dancing are also forbidden in the Church of Christ because it is believed that these activities will create lustful thoughts and lead to gambling and other sins that are unforgivable.

According to the Church of Christ, the Catholic Church is the scourge of the planet and many things we learned were of an anti-Catholic sentiment. These teachings greatly disturbed me and my face was smacked more than once for asking why, as true Christians, we would hate people of other faiths.

I was taught that we should call no man *father* because that title is reserved for God alone, and was told that Catholics worship statues and Mary, and not Jesus and God. I learned that the Catholic Church does not teach from Scripture, but from a different book, which I now realize is the *Catechism of the Catholic Church*. Also, reciting written prayers is considered a sin that Catholics often commit.

Baptism is another area where the Church of Christ differs from the Catholic Church. I learned that Catholics *sprinkle* babies, a type of baptism that is not valid because the word baptism means immersion or submersion, and unless you are completely submersed, your baptism is not legitimate. Also, since a baby cannot possibly understand what is going on, and since they are not at the age of reasoning or accountability, infant baptisms are not considered valid.

I do not want to sound like I am criticizing the Church of Christ and their beliefs, nor do I want to offend anyone with my testimony. My intent is to point out how strict the doctrines were that I was taught as a child, and how difficult it would be to have the courage to learn about other faiths.

Despite all of these intense religious beliefs deeply ingrained in me, I was not happy or satisfied with my faith. For many years I struggled daily with a great emptiness in my heart and soul. I felt guilty and lost. Finally, I decided that as long as I was lost, I might as well participate in worldly sins, and did all the things I had been taught were sinful…drinking, dancing, and going to movies.

The guilt I experienced was a terrible burden that made me feel emptier and even more lost. I prayed to God and was angry with Him for all the guilt I felt. When I was young, I was taught to have faith and never to question God. It wasn't until a few years ago that I understood that I had not been questioning God; I had been questioning the faith I learned as a child.

I began to realize that many things I learned in the Church of Christ weren't exactly what Scripture taught, and started to question those beliefs. I needed answers. At the same time I was afraid of what my family would do if I ventured outside of the faith, so I prayed with all my heart for the courage to explore other faith traditions. Something was missing in every faith I tried, until I stumbled into a relationship with a cradle Catholic who I would eventually marry.

My husband, Craig, and I met while we were both stationed in the military in Germany. At that time he only went to Mass on holy days of obligation. I asked him why he bothered going to church at all if he was only going on feast days a few times a year, and a short time later he began attending Mass more often.

When I returned to the United States, Craig came to Colorado where I was stationed. He immediately found a Catholic church and started going to Mass regularly. Each time he went, he came home from church very excited and on fire for his faith. After watching him return home from church several times filled with incredible peace and joy, I asked if I could go to Mass with him. He reminded me of how my family felt about the Catholic Church and I told him that they were hundreds of miles away and I didn't have to tell them, at least not yet.

Craig told me a few things about what to expect before I went to my first Mass, but there was not enough time for me to understand everything. Mass began and so did the genuflecting, standing, kneeling, and reciting of written prayers. I was overwhelmed. Then came the beginning of the consecration. The priest held up the Host and recited the words of Our Lord and Savior, "This is my body, which was given up for you, do this in remembrance of me." Then he took the cup and raised it up and said, "This is the cup of my blood. It was shed for all, do this in remembrance of me."

I began to cry and had to leave Mass so I wouldn't distract anyone. Outside I prayed and asked God why I was crying. The next week I went back to Mass, and then the week after that. I was able to control my crying but the tears continued to quietly flow, and I longed to be in communion with our Lord and Savior. I wanted the healing power of His body and blood, and had never desired anything so much in my life. At each Mass,

I prayed the blessing quietly to myself as the priest said it aloud. Finally I knew that this was what I had been searching for all those years.

I kept praying because I knew I would be leaving more than my childhood religion behind if I joined the Catholic Church. I talked with a few family members, giving them a scenario of a *friend* of mine joining the Catholic Church, and their angry reaction made it clear to me that I had a difficult choice to make. God knew I was struggling with this decision, and He soon allowed me to experience His healing power through my prayers before the Blessed Sacrament.

When our oldest son Justin was only six months old, he contracted spinal meningitis, and by the time we realized how sick he was, it was almost too late to save him. The doctors gave him a ten percent chance of surviving through the night. They asked me if I understood what they were telling me, and I sadly said yes, that they were telling me my son was more than likely going to die.

I told my husband that I needed to go to the church to pray. When we arrived, I knelt before the Blessed Sacrament and prayed with my whole heart. Instead of praying for a miracle, I prayed before my Lord as He prayed in the Garden of Gethsemane over two thousand years ago. I asked that His will be done with Justin, and that if He was to take my son, to give me the strength to accept and understand his death. I also promised that if he did live, I would raise him up to give him back to God, and that I would no longer hesitate in my conversion to Catholicism. Suddenly I understood that what I was about to loose here on earth was nothing compared to what I was to gain in heaven some day.

That night in the hospital was touch and go. When the doctor came in the next morning, he said Justin was alive not by anything he or his staff had done, but by the power of God. I knew exactly what he was talking about. I went back on my knees before the Blessed Sacrament in praise and thanks. Today my son is twenty years old and has no health problems. God truly blessed him and us with his life.

After that, I began my official journey into the Catholic Church. For a couple of years I attended RCIA, went to all of the Bible study and Church doctrine classes I could, and continuously learned about Catholicism. I spent time before the Blessed Sacrament asking for guidance, and each time I prayed, I felt His presence, love and compassion.

The transition was not easy because I struggled with what was to happen with my relationships with family members. I knew I had to put my faith in God, just as my family had taught me to do when I was a child. I prayed for the strength I would need when I told my family of my conversion, and asked Him to ease the pain they would have because of my decision to become Catholic.

On Holy Saturday, 1991, the sun was shining bright, the birds were singing, and spring was in full bloom. A new beginning was taking place all over the earth, and a new life in Christ was about to begin for me as well. Tears of joy and happiness streamed down my face as, for the first time, the priest held up the Host and then the chalice and said to me, "The body of Christ" and "The blood of Christ." I responded with a very profound, "Amen." At last my Lord and Savior was feeding me with the eternal food of His glory!

In no way do I deserve the gift of the Eucharist. It is only through His grace, mercy, and suffering on the cross that I humbly approach the altar to receive Communion at His beckoning. I realize that this was the blessing I had hungered and thirsted for all those years. I want everyone to know what the Eucharist truly is and what it can do for each and every one of us.

I cannot wait to go to Mass each week because the Eucharist is what sustains me. When I am in adoration of my Lord, I often remember the days of my searching, longing, and emptiness. I never want to forget how important it is for me to come to Christ in the Eucharist, to be fed and have my thirst quenched on earth until I go home to be with Him for eternity.

When I converted to Catholicism, some friends and family members disowned me. A few have reluctantly apologized, and many still cannot find it in their hearts to forgive me for leaving their faith. They do not understand why I became Catholic even though I tried to explain my decision. They told me I was going to hell for leaving the only true church. I told them that our Lord and Savior died on the cross for all of us, and suggested that they read and study to learn the real truth about His church.

I pray for my family and friends in the Church of Christ daily, and feel no resentment towards them. They are living by what they were taught growing up, just as I once did, and I only feel love and compassion towards them.

I thank God for leading me to His Son's sacrifice, His broken body, and Precious Blood that was poured out and now fills me completely. I pray a prayer of thanksgiving each time I have the humble honor and privilege of coming to His table to receive holy Communion.

This year I had the privilege of hearing Dr. Scott Hahn, a popular Catholic apologist who is a convert to our faith, give an inspiring talk. Afterwards as he was signing books, my husband told him I was also a convert. He smiled at me and said, "Welcome home!" I am thankful to God for the sacrifice of His body and blood, and how blessed we are as Catholics to share in the holy Eucharist. At home I am—praise be to God!

Kathy French   *Gilbert, Arizona*

Come then, good Shepherd, bread divine,
Still show to us thy mercy sign;
Oh, feed us, still keep us thine;
So we may see thy glories shine
in fields of immortality.

O thou, the wisest, mightiest, best,
Our present food, our future rest,
Come, make us each thy chosen guest,
Co-heirs of thine, and comrades blest
With saints whose dwelling is with thee.

A Parent's Communion

When I was a child, every Sunday morning our family would wake up and prepare to go to church. As a child, the impact of Communion was not totally understood, but the mystery and powerfulness of Communion and God's love was reinforced by my family to set roots into my soul and spirit that would help me to grow into a firmer and stronger journey with God.

Now, as an adult, whenever I read the story of the Last Supper, I see God's great and unconditional love. As a parent, I would gratefully and lovingly take my child's place so that they might not suffer.

God, our Father, saw His children suffering. He longed to be able to hold them in the safety of His arms, to envelop them in His all empowering love, but our sin was in the way.

So the Father sent His Son, Jesus, to bear all the sins and suffering of His children; past, present and future, so that He could embrace us wholly in His loving arms, so that we could spend eternity with Him.

When I say the prayer before Communion, I am reminded of God's Love. I remember Jesus' apostles and their imperfections; how Peter denied Him, how Judas betrayed Him, how His people mocked Him, persecuted Him and put Him to death. Yet, Jesus still loved them and He still loves us.

As a parent of teenagers, when I go to Communion, I pray to have the strength and power of God's love. I pray that I might be able to see beyond the parental rejection, the "I hate you!" and all the other typical teenage remarks a child has for their parents. I pray for God to enlighten me and to keep my spirit up as He did for His apostles at the Last Supper. He knew the ones He loved and trusted so dearly would turn away from Him.

I pray my children will someday follow the Lord because of my example and trust in the Lord.

"Take this cup and drink, the cup of my blood that will be shared for you and for all men so that sin can be forgiven. Do this in memory of me."

Heidi J. Guevara   *Holtsville, New York*

All Roads Lead to Home

Bayonne, New Jersey, where my story takes place, has had many incarnations. Once the heart of a thriving seaside resort, it later became the heart of one of Standard Oil's largest oil refining facilities. My focus, however, is how in the midst of this industrial city, the heart of Jesus Christ in the tabernacle spoke to me and led me into His most perfect will.

Over twenty years ago I felt called to the monastic life. I did not know exactly what kind of religious life the Lord was calling me to and tried to explore many possibilities by visiting several monasteries around the country.

As sometimes happens in life, things can become muddled and busy, and a person can get distracted. In my case, family needs became an urgency that couldn't wait. So I put what I believed was a calling to a religious vocation on hold for years. Years slipped by and no matter what I did or where I went, I always felt a quiet calling within me that I belonged in a monastery.

The last family need that kept me from pursuing a vocation was the sickness and subsequent death of my mother in 1997. After I had the great blessing of being at her bedside at what I can only call a most peaceful and blessed death, I felt yet again the calling in my heart to become a religious.

I attended daily Mass at St. Mary's where I would pray at the feet of several of the statues in the chapel. Beautiful one hundred-year-old wooden statues of Our Blessed Lady, St. Jude and The Sacred Heart were three of my favorite places to pray.

One day, however, I felt led to a rather dark corner of the chapel. When I approached the corner where I felt led to pray, I saw the tabernacle, which could not be seen from the main part of the chapel. A person had to know where it was to find it, as it was recessed and practically hidden on one of the walls. I did not know it was there as I approached it.

When I realized it was the tabernacle, I knelt before it and prayed. Then, every night afterwards, I would arrive at Mass thirty minutes early to kneel and pray before Our Lord in the tabernacle. I couldn't find the words to describe the joy I felt for having done so.

My friends began to comment that on my return from Mass I seemed happier and more at peace. They asked me several times, "What in the world are you so happy about?" The only words I could think of to describe even in part the joy I was feeling was, "I feel like I've met a friend I haven't seen in years and we're both extremely happy to be together again."

At that moment I realized what, or rather who, was making me so happy, and why. It was Jesus Christ Himself in the tabernacle! He was leading me to pray there, and was guiding me to the vocation that neither He nor I had ever forgotten about. A vocation that I had felt led to so many years before.

As I felt called to spend increasingly more time before the Eucharist, it slowly became apparent to me that Jesus was asking me if I would like to spend the rest of my life in eucharistic adoration. How could this be? I never knew there was a possibility of such a thing! I thought being a religious would mean becoming a teacher, or nurse, or missionary etc. Never in my wildest dreams did I think I would spend the rest of my life adoring Christ in the Eucharist as a vocation!

Miracles happen and the completion of this miracle came about through the use of the computer. I went home after Mass one night and simply typed the words "eucharistic adoration" into my search engine. The first web site that came up was *The Monks of Adoration*, a religious group of men whose charism is eucharistic adoration. Very soon I found myself visiting the monks and I never left!

It has been two years since I joined the Monks of Adoration. We are working hard to build our monastery through the help of St. Joseph, our patron saint. Through daily eucharistic adoration, I find Jesus who first called me so many years ago. He, who never stopped speaking to me during those many years of wandering, and He who, in the holy Eucharist, spoke to my heart, capturing not just my attention but my heart and soul as well.

Brother Mark Edward Debrizzi   *Venice, Florida*

Special Word from God

I love the celebration of the Eucharist, and because of the kindness of the Lord, I have been able to attend daily Mass most of my adult life. It was through the Mass, and the reception of the body and blood of Jesus, that I was able to get through an extremely difficult period in my life.

During this time, which was many years ago, God chose to reveal His great love for me through His gift of the Eucharist. Had it not been for His love, I don't think—no, I should say I know—I would not have made it. My whole world had fallen apart from something that I had no control over, and I became very depressed. I couldn't sleep or eat, and I had no energy. It seemed as if every drop of strength I ever had was gone. Sometimes it felt as if I couldn't take one more step.

The only thing I had going for me was my attendance at daily Mass. I have to admit, though, that my heart was so heavy that many times I was in a fog during the entire Mass, and at times I could barely focus. However, I continued going, and after a short time, I realized what was happening. Our dear Lord, in His mercy, was giving me eyes to see that He was indeed supporting me. At each eucharistic celebration, there would be a *special word* spoken directly to me. Sometimes it was a Scripture passage from one of the readings; other times it was from one of the many beautiful prayers we have in the Mass, and sometimes my word from the Lord came in the homily through the words of the priest.

When I heard it, I knew it! Throughout the day, I would think about my *special word from God* and it would give me the encouragement and strength I needed at that particular moment. It seemed like the Lord always gave me enough fuel at the morning Mass to get through the day, and just as my tank was about on empty, it was time to attend Mass again and be refueled with His love and mercy. Yes, it was through the Eucharist that I received the strength, grace, and power to get through each day.

In spite of the pain I was in, it was exciting to receive His words of comfort, and I began to look forward to receiving them. I knew it was His special gift to me, and He never failed me, not once. This went on for almost a year, and when the crisis was over, I was able to continue my journey with Him, knowing and believing that He would always be with me. I knew that even if my world might be crashing around me, I could always find Him in the Eucharist.

Many years have now gone by and I can never thank and praise our wonderful and awesome God enough for the way in which He nourished me daily with His gift of the Eucharist during that most painful time in my life. I am forever grateful to Him. And to think He chose to reveal His great love by speaking personally to me during the greatest prayer on earth—the Eucharist. How blessed I was then, and how blessed I am now. Praise God!

Anita Oberholtzer   *Clearwater, Florida*

Midnight Tryst

When I was a young sister teaching high school science in a business school setting, my love for science was not readily shared by the students, nor by the sisters with whom I lived. At the time I did not realize how much my self-image depended on how others approved and liked what I put a lot of energy into. Discouraged, I wondered if I had made the right choice in deciding to become a sister in a teaching order.

One night, when I was feeling particularly low, I got up about two in the morning and went to the chapel, which was two floors down from where I slept. I knelt before the Blessed Sacrament for what seemed a long time and prayed, "Lord, please give me a sign that you love me and want me to stay in the convent." I was moved to lift up my hands in prayer. I noticed a light band on the base of the fourth finger of my left hand. I turned my attention to what looked like a ring of light on my finger, like a wedding band.

Deeply moved, I stayed in that position and thanked Jesus for giving me a sign of His love for me. After about ten or fifteen minutes, being a true scientist, I looked to see where the light was coming from. There was a crack in the curtain, a space below the shade, a hole in the tree branches, and a bare bulb in a house on the next street.

I know God works in coincidences, but this one was compounded at least eight times. It was His plan that I was in the chapel in a certain place, that my hand was lifted to a certain level, that the curtain had a tiny crack, that the shade had not been pulled all the way down, that the tree was not in the way, and that the lone light bulb from such a distance could shed a small ring of light on only my left finger, and at the base of that finger. My faith was strengthened.

That happened forty years ago. I now work in an adult day care center with people from all cultures and walks of life, not as a scientist, but as one who uses activities in a therapeutic manner and helps people recognize that God works in strange ways.

Sister Marie Louise Pohlman, OSF   *Columbus, Ohio*

I Shed That Drop for You

As a scrupulous person, I agonized about receiving the Eucharist. Then the wine consecrated that day was white, and when I went to receive the precious blood, it appeared that the chalice was empty. I whispered to the eucharistic minister, "There isn't any left," and she replied, "There is." She was right, there was one drop left in the chalice.

As I made my way back through the pews, I was focused on finding my seat when I heard Jesus saying within me, "I shed that drop for you!" It was an awesome experience.

Stephanie S. Simon   *Danbury, Connecticut*

Aunt Jo and Jesus

My informal visits to Jesus in the Eucharist began on Sunday afternoons long before I was even in parochial school. It was with my Aunt Josephine, at a time when my cousin Joe and I would much rather enjoy playtime, not *pray time*.

Aunt Jo would call us from her backyard to the house, and quickly wash our hands and wipe our faces clean for an afternoon visit to church. As we walked, she'd remember to check our necks where, to her dismay, she'd usually find beads of sweat and dirt which she efficiently wiped off with one of her fancy handkerchiefs. We had to look presentable when we went to see Jesus and His Blessed Mother!

My aunt had different ideas for us at that time, and we disliked her disruption to our lives. There are so many times now—some forty years later—that I very gratefully remember her as I seek the solace and peace I can only find in church with the Blessed Mother and Jesus in the Eucharist at adoration.

I was also fortunate to have a mom and many teachers throughout my school years who encouraged us to go to daily Mass whenever we could attend. I have found that these non-Sunday encounters with Christ have been more beautiful and renewing than I could imagine. Recently, times have been unusually hard, and more and more I find myself drawn to morning Mass and eucharistic adoration, seeking answers and peace.

Early before Mass one morning, I knelt alone in church asking God to speak to me, to give me some answers. My head was so filled with worry that I couldn't hear anything. My mind wouldn't stop running. Then, as I prayed, silently begging for peace, Father Shelley came into church. For some reason, he came over to me, and I didn't even hear him approach.

He quietly excused himself for interrupting me, and asked if he could pray with me. I don't remember the entire prayer he said as he laid his hand on my head, but his last phrase lingers with me still: three times he repeated, "Lord Jesus, give me peace." At that time, I truly felt a peace wash over me that completely eased my mind and heart.

I know God answered me that day, and many times since, sometimes in similarly unusual ways. We know that His love and presence are both with us and within us at all times, but He is very specially there for us in church through the Eucharist. As I travel life's road, I pray I will never forget the lessons Aunt Jo taught me on those Sundays so long ago when we wanted to play, and instead we learned to pray.

Jeannie Paslawsky   *Willow Grove, Pennsylvania*

Precious Blood, Not Wine

It is my belief that we truly receive the body and blood of Jesus Christ in the consecrated bread and wine offered in the sacrifice of the holy Mass. One day I had an experience that confirmed this belief to me.

This particular experience happened shortly after I became a eucharistic minister. We were celebrating the Easter Vigil Mass, and I was one of the ministers of the cup. We had an overabundance of consecrated wine, and I knew it was required that the remaining precious blood was to be consumed. Therefore, I proceeded to drink what was remaining in my cup despite health issues that normally prevent me from drinking wine. I have Type II diabetes, and asthma that is triggered by drinking wine.

As a newly trained eucharistic minister, I had not been told we could share the excess precious blood with others, so that was the reason I consumed what was left in the cup. It was about two thirds of a cup, and I had no idea how it would affect my blood sugar or asthma, but I drank it anyway.

When I returned home, I checked my blood sugar and it was in the normal range. Drinking the wine had no affect on my asthma either. I believe that I truly received the body and blood of Christ, and that the wine was truly changed into His precious blood. If it was merely wine, I would have had a negative reaction to both my blood sugar level, and to my asthma condition because of the amount I had consumed.

Mary S. Gigstad   *Sacred Heart, Minnesota*

I Became a Eucharistic Minister

I never knew how powerful the Eucharist was to me until the fall of 2003 when I said "yes" to Our Lord. I was at St. Thomas More Catholic Church in Englewood, Colorado, when a parishioner, Tom Bennett, approached me and asked if I'd like to become a eucharistic minister. Flattered, yet not wanting to answer the call, I said, "I'll think about it."

When I saw him in church during the following months, I smiled politely, but never gave an indication of wanting to serve. After all, I had been a religious education teacher for nearly nine years, and thought that between that and taking care of my family affairs, I was doing my share of good deeds.

One Sunday after Mass, Tom approached me and asked, "Have you thought about becoming a eucharistic minister yet?" "Well…," I stammered. He said, "Look, there is no burning bush to give you a clear picture here, but I think you should consider it more strongly." "Alright," I promised.

Just then a good friend and fellow parishioner, Rosemary Connor, who was listening from her wheelchair, smiled with excitement. She was a eucharistic minister too, but it was getting harder for her to serve due to her disabilities. Even though she was in great pain at times, she continued to serve our parish of about six thousand families, and never ceased to serve with a smile. This motivated me into calling Tom and asking when the next training class was scheduled.

The following week at Mass, Rosemary introduced me as her *replacement* to one of her many friends. I was almost moved to tears that such a wonderful woman held me in such high esteem. This got the fire burning in me even brighter.

I attended classes and was mandated. It was Tom's plan to have me serve the 12:30 Mass, but in addition, I was moved to ask about ministering to the hospitals. In his surprise, he said an enthusiastic, "Yes!"

I told him that my offer was a package deal because I wanted to bring my eleven-year-old daughter, Emily, with me. He was very pleased and said that it would bring joy to the patients' eyes to see a child with such a clear vocation and love for Christ.

We were not prepared for the many blessings Our Lord had in store for us as we served Him in such a beautiful way. It was so moving to see the patients' eyes light up when they saw Emily come into their room with me, and they encouraged her in many ways to continue her journey.

Though there were many memorable experiences we encountered, as each room had a new story, there is one in particular that will always live in our hearts.

We went into the critical care unit one Tuesday at Swedish Medical Center, and met a man who was bruised from head to toe. It is to our discretion to never ask the patient about their condition, but we could clearly see that he was in great pain because of the many tubes all over him.

It was understandable that he was not in the best of spirits because of the great amount of pain he was in. We gave him Communion and told him we would pray the rosary for him that evening. Then we continued visiting the other patients on our list, and left.

The following week we saw this same man again, and he appeared to be in more pain and getting weaker. As he was moving in pain, I asked him if he wanted to receive Communion. I mentioned that since he couldn't make it to Jesus, Jesus had found a way to make it to him. He received the Eucharist and Emily and I went on our way, the same as the week before.

The following Tuesday we went to see this remarkable man again, and his wife was with him. She was very excited to see us and said, "We have been waiting for someone to come and bring him Communion." It was clear that he was getting closer to going home to our heavenly Father.

To myself, I quietly asked the Holy Spirit to work through my daughter and me, because I knew we might be some of the last people this patient would see before he died. When I gave Communion to him and his wife, she broke down into tears. At that time the patient was in too much pain to talk, but his wife said that the Eucharist was very important to him. "You see," she said, "he used to be an altar boy, and served at Mass every day since he was seven years old. He is very close to his faith." It was clear that she, too, shared the same passion for Our Lord.

After that, Emily and I went to see the other patients, and then went to the cafeteria for lunch. It was at lunchtime that we decided to go see them again and give them a scapular.

When we went back into the room, the wife jumped up and said that the first time we had visited them, it felt like two angels had entered the room. Emily, being so moved, gave the wife the scapular. Then the wife smiled tearfully and pulled out something from the patient's pocket of belongings. It was an old, worn, and very much loved green scapular.

"He carries this with him everywhere, but it's too old and torn for him to wear," she told us.

I took the new scapular, tied it around his wrist, and said, "There, now you're doubly covered." The next day I learned that the gentleman had gone home to Our Lord.

I cannot express the gratitude and love I feel in saying "yes" to Jesus' call to serve Him in such a humble ministry. Being a eucharistic minister leads us down such an inspiring pathway where we meet many beautiful people. What an honor it is to bring Our Lord to the sick and suffering.

My daughter and I have been changed forever by saying "yes" to the closest physical contact of Our Lord—the Eucharist. She is now homeschooled, so we are able to free up our time to go to the retirement home and occasional hospices, bringing Jesus with us. Emily aspires to be a saint, and feels a special closeness with Jesus because she helps bring Him to the ones who can't come to Him. What a joy it is to see their faces light up, and to see them eager to receive Him in such a wonderful way.

Kelly M. Westover   *Centennial, Colorado*

Sharing My Love

I want to tell you what happened to my husband and me a few years ago. We were engaged at the time, and I really wanted to share my love for the holy Eucharist with my future husband. We went to a little chapel out in the country and knelt before the exposed Blessed Sacrament.

As we were praying, in an instant, I saw Our Lord as one without faith would see Him. I looked upon the Eucharist as only a piece of bread. I knew it was Jesus, but all sensible knowing was gone. I don't know how to explain it except that the good God allowed me to experience what it is like to not have any faith at all. I was so disgusted with the way I felt that I got up and walked to the bookshelf and started thumbing through a book. I was thinking to myself, "Good job, Robin! You brought your fiancé here to ask Our Lord to give him a great love for Himself in the holy Eucharist and you can't even pray! You're just walking around like an idiot!"

I must have been up less than a minute when John called out, "Robin, I see God! I see the face of God in the Blessed Sacrament!" Praise God! I believe he *borrowed* my faith to give the gift of faith to John that day.

Robin Dupre   *Ville Platte, Louisiana*

Each One

Once, during the Eucharist, I was kneeling and could hear the priest say, "The body of Christ," to the people receiving Communion. It occurred to me then that not only is the Eucharist the body of Christ, but each one of us is the body of Christ too! That insight left me with an *ah ha!* type of feeling, and I remember it every time I go to Mass.

Denise Parenteau   *Edmonton, Alberta, Canada*

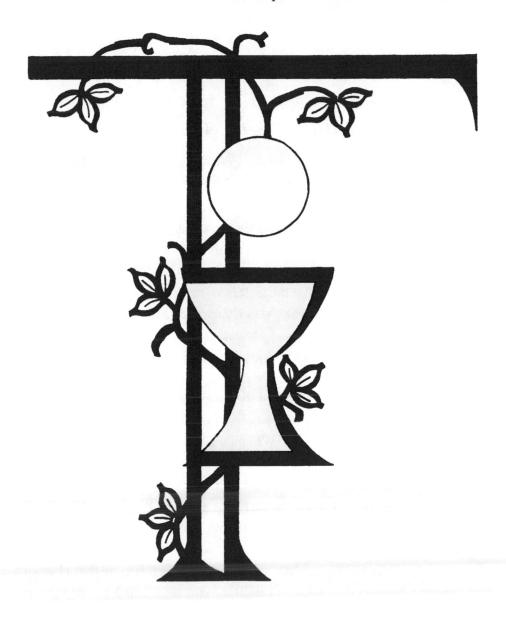

The following stories are from some of my fellow Poor Clare Sisters around the world. Our life is one of prayer and contemplation with special devotion to the Eucharist. Visit us on the web at www.poorclare.org

Kindness in a Call

I have heard people say that they received their vocation at the time of their first holy Communion. I think that is what happened to me.

I distinctly remember deciding not to become a sister when I was in the third grade. That was four or five months after my first holy Communion, so I think that Our Lord must have called me to Himself on that special day. The reason I decided I did not want to become a religious was simple. Someone told me that the sisters who taught us woke up at four-thirty every morning. That was too early for me! My mother had trouble waking me at seven.

I continued through school enjoying the religious education we received daily, and taking advantage of the visits we could make to the Blessed Sacrament during recess or the lunch hour. I remember kneeling at the altar rail to be with Jesus, who was in the domed tabernacle with sheer curtains and a cross on top. When I was twelve or thirteen years old, I even rose early to attend daily Mass during Lent. That fifteen-minute earlier rising was not as hard as the 8:45 p.m. retiring time required by my parents if I was going to wake up early and ride my bicycle to Mass.

I went to a public high school, and then a secular college, and do not think the idea of religious vocation crossed my mind during this time. Afterwards, I worked for a while and it was during this time that I began to wonder if I should consider a religious vocation. I had no idea about how to go about this though.

One day I was asked by a friend to drive her to an interview at a monastery. Curious, I asked her if I could go in with her and listen. She was happy to have me come along with her. While the sister behind the grill was describing life in a monastery, I had tears in my eyes. I did not realize that this life still existed!

My friend took me with her to a solemn profession at this same monastery a week later. Then she arranged an interview for me the following week. Seven and a half weeks later I entered. I had never wanted anything so much in my life, and this was a most joyful period for me.

Looking back, I realize that my clothing (receiving the habit) as a Poor Clare was twenty-five years after my decision to decline our Lord's generous offering of a life with Him on my first Communion day. He was so kind to ask me again. It is said that He cannot be outdone in generosity, and I think that He remembers those recesses I spent with Him, and those lunch hours during which I chose His company over games with my classmates.

Now, as a Poor Clare with our special devotion to Him in the Blessed Sacrament, a great part of my day is spent before the tabernacle, and the rest of the day I arrange so that my heart may remain there.

Sister Mary Seraphim, PCC   *Los Altos Hills, California*

A Eucharistic Calling

"Telephone, Mommy!" My voice shattered the silence of the church. The priest had just elevated the Host during the morning Eucharist, and the server was ringing the bells. As a child, each day I accompanied my mother the half mile walk to our parish church, St. Teresa of Avila in Cincinnati, Ohio. It was the late 1940s, and our pastor, Father Anthony, had a great devotion to the Eucharist that he passed on to his parishioners.

On days when my mother took me downtown for shopping, we would stop in the corner drugstore after Mass to order toast, jelly and tea. Then we would climb on the bus, and be the first customers as the department store doors were opened. Fond memories!

On days when my mother couldn't attend the morning Mass, she would call out to me as I left for grade school, "Pray for Aunt Annetta, her anniversary, or remember Uncle Aid, he is sick." At St. Teresa's, all the grades started the day with daily Eucharist. When I eventually entered religious life, I didn't need to learn the Gregorian Masses because I already knew them by heart. Even more than that, a love for daily Mass was a part of my whole being.

The parish had a yearly Corpus Christi outdoor procession. The first communicants led the procession, and eighth-grade graduates wore suits and long dresses. The streets were blocked off by the police, and four houses along the route were selected as *stations* for prayer. The last *station* was elaborately decorated for the ending Corpus Christi Benediction. Even those who weren't Catholic would sit quietly on their porches. In all the years that I can remember, it was never cancelled by inclement weather.

On Saturdays I would stay after Mass to watch the brides and their bridesmaids walk down the aisle. No doubt the bride's family was probably wondering how I had received an invitation. After watching, I would scurry out the side door, hoping not to be seen.

The real test of my devotion came in the summer months. Mass was early for a teenager, but something always drew me to attend. That was when I began high school. Seton High in Cincinnati had a beautiful chapel located to the right as you first came in. It was a place of silence, and I found myself stopping in during the day, and for times of exposition of the Blessed Sacrament.

When I needed to do research for papers, I would go downtown to our main library. At lunchtime, the cathedral had a noon Mass and then you could stay on for exposition in the Blessed Sacrament chapel. The chapel was being renovated at the same time my father, a skilled carpenter, was building a new home for us. I mentioned that they were putting up beautiful black marble in the chapel. My father knew the construction supervisor, so now the pieces of marble that were too small to be used in the chapel still adorn the fireplace in our family home. It's a nice reminder of the Eucharist being bread for our everyday lives.

When I felt the call to the Poor Clare way of life, it was natural for me to feel at home with women who love daily Eucharist, and exposition of the Blessed Sacrament. I know that I am continuing the eucharistic life passed on to me from my parents and pastor. I know my vocation was planted during those early hours of Mass and visits in grade and high school. "Telephone, Mommy," was for real. Jesus did *call* me through the Eucharist.

Sister Doris Gerke, OSC   *Cincinnati, Ohio*

A Special First Communion

When I was a junior in high school, I wanted my nine-year-old sister, Mary, to be able to receive her first Communion with the other children of her age group at church. Mary was in special education classes at the public school and was not able to be a part of the regular catechism classes in our church.

I knew Mary well, though, and although it was true she had difficulty learning things quickly, I felt that with patient instruction she would be able to understand this beautiful gift of Jesus coming to her in the Host. So one Sunday after Mass, I went with Mary and talked to our pastor to see if this would be possible.

Our pastor was very kind and understanding. He questioned me a bit and talked to Mary, and then gave me some material so I could instruct her during the next week. He also gave me an unconsecrated Host to take with me, so that I could teach her how Jesus would come to her after the consecration in this ordinary bread. Every day after school we carefully went over the instructions that he gave us. I would show Mary the ordinary Host and explain to her how it would be changed into Jesus' true body and blood after the consecration. By the next Sunday I felt she was ready, and both of us went back to the priest after Mass. He questioned her and then smiling, said yes, she would be able to make her first Communion with the other children.

Two weeks later, Mary, in her beautiful white dress, was part of the young children who made their first Communion. As she came back after receiving, she had a most beautiful smile on her face, and pointing to her mouth, she said in a loud voice so that everyone could hear, "Jesus!"

I know that she truly believed and understood what receiving Communion meant. Perhaps better than most of us!

Sister Jane Wade, OSC   *Spokane, Washington*

Face to Face

During the summer of 1995, I attended the "Come and See" program with the Missionaries of Charity in Gallup, New Mexico. I lived with the novices who spent an hour each day in adoration before the Blessed Sacrament exposed on the altar. They prayed the rosary together during the first half hour, and then spent the rest of the time in silent prayer.

One day I was late for adoration and Our Lord was already exposed on the altar. The small room that was used as a chapel was full except for one place. I was motioned to the vacant area directly in front of Our Lord.

Being shy and somewhat insecure, I was horrified at having to go to that spot, but silently crept up to the place, hoping no one would notice me. I knelt down and found myself face to face and at the same level as the sacred Host. There was no more than three feet between us.

I forgot about the sisters around me. At home, my kneeling posture during the family rosary included a gentle sway from side to side. I suppose it was a nervous habit displaying my desire to be doing something else. This time was different. I was so absorbed by His presence that I did not move during the whole hour. No formulated prayers passed from me to Him. He just looked at me and I looked at Him.

I never learned if this was the normal procedure, to set an applicant up before the Blessed Sacrament, and have Him *work on her*. Looking back, I would attribute more than just an isolated gift of consolation to this experience. Perhaps my contemplative vocation was truly strengthened, for in February I entered the Poor Clares in Los Altos Hills, California. Even today, when I am distracted and it is hard to pray, I find it helpful to imagine the Host that close again. I am very grateful to the Missionaries of Charity for this experience and, above all, their unsurpassed witness of joy.

Sister Mary Bernadette, PCC   *Los Altos Hills, California*

Healing Presence

When my best friend, June, became critically ill from lupus, I found myself very torn between my vow of enclosure as a Poor Clare and wanting to be with to her to give her my presence in heart and body. Yes, I could tell my head the facts of my first choice to enclosure, but it was hard on my heart to grasp and accept this reality.

I resolved it by taking my sorrow to the Lord during our daily eucharistic adoration. Within my troubled heart, I quietly heard the Lord say, "Bring her to Me." I immediately had this inner image of myself standing before the tabernacle and having June on a mat facing the eucharistic Lord. This image stayed with me, and each day I began my holy hour holding June on this mat.

Despite June's many setbacks over the months, which included a coronary, acute renal failure, aggressive steroid treatment, persistent electrolyte imbalance, and several hospitalizations, this image never left my mind and heart. To me, bringing June to the Lord daily seemed to be her best medicine, and mine too.

After almost nine months of daily prayer, June's body began to respond to treatment. I praise God that she is now in remission and her body is healing. Over those months, I came to realize that I did, after all, give June my presence. However, my presence was to the Divine Healer rather than to her directly.

The size of my healing mat is larger now. Daily I place on the mat those who are close as well as those who are far away who need the healing presence of God to make them whole. As a Poor Clare committed to a life of prayer, I place on the mat those who call, write, or stop by to request being remembered before the Lord. I also place those who make the headlines of our paper, or the lead story on our local or national news on this mat. We are people in need of healing. We all get by with a little help from our friends.

Sister Marilyn Trowbridge, OSC   *Cincinnati, Ohio*

I Am With You Always

The greatest gift God ever gave me was the gift of His presence in the Eucharist when I became a Catholic at the age of fifteen. From that time on, His true presence in the Eucharist has become the *home* of my heart. Through the many difficulties and struggles I had as a young person, and throughout my whole life, I could always come before Him and be strengthened with His love.

I entered the Poor Clare Monastery in Minneapolis, Minnesota, in 1955. There, too, my life was centered on the Eucharist through Mass and daily exposition of the Blessed Sacrament.

In 1968, I was part of a group of sisters from the monastery that made a new foundation in Korea. In the midst of uncertainty as to whether or not I would have the grace and inner strength needed for this endeavor, the one thought that gave me the courage to volunteer for the foundation was this: "Even though I am weak, the Blessed Sacrament will be there. Just as Jesus has given me His grace and strength here, He will continue to be with me in Korea just as much as He has been with me throughout my life."

Although I have received countless graces and insights through Jesus' eucharistic presence, one experience in particular stands out in my memory. I was making a private directed retreat here in Korea, and as I recall, the many hours of prayer each day were not easy. I was pretty much struggling along.

One night, during my hour of prayer in chapel, nothing seemed to be happening, and I dozed off for a while. Suddenly I woke up, and there was Jesus! Of course, I did not see Him, but His presence was more real to me than I had ever experienced in being with any other person. I was overwhelmed with joy!

My retreat director had told me that I was not to pray for more than an hour, and my hour was at an end. What should I do? I could have stayed there forever, but thought the Lord would be more pleased if I followed what my director had indicated. So, I reluctantly dragged myself away and went to my room where the experience of the Lord and His love lingered on for a while.

I woke up the next day very eager to meet Jesus again as I had the previous night. However, when I went to chapel to pray, the tabernacle seemed totally empty, and I was as dry as a stick. Five minutes of prayer seemed like an hour, and I could barely endure the time. Then, the Lord's grace touched my heart in a different way. The happy thought came to me that Jesus was just as much present now in my darkness and dryness as He was the night before when I experienced Him in such a felt way.

His presence does not depend on my feelings. He does not change, but is with us in times of difficulty and suffering as much as He is with us in times of joy and consolation. It is a matter of faith. This thought has continued to strengthen me at different times throughout my life. Whatever our situation is, whatever we are feeling or experiencing, the Lord is truly with us, embracing us, loving us, and giving us His grace.

It has been such a great privilege to live in the house of the Lord. Just as Jesus has been the *home* of my heart, I pray that this poor heart of mine may always be a *home* for Him where He is pleased to dwell.

Sister Mary Diane Ackerman, OSC　　　　　　　*Cheju Island, South Korea*

The Letter Made a Difference

A few years ago my dad's younger brother was critically ill in the hospital. As a cloistered nun I was not able to visit him, but I did send him a letter. I can no longer recall the exact wording, but I remember telling my uncle to keep looking at the cross and to unite his suffering with Jesus' suffering. Jesus would give him strength. Jesus would be his way.

My uncle had always been strong in practicing his faith, and in receiving the Eucharist frequently. He was also very active in his parish. I remember writing that even if it was time for Sister Death, he need not fear because he had received Our Lord in holy Communion many times over the years. Jesus was living in him.

In my letter to my uncle, I wrote that when "God the Father" looked at him, He would see His beloved son, and eagerly embrace him with eternal love. When "God the Son" looked at him, Jesus would see His beloved bride—the Church. Jesus would welcome him with joy into the wedding of heaven. Soon after sending the letter I received the news that my uncle had died peacefully. He was in his early sixties.

Months later, the Christmas mail brought the good news that my uncle's wife had returned to the Church and was receiving holy Communion frequently. She had read my final letter to her husband in his dying hours and the reality of the mystery of the Eucharist had struck a deep chord in her heart. Her husband's example had brought her home. She could face widowhood with serenity. She was alone, but not lonely. Jesus was living in her. She is once again a vital member of the Church community, which is Jesus' bride.

"Poor Clare Nun"

God's Choice

The Lord sought to get my attention from the busy life that goes with family and full-time work as a nurse. I felt a deep yearning to visit Him, to be present before Him. That was when I looked about and found an open chapel in the town I was living that was called The Power of Prayer. I immediately started to make weekly visits.

Before the year was out, I was finding so much comfort in my visits that I increased them to several times a week. To my surprise, my routine opened enough to allow me to stay for hourly visits. In the quiet and stillness of the chapel, I could think and talk to Jesus like a friend. Then it occurred to me that I could commit to a set hour, and sure enough, soon this was not enough for me. I was thirsting to be in His real presence, sharing my life with Him.

The years that followed were a commitment of an hour a day. These hours allowed me to build a bond with the beautiful group of people who also attended. I felt that I was truly living the life I was baptized for.

Nothing goes unseen by the Lord. We talked about many hard issues, and each of them was resolved. I knew I could always stand before Him in His love and mercy.

Once, while before the Eucharist, I was thanking Jesus for an especially spirit-filled weekend, and found myself saying that I was ready to give myself to Him as a consecrated woman. A deep knowing filled my being, and these words were impressed upon my soul: "I want you to be my bride." I responded with a most joyous "Yes!" Suddenly, my life seemed to leap into a most wonderful level of awareness. Jesus wanted me to be His wife. What came next was joy-filled also.

I answered this call to religious life in June of 2000. Then, I experienced life as an aspirant until the following early spring when I became a postulant at the Santa Clara Monastery in Canton, Ohio. During that live-in year, I felt the calling was real, and confirmation came from the sisters as well. I asked to be accepted into the novitiate of this fourteen-member community.

My approval came on February 2, 2001. In preparation, I was informed it was the community's custom to allow the postulant to pick her chosen religious name. I have long been aware of the beauty and meaningfulness in a name, so I went about examining why this or that name might be my choice.

Having a close relationship with my mother, I asked her opinion. She said, "Oh, it would be nice to take your grandmother's name, Mary Ellen." As I was presently called Ellen, and as I mused over other options, I liked the idea of pleasing mom. Plus, I had very fond memories of both of my grandmothers who shared the name Mary. So, I was very content that my new name would be Mary Ellen. "That will keep others clear on who I am," I thought. My current name on my car and nursing licenses were similar, so there would be less confusion when I took my new name. I had heard many stories of sisters being refused insurance because of their male name, etc., and now that wouldn't be a problem I'd incur.

The name rested easy but then I thought, "What about asking Jesus what name I should take?" In a teasing way, I asked myself "Isn't He a valid source?" With a smile I agreed and shook my head with an affirmative nod.

On December 25, 2001 at the Christmas Mass in the beautiful Franciscan church in Santa Clara, Father Nick, the full-time friar chaplain at the convent, elevated the Host with great reverence. It was then that the thought came to me, "Ask Jesus now." As I gazed upon the Eucharist, I received the clear impression of the name *Ishmael*. I was surprised, yet sure it was my answer. I did not even know how to spell the name, nor could I recall where I had heard it before, so I did some research in the convent library. I found the name in the Old Testament, in a section that spoke of Abraham's oldest son, Ishmael.

Now it was time to speak with my long time friend and spiritual advisor, Father Ken Tietgen. Predictably, he said he would pray on the use of Ishmael as my religious name. Confirmation was slow to come, and in time my abbess, Sister Marion, became aware of the name I was considering. With guarded words, she declined the request. "How could this be?" I thought. "The name was not my choice. It came from the Lord!" I quickly decided I would pray to Him for assurance. It came, and I returned with gentleness to open the issue again.

Father Ken and Sister Marion both said they would put it to prayer, which they did, but yet once again the answer was, "No."

"Why am I so sure," I wondered, "What am I to do?" I returned to Jesus in the Blessed Sacrament which is perpetually exposed at Santa Clara Monastery. I talked with Him about these feelings. I heard myself issuing forth the lament, "I need you. I need you to tell them because I can't. I know you want this name. Please let their hearts know."

With less than three hours left before the community meeting about my novitiate request, I received a long distance call from Father Ken. He told me he had spent prayerful time before the Eucharist in their Trappist

Infirmary, and now gave his approval on the name Ishmael. One half hour later, Sister Marion shared that she woke up and went to Jesus in the Eucharist, and became aware that she could now stand before community and ask approval for this name.

Jesus' eucharistic presence was the source of my calling to the religious life. The reception of my new religious name became the inspiring touch for others, and remains my continued affirmation of His real presence. I took the accompanying title of *Real Presence* so that I am now called Sister Ishmael of the Real Presence.

I am now prayerfully awaiting my simple vows as a Sister of Perpetual Adoration. To be with Jesus in the Eucharist is everything to me.

Sister Mary Ishmael, CAC   *Canton, Ohio*

A New Church

My mother died when I was only ten years old. She had been sick for a long time, and my sister and I grew up taking care of her. When I was thirteen, my dad got married in July, and for the rest of the summer, I stayed with my new mom's sister. My new aunt had five children, and was pregnant with a sixth. I fit somewhere in the middle. The plan was that I would stay with my aunt and cousins until school started in the fall.

My new family was very nice to me, but they were of an entirely different culture. I had been baptized as a Methodist, sent to Sunday school, and attended church as often as we could. My mother had been a good church going Methodist. No one at our church drank beer or believed in smoking. I had been taught that we didn't need those things, but not to judge anyone who used them; after all, my dad smoked.

My new family was loud and boisterous. My aunt and uncle actually drank beer and smoked! And, they were Catholic. I stayed quiet and watched how they lived.

No matter where I was, I knew it was important to always go to church on Sunday. I loved going to church. My new aunt said that they would drive me into town to the Methodist church, or I could go with them to the Catholic church. Since I was their houseguest, I felt it was not nice to impose, so I said I would go to church with them.

It was so funny watching all those kids trying to get themselves ready at the same time. Some of them seemed so helpless, even though we were all close in age. I was more accustomed to being independent out of necessity.

We arrived at the church early, so we stood in a line and watched until the first service was over. I was busy taking all this in when suddenly my interest was drawn to the altar like a magnet. The priest was holding this white thing high above his head. I couldn't take my eyes off of it. I was in awe. This was so beautiful, and I wanted to see it again, but it was gone. The saddest feeling came over me.

After the people from the first service left, we all filed in and sat in the first and second rows. One of my new cousins pointed to the page in our books, and it was in Latin! The other side was in English. Now that is strange, I thought. Why would they ever do that? My cousins didn't know Latin. What if you lost your place? How would you ever find it again?

I watched the priest's back and wondered if he was ever going to turn around. He did, and even preached in English. I felt good when he read the Bible to us. Shortly after that, it happened again. The priest held up the Host, and again I was deeply touched, and in awe.

I watched as everybody else got to go up to the altar and share in this Communion, and how they prayed very deeply. I thought about that all summer, and liked going to Mass with my new relatives on Sundays. Jesus in the form of the holy Eucharist was drawing me ever so gently to the Catholic Church.

In the fall I went home to a new mom, and my dad seemed very happy. Sometimes I went to the Catholic church with them, and sometimes my sister and I rode the bus into town to the Methodist church.

Sometime later, I was sitting on the front steps of our house, talking to Jesus about something on my mind. He had been my best friend since my grandmother had introduced me to Him in her best Baptist way. That day, I was talking to Him about people dying, like the boy in my class who I'd had a crush on. It didn't seem fair.

Jesus interjected into my commiseration, "I want you." That seemed strange because I've always loved Him. Then it came clearer, "I want all of you." I told Him that He was all Spirit and I wasn't, and I couldn't see how that was possible.

I decided this was something I would have to think about more because I just couldn't understand what He meant. Besides, He already had me. What would become of me if I just melted into His Spirit? Hmmm? "There must be something more," is what I thought.

At twenty years old, when I was in my last year of college, I completed my studies of the Catholic Church and received my first holy Communion and confirmation. Finally, I felt like I had arrived. This cannot be explained, but I understood. There is no question in my mind that the presence of Our Lord is truly in the Eucharist. He leads me ever so gently. We meet in the Eucharist in such a special way. This was and is a most loving and awesome event.

Sister Jane M. Deland, OSC   *Evansville, Indiana*

God is Here

When I was sixteen years old, I was a junior counselor at a summer camp in Rhinebeck, New York. One day early that summer, I had a weekday off and was taken to town to spend some of my free hours there.

While in town, I felt the need to find a church to pray in. My own Protestant church was closed, but the Catholic church was open. Even after all these decades, I vividly remember entering the church and feeling the presence of God. I recall saying to myself, "God is here," and how I went forward to the Communion rail because God's presence felt even stronger there in the front of the church.

Sometime later that summer, I saw the camp nurse reading a copy of the recently published *Seven Storey Mountain*, which she lent me. In that book, which I devoured, I read of Thomas Merton's journey to the Catholic faith, and of his love for the Eucharist. I knew then that I wanted to become a Catholic, and that I longed to receive the Blessed Sacrament.

Until I read that book, I didn't know that people could change the church they belonged to, nor did I know about taking instructions to join the Catholic Church. I also didn't know about the Real Presence because my Protestant Church taught a symbolic Communion.

When camp was over I returned to New York City. I went to the Catholic Information Center at St. Francis Xavier Church. This church is one that Thomas Merton mentions in his book as one he visited. I took instructions and was baptized there.

Many years went by and I loved being a Catholic. Eventually, after some years, I began to go to Mass and Communion every day. Then, much later in life, I felt God calling me to religious life.

After months of prayer and asking God over and over if I was hearing Him right, I was led to a spiritual director who assured me, "God is speaking very clearly." Then I visited and wrote to several religious communities, and found after a week of *live-in* that my spirit felt at home at the Poor Clare Monastery in Evansville, Indiana.

Before I entered the Poor Clares, I worked for thirty-one years at Oxford University Press in New York City. Now I am the librarian at my monastery, and am also serving as sacristan this year. As sacristan, I take care of the chalices, hosts, and linens before and after Mass, and I decorate the chapel.

It was a great surprise to be called to monastic life so late in life; I entered at the age of fifty-two! Now I am sixty-eight, and a professed Poor Clare Nun. I attend Mass every day of my life, and have the joy of living where the Blessed Sacrament dwells.

Sister Catherine K. Janeway, OSC   *Evansville, Indiana*

Faith and Science Do Mix

When I met the Poor Clare Sisters in Spokane, I had just started an internship to be certified as a medical technologist (in other words, lab tech). The yearlong internship consisted of rotations through the various departments in the hospital laboratory. In all the different departments there were bottles of distilled water on the countertops, which were used frequently. One of my lab partners discovered that the distilled water helped to dissolve the blood stains on his lab coat before he washed it. Of course, it was simple. The distilled water caused the red blood cells to lyse (burst), so the stain broke up very quickly. I tucked that little piece of practical information away for future reference.

After completing my internship, I made up my mind to join the sisters and did so within a few months. A few years later I was assigned to the laundry. I was responsible for the laundry for the sisters, the sacristy, the kitchen and other areas of the monastery.

The sacristy laundry primarily consists of washing the items the priest used on the altar—the purificator, corporal, finger towel and alb, as well as the altar linens. The purificators and corporals are washed together as the purificator comes directly in contact with the precious blood, and the corporal with the body of the Lord in the consecrated Hosts.

Before these items come to me in the laundry, they are rinsed in a special way and checked for stains. Sometimes, even after that, there are still stains that come through that look like wine stains. Normally, one would treat them like wine stains, but after the consecration, they are not wine stains anymore, but blood stains. I have tried treating them as wine stains but that is not effective. The stains only respond to distilled water like any other blood stain does.

Our Lord's blood is just like yours and mine in its basic composition.

Sister Colleen Byrne, OSC   *Spokane, Washington*

He Dwelt Among Us

Vespers is the evening song of the Church. As the last cadences of the chanted psalms are heard, the sun is setting behind the surrounding hill, and a deep quiet settles upon the heart as well as throughout the monastery. The community was gathered in prayer before the Blessed Sacrament in this post-vespers stillness when what sounded like a huge bowling ball rumbled down the long choir hall.

We were all in the choir except for our ninety-eight-year-old Sister Felix who was taking her evening meal in the infirmary. We had no idea where the sound could have come from until the whole building began to shake.

Living on an earthquake fault, we are somewhat familiar with the tremors that are part and parcel of life in California, but this was no ordinary tremor. Within moments, the entire choir was in movement from the lights above us that swung on their chains like swings at a city park, to the statue of Our Lady and Saint Joseph, which greatly swayed back and forth until they fell with a crash from their pedestals.

The sister next to me jumped out of her choir stall and grabbed my arm gasping, "Jesus and Mary!"

We kept our eyes glued to the tabernacle as the doors opened and closed from the quakes movements. Inside, our eucharistic king remained calm and serene in His standing pyx, which miraculously remained standing. Even the floor was undulating like a wooden sea. Then, just as suddenly as it had begun, the vespers stillness returned, except for the sound of falling glass.

As we continued our prayers before the Blessed Sacrament, we were reminded of the psalm verse, "Though the earth and all who dwell in it may rock, it is I who uphold its pillars" (Psalm 75). That Divine "I" was present with us.

It was then that we noticed one of the sisters was missing: Sister Regina. She must have gone to check upon Sister Felix. We had no idea how she could have managed to walk those wooden waves to reach the infirmary, but that was our only explanation for her absence. Quickly we made our way to the infirmary to see. She was there, and so was dear Sister Felix, safe but frightened and suffering a small burn from the hot soup that had been shaken out of her bowl and onto her arm. She quickly regained her Irish sense of humor to tell us that if there were any future tremors she would just shake with them.

There were many tremors. We remained together, going from room to room, to survey the damage. Lots of broken glass, fallen cupboards with their contents spread all over the floor, and much that simply needed to be picked up. We discovered that an unused chimney had fallen from the roof, leaving a large hole in another part of the roof during its downward plunge, and had landed with a crash in our garden courtyard. The larger-than-life-size statue of the Immaculate Heart of Mary that was in the garden had also fallen over, giving us an idea of the strength of the quake as this image is made of solid concrete.

That was October 1, 1989, a day that we would long remember. It didn't take long to clean up the glass and pick up what had fallen. Our good contractor, Mr. Bill Portman, was out the next day to survey the damage and begin repairs. Within a few weeks, everything was back in place and all was well. Or so we thought.

On a June day in 2002, within the novena to the Sacred Heart of Jesus, over half of our monastery was demolished. No, there wasn't another earthquake. This *quake* was planned.

Whether the structural difficulties were caused by the 1989 earthquake or not, there were definite and irreparable problems. We know for certain that some of them were caused by lack of construction knowledge when the buildings were first built in the 1920s. Although, maybe they just forgot to put the foundations in? Whatever the cause, demolition and rebuilding were prescribed as the best cure.

We still had a fraction of the monastery intact where we could live. Both Sister Felix and Sister Regina were safely in this part along with our three other older sisters. The rest of us were relatively young and ready to meet the challenges of living as best we could on the building site. The small section of the monastery that would not be demolished included the choir where Jesus remained, our anchor and our hope.

We squared our shoulders and set the monastic schedule into motion, meaning that it changed as the need arose. Then came one more thing in all of the already unplanned activity that we could not even have imagined. It all started with a simple need to remove an awning behind the choir so the diseased wood could go with all the other debris from the demolition. Only it wasn't just the awning that was diseased. The carpenter delivered the prognosis: termites in the only building that was left standing.

Our good contractor was back on site to meet with the termite extermination crew. "Isn't there any way the sisters could stay here while you do your work?" we asked hopefully. No way. So, where were we going to go? Sixteen cloistered nuns with no place to lay their heads.

We opted for camping out during the day and accepted a very kind invitation from the Daughters of Charity just down the road for night time accommodations. We pitched tents in the lower part of the garden, away from the construction work, and the work of extermination which was going on simultaneously. From there we could watch the billowing circus-like tent that covered all we had left of our monastery.

Because we could not leave the Blessed Sacrament within the monastery during the extermination process, the tabernacle was left empty after our chaplain offered holy Mass for us that momentous morning. Each sister became the tabernacle of Jesus for every other sister as we set out from our *Promised Land* to *Egypt*.

We worked in the garden during the day, praying the divine office from two long lines of folding chairs. We had picnic meals for lack of any kitchen other than a trailer loaned to us by another good friend. The following morning, after a pleasant night within the embrace of the hospitality of the Daughters of Charity, we attended holy Mass in their chapel offered by our own chaplain, Father James Hanley, S.J.

After the Mass, our eucharistic Jesus was carried in His standing pyx in the car caravan to our monastery. We drove past the billowing tents and the busy carpenter, and formed a procession singing Eucharist hymns as we carried our Ark of the Covenant, the Lord Himself, to His tenting place among us. He had His own tent where we were able to have our usual eucharistic adoration all day long.

Although the termite extermination company could not allow us to remain in the monastery during the tenting process, they did cut the time as short as possible and we were able to return to the monastery after only two days and one night in exile. Who do you think entered the monastery first? Our eucharistic king! He is the faithful one, who is always with us.

Sister Marie Colette, PCC   *Los Altos Hills, California*

I Knew Him in the Breaking of Bread

Having spent over a year traveling and hitchhiking around Europe and working in Switzerland, I thought it would be great to live where there were mountains and the ocean. That's when I decided to move to Vancouver, British Columbia. On my return to Canada, I left my home in Sudbury, Ontario, took the train out west, and found work in a lawyer's office. I settled down in the West End and proceeded to enjoy myself. It was 1970 and I was twenty-three years old.

About a year later our heavenly Father started trying to get my attention. He spoke so clearly that I started to listen and responded by adjusting my lifestyle. It was at the end of October, 1971, when I made a Young Adults Retreat with the Cenacle Sisters, who were then still in their beautiful Tudor mansion on Selkirk Street in Vancouver, British Columbia. Father Pat, a Jesuit from Seattle, Washington, facilitated our time together. He and our Cenacle Sisters put together renewal days that we would remember for years to come.

Our Mass was celebrated in a small chapel, where we were invited to form a circle around the altar during the Eucharistic Prayer. I found myself on Father Pat's immediate left, as the space behind the altar was quite limited. Since I had never witnessed the awesome mystery of the moment of consecration at such close quarters, my attention was riveted on the sacred species and our priest's liturgical movements. When Father spoke the words, "Take this, all of you, and eat it; this is my body which will be given up for you," I was suddenly overcome by the truth that Jesus was speaking to me personally.

It was then that I realized He was giving up His life for me; that He was loving me as if I was the only one there and, for that matter, the only one in the whole universe. Tears started flowing down my cheeks as that reality washed over me and filled me with intense joy and gratitude.

Later during the day I was able to share with Father Pat what I had experienced, and he asked if I would be comfortable sharing it with the rest of the group. When I did, I was again moved to tears, and I know that many of them were touched by my experience as we reflected on it together.

Shortly after, the Lord gave me the grace to give my life to Him and *return love for love* as a Poor Clare Nun in Mission, British Columbia, where we live out the eucharistic spirituality of St. Clare of Assisi. This special favor from the Lord happened thirty-three years ago but is as fresh today as on that beautiful fall day when He revealed His love for me. "How can I repay the Lord for His goodness to me? The cup of salvation I will raise; I will call on the Lord's Name." (Psalm 116)

Sister Claire Marie Blondin, OSC   *Mission, British Columbia, Canada*

Always a Missionary

My experience took place on December 8, 1974, in a little African village called Dungu. The village was situated in the northeastern part of Zaire, a central African country that was known as the Belgian Congo from 1960 to 1971, when it became the Republic of Zaire. It is now called the Democratic Republic of Congo. At that time I was a thirty-year-old Grey Nun of Montreal. In 1971, the community had accepted the request to start and direct the "Ecole Technique Medicale" (Technical Medical School), which opened its doors on September 30, 1973, in the village of Dungu. The community asked me to be one of the teachers.

There were many religious houses around our convent. To the right was the minor seminary, in front of us was the college headed by the Christian Instruction Brothers (F.I.C.), and a little distance to the west were the Franciscan Sisters and the cathedral. With so many other Catholic religious houses surrounding us, Bishop Theo William Van den Elzen, OSA, did not want us to have a chapel because it meant having Mass at our convent once a week.

We did not take "no" as an answer and kept asking. The brothers, seeing our distress, said they were willing to pack the twelve of them plus the four of us into our tiny chapel for a weekly Eucharist. After a year, the bishop gave in to our request and on December 8, 1974, the Lord came to dwell among us. We had asked our Blessed Mother to help us, so it was fitting that Our Lord, Jesus, came to us on the Feast of the Immaculate Conception. It was a day of joy beyond words.

During this time, President Mobutu had ordered all crucifixes, images, and statues in schools and public places throughout Zaire to be removed on the day of the proclamation of the law, which was November 25, 1974. One of the consequences of this edict was that religious feast days, such as Christmas and Good Friday, were no longer holidays. They became workdays.

In that first year of interdiction, the Church of Zaire suffered a terrible blow with the news of the murder of Father Luc Viane, O.S.A., on December 30, 1974. The whole population of Dungu grieved deeply and feared for the safety of the rest of the population.

During this time of great insecurity and religious persecution, the bishop, as well as the major superior of each of our communities, offered the missionaries the option of returning to their country of origin. Of the thirty missionaries in our diocese of Dungu-Dorema, only one left. The others put their trust in divine providence and continued to serve the people.

After the Lord came to stay with us in the Eucharist, I never felt alone or insecure. It was a great comfort to spend time with Jesus in the Eucharist and to talk to Him about all of my difficulties. He always brought peace to my heart.

It was through these hours spent with our eucharistic Lord that the call to a life of contemplation became clear. In late September of 1978, I left Dungu via a stopover in Germany to return to Canada for a time of discernment. On August 2, 1979, I transferred to the Monastery of Saint Clare in Mission, British Columbia. I did not return to a mission land, but the Lord sent me to Mission where, through a life of prayer centered on the Eucharist, I became a missionary without frontiers. Who can compare with our heavenly Father?

Sister Marie-Celine Campeau, OSC *Mission, British Columbia, Canada*

His Mysterious Presence

I grew up as a Fundamentalist Protestant in the small suburb of Liverpool, New York. My parents had belonged to this church from its inception and it was very much a part of my life during my early teenage years. There was a deep sense of fellowship there that I clung to during those very difficult years. But as I grew out of that period of adolescence, I began to feel that church was just not enough. There was something missing, but I didn't know what.

I attended public schools all my life and there was not too much mentioning of God, nor did there seem to be anybody there who was remotely interested in the subject. Then, one day, I was going to walk home with a friend of mine when, all of a sudden, she had to stay after school for some reason. She told me to walk home with her friend Christina instead. Christina seemed like a nice enough person, so off we went. During the course of this journey home the subject of God came up somehow, and much to my surprise, she was very interested in God and prayer.

Wow! I thought this was great. From that moment on we became fast friends and still are to this day. Christina was a Catholic, but I was willing to overlook this *fault* and maybe convert her to the *truth*. But what was the *truth*? What I did not quite realize at the time was that I was searching for something, but I did not know what. My Protestant faith was just not complete. I wanted more, but more of what? I did not know. The only thing I did know was that I was very drawn to Christina's Catholic faith.

The idea of going to Mass did not enter my mind right away. For one thing, I knew my parents would be very upset. They had encouraged me to try another Protestant church, like Lutheran or Methodist. That did not satisfy me. I had to try the Catholic Mass. So, one day I went with a few friends to Mass in a convent in Watertown, New York. I find it amusing that Our Lord would choose a convent to reveal His eucharist presence to me, but that is just what He did.

I remember it was early in the morning, as Masses usually are in convents, and it was still dark outside. Everyone was very quiet and the sisters all seemed to slide across the floor in silence. The atmosphere was one of profound reverence. This felt like a place of prayer, but there was something more here.

What was this presence? What was here that was not in my church at home? At the time I did not have any idea of what the Eucharist was. All I knew was that there was something here that drew me. Mass began. I cannot describe exactly what happened in words, as sometimes deep experiences are difficult to articulate.

I began to cry, and cried through the entire Mass even though I didn't know what was going on, or why or when everyone stood or knelt or sat. I was home. I felt like someone very lost who had finally found *home*. God was there so strongly, I had never felt so close to Him before. He was in that convent; He was in that Mass like I had never known before.

Of course, I had to go to another Mass, and another, and another. There was a Catholic church within walking distance from my house with a small adoration chapel with the Blessed Sacrament. I used to go there and pray and sing to Him, for I had come to believe through prayer and instruction that this was Jesus. I tried to go back to my Protestant church to see if this was just a passing thing, but it felt like an empty room to me. He was not there in the same way that He was in that little chapel, or in any Catholic church. It was not long before I longed to receive the Eucharist, so I asked for formal instruction and was baptized shortly after.

That was almost fifteen years ago and He has continued to lead me to Himself. About eight years after my conversion, I began to experience this longing for something again. As before, it was a convent that held the answer. I had begun to consider the possibility of entering religious life when I graduated from college. I looked at several different places but when I visited the Poor Clares in Cleveland, Ohio, again I was home. He was here, and wanted me to live day and night in His presence, forever.

As I reflect on the Eucharist in my life, I can see that our blessed Lord has continued to draw me closer and closer to Him through this wonderful gift that He left us. It brings home the Scripture passage: "It was not you who chose me but I that chose you." Thank you, Jesus, for your wonderful gift of the Blessed Sacrament! Amen!

Sister Maria Christina LaDieu, PCC   *Cleveland, Ohio*

This Is Proof

The date was probably somewhere around 1950 and 1952, during my early Catholic elementary school days. It was Sunday Mass, and I clearly remember kneeling with the other school children during the time of the consecration. As the priest lifted up the sacred Host that he had just said the special words over, the little bells rang. The very same thing happened when he lifted up the chalice containing the blood of Jesus. In my little mind I thought, "This is proof that the Catholic Church is the true Church of Jesus. Every time holy Mass is offered and the priest raises up the sacred Host and the chalice, the angels ring the bells. How could the Protestants not believe when this miracle happens every single day?"

Now, even though the day would come when I would learn the *truth* about just who rings the little bells during Mass, the mystery of and my love for the holy Eucharist never lessened. In fact, if anything, it only deepened with the passage of time. It was this mysterious *drawing* and *awareness* that would come upon me whenever I would go into church for a visit. Here was a presence that somehow just wasn't anywhere else. In my young mind I could only understand that it was Jesus. He was really present in the tabernacle and it felt so good to be there with Him.

The call from Jesus to go apart with Him in the cloistered contemplative life grew and developed within me over the years. It was a great joy for me on my first visit to the Poor Clare monastery back in 1962, to walk into the public chapel and see the Blessed Sacrament exposed on the altar, and to learn that He remains this way both day and night. What a great privilege we have in our Community of Perpetual Adoration of the Blessed Sacrament, a privilege that has been ours for many decades.

As I later learned, this mysterious *drawing* was not something unique to me. It is something that almost everyone experiences upon entering a Catholic church or chapel where the Blessed Sacrament is either exposed on the altar or reserved in the tabernacle. That is because it is Jesus, Himself, present for us, awaiting us, patiently waiting for our love and adoration.

Mother Mary Jude, PCC   *Cleveland, Ohio*

By This Mystery

I grew up in Keewaydin, Pennsylvania, a small village in the western part of the state. I did not have the opportunity of attending Catholic schools, but had good parents who saw to it that their children attended catechism classes in our parish church in Frenchville, about four miles from our home. I was a devout child and read with interest the Catholic magazine to which my parents subscribed. I noticed advertisements for religious orders in these magazines. Although I did not know any sisters, these ads interested me. I never sent for any information because I thought I was not good enough to belong to a religious order.

Later, I attended the public high school in Clearfield, and the State Teachers College in Bloomsburg, Pennsylvania. While in college I mentioned to a friend my interest in religious life, and she gave me a prayer for a vocation. I kept this card in my prayer book and sometimes prayed it when attending Mass on Sundays or First Fridays.

It was during my second year of teaching in Bristol, Pennsylvania, while I lived with relatives in Trenton, New Jersey, that I began attending daily Mass at Sts. Peter and Paul Church, a short distance from their home. Up until that time, I don't think I realized there was such a thing as a daily missal. I usually prayed the rosary or prayed from a prayer book during Mass. (This was in the early 1950s when Mass was said in Latin and the priest had his back to the congregation.) A friend noticed that I did not use a missal at Mass, so she presented me with one. I was delighted and always used the missal after that when attending Mass.

One day, shortly after being introduced to the daily missal, I came upon these words: "By the mystery of this water and wine may we come to share in the divinity of Christ, who humbled Himself to share in our humanity." I was astounded! What could these words mean? Was it possible that we human beings could actually share in the divinity of Christ? For days and weeks I pondered these words, and I prayed to understand their meaning.

During this second year of teaching I had come to know the sisters at the Monastery of Saint Clare in Bordentown, New Jersey. Upon the advice of the priest who had become my spiritual director, I entered the monastery in September of 1953. Through the years, these beautiful words of the Mass continue to thrill me as I strive to deepen my life of prayer and union with God.

Sister Agnes Valimont, OSC   *Columbus, New Jersey*

ENCYCLICAL LETTER
ECCLESIA DE EUCHARISTIA
OF HIS HOLINESS
POPE JOHN PAUL II
TO THE BISHOPS, PRIESTS AND DEACONS
MEN AND WOMEN IN THE CONSECRATED LIFE
AND ALL THE LAY FAITHFUL
ON THE EUCHARIST IN ITS RELATIONSHIP TO THE CHURCH

INTRODUCTION

1. The Church draws her life from the Eucharist. This truth does not simply express a daily experience of faith, but recapitulates *the heart of the mystery of the Church*. In a variety of ways she joyfully experiences the constant fulfilment of the promise: "Lo, I am with you always, to the close of the age" (*Mt* 28:20), but in the Holy Eucharist, through the changing of bread and wine into the body and blood of the Lord, she rejoices in this presence with unique intensity. Ever since Pentecost, when the Church, the People of the New Covenant, began her pilgrim journey towards her heavenly homeland, the Divine Sacrament has continued to mark the passing of her days, filling them with confident hope.

The Second Vatican Council rightly proclaimed that the Eucharistic sacrifice is "the source and summit of the Christian life".[1] "For the most holy Eucharist contains the Church's entire spiritual wealth: Christ himself, our passover and living bread. Through his own flesh, now made living and life-giving by the Holy Spirit, he offers life to men".[2] Consequently the gaze of the Church is constantly turned to her Lord, present in the Sacrament of the Altar, in which she discovers the full manifestation of his boundless love.

2. During the Great Jubilee of the Year 2000 I had an opportunity to celebrate the Eucharist in the Cenacle of Jerusalem where, according to tradition, it was first celebrated by Jesus himself. *The Upper Room was where this most holy Sacrament was instituted*. It is there that Christ took bread, broke it and gave it to his disciples, saying: "Take this, all of you, and eat it: this is my body which will be given up for you" (cf. *Mk* 26:26; *Lk* 22:19; *1 Cor* 11:24). Then he took the cup of wine and said to them: "Take this, all of you and drink from it: this is the cup of my blood, the blood of the new and everlasting covenant. It will be shed for you and for all, so that sins may be forgiven" (cf. *Mt* 14:24; *Lk* 22:20; *1 Cor* 11:25). I am grateful to the Lord Jesus for allowing me to repeat in that same place, in obedience to his command: "Do this in memory of me" (*Lk* 22:19), the words which he spoke two thousand years ago.

Did the Apostles who took part in the Last Supper understand the meaning of the words spoken by Christ? Perhaps not. Those words would only be fully clear at the end

---

1   Second Vatican Ecumenical Council, Dogmatic Constitution on the Church *Lumen Gentium,* 11.

2   Second Vatican Ecumenical Council, Decree on the Ministry and Life of Priests *Presbyterorum Ordinis,* 5.

of the *Triduum sacrum*, the time from Thursday evening to Sunday morning. Those days embrace the *mysterium paschale*; they also embrace the *mysterium eucharisticum*.

3. The Church was born of the paschal mystery. For this very reason the Eucharist, which is in an outstanding way the sacrament of the paschal mystery, *stands at the centre of the Church's life*. This is already clear from the earliest images of the Church found in the Acts of the Apostles: "They devoted themselves to the Apostles' teaching and fellowship, to the breaking of bread and the prayers" (2:42). The "breaking of the bread" refers to the Eucharist. Two thousand years later, we continue to relive that primordial image of the Church. At every celebration of the Eucharist, we are spiritually brought back to the paschal Triduum: to the events of the evening of Holy Thursday, to the Last Supper and to what followed it. The institution of the Eucharist sacramentally anticipated the events which were about to take place, beginning with the agony in Gethsemane. Once again we see Jesus as he leaves the Upper Room, descends with his disciples to the Kidron valley and goes to the Garden of Olives. Even today that Garden shelters some very ancient olive trees. Perhaps they witnessed what happened beneath their shade that evening, when Christ in prayer was filled with anguish "and his sweat became like drops of blood falling down upon the ground" (cf. *Lk* 22:44). The blood which shortly before he had given to the Church as the drink of salvation in the sacrament of the Eucharist, *began to be shed*; its outpouring would then be completed on Golgotha to become the means of our redemption: "Christ...as high priest of the good things to come..., entered once for all into the Holy Place, taking not the blood of goats and calves but his own blood, thus securing an eternal redemption" (*Heb* 9:11–12).

4. *The hour of our redemption.* Although deeply troubled, Jesus does not flee before his "hour". "And what shall I say? 'Father, save me from this hour?' No, for this purpose I have come to this hour" (*Jn* 12:27). He wanted his disciples to keep him company, yet he had to experience loneliness and abandonment: "So, could you not watch with me one hour? Watch and pray that you may not enter into temptation" (*Mt* 26:40–41). Only John would remain at the foot of the Cross, at the side of Mary and the faithful women. The agony in Gethsemane was the introduction to the agony of the Cross on Good Friday. *The holy hour,* the hour of the redemption of the world. Whenever the Eucharist is celebrated at the tomb of Jesus in Jerusalem, there is an almost tangible return to his "hour", the hour of his Cross and glorification. Every priest who celebrates Holy Mass, together with the Christian community which takes part in it, is led back in spirit to that place and that hour.

"He was crucified, he suffered death and was buried; he descended to the dead; on the third day he rose again". The words of the profession of faith are echoed by the words of contemplation and proclamation: *"This is the wood of the Cross, on which hung the Saviour of the world. Come, let us worship"*. This is the invitation which the Church extends to all in the afternoon hours of Good Friday. She then takes up her song during the Easter season in order to proclaim: *"The Lord is risen from the tomb; for our sake he hung on the Cross, Alleluia"*.

5. *"Mysterium fidei!"*—The Mystery of Faith!". When the priest recites or chants these words, all present acclaim: "We announce your death, O Lord, and we proclaim your resurrection, until you come in glory".

In these or similar words the Church, while pointing to Christ in the mystery of his passion, *also reveals her own mystery: Ecclesia de Eucharistia*. By the gift of the Holy Spirit at Pentecost the Church was born and set out upon the pathways of the world, yet a decisive moment in her taking shape was certainly the institution of the Eucharist in the Upper Room. Her foundation and wellspring is the whole *Triduum paschale*, but this is as it were gathered up, foreshadowed and "concentrated' for ever in the gift of the Eucharist. In this gift Jesus Christ entrusted to his Church the perennial making present of the paschal mystery. With it he brought about a mysterious "oneness in time" between that *Triduum* and the passage of the centuries.

The thought of this leads us to profound amazement and gratitude. In the paschal event and the Eucharist which makes it present throughout the centuries, there is a truly enormous "capacity" which embraces all of history as the recipient of the grace of the redemption. This amazement should always fill the Church assembled for the celebration of the Eucharist. But in a special way it should fill the minister of the Eucharist. For it is he who, by the authority given him in the sacrament of priestly ordination, effects the consecration. It is he who says with the power coming to him from Christ in the Upper Room: "This is my body which will be given up for you This is the cup of my blood, poured out for you…". The priest says these words, or rather *he puts his voice at the disposal of the One who spoke these words in the Upper Room* and who desires that they should be repeated in every generation by all those who in the Church ministerially share in his priesthood.

6. I would like to rekindle this Eucharistic "amazement" by the present Encyclical Letter, in continuity with the Jubilee heritage which I have left to the Church in the Apostolic Letter *Novo Millennio Ineunte* and its Marian crowning, *Rosarium Virginis Mariae*. To contemplate the face of Christ, and to contemplate it with Mary, is the "programme" which I have set before the Church at the dawn of the third millennium, summoning her to put out into the deep on the sea of history with the enthusiasm of the new evangelization. To contemplate Christ involves being able to recognize him wherever he manifests himself, in his many forms of presence, but above all in the living sacrament of his body and his blood. *The Church draws her life from Christ in the Eucharist*; by him she is fed and by him she is enlightened. The Eucharist is both a mystery of faith and a "mystery of light".[3] Whenever the Church celebrates the Eucharist, the faithful can in some way relive the experience of the two disciples on the road to Emmaus: "their eyes were opened and they recognized him" (*Lk* 24:31).

7. From the time I began my ministry as the Successor of Peter, I have always marked Holy Thursday, the day of the Eucharist and of the priesthood, by sending a letter to all the priests of the world. This year, the twenty-fifth of my Pontificate, I wish to involve the whole Church more fully in this Eucharistic reflection, also as a way of thanking the Lord for the gift of the Eucharist and the priesthood: "Gift and Mystery".[4] By proclaiming the Year of the Rosary, I wish to put this, my twenty-fifth anniversary, *under the aegis of the contemplation of Christ at the school of Mary*. Consequently, I

---

3   Cf. John Paul II, Apostolic Letter *Rosarium Virginis Mariae* (16 October 2002), 21: AAS 95 (2003), 19.

4   This is the title which I gave to an autobiographical testimony issued for my fiftieth anniversary of priestly ordination.

cannot let this Holy Thursday 2003 pass without halting before the "Eucharistic face" of Christ and pointing out with new force to the Church the centrality of the Eucharist. From it the Church draws her life. From this "living bread" she draws her nourishment. How could I not feel the need to urge everyone to experience it ever anew?

8. When I think of the Eucharist, and look at my life as a priest, as a Bishop and as the Successor of Peter, I naturally recall the many times and places in which I was able to celebrate it. I remember the parish church of Niegowic', where I had my first pastoral assignment, the collegiate church of Saint Florian in Krakow, Wawel Cathedral, Saint Peter's Basilica and so many basilicas and churches in Rome and throughout the world. I have been able to celebrate Holy Mass in chapels built along mountain paths, on lakeshores and seacoasts; I have celebrated it on altars built in stadiums and in city squares…This varied scenario of celebrations of the Eucharist has given me a powerful experience of its universal and, so to speak, cosmic character. Yes, cosmic! Because even when it is celebrated on the humble altar of a country church, the Eucharist is always in some way celebrated *on the altar of the world*. It unites heaven and earth. It embraces and permeates all creation. The Son of God became man in order to restore all creation, in one supreme act of praise, to the One who made it from nothing. He, the Eternal High Priest who by the blood of his Cross entered the eternal sanctuary, thus gives back to the Creator and Father all creation redeemed. He does so through the priestly ministry of the Church, to the glory of the Most Holy Trinity. Truly this is the *mysterium fidei* which is accomplished in the Eucharist: the world which came forth from the hands of God the Creator now returns to him redeemed by Christ.

9. The Eucharist, as Christ's saving presence in the community of the faithful and its spiritual food, is the most precious possession which the Church can have in her journey through history. This explains the *lively concern* which she has always shown for the Eucharistic mystery, a concern which finds authoritative expression in the work of the Councils and the Popes. How can we not admire the doctrinal expositions of the Decrees on the Most Holy Eucharist and on the Holy Sacrifice of the Mass promulgated by the Council of Trent? For centuries those Decrees guided theology and catechesis, and they are still a dogmatic reference-point for the continual renewal and growth of God's People in faith and in love for the Eucharist. In times closer to our own, three Encyclical Letters should be mentioned: the Encyclical *Mirae Caritatis* of Leo XIII (28 May 1902),[5] the Encyclical *Mediator Dei* of Pius XII (20 November 1947)[6] and the Encyclical *Mysterium Fidei* of Paul VI (3 September 1965).[7]

The Second Vatican Council, while not issuing a specific document on the Eucharistic mystery, considered its various aspects throughout its documents, especially the Dogmatic Constitution on the Church *Lumen Gentium* and the Constitution on the Sacred Liturgy *Sacrosanctum Concilium*.

I myself, in the first years of my apostolic ministry in the Chair of Peter, wrote the Apostolic Letter *Dominicae Cenae* (24 February 1980),[8] in which I discussed some

---

5   *Leonis XIII P.M. Acta*, XXII (1903), 115–136.

6   AAS 39 (1947), 521–595.

7   AAS 57 (1965), 753–774.

8   AAS 72 (1980), 113–148.

aspects of the Eucharistic mystery and its importance for the life of those who are its ministers. Today I take up anew the thread of that argument, with even greater emotion and gratitude in my heart, echoing as it were the word of the Psalmist: "What shall I render to the Lord for all his bounty to me? I will lift up the cup of salvation and call on the name of the Lord" (*Ps* 116:12–13).

10. The Magisterium's commitment to proclaiming the Eucharistic mystery has been matched by interior growth within the Christian community. Certainly *the liturgical reform inaugurated by the Council* has greatly contributed to a more conscious, active and fruitful participation in the Holy Sacrifice of the Altar on the part of the faithful. In many places, *adoration of the Blessed Sacrament* is also an important daily practice and becomes an inexhaustible source of holiness. The devout participation of the faithful in the Eucharistic procession on the Solemnity of the Body and Blood of Christ is a grace from the Lord which yearly brings joy to those who take part in it.

Other positive signs of Eucharistic faith and love might also be mentioned.

Unfortunately, alongside these lights, *there are also shadows*. In some places the practice of Eucharistic adoration has been almost completely abandoned. In various parts of the Church abuses have occurred, leading to confusion with regard to sound faith and Catholic doctrine concerning this wonderful sacrament. At times one encounters an extremely reductive understanding of the Eucharistic mystery. Stripped of its sacrificial meaning, it is celebrated as if it were simply a fraternal banquet. Furthermore, the necessity of the ministerial priesthood, grounded in apostolic succession, is at times obscured and the sacramental nature of the Eucharist is reduced to its mere effectiveness as a form of proclamation. This has led here and there to ecumenical initiatives which, albeit well-intentioned, indulge in Eucharistic practices contrary to the discipline by which the Church expresses her faith. How can we not express profound grief at all this? The Eucharist is too great a gift to tolerate ambiguity and depreciation.

It is my hope that the present Encyclical Letter will effectively help to banish the dark clouds of unacceptable doctrine and practice, so that the Eucharist will continue to shine forth in all its radiant mystery.

CHAPTER ONE

THE MYSTERY OF FAITH

11. "The Lord Jesus on the night he was betrayed" (*1 Cor* 11:23) instituted the Eucharistic Sacrifice of his body and his blood. The words of the Apostle Paul bring us back to the dramatic setting in which the Eucharist was born. The Eucharist is indelibly marked by the event of the Lord's passion and death, of which it is not only a reminder but the sacramental re-presentation. It is the sacrifice of the Cross perpetuated down the ages.[9] This truth is well expressed by the words with which the assembly in the Latin rite responds to the priest's proclamation of the "Mystery of Faith": *"We announce your death, O Lord"*.

---

9   Cf. Second Vatican Ecumenical Council, Constitution *Sacrosanctum Concilium*, 47: "...our Saviour instituted the Eucharistic Sacrifice of his body and blood, in order to perpetuate the sacrifice of the Cross throughout time, until he should return".

The Church has received the Eucharist from Christ her Lord not as one gift—however precious—among so many others, but as the *gift par excellence*, for it is the gift of himself, of his person in his sacred humanity, as well as the gift of his saving work. Nor does it remain confined to the past, since "all that Christ is—all that he did and suffered for all men—participates in the divine eternity, and so transcends all times".[10]

When the Church celebrates the Eucharist, the memorial of her Lord's death and resurrection, this central event of salvation becomes really present and "the work of our redemption is carried out".[11] This sacrifice is so decisive for the salvation of the human race that Jesus Christ offered it and returned to the Father only *after he had left us a means of sharing in it* as if we had been present there. Each member of the faithful can thus take part in it and inexhaustibly gain its fruits. This is the faith from which generations of Christians down the ages have lived. The Church's Magisterium has constantly reaffirmed this faith with joyful gratitude for its inestimable gift.[12] I wish once more to recall this truth and to join you, my dear brothers and sisters, in adoration before this mystery: a great mystery, a mystery of mercy. What more could Jesus have done for us? Truly, in the Eucharist, he shows us a love which goes "to the end" (cf. *Jn* 13:1), a love which knows no measure.

12. This aspect of the universal charity of the Eucharistic Sacrifice is based on the words of the Saviour himself. In instituting it, he did not merely say: "This is my body", "this is my blood", but went on to add: "which is given for you", "which is poured out for you" (*Lk* 22:19–20). Jesus did not simply state that what he was giving them to eat and drink was his body and his blood; he also expressed its *sacrificial meaning* and made sacramentally present his sacrifice which would soon be offered on the Cross for the salvation of all. "The Mass is at the same time, and inseparably, the sacrificial memorial in which the sacrifice of the Cross is perpetuated and the sacred banquet of communion with the Lord's body and blood".[13]

The Church constantly draws her life from the redeeming sacrifice; she approaches it not only through faith-filled remembrance, but also through a real contact, since *this sacrifice is made present ever anew*, sacramentally perpetuated, in every community which offers it at the hands of the consecrated minister. The Eucharist thus applies to men and women today the reconciliation won once for all by Christ for mankind in every age. "The sacrifice of Christ and the sacrifice of the Eucharist are *one single sacrifice*".[14] Saint John Chrysostom put it well: "We always offer the same Lamb, not one today and another tomorrow, but always the same one. For this reason the sacrifice

---

10 *Catechism of the Catholic Church*, 1085.

11 Second Vatican Ecumenical Council, Dogmatic Constitution on the Church *Lumen Gentium*, 3.

12 Cf. Paul VI, *Solemn Profession of Faith*, 30 June 1968, 24: AAS 60 (1968), 442; John Paul II, Apostolic Letter *Dominicae Cenae* (24 February 1980), 12: AAS 72 (1980), 142.

13 *Catechism of the Catholic Church*, 1382.

14 *Catechism of the Catholic Church*, 1367.

is always only one...Even now we offer that victim who was once offered and who will never be consumed".[15]

The Mass makes present the sacrifice of the Cross; it does not add to that sacrifice nor does it multiply it.[16] What is repeated is its *memorial* celebration, its "commemorative representation" (*memorialis demonstratio*),[17] which makes Christ's one, definitive redemptive sacrifice always present in time. The sacrificial nature of the Eucharistic mystery cannot therefore be understood as something separate, independent of the Cross or only indirectly referring to the sacrifice of Calvary.

13. By virtue of its close relationship to the sacrifice of Golgotha, the Eucharist is *a sacrifice in the strict sense*, and not only in a general way, as if it were simply a matter of Christ's offering himself to the faithful as their spiritual food. The gift of his love and obedience to the point of giving his life (cf. *Jn* 10:17–18) is in the first place a gift to his Father. Certainly it is a gift given for our sake, and indeed that of all humanity (cf. *Mt* 26:28; *Mk* 14:24; *Lk* 22:20; *Jn* 10:15), yet it is *first and foremost a gift to the Father*: "a sacrifice that the Father accepted, giving, in return for this total self-giving by his Son, who 'became obedient unto death' (*Phil* 2:8), his own paternal gift, that is to say the grant of new immortal life in the resurrection".[18]

In giving his sacrifice to the Church, Christ has also made his own the spiritual sacrifice of the Church, which is called to offer herself in union with the sacrifice of Christ. This is the teaching of the Second Vatican Council concerning all the faithful: "Taking part in the Eucharistic Sacrifice, which is the source and summit of the whole Christian life, they offer the divine victim to God, and offer themselves along with it".[19]

14. Christ's passover includes not only his passion and death, but also his resurrection. This is recalled by the assembly's acclamation following the consecration: *"We proclaim your resurrection"*. The Eucharistic Sacrifice makes present not only the mystery of the Saviour's passion and death, but also the mystery of the resurrection which crowned his sacrifice. It is as the living and risen One that Christ can become in the Eucharist the "bread of life" (*Jn* 6:35, 48), the "living bread" (*Jn* 6:51). Saint Ambrose reminded the newly-initiated that the Eucharist applies the event of the resurrection to their lives: "Today Christ is yours, yet each day he rises again for you".[20] Saint Cyril of Alexandria also makes clear that sharing in the sacred mysteries

---

15 *In Epistolam ad Hebraeos Homiliae, Hom.* 17,3: PG 63, 131.

16 Cf. Ecumenical Council of Trent, Session XXII, *Doctrina de ss. Missae Sacrificio*, Chapter 2: DS 1743: "It is one and the same victim here offering himself by the ministry of his priests, who then offered himself on the Cross; it is only the manner of offering that is different".

17 Pius XII, Encyclical Letter *Mediator Dei* (20 November 1947): AAS 39 (1947), 548.

18 John Paul II, Encyclical Letter *Redemptor Hominis* (15 March 1979), 20: AAS 71 (1979), 310.

19 Dogmatic Constitution on the Church *Lumen Gentium*, 11.

20 *De Sacramentis*, V, 4, 26: CSEL 73, 70.

"is a true confession and a remembrance that the Lord died and returned to life for us and on our behalf".[21]

15. The sacramental representation of Christ's sacrifice, crowned by the resurrection, in the Mass involves a most special presence which—in the words of Paul VI—"is called 'real' not as a way of excluding all other types of presence as if they were 'not real', but because it is a presence in the fullest sense: a substantial presence whereby Christ, the God-Man, is wholly and entirely present".[22] This sets forth once more the perennially valid teaching of the Council of Trent: "the consecration of the bread and wine effects the change of the whole substance of the bread into the substance of the body of Christ our Lord, and of the whole substance of the wine into the substance of his blood. And the holy Catholic Church has fittingly and properly called this change transubstantiation".[23] Truly the Eucharist is a *mysterium fidei*, a mystery which surpasses our understanding and can only be received in faith, as is often brought out in the catechesis of the Church Fathers regarding this divine sacrament: "Do not see— Saint Cyril of Jerusalem exhorts—in the bread and wine merely natural elements, because the Lord has expressly said that they are his body and his blood: faith assures you of this, though your senses suggest otherwise".[24]

Adoro te devote, latens Deitas, we shall continue to sing with the Angelic Doctor. Before this mystery of love, human reason fully experiences its limitations. One understands how, down the centuries, this truth has stimulated theology to strive to understand it ever more deeply.

These are praiseworthy efforts, which are all the more helpful and insightful to the extent that they are able to join critical thinking to the "living faith" of the Church, as grasped especially by the Magisterium's "sure charism of truth" and the "intimate sense of spiritual realities"[25] which is attained above all by the saints. There remains the boundary indicated by Paul VI: "Every theological explanation which seeks some understanding of this mystery, in order to be in accord with Catholic faith, must firmly maintain that in objective reality, independently of our mind, the bread and wine have ceased to exist after the consecration, so that the adorable body and blood of the Lord Jesus from that moment on are really before us under the sacramental species of bread and wine".[26]

16. The saving efficacy of the sacrifice is fully realized when the Lord's body and blood are received in communion. The Eucharistic Sacrifice is intrinsically directed to the inward union of the faithful with Christ through communion; we receive the very One who offered himself for us, we receive his body which he gave up for us on the Cross and his blood which he "poured out for many for the forgiveness of sins" (*Mt*

---

21 *In Ioannis Evangelium*, XII, 20: PG 74, 726.

22 Encyclical Letter *Mysterium Fidei* (3 September 1965): AAS 57 (1965), 764.

23 Session XIII, *Decretum de ss. Eucharistia*, Chapter 4: DS 1642.

24 *Mystagogical Catecheses*, IV, 6: SCh 126, 138.

25 Second Vatican Ecumenical Council, Dogmatic Constitution on Divine Revelation *Dei Verbum*, 8.

26 *Solemn Profession of Faith*, 30 June 1968, 25: AAS 60 (1968), 442–443.

26:28). We are reminded of his words: "As the living Father sent me, and I live because of the Father, so he who eats me will live because of me" (*Jn* 6:57). Jesus himself reassures us that this union, which he compares to that of the life of the Trinity, is truly realized. *The Eucharist is a true banquet*, in which Christ offers himself as our nourishment. When for the first time Jesus spoke of this food, his listeners were astonished and bewildered, which forced the Master to emphasize the objective truth of his words: "Truly, truly, I say to you, unless you eat the flesh of the Son of Man and drink his blood, you have no life within you" (*Jn* 6:53). This is no metaphorical food: "My flesh is food indeed, and my blood is drink indeed" (*Jn* 6:55).

17. Through our communion in his body and blood, Christ also grants us his Spirit. Saint Ephrem writes: "He called the bread his living body and he filled it with himself and his Spirit...He who eats it with faith, eats Fire and Spirit...Take and eat this, all of you, and eat with it the Holy Spirit. For it is truly my body and whoever eats it will have eternal life".[27] The Church implores this divine Gift, the source of every other gift, in the Eucharistic epiclesis. In the *Divine Liturgy* of Saint John Chrysostom, for example, we find the prayer: "We beseech, implore and beg you: send your Holy Spirit upon us all and upon these gifts...that those who partake of them may be purified in soul, receive the forgiveness of their sins, and share in the Holy Spirit".[28] And in the *Roman Missal* the celebrant prays: "grant that we who are nourished by his body and blood may be filled with his Holy Spirit, and become one body, one spirit in Christ".[29] Thus by the gift of his body and blood Christ increases within us the gift of his Spirit, already poured out in Baptism and bestowed as a "seal" in the sacrament of Confirmation.

18. The acclamation of the assembly following the consecration appropriately ends by expressing the eschatological thrust which marks the celebration of the Eucharist (cf. *1 Cor* 11:26): *"until you come in glory"*. The Eucharist is a straining towards the goal, a foretaste of the fullness of joy promised by Christ (cf. *Jn* 15:11); it is in some way the anticipation of heaven, the "pledge of future glory".[30] In the Eucharist, everything speaks of confident waiting "in joyful hope for the coming of our Saviour, Jesus Christ".[31] Those who feed on Christ in the Eucharist need not wait until the hereafter to receive eternal life: *they already possess it on earth*, as the first-fruits of a future fullness which will embrace man in his totality. For in the Eucharist we also receive the pledge of our bodily resurrection at the end of the world: "He who eats my flesh and drinks my blood has eternal life, and I will raise him up at the last day" (*Jn* 6:54). This pledge of the future resurrection comes from the fact that the flesh of the Son of Man, given as food, is his body in its glorious state after the resurrection. With the Eucharist we digest, as it were, the "secret" of the resurrection. For this reason Saint

---

27 *Sermo IV in Hebdomadam Sanctam*: CSCO 413/Syr. 182, 55.

28 Anaphora.

29 Eucharistic Prayer III.

30 Solemnity of the Body and Blood of Christ, Second Vespers, Antiphon to the *Magnificat*.

31 *Missale Romanum*, Embolism following the Lord's Prayer.

Ignatius of Antioch rightly defined the Eucharistic Bread as "a medicine of immortality, an antidote to death".[32]

19. The eschatological tension kindled by the Eucharist *expresses and reinforces our communion with the Church in heaven*. It is not by chance that the Eastern Anaphoras and the Latin Eucharistic Prayers honour Mary, the ever-Virgin Mother of Jesus Christ our Lord and God, the angels, the holy apostles, the glorious martyrs and all the saints. This is an aspect of the Eucharist which merits greater attention: in celebrating the sacrifice of the Lamb, we are united to the heavenly "liturgy" and become part of that great multitude which cries out: "Salvation belongs to our God who sits upon the throne, and to the Lamb!" (*Rev* 7:10). The Eucharist is truly a glimpse of heaven appearing on earth. It is a glorious ray of the heavenly Jerusalem which pierces the clouds of our history and lights up our journey.

20. A significant consequence of the eschatological tension inherent in the Eucharist is also the fact that it spurs us on our journey through history and plants a seed of living hope in our daily commitment to the work before us. Certainly the Christian vision leads to the expectation of "new heavens" and "a new earth" (*Rev* 21:1), but this increases, rather than lessens, *our sense of responsibility for the world today*.[33] I wish to reaffirm this forcefully at the beginning of the new millennium, so that Christians will feel more obliged than ever not to neglect their duties as citizens in this world. Theirs is the task of contributing with the light of the Gospel to the building of a more human world, a world fully in harmony with God's plan.

Many problems darken the horizon of our time. We need but think of the urgent need to work for peace, to base relationships between peoples on solid premises of justice and solidarity, and to defend human life from conception to its natural end. And what should we say of the thousand inconsistencies of a "globalized" world where the weakest, the most powerless and the poorest appear to have so little hope! It is in this world that Christian hope must shine forth! For this reason too, the Lord wished to remain with us in the Eucharist, making his presence in meal and sacrifice the promise of a humanity renewed by his love. Significantly, in their account of the Last Supper, the Synoptics recount the institution of the Eucharist, while the Gospel of John relates, as a way of bringing out its profound meaning, the account of the "washing of the feet", in which Jesus appears as the teacher of communion and of service (cf. *Jn* 13:1–20). The Apostle Paul, for his part, says that it is "unworthy" of a Christian community to partake of the Lord's Supper amid division and indifference towards the poor (cf. *1 Cor* 11:17–22, 27–34).[34]

---

32 *Ad Ephesios*, 20: PG 5, 661.

33 Cf. Second Vatican Ecumenical Council, Pastoral Constitution on the Church in the Modern World *Gaudium et Spes*, 39.

34 "Do you wish to honour the body of Christ? Do not ignore him when he is naked. Do not pay him homage in the temple clad in silk, only then to neglect him outside where he is cold and ill-clad. He who said: 'This is my body' is the same who said: 'You saw me hungry and you gave me no food', and 'Whatever you did to the least of my brothers you did also to me'...What good is it if the Eucharistic table is overloaded with golden chalices when your brother is dying of hunger.

Proclaiming the death of the Lord "until he comes" (*1 Cor* 11:26) entails that all who take part in the Eucharist be committed to changing their lives and making them in a certain way completely "Eucharistic". It is this fruit of a transfigured existence and a commitment to transforming the world in accordance with the Gospel which splendidly illustrates the eschatological tension inherent in the celebration of the Eucharist and in the Christian life as a whole: "Come, Lord Jesus!" (*Rev* 22:20).

CHAPTER TWO

THE EUCHARIST BUILDS THE CHURCH

21. The Second Vatican Council teaches that the celebration of the Eucharist is at the centre of the process of the Church's growth. After stating that "the Church, as the Kingdom of Christ already present in mystery, grows visibly in the world through the power of God",[35] then, as if in answer to the question: "How does the Church grow?", the Council adds: "as often as the sacrifice of the Cross by which 'Christ our pasch is sacrificed' (*1 Cor* 5:7) is celebrated on the altar, the work of our redemption is carried out. At the same time in the sacrament of the Eucharistic bread, the unity of the faithful, who form one body in Christ (cf. *1 Cor* 10:17), is both expressed and brought about".[36]

A causal influence of the Eucharist is present at the Church's very origins. The Evangelists specify that it was the Twelve, the Apostles, who gathered with Jesus at the Last Supper (cf. *Mt* 26:20; *Mk* 14:17; *Lk* 22:14). This is a detail of notable importance, for the Apostles "were both the seeds of the new Israel and the beginning of the sacred hierarchy".[37] By offering them his body and his blood as food, Christ mysteriously involved them in the sacrifice which would be completed later on Calvary. By analogy with the Covenant of Mount Sinai, sealed by sacrifice and the sprinkling of blood,[38] the actions and words of Jesus at the Last Supper laid the foundations of the new messianic community, the People of the New Covenant.

The Apostles, by accepting in the Upper Room Jesus' invitation: "Take, eat", "Drink of it, all of you" (*Mt* 26:26–27), entered for the first time into sacramental communion with him. From that time forward, until the end of the age, the Church is built up through sacramental communion with the Son of God who was sacrificed for

---

Start by satisfying his hunger and then with what is left you may adorn the altar as well": Saint John Chrysostom, *In Evangelium S. Matthaei, hom.* 50:3–4: PG 58, 508–509; cf. John Paul II, Encyclical Letter *Sollicitudo Rei Socialis* (30 December 1987), 31: AAS 80 (1988), 553–556.

35 Dogmatic Constitution *Lumen Gentium*, 3.

36 *Ibid.*

37 Second Vatican Ecumenical Council, Decree on the Missionary Activity of the Church *Ad Gentes*, 5.

38 "Moses took the blood and threw it upon the people, and said: 'Behold the blood of the Covenant which the Lord has made with you in accordance with all these words'" (*Ex* 24:8).

our sake: "Do this is remembrance of me…Do this, as often as you drink it, in remembrance of me" (*1 Cor* 11:24–25; cf. *Lk* 22:19).

22. Incorporation into Christ, which is brought about by Baptism, is constantly renewed and consolidated by sharing in the Eucharistic Sacrifice, especially by that full sharing which takes place in sacramental communion. We can say not only that *each of us receives Christ*, but also that *Christ receives each of us*. He enters into friendship with us: "You are my friends" (*Jn* 15:14). Indeed, it is because of him that we have life: "He who eats me will live because of me" (*Jn* 6:57). Eucharistic communion brings about in a sublime way the mutual "abiding" of Christ and each of his followers: "Abide in me, and I in you" (*Jn* 15:4).

By its union with Christ, the People of the New Covenant, far from closing in upon itself, becomes a "sacrament" for humanity,[39] a sign and instrument of the salvation achieved by Christ, the light of the world and the salt of the earth (cf. *Mt* 5:13–16), for the redemption of all.[40] The Church's mission stands in continuity with the mission of Christ: "As the Father has sent me, even so I send you" (*Jn* 20:21). From the perpetuation of the sacrifice of the Cross and her communion with the body and blood of Christ in the Eucharist, the Church draws the spiritual power needed to carry out her mission. The Eucharist thus appears as both *the source* and *the summit* of all evangelization, since its goal is the communion of mankind with Christ and in him with the Father and the Holy Spirit.[41]

23. Eucharistic communion also confirms the Church in her unity as the body of Christ. Saint Paul refers to this *unifying power* of participation in the banquet of the Eucharist when he writes to the Corinthians: "The bread which we break, is it not a communion in the body of Christ? Because there is one bread, we who are many are one body, for we all partake of the one bread" (*1 Cor* 10:16–17). Saint John Chrysostom's commentary on these words is profound and perceptive: "For what is the bread? It is the body of Christ. And what do those who receive it become? The Body of Christ—not many bodies but one body. For as bread is completely one, though made of up many grains of wheat, and these, albeit unseen, remain nonetheless present, in such a way that their difference is not apparent since they have been made a perfect whole, so too are we mutually joined to one another and together united with Christ".[42] The argument is compelling: our union with Christ, which is a gift and grace for each of us, makes it possible for us, in him, to share in the unity of his body which is the Church. The Eucharist reinforces the incorporation into Christ which took place in Baptism though the gift of the Spirit (cf. *1 Cor* 12:13, 27).

---

39 Cf. Second Vatican Ecumenical Council, Dogmatic Constitution on the Church *Lumen Gentium*, 1.

40 Cf. *ibid.*, 9.

41 Cf. Second Vatican Ecumenical Council, Decree on the Life and Ministry of Priests *Presbyterorum Ordinis*, 5. The same Decree, in No. 6, says: "No Christian community can be built up which does not grow from and hinge on the celebration of the most holy Eucharist".

42 *In Epistolam I ad Corinthios Homiliae*, 24, 2: PG 61, 200; Cf. *Didache*, IX, 4: F.X. Funk, I, 22; Saint Cyprian, *Ep.* LXIII, 13: PL 4, 384.

The joint and inseparable activity of the Son and of the Holy Spirit, which is at the origin of the Church, of her consolidation and her continued life, is at work in the Eucharist. This was clearly evident to the author of the *Liturgy of Saint James*: in the epiclesis of the Anaphora, God the Father is asked to send the Holy Spirit upon the faithful and upon the offerings, so that the body and blood of Christ "may be a help to all those who partake of it…for the sanctification of their souls and bodies".[43] The Church is fortified by the divine Paraclete through the sanctification of the faithful in the Eucharist.

24. The gift of Christ and his Spirit which we receive in Eucharistic communion superabundantly fulfils the yearning for fraternal unity deeply rooted in the human heart; at the same time it elevates the experience of fraternity already present in our common sharing at the same Eucharistic table to a degree which far surpasses that of the simple human experience of sharing a meal. Through her communion with the body of Christ the Church comes to be ever more profoundly "in Christ in the nature of a sacrament, that is, a sign and instrument of intimate unity with God and of the unity of the whole human race".[44]

The seeds of disunity, which daily experience shows to be so deeply rooted in humanity as a result of sin, are countered by *the unifying power* of the body of Christ. The Eucharist, precisely by building up the Church, creates human community.

25. The *worship of the Eucharist outside of the Mass* is of inestimable value for the life of the Church. This worship is strictly linked to the celebration of the Eucharistic Sacrifice. The presence of Christ under the sacred species reserved after Mass—a presence which lasts as long as the species of bread and of wine remain [45]—derives from the celebration of the sacrifice and is directed towards communion, both sacramental and spiritual.[46] It is the responsibility of Pastors to encourage, also by their personal witness, the practice of Eucharistic adoration, and exposition of the Blessed Sacrament in particular, as well as prayer of adoration before Christ present under the Eucharistic species.[47]

It is pleasant to spend time with him, to lie close to his breast like the Beloved Disciple (cf. *Jn* 13:25) and to feel the infinite love present in his heart. If in our time Christians must be distinguished above all by the "art of prayer",[48] how can we not feel a renewed need to spend time in spiritual converse, in silent adoration, in heartfelt love before Christ present in the Most Holy Sacrament? How often, dear brother and sisters, have I experienced this, and drawn from it strength, consolation and support!

43 PO 26, 206.

44 Second Vatican Ecumenical Council, Dogmatic Constitution on the Church *Lumen Gentium*, 1.

45 Cf. Ecumenical Council of Trent, Session XIII, *Decretum de ss. Eucharistia*, Canon 4: DS 1654.

46 Cf. *Rituale Romanum: De sacra communione et de cultu mysterii eucharistici extra Missam*, 36 (No. 80).

47 Cf. *ibid.*, 38–39 (Nos. 86–90).

48 John Paul II, Apostolic Letter *Novo Millennio Ineunte* (6 January 2001), 32: AAS 93 (2001), 288.

This practice, repeatedly praised and recommended by the Magisterium,[49] is supported by the example of many saints. Particularly outstanding in this regard was Saint Alphonsus Liguori, who wrote: "Of all devotions, that of adoring Jesus in the Blessed Sacrament is the greatest after the sacraments, the one dearest to God and the one most helpful to us".[50] The Eucharist is a priceless treasure: by not only celebrating it but also by praying before it outside of Mass we are enabled to make contact with the very wellspring of grace. A Christian community desirous of contemplating the face of Christ in the spirit which I proposed in the Apostolic Letters *Novo Millennio Ineunte* and *Rosarium Virginis Mariae* cannot fail also to develop this aspect of Eucharistic worship, which prolongs and increases the fruits of our communion in the body and blood of the Lord.

CHAPTER THREE

THE APOSTOLICITY OF THE EUCHARIST AND OF THE CHURCH

26. If, as I have said, the Eucharist builds the Church and the Church makes the Eucharist, it follows that there is a profound relationship between the two, so much so that we can apply to the Eucharistic mystery the very words with which, in the Nicene-Constantinopolitan Creed, we profess the Church to be "one, holy, catholic and apostolic". The Eucharist too is one and catholic. It is also holy, indeed, the Most Holy Sacrament. But it is above all its apostolicity that we must now consider.

27. The *Catechism of the Catholic Church*, in explaining how the Church is apostolic—founded on the Apostles—sees *three meanings* in this expression. First, "she was and remains built on 'the foundation of the Apostles' (*Eph* 2:20), the witnesses chosen and sent on mission by Christ himself".[51] The Eucharist too has its foundation in the Apostles, not in the sense that it did not originate in Christ himself, but because it was entrusted by Jesus to the Apostles and has been handed down to us by them and by their successors. It is in continuity with the practice of the Apostles, in obedience to the Lord's command, that the Church has celebrated the Eucharist down the centuries.

The second sense in which the Church is apostolic, as the *Catechism* points out, is that "with the help of the Spirit dwelling in her, the Church keeps and hands on the teaching, the 'good deposit', the salutary words she has heard from the Apostles".[52] Here too the Eucharist is apostolic, for it is celebrated in conformity with the faith of the Apostles. At various times in the two-thousand-year history of the People of the

---

49 "In the course of the day the faithful should not omit visiting the Blessed Sacrament, which in accordance with liturgical law must be reserved in churches with great reverence in a prominent place. Such visits are a sign of gratitude, an expression of love and an acknowledgment of the Lord's presence": Paul VI, Encyclical Letter *Mysterium Fidei* (3 September 1965): AAS 57 (1965), 771.

50 *Visite al SS. Sacramento e a Maria Santissima*, Introduction: *Opere Ascetiche, Avellino*, 2000, 295.

51 No. 857.

52 *Ibid.*

New Covenant, the Church's Magisterium has more precisely defined her teaching on the Eucharist, including its proper terminology, precisely in order to safeguard the apostolic faith with regard to this sublime mystery. This faith remains unchanged and it is essential for the Church that it remain unchanged.

28. Lastly, the Church is apostolic in the sense that she "continues to be taught, sanctified and guided by the Apostles until Christ's return, through their successors in pastoral office: the college of Bishops assisted by priests, in union with the Successor of Peter, the Church's supreme pastor".[53] Succession to the Apostles in the pastoral mission necessarily entails the sacrament of Holy Orders, that is, the uninterrupted sequence, from the very beginning, of valid episcopal ordinations.[54] This succession is essential for the Church to exist in a proper and full sense.

The Eucharist also expresses this sense of apostolicity. As the Second Vatican Council teaches, "the faithful join in the offering of the Eucharist by virtue of their royal priesthood",[55] yet it is the ordained priest who, "acting in the person of Christ, brings about the Eucharistic Sacrifice and offers it to God in the name of all the people".[56] For this reason, the Roman Missal prescribes that only the priest should recite the Eucharistic Prayer, while the people participate in faith and in silence.[57]

29. The expression repeatedly employed by the Second Vatican Council, according to which "the ministerial priest, acting in the person of Christ, brings about the Eucharistic Sacrifice",[58] was already firmly rooted in papal teaching.[59] As I have pointed out on other occasions, the phrase *in persona Christi* "means more than offering 'in the name of' or 'in the place of' Christ. *In persona* means in specific sacramental identification with the eternal High Priest who is the author and principal subject of this sacrifice of his, a sacrifice in which, in truth, nobody can take his place".[60] The ministry of priests who have received the sacrament of Holy Orders, in the economy of salvation chosen by Christ, makes clear that the Eucharist which they celebrate is a *gift which*

---

53 *Ibid.*

54 Cf. Congregation for the Doctrine of the Faith, Letter *Sacerdotium Ministeriale* (6 August 1983), III.2: AAS 75 (1983), 1005.

55 Second Vatican Ecumenical Council, Dogmatic Constitution on the Church *Lumen Gentium*, 10.

56 *Ibid.*

57 Cf. *Institutio Generalis*: Editio typica tertia, No. 147.

58 Cf. Dogmatic Constitution on the Church *Lumen Gentium*, 10 and 28; Decree on the Ministry and Life of Priests *Presbyterorum Ordinis*, 2.

59 "The minister of the altar acts in the person of Christ inasmuch as he is head, making an offering in the name of all the members": Pius XII, Encyclical Letter *Mediator Dei* (20 November 1947): AAS 39 (1947), 556; cf. Pius X, Apostolic Exhortation *Haerent Animo* (4 August 1908): *Acta Pii X*, IV, 16; Pius XI, Encyclical Letter *Ad Catholici Sacerdotii* (20 December 1935): AAS 28 (1936), 20.

60 Apostolic Letter *Dominicae Cenae* (24 February 1980), 8: AAS 72 (1980), 128–129.

radically transcends the power of the assembly and is in any event essential for validly linking the Eucharistic consecration to the sacrifice of the Cross and to the Last Supper. The assembly gathered together for the celebration of the Eucharist, if it is to be a truly Eucharistic assembly, absolutely requires the presence of an ordained priest as its president. On the other hand, the community is by itself incapable of providing an ordained minister. This minister is a gift which the assembly *receives through episcopal succession going back to the Apostles*. It is the Bishop who, through the Sacrament of Holy Orders, makes a new presbyter by conferring upon him the power to consecrate the Eucharist. Consequently, "the Eucharistic mystery cannot be celebrated in any community except by an ordained priest, as the Fourth Lateran Council expressly taught".[61]

30. The Catholic Church's teaching on the relationship between priestly ministry and the Eucharist and her teaching on the Eucharistic Sacrifice have both been the subject in recent decades of a fruitful dialogue *in the area of ecumenism*. We must give thanks to the Blessed Trinity for the significant progress and convergence achieved in this regard, which lead us to hope one day for a full sharing of faith. Nonetheless, the observations of the Council concerning the Ecclesial Communities which arose in the West from the sixteenth century onwards and are separated from the Catholic Church remain fully pertinent: "The Ecclesial Communities separated from us lack that fullness of unity with us which should flow from Baptism, and we believe that especially because of the lack of the sacrament of Orders they have not preserved the genuine and total reality of the Eucharistic mystery. Nevertheless, when they commemorate the Lord's death and resurrection in the Holy Supper, they profess that it signifies life in communion with Christ and they await his coming in glory".[62]

The Catholic faithful, therefore, while respecting the religious convictions of these separated brethren, must refrain from receiving the communion distributed in their celebrations, so as not to condone an ambiguity about the nature of the Eucharist and, consequently, to fail in their duty to bear clear witness to the truth. This would result in slowing the progress being made towards full visible unity. Similarly, it is unthinkable to substitute for Sunday Mass ecumenical celebrations of the word or services of common prayer with Christians from the aforementioned Ecclesial Communities, or even participation in their own liturgical services. Such celebrations and services, however praiseworthy in certain situations, prepare for the goal of full communion, including Eucharistic communion, but they cannot replace it.

The fact that the power of consecrating the Eucharist has been entrusted only to Bishops and priests does not represent any kind of belittlement of the rest of the People of God, for in the communion of the one body of Christ which is the Church this gift redounds to the benefit of all.

31. If the Eucharist is the centre and summit of the Church's life, it is likewise the centre and summit of priestly ministry. For this reason, with a heart filled with gratitude

---

61 Congregation for the Doctrine of the Faith, Letter *Sacerdotium Ministeriale* (6 August 1983), III.4: AAS 75 (1983), 1006; cf. Fourth Lateran Ecumenical Council, Chapter 1, Constitution on the Catholic Faith *Firmiter Credimus*: DS 802.

62 Second Vatican Ecumenical Council, Decree on Ecumenism *Unitatis Redintegratio*, 22.

to our Lord Jesus Christ, I repeat that the Eucharist "is the principal and central *raison d'être* of the sacrament of priesthood, which effectively came into being at the moment of the institution of the Eucharist".[63]

Priests are engaged in a wide variety of pastoral activities. If we also consider the social and cultural conditions of the modern world it is easy to understand how priests face the very real *risk of losing their focus* amid such a great number of different tasks. The Second Vatican Council saw in pastoral charity the bond which gives unity to the priest's life and work. This, the Council adds, "flows mainly from the Eucharistic Sacrifice, which is therefore the centre and root of the whole priestly life".[64] We can understand, then, how important it is for the spiritual life of the priest, as well as for the good of the Church and the world, that priests follow the Council's recommendation to celebrate the Eucharist daily: "for even if the faithful are unable to be present, it is an act of Christ and the Church".[65] In this way priests will be able to counteract the daily tensions which lead to a lack of focus and they will find in the Eucharistic Sacrifice— the true centre of their lives and ministry—the spiritual strength needed to deal with their different pastoral responsibilities. Their daily activity will thus become truly Eucharistic.

The centrality of the Eucharist in the life and ministry of priests is the basis of its centrality in the *pastoral promotion of priestly vocations*. It is in the Eucharist that prayer for vocations is most closely united to the prayer of Christ the Eternal High Priest. At the same time the diligence of priests in carrying out their Eucharistic ministry, together with the conscious, active and fruitful participation of the faithful in the Eucharist, provides young men with a powerful example and incentive for responding generously to God's call. Often it is the example of a priest's fervent pastoral charity which the Lord uses to sow and to bring to fruition in a young man's heart the seed of a priestly calling.

32. All of this shows how distressing and irregular is the situation of a Christian community which, despite having sufficient numbers and variety of faithful to form a parish, does not have a priest to lead it. Parishes are communities of the baptized who express and affirm their identity above all through the celebration of the Eucharistic Sacrifice. But this requires the presence of a presbyter, who alone is qualified to offer the Eucharist *in persona Christi*. When a community lacks a priest, attempts are rightly made somehow to remedy the situation so that it can continue its Sunday celebrations, and those religious and laity who lead their brothers and sisters in prayer exercise in a praiseworthy way the common priesthood of all the faithful based on the grace of Baptism. But such solutions must be considered merely temporary, while the community awaits a priest.

The sacramental incompleteness of these celebrations should above all inspire the whole community to pray with greater fervour that the Lord will send labourers into his harvest (cf. *Mt* 9:38). It should also be an incentive to mobilize all the resources needed

---

63 Apostolic Letter *Dominicae Cenae* (24 February 1980), 2: AAS 72 (1980), 115.

64 Decree on the Life and Ministry of Priests *Presbyterorum Ordinis*, 14.

65 *Ibid.*, 13; cf. *Code of Canon Law*, Canon 904; *Code of Canons of the Eastern Churches*, Canon 378.

for an adequate pastoral promotion of vocations, without yielding to the temptation to seek solutions which lower the moral and formative standards demanded of candidates for the priesthood.

33. When, due to the scarcity of priests, non-ordained members of the faithful are entrusted with a share in the pastoral care of a parish, they should bear in mind that— as the Second Vatican Council teaches—"no Christian community can be built up unless it has its basis and centre in the celebration of the most Holy Eucharist".[66] They have a responsibility, therefore, to keep alive in the community a genuine "hunger" for the Eucharist, so that no opportunity for the celebration of Mass will ever be missed, also taking advantage of the occasional presence of a priest who is not impeded by Church law from celebrating Mass.

CHAPTER FOUR

THE EUCHARIST AND ECCLESIAL COMMUNION

34. The Extraordinary Assembly of the Synod of Bishops in 1985 saw in the concept of an "ecclesiology of communion" the central and fundamental idea of the documents of the Second Vatican Council.[67] The Church is called during her earthly pilgrimage to maintain and promote communion with the Triune God and communion among the faithful. For this purpose she possesses the word and the sacraments, particularly the Eucharist, by which she "constantly lives and grows"[68] and in which she expresses her very nature. It is not by chance that the term *communion* has become one of the names given to this sublime sacrament.

The Eucharist thus appears as the culmination of all the sacraments in perfecting our communion with God the Father by identification with his only-begotten Son through the working of the Holy Spirit. With discerning faith a distinguished writer of the Byzantine tradition voiced this truth: in the Eucharist "unlike any other sacrament, the mystery [of communion] is so perfect that it brings us to the heights of every good thing: here is the ultimate goal of every human desire, because here we attain God and God joins himself to us in the most perfect union".[69] Precisely for this reason it is good to *cultivate in our hearts a constant desire for the sacrament of the Eucharist*. This was the origin of the practice of "spiritual communion", which has happily been established in the Church for centuries and recommended by saints who were masters of the spiritual life. Saint Teresa of Jesus wrote: "When you do not receive communion and you do not attend Mass, you can make a spiritual communion, which is a most beneficial practice; by it the love of God will be greatly impressed on you".[70]

35. The celebration of the Eucharist, however, cannot be the starting-point for communion; it presupposes that communion already exists, a communion which it

---

66 Decree on the Ministry and Life of Priests *Presbytero- rum Ordinis*, 6.

67 Cf. Final Report, II.C.1: *L'Osservatore Romano*, 10 December 1985, 7.

68 Second Vatican Ecumenical Council, Dogmatic Constitution on the Church *Lumen Gentium*, 26.

69 Nicolas Cabasilas, *Life in Christ*, IV, 10: SCh 355, 270.

70 *Camino de Perfección*, Chapter 35.

seeks to consolidate and bring to perfection. The sacrament is an expression of this bond of communion both in its *invisible* dimension, which, in Christ and through the working of the Holy Spirit, unites us to the Father and among ourselves, and in its *visible* dimension, which entails communion in the teaching of the Apostles, in the sacraments and in the Church's hierarchical order. The profound relationship between the invisible and the visible elements of ecclesial communion is constitutive of the Church as the sacrament of salvation.[71] Only in this context can there be a legitimate celebration of the Eucharist and true participation in it. Consequently it is an intrinsic requirement of the Eucharist that it should be celebrated in communion, and specifically maintaining the various bonds of that communion intact.

36. Invisible communion, though by its nature always growing, presupposes the life of grace, by which we become "partakers of the divine nature" (*2 Pet* 1:4), and the practice of the virtues of faith, hope and love. Only in this way do we have true communion with the Father, the Son and the Holy Spirit. Nor is faith sufficient; we must persevere in sanctifying grace and love, remaining within the Church "bodily" as well as "in our heart"; [72] what is required, in the words of Saint Paul, is "faith working through love" (*Gal* 5:6).

Keeping these invisible bonds intact is a specific moral duty incumbent upon Christians who wish to participate fully in the Eucharist by receiving the body and blood of Christ. The Apostle Paul appeals to this duty when he warns: "Let a man examine himself, and so eat of the bread and drink of the cup" (*1 Cor* 11:28). Saint John Chrysostom, with his stirring eloquence, exhorted the faithful: "I too raise my voice, I beseech, beg and implore that no one draw near to this sacred table with a sullied and corrupt conscience. Such an act, in fact, can never be called 'communion', not even were we to touch the Lord's body a thousand times over, but 'condemnation', 'torment' and 'increase of punishment'".[73]

Along these same lines, the *Catechism of the Catholic Church* rightly stipulates that "anyone conscious of a grave sin must receive the sacrament of Reconciliation before coming to communion".[74] I therefore desire to reaffirm that in the Church there remains in force, now and in the future, the rule by which the Council of Trent gave concrete expression to the Apostle Paul's stern warning when it affirmed that, in order to receive the Eucharist in a worthy manner, "one must first confess one's sins, when one is aware of mortal sin".[75]

---

71 Cf. Congregation for the Doctrine of the Faith, Letter to the Bishops of the Catholic Church on Some Aspects of the Church Understood as Communion *Communionis Notio* (28 May 1992), 4: AAS 85 (1993), 839–840.

72 Cf. Second Vatican Ecumenical Council, Dogmatic Constitution on the Church *Lumen Gentium*, 14.

73 *Homiliae in Isaiam*,6, 3: PG 56, 139.

74 No. 1385; cf. *Code of Canon Law*, Canon 916; *Code of Canons of the Eastern Churches*, Canon 711.

75 Address to the Members of the Sacred Apostolic Penitentiary and the Penitentiaries of the Patriarchal Basilicas of Rome (30 January 1981): AAS 73 (1981), 203. Cf. Ecumenical Council of Trent, Sess. XIII, *Decretum de ss. Eucharistia*, Chapter 7 and Canon 11: DS 1647, 1661.

37. The two sacraments of the Eucharist and Penance are very closely connected. Because the Eucharist makes present the redeeming sacrifice of the Cross, perpetuating it sacramentally, it naturally gives rise to a continuous need for conversion, for a personal response to the appeal made by Saint Paul to the Christians of Corinth: "We beseech you on behalf of Christ, be reconciled to God" (2 Cor 5:20). If a Christian's conscience is burdened by serious sin, then the path of penance through the sacrament of Reconciliation becomes necessary for full participation in the Eucharistic Sacrifice.

The judgment of one's state of grace obviously belongs only to the person involved, since it is a question of examining one's conscience. However, in cases of outward conduct which is seriously, clearly and steadfastly contrary to the moral norm, the Church, in her pastoral concern for the good order of the community and out of respect for the sacrament, cannot fail to feel directly involved. The *Code of Canon Law* refers to this situation of a manifest lack of proper moral disposition when it states that those who "obstinately persist in manifest grave sin" are not to be admitted to Eucharistic communion.[76]

38. Ecclesial communion, as I have said, is likewise *visible*, and finds expression in the series of "bonds" listed by the Council when it teaches: "They are fully incorporated into the society of the Church who, possessing the Spirit of Christ, accept her whole structure and all the means of salvation established within her, and within her visible framework are united to Christ, who governs her through the Supreme Pontiff and the Bishops, by the bonds of profession of faith, the sacraments, ecclesiastical government and communion".[77]

The Eucharist, as the supreme sacramental manifestation of communion in the Church, demands to be celebrated in a *context where the outward bonds of communion are also intact*. In a special way, since the Eucharist is "as it were the summit of the spiritual life and the goal of all the sacraments",[78] it requires that the bonds of communion in the sacraments, particularly in Baptism and in priestly Orders, be real. It is not possible to give communion to a person who is not baptized or to one who rejects the full truth of the faith regarding the Eucharistic mystery. Christ is the truth and he bears witness to the truth (cf. *Jn* 14:6; 18:37); the sacrament of his body and blood does not permit duplicity.

39. Furthermore, given the very nature of ecclesial communion and its relation to the sacrament of the Eucharist, it must be recalled that "the Eucharistic Sacrifice, while always offered in a particular community, is never a celebration of that community alone. In fact, the community, in receiving the Eucharistic presence of the Lord, receives the entire gift of salvation and shows, even in its lasting visible particular form, that it is the image and true presence of the one, holy, catholic and apostolic Church".[79] From this it follows that a truly Eucharistic community cannot be closed in upon itself,

---

76 Canon 915; *Code of Canons of the Eastern Churches*, Canon 712.

77 Dogmatic Constitution on the Church *Lumen Gentium*, 14.

78 Saint Thomas Aquinas, *Summa Theologiae*, III, q. 73, a. 3c.

79 Congregation for the Doctrine of the Faith, Letter to the Bishops of the Catholic Church on Some Aspects of the Church Understood as Communion *Communionis Notio* (28 May 1992), 11: AAS 85 (1993), 844.

as though it were somehow self-sufficient; rather it must persevere in harmony with every other Catholic community.

The ecclesial communion of the Eucharistic assembly is a communion with its own *Bishop* and with the *Roman Pontiff*. The Bishop, in effect, is the *visible* principle and the foundation of unity within his particular Church.[80] It would therefore be a great contradiction if the sacrament *par excellence* of the Church's unity were celebrated without true communion with the Bishop. As Saint Ignatius of Antioch wrote: "That Eucharist which is celebrated under the Bishop, or under one to whom the Bishop has given this charge, may be considered certain".[81] Likewise, since "the Roman Pontiff, as the successor of Peter, is the perpetual and visible source and foundation of the unity of the Bishops and of the multitude of the faithful",[82] communion with him is intrinsically required for the celebration of the Eucharistic Sacrifice. Hence the great truth expressed which the Liturgy expresses in a variety of ways: "Every celebration of the Eucharist is performed in union not only with the proper Bishop, but also with the Pope, with the episcopal order, with all the clergy, and with the entire people. Every valid celebration of the Eucharist expresses this universal communion with Peter and with the whole Church, or objectively calls for it, as in the case of the Christian Churches separated from Rome".[83]

40. The Eucharist *creates communion* and *fosters communion*. Saint Paul wrote to the faithful of Corinth explaining how their divisions, reflected in their Eucharistic gatherings, contradicted what they were celebrating, the Lord's Supper. The Apostle then urged them to reflect on the true reality of the Eucharist in order to return to the spirit of fraternal communion (cf. *1 Cor* 11:17– 34). Saint Augustine effectively echoed this call when, in recalling the Apostle's words: "You are the body of Christ and individually members of it" (*1 Cor* 12: 27), he went on to say: "If you are his body and members of him, then you will find set on the Lord's table your own mystery. Yes, you receive your own mystery".[84] And from this observation he concludes: "Christ the Lord...hallowed at his table the mystery of our peace and unity. Whoever receives the mystery of unity without preserving the bonds of peace receives not a mystery for his benefit but evidence against himself".[85]

41. The Eucharist's particular effectiveness in promoting communion is one of the reasons for the importance of Sunday Mass. I have already dwelt on this and on the other reasons which make Sunday Mass fundamental for the life of the Church and of

---

80 Cf. Second Vatican Ecumenical Council, Dogmatic Constitution on the Church *Lumen Gentium*, 23.

81 *Ad Smyrnaeos*, 8: PG 5, 713.

82 Second Vatican Ecumenical Council, Dogmatic Constitution on the Church *Lumen Gentium*, 23.

83 Congregation for the Doctrine of the Faith, Letter to the Bishops of the Catholic Church on Some Aspects of the Church Understood as Communion *Communionis Notio* (28 May 1992), 14: AAS 85 (1993), 847.

84 *Sermo* 272: PL 38, 1247.

85 *Ibid.*, 1248.

individual believers in my Apostolic Letter on the sanctification of Sunday *Dies Domini*.[86] There I recalled that the faithful have the obligation to attend Mass, unless they are seriously impeded, and that Pastors have the corresponding duty to see that it is practical and possible for all to fulfil this precept.[87] More recently, in my Apostolic Letter *Novo Millennio Ineunte*, in setting forth the pastoral path which the Church must take at the beginning of the third millennium, I drew particular attention to the Sunday Eucharist, emphasizing its effectiveness for building communion. "It is"—I wrote—"the privileged place where communion is ceaselessly proclaimed and nurtured. Precisely through sharing in the Eucharist, *the Lord's Day* also becomes *the Day of the Church*, when she can effectively exercise her role as the sacrament of unity".[88]

42. The safeguarding and promotion of ecclesial communion is a task of each member of the faithful, who finds in the Eucharist, as the sacrament of the Church's unity, an area of special concern. More specifically, this task is the particular responsibility of the Church's Pastors, each according to his rank and ecclesiastical office. For this reason the Church has drawn up norms aimed both at fostering the frequent and fruitful access of the faithful to the Eucharistic table and at determining the objective conditions under which communion may not be given. The care shown in promoting the faithful observance of these norms becomes a practical means of showing love for the Eucharist and for the Church.

43. In considering the Eucharist as the sacrament of ecclesial communion, there is one subject which, due to its importance, must not be overlooked: I am referring to the *relationship of the Eucharist to ecumenical activity*. We should all give thanks to the Blessed Trinity for the many members of the faithful throughout the world who in recent decades have felt an ardent desire for unity among all Christians. The Second Vatican Council, at the beginning of its Decree on Ecumenism, sees this as a special gift of God.[89] It was an efficacious grace which inspired us, the sons and daughters of the Catholic Church and our brothers and sisters from other Churches and Ecclesial Communities, to set forth on the path of ecumenism.

Our longing for the goal of unity prompts us to turn to the Eucharist, which is the supreme sacrament of the unity of the People of God, in as much as it is the apt expression and the unsurpassable source of that unity.[90] In the celebration of the Eucharistic Sacrifice the Church prays that God, the Father of mercies, will grant his children the fullness of the Holy Spirit so that they may become one body and one spirit in Christ.[91] In raising this prayer to the Father of lights, from whom comes every good endowment and every perfect gift (cf. *Jas* 1:17), the Church believes that she will

---

86 Cf. Nos. 31–51: AAS 90 (1998), 731–746.

87 Cf. *ibid.*, Nos. 48–49: AAS 90 (1998), 744.

88 No. 36: AAS 93 (2001), 291–292.

89 Cf. Decree on *Ecumenism Unitatis Redintegratio*, 1.

90 Cf. Dogmatic Constitution on the Church *Lumen Gentium*, 11.

91 "Join all of us, who share the one bread and the one cup, to one another in the communion of the one Holy Spirit": *Anaphora of the Liturgy of Saint Basil*.

be heard, for she prays in union with Christ her Head and Spouse, who takes up this plea of his Bride and joins it to that of his own redemptive sacrifice.

44. Precisely because the Church's unity, which the Eucharist brings about through the Lord's sacrifice and by communion in his body and blood, absolutely requires full communion in the bonds of the profession of faith, the sacraments and ecclesiastical governance, it is not possible to celebrate together the same Eucharistic liturgy until those bonds are fully reestablished. Any such concelebration would not be a valid means, and might well prove instead to be an *obstacle, to the attainment of full communion*, by weakening the sense of how far we remain from this goal and by introducing or exacerbating ambiguities with regard to one or another truth of the faith. The path towards full unity can only be undertaken in truth. In this area, the prohibitions of Church law leave no room for uncertainty,[92] in fidelity to the moral norm laid down by the Second Vatican Council.[93]

I would like nonetheless to reaffirm what I said in my Encyclical Letter *Ut Unum Sint* after having acknowledged the impossibility of Eucharistic sharing: "And yet we do have a burning desire to join in celebrating the one Eucharist of the Lord, and this desire itself is already a common prayer of praise, a single supplication. Together we speak to the Father and increasingly we do so 'with one heart'".[94]

45. While it is never legitimate to concelebrate in the absence of full communion, the same is not true with respect to the administration of the Eucharist *under special circumstances, to individual persons* belonging to Churches or Ecclesial Communities not in full communion with the Catholic Church. In this case, in fact, the intention is to meet a grave spiritual need for the eternal salvation of an individual believer, not to bring about an *intercommunion* which remains impossible until the visible bonds of ecclesial communion are fully reestablished.

This was the approach taken by the Second Vatican Council when it gave guidelines for responding to Eastern Christians separated in good faith from the Catholic Church, who spontaneously ask to receive the Eucharist from a Catholic minister and are properly disposed.[95] This approach was then ratified by both Codes, which also consider—with necessary modifications—the case of other non-Eastern Christians who are not in full communion with the Catholic Church.[96]

---

92 Cf. *Code of Canon Law*, Canon 908; *Code of Canons of the Eastern Churches*, Canon 702; Pontifical Council for the Promotion of Christian Unity, *Ecumenical Directory*, 25 March 1993, 122–125, 129–131: AAS 85 (1993), 1086–1089; Congregation for the Doctrine of the Faith, Letter *Ad Exsequendam*, 18 May 2001: AAS 93 (2001), 786.

93 "Divine law forbids any common worship which would damage the unity of the Church, or involve formal acceptance of falsehood or the danger of deviation in the faith, of scandal, or of indifferentism": Decree on the Eastern Catholic Churches *Orientalium Ecclesiarum*, 26.

94 No. 45: AAS 87 (1995), 948.

95 Decree on the Eastern Catholic Churches *Orientalium Ecclesiarum*, 27.

96 Cf. *Code of Canon Law*, Canon 844 §§ 3–4; *Code of Canons of the Eastern Churches*, Canon 671 §§ 3–4.

46. In my Encyclical *Ut Unum Sint* I expressed my own appreciation of these norms, which make it possible to provide for the salvation of souls with proper discernment: "It is a source of joy to note that Catholic ministers are able, in certain particular cases, to administer the sacraments of the Eucharist, Penance and Anointing of the Sick to Christians who are not in full communion with the Catholic Church but who greatly desire to receive these sacraments, freely request them and manifest the faith which the Catholic Church professes with regard to these sacraments. Conversely, in specific cases and in particular circumstances, Catholics too can request these same sacraments from ministers of Churches in which these sacraments are valid".[97]

These conditions, from which no dispensation can be given, must be carefully respected, even though they deal with specific individual cases, because the denial of one or more truths of the faith regarding these sacraments and, among these, the truth regarding the need of the ministerial priesthood for their validity, renders the person asking improperly disposed to legitimately receiving them. And the opposite is also true: Catholics may not receive communion in those communities which lack a valid sacrament of Orders.[98]

The faithful observance of the body of norms established in this area[99] is a manifestation and, at the same time, a guarantee of our love for Jesus Christ in the Blessed Sacrament, for our brothers and sisters of different Christian confessions—who have a right to our witness to the truth—and for the cause itself of the promotion of unity.

CHAPTER FIVE

THE DIGNITY OF THE EUCHARISTIC CELEBRATION

47. Reading the account of the institution of the Eucharist in the Synoptic Gospels, we are struck by the simplicity and the "solemnity" with which Jesus, on the evening of the Last Supper, instituted this great sacrament. There is an episode which in some way serves as its prelude: *the anointing at Bethany*. A woman, whom John identifies as Mary the sister of Lazarus, pours a flask of *costly ointment* over Jesus' head, which provokes from the disciples—and from Judas in particular (cf. Mt 26:8; *Mk* 14:4; *Jn* 12:4)—an indignant response, as if this act, in light of the needs of the poor, represented an intolerable "waste". But Jesus' own reaction is completely different. While in no way detracting from the duty of charity towards the needy, for whom the disciples must always show special care—"the poor you will always have with you" (*Mt* 26, 11; *Mk* 14:7; cf. *Jn* 12:8)—he looks towards his imminent death and burial, and sees this act of anointing as an anticipation of the honour which his body will continue to merit even after his death, indissolubly bound as it is to the mystery of his person.

---

97 No. 46: AAS 87 (1995), 948.

98 Cf. Second Vatican Ecumenical Council, Decree on *Ecumenism Unitatis Redintegratio*, 22.

99 *Code of Canon Law*, Canon 844; *Code of Canons of the Eastern Churches*, Canon 671.

The account continues, in the Synoptic Gospels, with Jesus' charge to the disciples to *prepare carefully the "large upper room"* needed for the Passover meal (cf. *Mk* 14:15; *Lk* 22:12) and with the narration of the institution of the Eucharist. Reflecting at least in part the *Jewish rites* of the Passover meal leading up to the singing of the Hallel (cf. *Mt* 26:30; *Mk* 14:26), the story presents with sobriety and solemnity, even in the variants of the different traditions, the words spoken by Christ over the bread and wine, which he made into concrete expressions of the handing over of his body and the shedding of his blood. All these details are recorded by the Evangelists in the light of a praxis of the "breaking of the bread" already well-established in the early Church. But certainly from the time of Jesus on, the event of Holy Thursday has shown visible traces of a liturgical "sensibility" shaped by Old Testament tradition and open to being reshaped in Christian celebrations in a way consonant with the new content of Easter.

48. Like the woman who anointed Jesus in Bethany, *the Church has feared no "extravagance"*, devoting the best of her resources to expressing her wonder and adoration before the *unsurpassable gift of the Eucharist*. No less than the first disciples charged with preparing the "large upper room", she has felt the need, down the centuries and in her encounters with different cultures, to celebrate the Eucharist in a setting worthy of so great a mystery. In the wake of Jesus' own words and actions, and building upon the ritual heritage of Judaism, the *Christian liturgy was born*. Could there ever be an adequate means of expressing the acceptance of that self-gift which the divine Bridegroom continually makes to his Bride, the Church, by bringing the Sacrifice offered once and for all on the Cross to successive generations of believers and thus becoming nourishment for all the faithful? Though the idea of a "banquet" naturally suggests familiarity, the Church has never yielded to the temptation to trivialize this "intimacy" with her Spouse by forgetting that he is also her Lord and that the "banquet" always remains a sacrificial banquet marked by the blood shed on Golgotha. *The Eucharistic Banquet is truly a "sacred" banquet*, in which the simplicity of the signs conceals the unfathomable holiness of God: *O sacrum convivium, in quo Christus sumitur!* The bread which is broken on our altars, offered to us as wayfarers along the paths of the world, is *panis angelorum*, the bread of angels, which cannot be approached except with the humility of the centurion in the Gospel: "Lord, I am not worthy to have you come under my roof " (*Mt* 8:8; *Lk* 7:6).

49. With this heightened sense of mystery, we understand how the faith of the Church in the mystery of the Eucharist has found historical expression not only in the demand for an interior disposition of devotion, but also *in outward forms* meant to evoke and emphasize the grandeur of the event being celebrated. This led progressively to the development of a *particular form of regulating the Eucharistic liturgy*, with due respect for the various legitimately constituted ecclesial traditions. On this foundation a *rich artistic heritage* also developed. Architecture, sculpture, painting and music, moved by the Christian mystery, have found in the Eucharist, both directly and indirectly, a source of great inspiration.

Such was the case, for example, with architecture, which witnessed the transition, once the historical situation made it possible, from the first places of Eucharistic celebration in the *domus* or "homes" of Christian families to the solemn *basilicas* of the early centuries, to the imposing *cathedrals* of the Middle Ages, and to the *churches*, large and small, which gradually sprang up throughout the lands touched by Christianity. The designs of altars and tabernacles within Church interiors were often not simply motivated by artistic inspiration but also by a clear understanding of the mystery. The same could be said for *sacred music*, if we but think of the inspired Gregorian melodies and the many, often great, composers who sought to do justice to the liturgical texts of the Mass. Similarly, can we overlook the enormous quantity of *artistic production*, ranging from fine craftsmanship to authentic works of art, in the area of Church furnishings and vestments used for the celebration of the Eucharist?

It can be said that the Eucharist, while shaping the Church and her spirituality, has also powerfully affected "culture", and the arts in particular.

50. In this effort to adore the mystery grasped in its ritual and aesthetic dimensions, a certain "competition" has taken place between Christians of the West and the East. How could we not give particular thanks to the Lord for the contributions to Christian art made by the great architectural and artistic works of the Greco-Byzantine tradition and of the whole geographical area marked by Slav culture? In the East, sacred art has preserved a remarkably powerful sense of mystery, which leads artists to see their efforts at creating beauty not simply as an expression of their own talents, but also as a *genuine service to the faith*. Passing well beyond mere technical skill, they have shown themselves docile and open to the inspiration of the Holy Spirit.

The architectural and mosaic splendours of the Christian East and West are a patrimony belonging to all believers; they contain a hope, and even a pledge, of the desired fullness of communion in faith and in celebration. This would presuppose and demand, as in Rublëv's famous depiction of the Trinity, *a profoundly Eucharistic Church* in which the presence of the mystery of Christ in the broken bread is as it were immersed in the ineffable unity of the three divine Persons, making of the Church herself an "icon" of the Trinity.

Within this context of an art aimed at expressing, in all its elements, the meaning of the Eucharist in accordance with the Church's teaching, attention needs to be given to the norms regulating *the construction and decor of sacred buildings*. As history shows and as I emphasized in my *Letter to Artists*,[100] the Church has always left ample room for the creativity of artists. But sacred art must be outstanding for its ability to express adequately the mystery grasped in the fullness of the Church's faith and in accordance with the pastoral guidelines appropriately laid down by competent Authority. This holds true both for the figurative arts and for sacred music.

51. The development of sacred art and liturgical discipline which took place in lands of ancient Christian heritage is also taking place *on continents where Christianity is younger*. This was precisely the approach supported by the Second Vatican Council on the need for sound and proper "inculturation". In my numerous Pastoral Visits I have seen, throughout the world, the great vitality which the celebration of the Eucharist can have when marked by the forms, styles and sensibilities of different cultures. By adaptation to the changing conditions of time and place, the Eucharist offers sustenance not only to individuals but to entire peoples, and it shapes cultures inspired by Christianity.

It is necessary, however, that this important work of adaptation be carried out with a constant awareness of the ineffable mystery against which every generation is called

---

100 Cf. AAS 91 (1999), 1155–1172.

to measure itself. The "treasure" is too important and precious to risk impoverishment or compromise through forms of experimentation or practices introduced without a careful review on the part of the competent ecclesiastical authorities. Furthermore, the centrality of the Eucharistic mystery demands that any such review must be undertaken in close association with the Holy See. As I wrote in my Post-Synodal Apostolic Exhortation *Ecclesia in Asia*, "such cooperation is essential because the Sacred Liturgy expresses and celebrates the one faith professed by all and, being the heritage of the whole Church, cannot be determined by local Churches in isolation from the universal Church".[101]

52. All of this makes clear the great responsibility which belongs to priests in particular for the celebration of the Eucharist. It is their responsibility to preside at the Eucharist *in persona Christi* and to provide a witness to and a service of communion not only for the community directly taking part in the celebration, but also for the universal Church, which is a part of every Eucharist. It must be lamented that, especially in the years following the post-conciliar liturgical reform, as a result of a misguided sense of creativity and adaptation there have been a number of *abuses* which have been a source of suffering for many. A certain reaction against "formalism" has led some, especially in certain regions, to consider the "forms" chosen by the Church's great liturgical tradition and her Magisterium as nonbinding and to introduce unauthorized innovations which are often completely inappropriate.

I consider it my duty, therefore to appeal urgently that the liturgical norms for the celebration of the Eucharist be observed with great fidelity. These norms are a concrete expression of the authentically ecclesial nature of the Eucharist; this is their deepest meaning. Liturgy is never anyone's private property, be it of the celebrant or of the community in which the mysteries are celebrated. The Apostle Paul had to address fiery words to the community of Corinth because of grave shortcomings in their celebration of the Eucharist resulting in divisions (*schismata*) and the emergence of factions (*haireseis*) (cf. *1 Cor* 11:17–34). Our time, too, calls for a renewed awareness and appreciation of liturgical norms as a reflection of, and a witness to, the one universal Church made present in every celebration of the Eucharist. Priests who faithfully celebrate Mass according to the liturgical norms, and communities which conform to those norms, quietly but eloquently demonstrate their love for the Church. Precisely to bring out more clearly this deeper meaning of liturgical norms, I have asked the competent offices of the Roman Curia to prepare a more specific document, including prescriptions of a juridical nature, on this very important subject. No one is permitted to undervalue the mystery entrusted to our hands: it is too great for anyone to feel free to treat it lightly and with disregard for its sacredness and its universality.

CHAPTER SIX

AT THE SCHOOL OF MARY, "WOMAN OF THE EUCHARIST"

53. If we wish to rediscover in all its richness the profound relationship between the Church and the Eucharist, we cannot neglect Mary, Mother and model of the Church. In my Apostolic Letter *Rosarium Virginis Mariae*, I pointed to the Blessed

---

101 No. 22: AAS 92 (2000), 485.

Virgin Mary as our teacher in contemplating Christ's face, and among the mysteries of light I included the *institution of the Eucharist*.[102] Mary can guide us towards this most holy sacrament, because she herself has a profound relationship with it.

At first glance, the Gospel is silent on this subject. The account of the institution of the Eucharist on the night of Holy Thursday makes no mention of Mary. Yet we know that she was present among the Apostles who prayed "with one accord" (cf. *Acts* 1:14) *in the first community which gathered after the Ascension in expectation of Pentecost*. Certainly Mary must have been present at the Eucharistic celebrations of the first generation of Christians, who were devoted to "the breaking of bread" (*Acts* 2:42).

But in addition to her sharing in the Eucharistic banquet, an indirect picture of Mary's relationship with the Eucharist can be had, beginning with her interior disposition. *Mary is a "woman of the Eucharist" in her whole life*. The Church, which looks to Mary as a model, is also called to imitate her in her relationship with this most holy mystery.

54. *Mysterium fidei!* If the Eucharist is a mystery of faith which so greatly transcends our understanding as to call for sheer abandonment to the word of God, then there can be no one like Mary to act as our support and guide in acquiring this disposition. In repeating what Christ did at the Last Supper in obedience to his command: "Do this in memory of me!", we also accept Mary's invitation to obey him without hesitation: "Do whatever he tells you" (*Jn* 2:5). With the same maternal concern which she showed at the wedding feast of Cana, Mary seems to say to us: "Do not waver; trust in the words of my Son. If he was able to change water into wine, he can also turn bread and wine into his body and blood, and through this mystery bestow on believers the living memorial of his passover, thus becoming the 'bread of life'".

55. In a certain sense Mary lived her *Eucharistic faith* even before the institution of the Eucharist, by the very fact that *she offered her virginal womb for the Incarnation of God's Word*. The Eucharist, while commemorating the passion and resurrection, is also in continuity with the incarnation. At the Annunciation Mary conceived the Son of God in the physical reality of his body and blood, thus anticipating within herself what to some degree happens sacramentally in every believer who receives, under the signs of bread and wine, the Lord's body and blood.

As a result, there is a profound analogy between the *Fiat* which Mary said in reply to the angel, and the *Amen* which every believer says when receiving the body of the Lord. Mary was asked to believe that the One whom she conceived "through the Holy Spirit" was "the Son of God" (*Lk* 1:30–35). In continuity with the Virgin's faith, in the Eucharistic mystery we are asked to believe that the same Jesus Christ, Son of God and Son of Mary, becomes present in his full humanity and divinity under the signs of bread and wine.

"Blessed is she who believed" (*Lk* 1:45). Mary also anticipated, in the mystery of the incarnation, the Church's Eucharistic faith. When, at the Visitation, she bore in her womb the Word made flesh, she became in some way a "tabernacle"—the first "tabernacle"—in history—in which the Son of God, still invisible to our human gaze, allowed himself to be adored by Elizabeth, radiating his light as it were through the eyes and

---

102 Cf. No. 21: AAS 95 (2003), 20.

the voice of Mary. And is not the enraptured gaze of Mary as she contemplated the face of the newborn Christ and cradled him in her arms that unparalleled model of love which should inspire us every time we receive Eucharistic communion?

56. Mary, throughout her life at Christ's side and not only on Calvary, made her own *the sacrificial dimension of the Eucharist*. When she brought the child Jesus to the Temple in Jerusalem "to present him to the Lord" (*Lk* 2:22), she heard the aged Simeon announce that the child would be a "sign of contradiction" and that a sword would also pierce her own heart (cf. *Lk* 2:34–35). The tragedy of her Son's crucifixion was thus foretold, and in some sense Mary's *Stabat Mater* at the foot of the Cross was foreshadowed. In her daily preparation for Calvary, Mary experienced a kind of "anticipated Eucharist"—one might say a "spiritual communion"—of desire and of oblation, which would culminate in her union with her Son in his passion, and then find expression after Easter by her partaking in the Eucharist which the Apostles celebrated as the memorial of that passion.

What must Mary have felt as she heard from the mouth of Peter, John, James and the other Apostles the words spoken at the Last Supper: "This is my body which is given for you" (*Lk* 22:19)? The body given up for us and made present under sacramental signs was the same body which she had conceived in her womb! For Mary, receiving the Eucharist must have somehow meant welcoming once more into her womb that heart which had beat in unison with hers and reliving what she had experienced at the foot of the Cross.

57. "Do this in remembrance of me" (*Lk* 22:19). In the "memorial" of Calvary all that Christ accomplished by his passion and his death is present. Consequently *all that Christ did with regard to his Mother* for our sake is also present. To her he gave the beloved disciple and, in him, each of us: "Behold, your Son!". To each of us he also says: "Behold your mother!" (cf. *Jn* 19: 26–27).

Experiencing the memorial of Christ's death in the Eucharist also means continually receiving this gift. It means accepting—like John—the one who is given to us anew as our Mother. It also means taking on a commitment to be conformed to Christ, putting ourselves at the school of his Mother and allowing her to accompany us. Mary is present, with the Church and as the Mother of the Church, at each of our celebrations of the Eucharist. If the Church and the Eucharist are inseparably united, the same ought to be said of Mary and the Eucharist. This is one reason why, since ancient times, the commemoration of Mary has always been part of the Eucharistic celebrations of the Churches of East and West.

58. In the Eucharist the Church is completely united to Christ and his sacrifice, and makes her own the spirit of Mary. This truth can be understood more deeply by *rereading the Magnificat* in a Eucharistic key. The Eucharist, like the Canticle of Mary, is first and foremost praise and thanksgiving. When Mary exclaims: "My soul magnifies the Lord and my spirit rejoices in God my Saviour", she already bears Jesus in her womb. She praises God "through" Jesus, but she also praises him "in" Jesus and "with" Jesus. This is itself the true "Eucharistic attitude".

At the same time Mary recalls the wonders worked by God in salvation history in fulfilment of the promise once made to the fathers (cf. *Lk* 1:55), and proclaims the wonder that surpasses them all, the redemptive incarnation. Lastly, the *Magnificat* reflects the eschatological tension of the Eucharist. Every time the Son of God comes again to us in the "poverty" of the sacramental signs of bread and wine, the seeds of that new history wherein the mighty are "put down from their thrones" and "those of low degree are exalted" (cf. *Lk* 1:52), take root in the world. Mary sings of the "new heavens" and the "new earth" which find in the Eucharist their anticipation and in some sense their programme and plan. The *Magnificat* expresses Mary's spirituality, and there is nothing greater than this spirituality for helping us to experience the mystery of the Eucharist. The Eucharist has been given to us so that our life, like that of Mary, may become completely a *Magnificat!*

CONCLUSION

59. *Ave, verum corpus natum de Maria Virgine!* Several years ago I celebrated the fiftieth anniversary of my priesthood. Today I have the grace of offering the Church this Encyclical on the Eucharist on the Holy Thursday which falls *during the twenty-fifth year of my Petrine ministry.* As I do so, my heart is filled with gratitude. For over a half century, every day, beginning on 2 November 1946, when I celebrated my first Mass in the Crypt of Saint Leonard in Wawel Cathedral in Krakow, my eyes have gazed in recollection upon the host and the chalice, where time and space in some way "merge" and the drama of Golgotha is represented in a living way, thus revealing its mysterious "contemporaneity". Each day my faith has been able to recognize in the consecrated bread and wine the divine Wayfarer who joined the two disciples on the road to Emmaus and opened their eyes to the light and their hearts to new hope (cf. *Lk* 24:13–35).

Allow me, dear brothers and sisters, to share with deep emotion, as a means of accompanying and strengthening your faith, my own testimony of faith in the Most Holy Eucharist. *Ave verum corpus natum de Maria Virgine, vere passum, immolatum, in cruce pro homine!* Here is the Church's treasure, the heart of the world, the pledge of the fulfilment for which each man and woman, even unconsciously, yearns. A great and transcendent mystery, indeed, and one that taxes our mind's ability to pass beyond appearances. Here our senses fail us: *visus, tactus, gustus in te fallitur,* in the words of the hymn *Adoro Te Devote*; yet faith alone, rooted in the word of Christ handed down to us by the Apostles, is sufficient for us. Allow me, like Peter at the end of the Eucharistic discourse in John's Gospel, to say once more to Christ, in the name of the whole Church and in the name of each of you: "Lord to whom shall we go? You have the words of eternal life" (*Jn* 6:68).

60. At the dawn of this third millennium, we, the children of the Church, are called to undertake with renewed enthusiasm the journey of Christian living. As I wrote in my Apostolic Letter *Novo Millennio Ineunte,* "it is not a matter of inventing a 'new programme'. The programme already exists: it is the plan found in the Gospel and in the living Tradition; it is the same as ever. Ultimately, it has its centre in Christ himself, who is to be known, loved and imitated, so that in him we may live the life of the Trinity, and with him transform history until its fulfilment in the heavenly Jerusalem".[103] The implementation of this programme of a renewed impetus in Christian living passes through the Eucharist.

Every commitment to holiness, every activity aimed at carrying out the Church's mission, every work of pastoral planning, must draw the strength it needs from the

---

103 No. 29: AAS 93 (2001), 285.

Eucharistic mystery and in turn be directed to that mystery as its culmination. In the Eucharist we have Jesus, we have his redemptive sacrifice, we have his resurrection, we have the gift of the Holy Spirit, we have adoration, obedience and love of the Father. Were we to disregard the Eucharist, how could we overcome our own deficiency?

61. The mystery of the Eucharist—sacrifice, presence, banquet—*does not allow for reduction or exploitation*; it must be experienced and lived in its integrity, both in its celebration and in the intimate converse with Jesus which takes place after receiving communion or in a prayerful moment of Eucharistic adoration apart from Mass. These are times when the Church is firmly built up and it becomes clear what she truly is: one, holy, catholic and apostolic; the people, temple and family of God; the body and bride of Christ, enlivened by the Holy Spirit; the universal sacrament of salvation and a hierarchically structured communion.

The path taken by the Church in these first years of the third millennium is also a *path of renewed ecumenical commitment*. The final decades of the second millennium, culminating in the Great Jubilee, have spurred us along this path and called for all the baptized to respond to the prayer of Jesus *"ut unum sint "* (*Jn* 17:11). The path itself is long and strewn with obstacles greater than our human resources alone can overcome, yet we have the Eucharist, and in its presence we can hear in the depths of our hearts, as if they were addressed to us, the same words heard by the Prophet Elijah: "Arise and eat, else the journey will be too great for you" (*1 Kg* 19:7). The treasure of the Eucharist, which the Lord places before us, impels us towards the goal of full sharing with all our brothers and sisters to whom we are joined by our common Baptism. But if this treasure is not to be squandered, we need to respect the demands which derive from its being the sacrament of communion in faith and in apostolic succession.

By giving the Eucharist the prominence it deserves, and by being careful not to diminish any of its dimensions or demands, we show that we are truly conscious of the greatness of this gift. We are urged to do so by an uninterrupted tradition, which from the first centuries on has found the Christian community ever vigilant in guarding this "treasure". Inspired by love, the Church is anxious to hand on to future generations of Christians, without loss, her faith and teaching with regard to the mystery of the Eucharist. There can be no danger of excess in our care for this mystery, for "in this sacrament is recapitulated the whole mystery of our salvation".[104]

62. Let us take our place, dear brothers and sisters, *at the school of the saints*, who are the great interpreters of true Eucharistic piety. In them the theology of the Eucharist takes on all the splendour of a lived reality; it becomes "contagious" and, in a manner of speaking, it "warms our hearts". Above all, let us *listen to Mary Most Holy*, in whom the mystery of the Eucharist appears, more than in anyone else, as a *mystery of light*. Gazing upon Mary, we come to know *the transforming power present in the Eucharist*. In her we see the world renewed in love. Contemplating her, assumed body and soul into heaven, we see opening up before us those "new heavens" and that "new earth" which will appear at the second coming of Christ. Here below, the Eucharist represents their pledge, and in a certain way, their anticipation: *"Veni, Domine Iesu!"* (*Rev* 22:20).

In the humble signs of bread and wine, changed into his body and blood, Christ walks beside us as our strength and our food for the journey, and he enables us to

---

104 Saint Thomas Aquinas, *Summa Theologiae*, III, q. 83, a. 4c.

become, for everyone, witnesses of hope. If, in the presence of this mystery, reason experiences its limits, the heart, enlightened by the grace of the Holy Spirit, clearly sees the response that is demanded, and bows low in adoration and unbounded love.

Let us make our own the words of Saint Thomas Aquinas, an eminent theologian and an impassioned poet of Christ in the Eucharist, and turn in hope to the contemplation of that goal to which our hearts aspire in their thirst for joy and peace:

Bone pastor, panis vere,
Iesu, nostri miserere…

> *Come then, good Shepherd, bread divine,*
> *Still show to us thy mercy sign;*
> *Oh, feed us, still keep us thine;*
> *So we may see thy glories shine*
> *in fields of immortality.*
>
> *O thou, the wisest, mightiest, best,*
> *Our present food, our future rest,*
> *Come, make us each thy chosen guest,*
> *Co-heirs of thine, and comrades blest*
> *With saints whose dwelling is with thee.*

Given in Rome, at Saint Peter's, on 17 April, Holy Thursday, in the year 2003, the Twenty-fifth of my Pontificate, the Year of the Rosary.

IOANNES PAULUS II

By

Rev. Lawrence G. Lovasik, S.V.D.

Divine Word Missionary

Used by permission from Tan Publishing.

Tan Publishing has republished Father Lovasik's
A Novena of Holy Communions (1960 edition)
as a booklet and it is currently available.

B.1

In Loving Memory of

Rev. Lawrence G. Lovasik

Born: June 22, 1913
Ordained: August 14, 1938
Died: June 9, 1986

O God, grant that your servant, whom you raised to priestly dignity in the priesthood of the apostles, may now be admitted into their company forever. Through Jesus Christ, our Lord. Amen.

Eternal rest grant unto him, O Lord; and let perpetual light shine upon him. May he rest in peace. Amen.

CONTENTS

PART I—DEVOTIONS FOR EACH DAY OF THE WEEK

Sunday

BEFORE COMMUNION

Faith

Lord Jesus Christ, you have loved me and given yourself not only to suffer and die, but also to the food of my soul, to remain with me throughout my life. Having taken bread, given thanks, and blessed it, you gave it to your disciples, saying: "Take and eat; this is my body." And likewise you took the chalice and said: "All of you drink of this; for this is my blood." And by commanding them, "Do this in remembrance of Me," you gave them the power to do what you did, to change bread into your body and wine into your blood; for if we do not eat your flesh and drink your blood, we shall not have life in us. Eternal God, who can understand the depths of your wisdom, the measure of your power, and the greatness of your love?

I believe that you, the Son of God, are the living bread from heaven. I believe that you are present, really and truly, body and soul, divinity and humanity, in the Holy Sacrament of the Altar. I believe that your body is really food and your blood is really drink. I believe that today I shall really partake of your holy table. All this I believe because you have revealed it. Strengthen my faith, dear Jesus!

Hope

Jesus, with this firm belief I approach your holy table, where you are ready to give me yourself, God and man. I rely on your mercy and love and your infallible promises. From you I dare hope everything for you are almighty.

You have said, "My flesh is food indeed, and my blood in drink indeed." I firmly hope it will nourish and strengthen my soul in virtue.

You have said: "He who eats my flesh and drinks my blood abides in me and I in him." I hope that I shall remain in you and you in me.

You have said: "He who eats my flesh and drinks my blood has life everlasting, and I will raise him up on the last day." I rely on this promise.

You have said: "He who eats me, he also shall live because of me. He who eats this bread shall live forever." For this I hope. Strengthen my hope, dear Jesus!

Charity

Jesus, inflame my heart with love that I may love you above all things and with my whole heart. Help me ever to remember your love for me. You have loved me so much as to deliver yourself for me into the hands of your cruel enemies. You humbled yourself to death for me, even to death on a cross. Wounded and weary, you meekly climbed the mount of Calvary. There you were nailed to the cross and raised between heaven and earth. At last, exhausted with pain, you bowed your head and died between two criminals.

At the sight of your great love for me and my coldness and ingratitude towards you, I am deeply ashamed of myself. Let me never grow weary of loving and thanking you for your infinite mercy and love.

My Savior, I love you with my whole heart, with my whole soul, with all my strength. Enkindle your own love in me. I love you because for love of me you are ever present in this holy sacrament in order to be with me and to help me. I love you because in the worthy receiving of your body and blood you will give me a pledge of eternal life.

Humility

Jesus, who am I that you should work such wonders for my sake? How dare I, a poor sinner, approach you, my God and Savior, the source of infinite purity and sanctity? St. John, pure and holy, considered himself unworthy to loose the traps of your sandals. The angels conceal their faces out of reverence for you, but I am to receive you into my soul. My extreme need of you must be my excuse. I rely upon your mercy and goodness; I cast myself upon your love.

Help me, my Jesus, and fill up the emptiness of my heart. Take out of it every sinful affection. Wash my soul from sin by the grace of this holy Communion, and graciously remove everything that might hinder your grace from changing me from the poor sinner that I am, into a saint.

Lord, I am not worthy that you should come to me. I would not dare approach your holy table if you had not commanded me. Obedient to your wish and command, because I love you and desire my salvation, I approach, feeling keenly my unworthiness and confessing: Lord, I am not worthy that you should come to me.

Contrition

Jesus, I am a poor weak creature. How often has sin stained my soul! I am easily inclined to evil; I am inconstant in doing good. How many graces you have given me; how many times I have been unfaithful to you!

I am truly sorry, O God of my heart, not only for not having loved you in the past, but for having rejected your grace and friendship, turned my back on you, and offended you.

Merciful Lord, I grieve with all my heart for this ingratitude. I sincerely detest all the sins that I have committed, because by them I have offended you, infinite Goodness. I trust that you have already forgiven me. Let me not hurt you again. Wash with your most precious blood this soul in which you are about to dwell.

Desire

Jesus, give me the grace to appreciate the privilege of having you come to me. Hidden in this sacrament in the form of bread. You are visible to faith alone. I believe that you are coming to be the food of my soul, to live in me, and to bring grace and salvation to my soul.

I rejoice that you are about to enter into my soul. I long for you. In you I posses all things. You are my God, my Redeemer, my Savior. Nourish and strengthen my soul. Come, Lamb of God. Come and take away my weakness and my sin. Come, Jesus, help me, save me.

Most holy virgin and my Mother Mary, how I wish I could receive your Son with a heart like yours! Be with me in this most sacred hour, and pray for me. Give me Jesus this morning as you gave Him to the shepherds and the three kings. I wish to receive Him from your most pure hands.

Jesus, Thou comest to me,
　　Thou word made flesh for me,
Thou Lord who died for me,
　　Thou love made food for me.
　　　　O come, abide in me!

Come, Jesus, ev'n to me,
　　To one redeemed by thee,
To one in love with thee,
　　To one who longs for thee.
　　　　O come, abide in me!

My Jesus, come to me
　　To reign upon thy throne,
To reign supreme alone,
　　To make me all thine own.
　　　　O come, abide in me!

AFTER HOLY COMMUNION

Welcome

My Jesus, my love, my treasure, my all, welcome to my poor heart! It is full of earthly affections, of self-love, of evil desires. How can you consent to dwell in so wretched a place? I must say with St. Peter: "Depart from me, O Lord, for I am a sinful man." I am indeed unworthy to receive you, the God of infinite holiness.

But do not leave me, dearest Jesus, I welcome you, I embrace you, I am happy to have you so close to me. How foolish have I been in the past! For the love of creatures I turned away from you and drove you from me by my sins. I regret my folly. I am determined never more to separate myself from you, my only treasure. My most earnest desire is to live and die united with you. Most Blessed Virgin Mary, all you angels and saints, teach me to converse worthily with my beloved Jesus.

Adoration

Jesus, my God and Savior, I believe that you have come to visit me; you are now within me. You have become mine; you wish to make me all yours. O infinite Goodness! O infinite Mercy! O infinite Love! With the angels who are now around you adoring their God, I adore you as my God.

Divine Jesus, behold me kneeling before your infinite majesty. I acknowledge my nothingness before you, my complete dependence upon you. O make me your willing and loving creature. Grant me the grace to be perfectly obedient to you, my Lord and my God. In union with your loving Mother Mary, I offer you my humble adoration.

　　Hail, holy Host! Hail, living bread from heaven.
　　　　Thou art our God, the God that made us all.
　　Hail, blood of Christ, in love for sinners given.
　　　　Lord, we believe and on thy mercy call.

Thou art our pledge that men shall perish never,
  Rise from the grave unto eternal day.
"He that shall eat this bread shall live forever."
  These are thy words, they cannot pass away.

Thy love for us has set a banquet royal,
  And in return it asks one single thing.
Take then our love, receive our homage loyal;
  Reign in our hearts, O eucharistic King.

Thanksgiving

Jesus, my God, I thank you for all your mercy to me. I thank you for all the graces and favors which you have granted me from the very beginning of my existence. You have bestowed upon me the great grace of the true faith and a Christian education. How many opportunities I have had to draw near to you and to live in your presence! How many times I have been indifferent to you and neglected these graces! I thank you for your patience with me in spite of my unfaithfulness.

My dearest Jesus, after bestowing on me so many great favors which I can never really appreciate as I should, you have been so kind as to give me even your own self. My Lord and my God, I thank you with all my heart for the unspeakable favor of coming to dwell in my soul. Would that I could thank you worthily for this great gift! With the priest in this Mass I pray: "What shall I render to the Lord for all that He has bestowed on me?" I call on your Mother Mary, my holy patron saints, my guardian angel, and all the angels and saints of heaven to join me in thanking you for the wonderful things you have done for me.

Most merciful Father, I thank you for having loved me so much as to give me your only begotten Son to be my foods and drink. You have given me all things with Him. Look upon the face of your anointed one in whom you are well pleased. Behold, heavenly Father, the one mediator between God and men, your own Son Jesus Christ, my advocate and high-priest who intercedes for me. He bore the sins of the world, and by His wounds we are healed. Accept, therefore, holy Father, this spotless victim, for the honor and glory of your name, in thanksgiving for all the blessings you have ever bestowed upon me, for the remission of my sins, and in atonement for all my wrongdoings.

Offering

My beloved Jesus, since you have stooped so low as to visit the poor dwelling of my soul, with a heart overflowing with gratitude I offer you myself—all that I am and have, now and forever. You have given yourself entirely to me; I give myself entirely to you. From now on I shall no longer be mine, but yours, all yours. May my senses serve me only to please you. What great joy can I have than to please you, my loving God.

I offer you all the powers of my soul that they may ever serve you alone. I will use my memory to recall your mercy and your love toward me; I will use my understanding in thinking of you who are always thinking of my welfare. I will use my will to love you, my God and my all, and in willing only what you will.

Most sweet Jesus, through the hands of your loving Mother Mary I consecrate my whole being, body and soul to you. At least for her sake, accept this offering of one who has so often offended you. Do with me whatever you wish. Consume in me whatever is mine—my sinfulness, my misery, and whatever is displeasing to you, so that henceforth I may be all yours and may live only to do your most holy will.

Most holy Mary, my Mother, with your pure hands offer this gift of myself to Jesus. Obtain for me the grace to remain faithful to my God until death.

Petition

Adorable Savior, in whose Sacred Heart are hidden all the treasures of wisdom and knowledge, you have promised an answer to my prayers when you said: "Ask and you shall receive." And again at the Last Supper, after having given me yourself in this sacrament of love, you promised: "If you abide in me, and if my words abide in you, ask whatever you will and it shall be done to you" (John 15,17). Confiding in your promises, which never fail, I present to you the needs of my poor soul.

Jesus, you know how weak and sinful I am. I am often tempted, troubled, and discouraged. To you I come for remedy. I pray to you for comfort and help. You alone can help me. Inflame my coldness with the fire of your love; enlighten my blindness with the brightness of your presence; fill my poor soul with the treasures of your grace. Enlighten my faith, strengthen my hope, and inflame my love, that all sinful inclinations may disappear in me, and that I may prefer death to ever again committing a single sin. Fill my heart with a truly Christian love for my neighbor. Grant me the grace patiently to bear my cross, and by the faithful fulfillment of the duties of my state of life, to render them meritorious for eternity.

My divine Redeemer, change my heart, detach it from all dangerous affection. Make it like your own in all things, that I may seek only what is most pleasing to you, and may desire only your holy love. Give me all the graces which I need to save my soul. I do not deserve these graces. I ask for them through your merits and the merits of your most holy Mother. I ask for these graces for the love you have for your heavenly Father.

If it should be your holy will, grant me also the favors which I now present to you. (*Mention them.*)

Dear Lord, shed the abundance of your blessings also upon my whole family and all those I love. Guide them in the right path, restrain them from evil, and preserve them from misfortune of soul and body. Be their protector upon earth, their hope at the hour of death. Be to them a gracious judge and Savior. Preserve us in peace and harmony, that we may live here upon earth as we hope hereafter to do in heaven, and let not one of us be lost.

Bless the holy Catholic Church, our holy father the pope, and all the bishops and priests. Bring heretics back to your fold and sinners to the mercy of your Sacred Heart. Have pity on the poor pagans and lead them to the true faith.

Have mercy on the souls in purgatory, especially…Send them heavenly refreshment in their pains, and grant that they may soon see you face to face in the bliss of your heavenly kingdom.

Eternal Father, your loving Son Jesus has said: "If you ask the Father anything in my name, He will give it to you." For the love of your only begotten Son, who is now dwelling in my heart, graciously hear me and grant my requests. Amen

Monday: In Union with the Holy Spirit

BEFORE COMMUNION

Faith

Jesus, my God, I firmly believe that you are present in the Holy Sacrament of the Altar. You give me this heavenly bread to unite yourself with me and to preserve and increase your divine life in my soul. You said: "He who eats my flesh, and drinks my blood, abides in me and I in him" (John 6,57).

I believe that a *wonderful union takes place at holy Communion.* Nothing on earth can be compared with it. It is a union of love between you and my soul.

Jesus, I believe that *you come to me in holy Communion as man.* The sacred Host contains the *body* which you took of your most pure Virgin Mother, and which arose in glory from the tomb. It contains your precious *blood,* with which you redeemed me, and one drop of which would have been enough to redeem a thousand worlds. It contains your most sacred *soul,* the abode of graces and virtues in absolute perfection. In the heavens the sight of your glorified humanity fills the angels and saints with joy. This glorified body, animated by your Sacred Heart which is an abyss of love, and by your soul unspeakably beautiful, radiating light, life, grace, peace and joy, becomes my banquet.

Jesus, I believe that *you come to me in holy Communion even as God.* You are the Word, eternally begotten in the bosom of the divinity. You share in His divine life as the Divine Word, as the only Son of the Father. You receive the life which the Father gives to you, His Son, from all eternity. I can posses your divinity in my soul at all times by remaining in the state of grace. But it is only at the time of holy Communion—as long as the species of bread lasts—that I enjoy the great privilege of being intimately united with your human nature also: your body, your blood, your soul. At holy Communion I am really in possession of you, my Jesus, God and man, with all the treasures of your divinity, and all the graces of your humanity. I thank you for this greatest of all privileges.

Jesus, I believe that *you come to me together with the Father and the Holy Spirit.* Where you are, your Father is also, and where the Father and the Son are present, there also is the Holy Spirit. I firmly believe that the adorable Trinity dwells in my heart at holy Communion, for you said, "If anyone love me, he will keep my word, and my Father will love him, and we will come to him and make our abode with him" (John 14,23). By sanctifying grace, the entire Trinity is the guest of my soul. Yet this is, if possible, more true at the moment of Communion because you come to me as the bread of life, expressly to bestow upon me that life which you receive from your Father.

Jesus, how wonderful are the effects of holy Communion! Only an infinite love could have devised them. And I have been so privileged as to be chosen by you to enjoy these marvelous fruits of the Eucharist for the salvation of my soul. I thank you for this infinite generosity and love towards me, your poor sinful creature.

Temple of the Holy Spirit

Holy Spirit, I believe that you sanctify me especially through the sacraments of the Catholic Church, which are like sevenfold streams of grace whereby my soul is continually refreshed. *But above all in holy Communion you dwell within that temple that is sanctified by the presence of Christ.* Through sanctifying grace, which is increase in my soul in holy Communion, you are present within me, inspiring me, and leading me on to that goal for which I was created—union with God. You give me a foretaste of the union in the sacrament of the holy Eucharist. Whenever I pass from sin to grace; whenever I resist temptation; whenever I perform a good act which leads to salvation, then and there you are at work. I thank you for your love and generosity toward me.

Holy Spirit, Divine Paraclete, I adore you in the temple of my soul. May the holy Communion which I am about to receive, unite me more intimately with you. Spirit of Jesus, you are my heart and soul, my innermost life and deepest strength which unite me to the Son of God. *I cannot come to a special union with Jesus and be His own without possessing you.* St. Paul reminds me: "But if anyone does not have the Spirit of Christ, he does not belong to Christ" (Rom. 8,9). I cannot be transformed into the image of the Savior except by you. May that transformation take place in me through my holy Communions.

Purest and holiest heart of Mary, in whom Jesus lives through the Holy Spirit, implore for me from this Holy Spirit, that the Sacred Heart of Jesus, through Him, may live in my heart and in the hearts of all men.

> Holy Spirit, Love Divine!
> Through that spotless Spouse of Thine,
> With the Lamb's oblation:
> All I have to thee I bring,
> Choosing thee to be my King,
> God of my salvation.
>
> O thou bright, consuming fire
> Hear my fervent heart's desire
> To thy throne ascending:
> One delight my soul can fill:
> Evermore to do thy will,
> God of light unending!
>
> Queen Immaculate, oh, pray
> That thy Spouse with me may stay,
> One, united ever:
> That through Him the word may deign,
> As in thee, in me to reign,
> King of Love forever.

Holy Spirit, be my guide and helper in this most sacred hour, as I prepare myself to receive the most holy sacrament. Only through confidence in you, my God and sanctifier, who are infinite love itself, do I, a poor sinner, dare to approach your altar. Enlighten my understanding, purify my heart, direct my will, strengthen my faith, enliven my hope, inflame my desire, enkindle my love, that I may receive the gift of heaven worthily.

Come, Holy Spirit, fill the hearts of your faithful and enkindle in them the fire of your love.

V. Send forth your Spirit and they shall be created.

R. And you shall renew the face of the earth.

Let us pray:

Visit us, O Lord, we beg of you, and purify our conscience, that our Lord Jesus Christ may find a dwelling-place prepared for Him in our hearts, who lives and reigns with you in the unity of the Holy Spirit, God forever and ever. Amen.

Desire

My eucharistic God, be merciful to me a sinner, and take me to the arms of your infinite love. Your mercy calling me to your holy table is greater than my unworthiness, which discourages me from approaching it. I come to you with a contrite and humble heart.

Jesus, lover of my soul, take into your possession what you have purchased so dearly. I love you and you alone. Come, heavenly Physician, enter into the dwelling of my soul and make it acceptable to you. Heal my heart, wounded, sick, and wretched from sin.

Come, my most generous friend, and enrich my poverty from the riches of your Sacred Heart. Fill it with the treasures of your grace. Come, Divine Light, and dispel the darkness of my soul.

Jesus, my love, I await you with fervent devotion. Behold a poor sinner, unworthy to appear before you, comes to you imploring you to pour your love into his heart as you did into the heart of your dearest Mother Mary.

AFTER COMMUNION

Thanksgiving

Jesus, my God, I adore you now really present in my soul as God and as man. With your dearest Mother Mary, and all the angels and saints I adore you and I thank you for the unspeakable grace of your personal visit to my poor soul.

From the blessed Trinity to holy Communion: such was the route you took to give me your divine life, the path made by divine love in descending to me whom you wished to save.

From holy Communion to the blessed Trinity: such is the ascent by which I, purified and strengthened by union with you, must make to the eternal possession of God. I thank you most sincerely for this holy Communion which is my surest way to God.

I thank you, my beloved Savior, for coming to be the guest of my soul. You are the Word, the eternal Word who fills my soul with your light. May your grace take possession of me through the action of the Holy Spirit who also dwells in me. In this eucharistic union apply to my soul the infinite merits of your death and give me the pledge of future life. What gracious assurance and what peace you bring to my soul in coming to it! I thank you for your infinite generosity.

Through the Holy Spirit, my sanctifier, enkindle your love in me! May each Communion bring me nearer and nearer to you, my model; above all, may it make me penetrate more intimately into the knowledge, the love, and the mercy of your Sacred Heart.

O Bread of Life, the bread which makes me live. May the works that I do be the works of life, the works of a child of God, after having been nourished with this divine bread in order to be changed into you. Do not let me, from want of generosity, and in order to excuse my laziness, say that I am weak. This is more true even than I think. But by the side of the abyss of my weakness, there is the abyss of your merits and treasures; and, by Communion, all this is mine, because you are mine. Accept, then, my good will and my confidence in you, my Lord and my God. Accept my sincerest thanks for your most generous love for me.

Petitions for the Seven Gifts

Sacred Heart of Jesus, you have not left us orphans, but you kept your promise to remain with us to the end of the world, not only by your abiding presence in the Blessed Sacrament, but also by sending us from the Father the Holy Spirit to be our light and strength on our earthly pilgrimage. "I will ask the Father and He will give you another Advocate to dwell with you forever, the spirit of truth whom the world cannot receive" (John 14,16).

Lord, through this holy Communion I have become more closely united not only with you, but also with the Father and the Holy Spirit, for you and the Father are one in the love of the Holy Spirit. I thank you for meriting for me the abiding help of the Holy Spirit; I implore you that I may ever know and love this sweet guest of my soul, and become more and more worthy of His divine indwelling.

Jesus, through the ardent love of your most Sacred Heart, *I beg you to obtain for me from the Father the Holy Spirit, the comforter, that he may make my heart more like to yours.*

Through the hatred of your divine heart for the least shadow of sin and through all the sacrifices of love which it has made for sinners, I implore you, most humble Jesus, fill me with the *spirit of fear of the Lord* that I may flee from sin and, through a salutary fear of the judgments of God, arrive at true humility.

By the filial love which your divine heart bears to the Father and by the constant tenderness with which it ever regards mankind, I implore you, most loving Jesus, fill me with the *spirit of piety* that I may crush all feeling of unkindness and serve God with childlike love.

Through the compassion which your tender heart always feels for the miseries of mankind, I implore you, most faithful Jesus, give me the *spirit of knowledge* that, realizing the vanity of all earthly things, I may strive solely for those which are eternal.

Through the courage with which your most holy heart bore so many great sufferings, I implore you, most noble Jesus, give me the *spirit of fortitude* that, detesting all carelessness, I may ever serve you with zeal and fidelity.

Through the mercy which your loving heart ever showed for mankind, I implore you, kind Jesus, give me the *spirit of counsel* that I may renounce all attachment to creatures and earthly goods to follow you in the way of perfection.

Through the purity of your most Sacred Heart, I implore you, sweet Jesus, eternal splendor of the Father, give me the *spirit of understanding* that I may clearly understand the truths of faith and steadily increase in the knowledge of the most holy Trinity.

Through the sweet peace which your adorable heart ever enjoyed in the love of God, I implore you, dear Jesus, eternal wisdom, give me the *spirit of wisdom*, that for your sake I may be indifferent to all created things and strive only to increase in our divine love.

Send your Holy Spirit with His life-giving graces and blessings also to my parents, my family, relatives, benefactors, friends, and to all those for whom I am bound to pray or who have recommended themselves to my prayers.

My Indwelling Guest

Divine Spirit, so intimately united to me in this holy Communion, I adore you dwelling in my soul with the Father and the Son. You are my sanctifier. By your holy grace in this sacrament make me more like Jesus, my Savior. I can be holy only in so far as I become similar to Him, Who is "the way and the truth and the life." God has laid no other foundation for my salvation, perfection, and glory. You alone can bring me to Christ and affect the union of my soul with the Son of God. Infuse your grace into my mind and heart in this holy Communion.

Living Fire, I desire to offer myself to you with the same love with which Jesus offers Himself in this holy Mass and in all the holy Masses that are celebrated throughout the entire world. I beg you through the merits of this holy sacrifice, have mercy on me and make me a living, pleasing sacrifice to you. Transform my spirit into the spirit of Jesus, and grant that I may have a share in the abundance of graces hidden in His Sacred Heart so that my heart may become your pleasing temple. *Live in my heart as you live in the Sacred Heart of Jesus and in the immaculate heart of Mary, that the fullness of your light and the power of your grace may reign in me.*

Spirit of the Father and of the Son; let the might of your love be felt ever more in the hearts of men. Let your light shine upon the souls of those who are wandering in darkness. Turn them to the life-giving heart of Jesus and to the healing streams of His most Precious Blood. Strengthen souls that love you; perfect in them your seven gifts and your twelve fruits. Make them your temples here, that you may be adored by them forever in heaven. Amen.

> Spirit of my soul's redeemer,
>   Blest, life-giving dove,
> Hov'ring o'er the Word Incarnate,
>   In thy work of love.
> Come, posses my heart and mold it,
>   Like the heart of God's own Son;
> Bind my will to thine and hold it
>   With His ever one.

> Jesus was thine art's perfection,
>   Formed in Mary's womb;
> By thy grace His hidden Godhead
>   Shone in manhood's bloom.
> Lead me, too, in my vocation;
>   To thy hand by faith I cling,
> Guide me in my imitation
>   Of my Lord and King.

> Thou hast led our blessed Savior
>   To the hill of pain;

Rais'd Him up again in glory
Evermore to reign.
In my soul this hope is burning,
As I tread life's Calvary;
Thou wilt still my ardent yearning
for eternity.

Holy Spirit, Fount of Holiness, you have rested upon our divine Savior in all the fullness of your gifts; give me a share in these gifts and make me a partaker of the grace that is in Jesus. Let Jesus be my way, my truth, my resurrection, my life.

Loving Comforter, whom my divine Redeemer has promised to His disciples, be also my paraclete, my assistance, my consolation in this life. Bring home to my mind the truths of salvation which our Savior has taught us. Give me peace which the world cannot give. Enable me to shun sin, practice virtue, and escape the judgment of this world. Confirm me, giver of all grace, in a living faith an immaculate life that I may give testimony to Jesus Christ and love Him with all my heart.

Holy Spirit, my delight and my love! *Abide in my soul as in your temple as you ever lived in Jesus.* Divine Fire, melt the icy coldness of my poor heart and help me to love my Jesus with all my heart. Give me the spirit of Jesus, ever striving to please you as He did. In Jesus I offer you my labors of each day, all the love of my soul, and every beat of my heart, that through the gentle power of your grace in this holy Communion I may become "Another Christ."

Tuesday: In Union With the Church

BEFORE COMMUNION

Faith

Jesus, I come to you. You are *the way* that I want to follow in obedience to your commandments, your counsels and your example. Let me walk after you in the way of obedience, self-denial and sacrifice, which leads to heaven and to you.

Jesus, you are *the truth*. You are "the true light which enlightens every man who comes into this world." I believe in you. I believe in your Gospel. I want to know you that I may love you. I want to make you known in order to make you loved.

Jesus, you are *the life* through your sanctifying grace which is the life of our souls; through your words which are "the words of everlasting life;" through your Eucharist which is "the living bread which has come down from heaven;" through your heart which is the foundation of life for individual souls and for society.

I cling to your word with all my heart. I hunger for the living bread of your Eucharist. I open my heart eagerly to the life-giving streams from your Sacred Heart. I unite myself inwardly to all its intentions. May this divine heart reign universally over the children of the Church and over all humanity. Amen.

Adoration and Thanksgiving

I adore you, *Eternal Father*, and I give you thanks for the infinite love with which you have deigned to send your only begotten Son to redeem me and to become the food of my soul.

I offer you all the acts of adoration and thanksgiving that are offered to you by your angels and saints in heaven and by the just on earth. I praise, love, and thank you with all the praise, love, and thanksgiving that are offered to you by your own Son in the Blessed Sacrament, and I beg you to grant that He may be known, loved, praised and worthily received by all in this most divine sacrament.

Our Father, Hail Mary, Glory be.

I adore you *Eternal Son*, and I thank you for the infinite love which caused you to become man for me, to be born in a stable, to live in poverty, to suffer hunger, thirst, heat and cold, weariness and hardships, contempt and persecutions, the scourging and the crowning with thorns, and a cruel death upon the hard wood of the cross.

I thank you with the Church militant and the Church triumphant for the infinite love with which you have instituted the most Blessed Sacrament to be the food of my soul. I adore you in all consecrated Hosts throughout the world, and I thank you for those who do not know you and do not thank you. Would that I were able to make you better known, loved, and honored by all in this sacrament of love, and to prevent the sacrileges that are committed against you!

I love you, divine Jesus, and I desire to receive you with the purity, love, and affection of your Blessed Mother and with the love and perfection of your own most pure heart. Grant, most amiable spouse of my soul, in coming to me in this most holy sacrament, that I may receive all the graces and blessings which you wish to bestow upon me. Let me rather die than receive you unworthily.

Our Father, Hail Mary, Glory be.

I adore you, *Eternal Holy Spirit*, and I give you thanks for the infinite love with which you worked the unspeakable mystery of the Incarnation.

With infinite love you formed out of the most pure blood of the Blessed Virgin Mary the sacred body of our Lord Jesus Christ, which in this sacrament is the food of my soul. I beg you to enlighten my mind and to purify my heart and the hearts of all men, that all may realize the benefits of your love and worthily receive this most Blessed Sacrament.

Our Father, Hail Mary, Glory be.

O sacred banquet in which Christ is received, the memory of His Passion is renewed, the mind is filled with grace, and a pledge of future glory is given to us.

V. You have given them bread from heaven:

R. Containing in itself all sweetness.

Let us pray.

O God, you have left us a remembrance of your Passion beneath the veils of this sacrament. Grant us, we pray, so to venerate the sacred mysteries of your body and blood that we may always enjoy the fruits of your redemption: Who live and reign forever. Amen.

Love

Behold, my most loving Jesus, how far your great love has reached! You have prepared for me a divine table of your own flesh and most precious blood in order to give yourself entirely to me. What has brought you to such generous love? Surely nothing else but your most loving heart.

Adorable heart of my Jesus, burning furnace of divine charity, receive my heart within your most sacred wound, that in this school of love I may learn to return love to the God who has given me such wondrous proofs of His own love. Amen.

> Very bread, good shepherd, tend us,
> Jesus of thy love befriend us,
> Thou refresh us, Thou defend us,
> Thine eternal goodness send us
> In the land of life to see.
>
> Thou who all things canst and knowest
> Who on earth such food bestowest,
> Grant us with thy saints, though lowest,
> Where the heavenly feast thou showest,
> Fellow-heirs and guests to be. Amen.
> —St. Thomas Aquinas

Humility

Lord Jesus Christ, Son of the living God, you have given life to the world by your death, according to the will of the Father and in union with the Holy Spirit. By your most sacred body, which I, unworthy as I am, dare to receive, deliver me from all my sins and from every evil. Help me ever to keep your commandments and never let me be separated from you.

Let the receiving of your body, Lord Jesus Christ, which I, though unworthy, dare to receive, not turn to me for judgment and condemnation, but, according to your mercy, let it be profitable to me for the protection and healing of soul and body: Who live and reign forever. Amen.

Lord, I am not worthy that you should enter under my roof, but only say the word and my soul shall be healed. (3 times)

Longing

Blessed is he that comes in the name of the Lord; Hosanna in the highest.
Jesus in the Blessed Sacrament, have mercy on us.
As the stag thirsts after the springs of water, so does my soul long or you, O God.
Come, O Lord, and do not delay.

AFTER COMMUNION

Love

My God and my all.
My God, my only good! You are all mine; may I be always yours.
Jesus, grant that I may be yours, entirely yours, forever yours.
Jesus, with all my heart I cling to you.
Sweetest Jesus, hide me in your Sacred Heart; do not let me be separated from you;
  defend me from the evil foe.

My God, I love you.

My God, grant that I may love you, and let the only reward of my love be to love you more and more.

Sweet Heart of Jesus, be my love.

Jesus, my God, I love you above all things.

Sacred Heart of Jesus, I believe in your love for me.

Sweet heart of my Jesus, grant that I may ever love you more.

Adoration

O my God, I firmly believe that you are really and bodily present in the Blessed Sacrament of the altar. I adore you here present from the very depths of my heart, and I worship your sacred presence with all possible humility.

O my soul, what joy to have Jesus Christ always with us, and to be able to speak to Him, heart to heart, with all confidence!

O Lord, grant that having adored your divine majesty here on earth in this wonderful sacrament, I may be able to adore it eternally in heaven. Amen.

Humbly kneeling before you and united in spirit with all the faithful on earth and all the saints in heaven, I adore you, Jesus, true God and true man, here present in the holy Eucharist. In deepest gratitude for so great a blessing, I love you, my Jesus, with my whole heart, for you are all perfect and all worthy of love.

Give me grace nevermore in any to offend you, and grant that, being refreshed by your eucharistic presence here on earth, I may be found worthy to come to the enjoyment with Mary of your eternal and ever blessed presence in heaven. Amen.

Consecration

My loving Jesus, out of the grateful love I bear you, and to make reparation for my unfaithfulness to grace, I give you my heart, and I consecrate myself entirely to you; and with your help I am determined to sin no more.

Most holy heart of Jesus, fountain of every blessing, I adore you, I love you, and with a lively sorrow for my sins, I offer you this poor heart of mine. Make me humble, patient, pure and wholly obedient to your will.

Grant, good Jesus, that I may live in you and for you. Protect me in the midst of danger; comfort me in my afflictions. Give me health of body, assistance in my temporal needs, your blessing on all that I do, and the grace of a holy death.

Reveal your Sacred Heart to me, O Jesus, and show me its attractions. Unite me to it forever. Grant that all my aspirations and all the beats of my heart, which do not cease even while I sleep, be a witness to you of my love for you and may say to you: Yes, Lord, I am yours! The pledge of my loyalty to you rests ever in my heart and will never cease to be there.

Accept the slight amount of good that I do and be pleased to repair all my wrongdoing, so that I may be able to praise you in time and in eternity. Amen.

Petition

I greet you, Sacred Heart of Jesus, living and life-giving fountain of eternal life, infinite treasure of divinity, glowing furnace of divine love! You are my place of rest and my most sure refuge.

My dear Savior, enkindle my heart with that burning love with which your own is on fire. Pour into my heart the manifold grace, of which your heart is the source. Let your will be mine, and let mine be forever obedient to yours. Amen.

My Lord Jesus Christ, most sweet and most kind, who even now have entered into this poor humble abode of your great goodness, adorn it and enrich it with your treasures, that it may be made worthy of your indwelling. Take up your rest in it that my heart may find its rest in you alone.

Let it not be enough for you, Lord, to have given me your sacred body. Give me also the treasures of grace which you bring with you; for it will profit me little to eat the bread of life, if I remain unnourished by your grace.

Lord, give me a heart completely transformed into you by love. Give me a life that shall be all yours, a quiet death that shall be the beginning of eternal life.

That is what I look for, pray and hope for from you, my eternal God, through the power of this Blessed Sacrament. Amen

> Teach me, O dearest Jesus,
>   In thine own sweet loving way,
> All *the lessons of perfection*
>   I must practice day by day.
>
> Teach me *meekness*, dearest Jesus,
>   Of thine own the counterpart;
> Not in words and actions only,
>   But the meekness of the heart.
>
> Teach *humility*, sweet Jesus,
>   To this poor proud heart of mine,
> Which yet wishes, O my Jesus,
>   To be modeled after thine.
>
> Teach me *fervor*, dearest Jesus,
>   To comply with every grace,
> So as never to look backwards,
>   Never slacken in the race.
>
> Teach me *poverty*, sweet Jesus,
>   That my heart may never cling
> To whate'er its love might sever
>   From my Savior and my King.
>
> Teach me *chastity*, sweet Jesus,
>   That my every day may see
> Something added to the likeness
>   That my soul should bear to thee.

Teach *obedience*, dearest Jesus,
　　Such as was thy daily food
In thy toilsome earthly journey
　　From the cradle to the rood.

Teach thy *heart* to me, dear Jesus,
　　Is my fervent final prayer;
For all beauties and perfections
　　Are in full perfection there.

Sweetest Jesus, you came into the world to give all souls the life of your grace, and to preserve and nourish it in them. You wanted to be at the same time the daily cure of their daily infirmities and their daily nourishment. We humbly beg of you, by your heart all on fire with love for us, to pour forth upon them all your divine spirit, so that those who are unhappily in mortal sin, may turn to you and regain the life of grace which they have lost, and those who through your grace are already living this divine life, may approach your holy table daily, if they can, and there receive the remedy for their daily venial sins by means of daily Communion, and each day foster within themselves the life of grace. Being thus ever more and more purified, may they at last reach that eternal life which is happiness with you. Amen.

Most holy heart of Jesus, shower your blessings abundantly upon your holy Church, upon the supreme pontiff and upon all the clergy. Grant perseverance to the just, convert sinners, and enlighten unbelievers. Bless our relatives, friends, and benefactors. Assist the dying, deliver the holy souls in purgatory, and extend over all hearts the sweet empire of your love. Amen.

I thank you, Lord, Almighty Father, Everlasting God, for having been pleased, through no merit of mind, but of your great mercy alone, to feed me, a sinner and your unworthy servant, with the precious body and blood of your Son, our Lord Jesus Christ. I pray that this holy Communion may not be for my judgment and condemnation, but for my pardon and salvation.

Let this holy Communion be to me an armor of faith and a shield of good will, a cleansing of all vices, and a rooting out of all evil desires. May it increase love and patience, humility and obedience, and all virtues. May it be a firm defense against the evil designs of all my visible and invisible enemies, a perfect quieting of all the desires of soul and body.

May this holy Communion bring about a perfect union with you, the one true God, and at last enable me to reach eternal bliss when you will call me. I pray that you being me, a sinner, to that unspeakable feast where you, with your Son and the Holy Spirit, are to your saints true light, full blessedness, everlasting joy, and perfect happiness. Through the same Christ our Lord. Amen.

　　—St. Thomas Aquinas

Wednesday: In Union With the Saints

BEFORE COMMUNION

Humility

Almighty and Eternal God, behold I come to the sacrament of your only begotten Son, our Lord Jesus Christ. As one sick I come to the physician of life; unclean, to the fountain of mercy; blind, to the light of eternal splendor; poor and needy, to the Lord of heaven and earth. Therefore, I beg of you, through your infinite mercy and generosity, heal my weakness, wash my uncleanness, give light to my blindness, enrich my poverty, and clothe my nakedness. May I thus receive the bread of angels, the King of Kings, Lord of Lord, with such reverence and humility, contrition and devotion, purity and faith, purpose and intention, as shall aid my soul's salvation.

Grant, I beg of you, that I may receive not only the sacrament of the body and blood of our Lord, but also its full grace and power. Give me the grace, most merciful God, to receive the body of your only Son, our Lord Jesus Christ, born of the Virgin Mary, in such manner that I may deserve to be intimately united with His mystical body and to be numbered among His members.

Most loving Father, grant that I may behold for all eternity face to face your beloved Son, whom now, on my pilgrimage, I am about to receive under the sacramental veil, who lives and reigns with you, in the unity of the Holy Spirit, God, world without end. Amen.

—St. Thomas Aquinas

Petition

I beg of you, O Lord, by this most holy mystery of your body and blood, with which you daily nourish us in your Church, that we may be cleansed and sanctified and made sharers in your divinity.

Grant to me your holy virtues, which will enable me a approach your altar with a clean conscience, so that this heavenly sacrament may be a means of salvation and life for me. You yourself have spoken: "I am the living bread that has come down from heaven. If anyone eat of this bread, he shall live forever; and the bread that I will give is my flesh for the life of the world."

Most sweet bread, heal my heart, that I may taste the sweetness of your love. Heal it from all weakness, that I may enjoy no sweetness but you. Most pure bread, containing every delight which ever refreshes us, may my heart consume you and may my soul be filled with your sweetness.

Holy bread, living bread, perfect bread, that has come down from heaven to give life to the world, come into my heart and cleanse me from every stain of body of soul. Enter into my soul; heal and cleanse me completely. Be the constant safeguard and salvation of my soul and body. Guard me from the enemies who lie in wait; may they flee from the protecting presence of your power, that, armed in soul and body by you, I may safely reach your kingdom. There we shall see you, not as now in mysteries, but face to face, when you will deliver the kingdom to God the Father, and will reign as God over all. Then you will satisfy the hunger of my soul perfectly with yourself, so that I shall neither hunger nor thirst again; who, with the same God the Father and the Holy Spirit, live and reign forever. Amen.

—St. Ambrose

O God, I love thee for thyself
    And not that I may heaven gain,
Nor yet that they who love thee not
    Must suffer hell's eternal pain.

Thou, O my Jesus, thou didst me
    Upon the cross embrace;
For me didst bear the nails and spear
    And manifold disgrace;

And griefs and torments numberless,
    And sweat of agony;
Even death itself—and all for one
    Who was thine enemy.

Then why, O dearest Jesus Christ,
    Should I not love thee well;
Not for the sake of winning heaven
    Or of escaping hell;

Not with the hope of gaining aught,
    Not seeking a reward;
But, as thyself hast loved me,
    O ever-loving Lord?

Even so I love thee, and will love,
    And in thy praise will sing;
Solely because thou art my God
    And my eternal King.
    —St. Francis Xavier

Love

Sweetest Lord Jesus Christ, pierce the depths of my soul with the most joyous and life-giving wound of your love, with true, serene, holy apostolic charity, that my heart may ever yearn for you, and melt with genuine love, and long for you; that it may desire you, sigh for your heavenly home, and earnestly yearn to become as nothing in order to be with you.

Grant that my soul may hunger for you, the bread of angels, the refreshment of holy souls, our daily and ever-satisfying bread, which contains all possible sweetness. Let my heart ever hunger after you and feed upon you, upon whom the angels desire to gaze, and may my whole soul be filled with your sweetness. May it ever thirst for you, the fountain of life, the source of wisdom and knowledge, the fountain of eternal light, the torrent of pleasure, the richness of the house of God. May it ever yearn for you, seek you, find you, stretch towards you, reach you, meditate upon you, speak of you, and do all things for the praise and glory of your holy name, with humility and prudence, with love and delight, with willingness and affection, with perseverance to the very end.

Be ever my hope and my whole confidence, my riches, my delight, my pleasure, and my joy. Be my rest, my peace, my sweetness and my delight. Be my spiritual enjoyment, my food and refreshment. Be my refuge and my help, my wisdom, my reward, my possession and my treasure, in whom my mind and my heart may ever remain fixed and firm now and forever. Amen.
—St. Bonaventure

Longing

Jesus, most ardently desired and longed for, behold the moment draws near, the happy moment in which I shall receive you, my God, into my soul.

My Jesus, behold, I come to you, and run to meet you with the sincerest devotion and reverence which I am able to show. Stretch forth your most sacred hands to embrace my soul, those pierced hands of yours which you have stretched forth amid the anguish of your Passion to embrace all sinners.

My crucified Jesus, I stretch forth not my hands only, but my heart and soul, to embrace you and to lead you into my inmost soul. Would that I had within me the greatest love and purity that have ever adorned the heart of man. Would that I were filled with virtues, with all holy desires, with perfect devotion! How I wish I had the purity of all your angels, the charity of all your apostles, the holiness of all confessors, the chastity of all virgins! I long to receive you now with all that devotion, reverence, and love with which your most Blessed Mother received you in your Incarnation, and in your adorable sacrament. Oh, would that I had your own Sacred Heart, that I might receive you into it as your divine majesty deserves.

Most chaste Virgin Mary, I beg of you, by that perfect purity with which you prepared for the Son of God a dwelling of delights in your virginal womb, that by your prayers I may be cleansed from every stain of sin.

Most humble Virgin Mary, I beg of you, by that most profound humility with which you merited to be raised high above all the choirs of angels and of saints, that by your prayers I may atone for all my faults.

Most loving Virgin Mary, I beg of you, by that unspeakable love which united you so closely and so inseparably to God, that by your prayers I may obtain an abundance of all merits. Amen
—St. Gertrude

AFTER COMMUNION

Love

Jesus, now you fill my heart to overflowing. My dear Savior, repose in my heart for it belongs to you. Only self-surrender places me in your arms and lets me feed on the bread of love reserved for your chosen ones.

Jesus, by loving you I come to the Father that my poor heart may keep Him forever! O holy Trinity, you are the prisoner of my love!

My beloved, supreme beauty, you have given yourself to me. I love you in return, my Savior. Only make of my life one great act of love. I cannot receive you in holy Communion as often as I wish, but, dear Lord, are you not all-powerful? Remain in my heart as in the Tabernacle, and never leave me.

Jesus, you are my peace, my happiness, my only love. My God, you know that I have desired nothing but to love you alone. I desire no other glory. I am weak and feeble, but it is my being like a child that makes me dare to offer my self as a sacrifice to your love, my Jesus.

Give me a thousand hearts, that I may love you; but even these are not enough, O supreme beauty. Give me your Sacred Heart itself with which to love you. May your heart preserve my innocence. I place my hope in you, O Lord, that after this life I may see you in heaven.

Although you have the seraphim in your heavenly court, yet you seek my love. You desire my heart. Jesus, I give it to you. I have no other way to prove my love for you but to throw flowers before you, that is, to let no sacrifice, word, or look escape; to draw profit from the smallest actions and to do them for love.

I love you, my Jesus, and I give myself to you forever. Give me the grace, O Lord, to live by love. You alone can satisfy my soul, for I must love you for all eternity.

The grace that I especially ask, my Jesus, is never to offend you. I fear only on thing, my God, to do my own will. Then take it, for I choose all that you choose. My gifts are all unworthy, and so I offer you my very soul, most loving Savior. I offer myself to you that you may perfectly accomplish in me your holy designs. I will not allow anything created to hinder you from doing your holy will in me.

—St. Therese of the Child Jesus

Adoro Te
　　O Godhead hid, devoutly I adore thee,
　　　　Who truly art within the forms before me;
　　To thee my heart I bow with bended knee,
　　　　At utter loss in contemplating thee.

　　Sight, touch and taste in thee are each deceived;
　　　　The ear alone most safely is believed.
　　I cling to all the Son of God has said,
　　　　Than truth's own word no truer word is read.

　　God only on the cross lay hid from view,
　　　　But here lies hid at once thy manhood too.
　　And I, in both professing my belief,
　　　　Repeat the longing of the contrite thief.

　　Thy wounds, as Thomas saw, I do not see,
　　　　Yet thee confess my Lord and God to be.
　　Make me believe thee ever more and more;
　　　　In thee my hope, in thee my love to store.

　　O thou memorial of our Lord's own dying!
　　　　O living bread, to mortals life supplying!
　　Make thou my soul henceforth on thee to live;
　　　　Ever a taste of heavenly sweetness give.

O loving pelican! O Son of God!
    Unclean I am, but cleanse me in thy blood,
Of which a single drop for sinners spilt,
    Can purge the whole wide world from all its guilt.

Jesus, whom for the present veiled I see,
    What I so thirst for, oh, vouchsafe to me:
That I may see thy countenance unfold
    And may be blest thy glory to behold. Amen.
    —St. Thomas Aquinas

Praise

Praise be to you, O Lord, who fill heaven and earth with your majesty, and yet you have been pleased to nourish me with this most holy sacrament. Cleanse me, my God, from every stain of soul and body, and teach me to walk in your fear and do good, so that my conscience my prove that I have been sanctified by the receiving of your holy body and blood, and my soul is indeed a temple of the Holy Spirit. Merciful Lord, let me not have increased my guilt through an unworthy reception of this sacrament, but grant that it may be a means of making me more pleasing to you.

Father of mercy and God of all consolation, graciously look upon me and impart to me the blessing which flows from this holy sacrament. Overshadow me with your loving kindness, and let this divine mystery bear fruit in me.

I thank you, almighty and merciful Father, I am deeply grateful to you for having had pity on me and cleansed me from sin and allowed me to have a share in this sacrament on which the angels desire to gaze. Grant that this sacred union with you may avail for the pardon of my past sins, as a remedy of those which I may still have, and a safeguard against those I might commit in the future, who live and reign as God forever. Amen
    —St. Blasé

Petition

O Eternal Word, only begotten Son of God, I beg of you, teach me to be truly generous. Teach me to serve you as you deserve, to give without counting the cost, to fight without heeding wounds, to labor without seeking rest, to sacrifice myself without looking for any reward except the knowledge of having done your holy will.
    —St. Ignatius

Lord, grant that I may always allow myself to be guided by you, always follow your plans, and perfectly accomplish your holy will. Grant that in all things, great and small, today and all the days of my life, I may do that which your sweet pleasure, your holy will, may require of me. Help me to respond to the slightest prompting of your grace, that I may become a trustworthy instrument for your honor, and that your holy will may be done in time and eternity by me, in me, and through me. Amen.
    —St. Teresa

Lord, make me an instrument of your peace. Where there is hatred, let me sow love; where there is injury, pardon; where the is doubt, faith; where there is despair, hope; where there is darkness, light; and where there is sadness, joy.

Divine master, grant that I may not so much seek to be consoled as to console; to be understood as to understand; to be loved as to love; for it is in giving that we receive, it is in pardoning that we are pardoned and it is in dying that we are born to eternal life.

—St. Francis of Assisi

Prayer of St. Augustine

O Lord Jesus, let me know myself, let me know you, and desire nothing but you alone.
Let me hate myself and love you, and do all things for the sake of you.
Let me humble myself and exalt you, and think of nothing but you alone.
Let me die to myself and live in you, and take whatever happens as coming from you.
Let me forsake myself and walk after you, and ever desire to follow you.
Let me flee from myself and turn to you, that thus I may merit to be defended by you.
Let me fear for myself, let me fear you, and be among those who are chosen by you.
Let me distrust myself and trust in you, and ever obey for love of you.
Let me cleave to nothing but only to you, and ever be poor for the sake of you.
Look upon me that I may love you. Call me that I may see you and forever possess you.
Amen.

—St. Augustine

Thursday: In Union with The Eucharistic Christ

BEFORE COMMUNION

Preparation

Lord Jesus Christ, you are about to give me yourself in holy Communion and to impart to my soul all the graces I need to sanctify and save my soul. My divine Savior, I humbly and earnestly beg of you to give me not only an increase of sanctifying grace, the life and beauty of my soul, in this holy Communion, but all the *actual graces* I need to live a life that is pleasing to you and to save my soul. Give me actual graces to increase my love for you and my neighbor and to put it into action that I may return love for love; actual graces to help me to do your holy will perfectly and to avoid sin; actual graces which will fill my soul with peace and joy. Through this holy Communion give me the graces I need to strengthen me in my struggle against the enemies of my soul that lead me into mortal sin—the world, the flesh, and the devil.

Jesus, I thank you for the marvelous effects which holy Communion produces in my soul. But since *these effects depend in a large measure on my dispositions and my preparation,* I earnestly desire to prepare for you a dwelling less unworthy of your divinity.

In the Gospel you rewarded the desires and efforts of Zachaeus. This prince of the publicans desired only to see you, and you went so far as to tell him you wanted to visit his home. Your visit brought him pardon and salvation. In this sacrament I can see you only by faith. But may your visit to my heart this morning bring pardon and salvation to my soul, for I am a sinner, but a sinner who trusts in your mercy and kindness.

In the house of Simon the Pharisee, where Magdalene washed your feet with her tears, you compared what she did for you with what the Pharisee had omitted in his hospitality towards you. You said of Magdalene: "Her sins, many as they are, shall be forgiven her, because she has loved much" (Luke 7,47). Being aware of my own sinfulness, I approach you with a loving heart, and I confidently hope that you will not only forgive my sins, but will fill my heart with many graces in this holy Communion, for I also want to love you very much. I know that you are attentive to the marks of love with which I receive you.

My Lord and my God, help me to prepare myself constantly for your visit by directing all my actions each day towards holy Communion, so that my union with you in the Eucharist may become truly the sun of my life. Aid me in making of every action of the day a preparation for the eucharistic sacrifice of the morrow.

Jesus Christ, Incarnate Word, I desire to prepare a dwelling for you within myself, but I am incapable of this work. Eternal Wisdom, by your infinite merits, prepare my soul to become your temple. Grant that I may attach myself to you alone! I offer you my actions and the sufferings of this day in order that you may render them pleasing in your divine sight, and that I may not come before you with empty hands in holy Communion.

Dearest Jesus, let me never forget that the Eucharist is the sacrament of union, and *the fewer obstacles I put into the way of this union with you, the more the grace of your sacrament acts in me.* Help me to receive holy Communion with a heart well-disposed and well-prepared that I may receive all the gifts of grace which you have in store for my soul.

Never let me put obstacles in the way of your grace, which will prevent these fruits of the Eucharist from being imparted to my soul. Mortal sin is the biggest obstacle to your grace because it brings about the death of my soul. Make me hate *mortal sin* as the greatest evil in the world.

I realize that to remain attached to *venial sin,* willful faults and negligences would mean to hinder the action of your grace in my soul. The faults that I am sorry for and strive to master will not prevent your action in my soul, for you come to help me to overcome these faults. But help me to overcome my bad habits which I am aware of and which I am not generous enough to attack. I ask in particular for the grace to overcome my willful faults against charity towards my neighbor, for since we are all members of your mystical body, holy Communion should unite us to each other and to you, our divine head.

Jesus, I want my union with you to be perfect, and, therefore, I do not wish to reserve any place in my heart for creatures loved for their own sake. Give me the grace to set myself apart from the world and all it has to offer, to long for the perfect coming of your kingdom within me by submitting all my being to your holy will and to the action of the Holy Spirit who will sanctify me. May my selfishness not be an obstacle to your complete reign in my soul. I want to die to my selfish life in order to live in the divine life. The Christ-life in me is a life of self-surrender and love. May love yield my will to you, and through it, my whole being and all my energies. I know what you give yourself to me according to the measure of my love. Help me to be detached both from myself and creatures, and to give myself to you unreservedly with a pure heart, that in exchange you may give yourself to me as only God is able to do.

Faith

Jesus, nowhere is faith so necessary as in the sacrament of the holy Eucharist, because neither my reason nor my senses perceive anything of you. When I look at the manger, I see you as a little child, but the angels sing your coming that they may make known your divinity and your mission as Savior of mankind. During your public life your miracles and your doctrine prove that you are the Son of God. On Thabor, your body is transfigured by your divinity. On the cross itself your divinity does not entirely disappear, for nature proclaims that you are the creator of the world. But on the altar I can see neither your humanity nor your divinity. For my senses, the sight, the taste, the touch, there are only the bread and wine. Give me the eye of faith to see through these appearances, to penetrate these veils and see you as you really are.

Dear Lord, may my faith supply what is lacking to my senses. You said: "This is my body, this is my blood." Your word is enough for me; I believe it. This bread that you give me is your own self, the beloved Son of the Father who became incarnate and was delivered up for me; this bread is Jesus the Son of the Virgin Mary, who was born at Bethlehem, dwelt in Nazareth, cured the sick and gave sight to the blind. You are the Jesus who forgave Magdalen and the good thief, who at the Last Supper permitted John to lay his head upon your heart. You are the way, the truth, and the life. You are the Jesus who died for love of me, who arose from the dead, ascended into heaven, and now, at the right hand of God the Father, reigns and intercedes unceasingly for us.

Jesus, Eternal Truth, you declare that you are present upon the altar, really and substantially, with your sacred humanity and all the treasures of your divinity. I believe it, and, because I believe it, I cast myself down and adore you. My God and my all, receive this homage of my faith and adoration.

My Daily Bread
 Give me my daily bread,
  O God, the bread of strength!
 For I have learnt to know
  How weak I am at length.
 As child I am so weak,
  As child I must be fed;—
 Give me your grace, O Lord,
  Oh, be my daily bread.

 Give me my daily bread,
  In bitter days of grief.
 I sought earth's poisoned feasts
  For pleasure and relief;
 I sought her deadly fruits,
  But now, O God, instead,
 I ask your healing grace,—
  Oh, be my daily bread.

 Give me my daily bread,
  To cheer my fainting soul;

The feast of comfort, Lord,
>And peace, to make me whole;
For I am sick of tears,
>The useless tears I shed;—
Now give me comfort, Lord.
>Oh, be my daily bread.

Give me my daily bread,
>The bread of angels, Lord,
For me, so many times,
>Broken, betrayed, adored:
Your body and your blood—
>The Feast that you have spread.
O Come—my life, my all—
>To be my daily bread!

Longing

Lord Jesus, do not look at my sins, which I detest, but at the faith of your Church, which tells me that you are here present under the veils of the Host in order to come to me. You have the power of drawing me entirely to yourself so that I may be transformed into you. I yield myself entirely to you that you may be the master of all my being, and of all my actions, that I may live only because of you and in you.

I open my soul to you by faith, by confidence, by love, by holy desires, by abandonment to you. Fill it with yourself, dear Lord. *Give me yourself entirely, with your divinity and your humanity, and the price of your Passion.*

Jesus, come to me, as you came on the earth in order to destroy the works of the devil. Offer with me divine homage to your Father. Give me a share in the treasure or your divinity, in the eternal life you hold from your Father and which your Father wills that you share with me that I may resemble you. Fill me with your grace so that you may become my wisdom, my sanctification, my way, my truth, my life. Let me become "Another Christ," so that like you, and because of you, I may become the object of your Father's delight. I open my soul to you, dear Jesus. Fill it with yourself and your graces. Amen.

The Bread of Life

Jesus speaks:

"As the living Father has sent me, and as I live because of the Father, so he who eats me, he also shall live because of me" (John 6,58). My desire is to share my divine life with you. I hold my being, my life, my all, from my Father. Hence I live only for Him. I earnestly desire that you, holding all from me, may live only for me. The life of your body is preserved and developed by food. I want to be the food of your soul, so as to preserve and develop its life. He that eats me, lives by my life. I have the fullness of grace, and I give you a share in this grace when I give myself to you as food in holy Communion. I am living bread that has come down from heaven to give you eternal life. You need that bread for the life of your soul. Remember my warning: "Unless you eat the flesh of the Son of Man, and drink his blood, you shall not have life in you."

Divine Jesus, I firmly believe that holy Communion is the sacred banquet in which you give yourself to me as the bread of life. You are present upon the altar not only to offer perfect homage to your Father by renewing in an unbloody manner your bloody sacrifice of Calvary, but also to make yourself, under the sacramental species, the food of my soul. You made known this intention of your Sacred Heart at the moment of instituting this sacrifice: "Take and eat; this is my body" (Matt. 26,26).

Faith tells me that you willed to institute this sacrament under the form of food in order to maintain your divine life in my soul. You are the vine; we are the branches; grace is the sap that rises up into the branches to make them bear fruit. I thank you for this gift of yourself in the Eucharist which makes grace abound within my soul. I long to receive this grace. Through your infinite love and mercy, grant it to me in this holy Communion which I am about to receive.

My eucharistic Savior, I thank you for this heavenly bread which is the food of my soul. May it preserve, heal, and rejoice my soul, and increase the life of grace within it, because holy Communion gives you to me, and you are the author of all grace.

Jesus Christ, Incarnate Word, in whom "dwells all the fullness of the Godhead bodily" (Col. 2,9), enter into me to make me a partaker of this fullness. This is divine life for me, since to receive you is to share in the life you have received from your Father. Through the grace of this holy Communion, may that same life overflow in my soul. Come to be my food, that I may live by your life.

> O bread of heav'n beneath this veil,
> > Thou dost my very God conceal.
> My Jesus dearest treasure, hail!
> > I love thee and adoring knell.
> Each loving soul by thee is fed,
> > With thine own self in form of bread.

> O Food of life, Thou who dost give,
> > The pledge of immortality.
> I live, no 'tis not I that live,
> > God gives me life, God lives in me;
> He feeds my soul, He guides my ways,
> > His joy all grief of soul repays.

> My dearest God, who dost so bind,
> > My heart with countless chains to thee.
> O sweetest love, my soul shall find
> > In thy dear bonds true liberty.
> Thyself thou has bestowed on me,
> > Thine, thine for ever I will be.

AFTER HOLY COMMUNION

Abiding in Christ

Jesus speaks:

"Abide in me and I in you…He who abides in me, and I in him, he bears much fruit; for without me you can do nothing. If anyone does not abide in me, he shall be cast outside as the branch and wither (John 15,5)…He who eats my flesh, and drinks my blood, abides in me and I in him (John 6,57). If you keep my commandments you will abide in my life, as I also have kept my Father's commandments, and abide in his love" (John 15,10).

Dearest Jesus, your words sum up not only the whole Christian life, but also all holiness. You instituted the holy Eucharist not only to be the heavenly bread which preserves and increases the divine life in my soul. You also wanted me to abide in you and you in me.

Through this holy Communion, which I have just received, *let me abide in you.* Let me abide in you by sharing in your divine sonship by sanctifying grace as a child of God. Let me abide in you by being one with you in *mind* by accepting with a simple act of faith all that you tell me, and all that you are. Let me abide in you in *will,* by submitting my will to yours and by making all my actions dependent on your grace. Help me to abide in your love by doing your will perfectly and by preferring your desires to my own. I am determined to make your interests my own and to yield myself to you entirely, without counting the cost, reserving nothing and taking nothing back. I rely with absolute confidence upon your wisdom, your power, your strength, and your love.

My eucharistic Lord, *I also beg you to abide in me* through holy Communion and the action of your Holy Spirit. You earnestly want to be in me the source of all activity of my soul as St. Paul says: "He who cleaves to the Lord is one spirit with him" (I Cor. 6,17). Grant that my soul may remain given up to you and your every wish, and that your action may become so powerful that my soul may be carried on to ever greater holiness.

Jesus, remain in my soul with your divinity, your merits, your riches, to be its light and way and truth, its wisdom, justice, and redemption. Be the life of my soul by living within my soul. Abide in it and transform it, little by little, into yourself, that like St. Paul I may exclaim: "It is now no longer I that live, but Christ lives in me" (Gal. 2,20).

Transformation into Christ

Jesus, Son of God, as last you have come to abide in my soul. I welcome you with all my heart. I thank you for giving me the privilege of receiving you entirely: your divinity and humanity: your body, your blood, your soul. May this holy Communion produce all the effects in my soul which you intended it to produce. Let nothing stand in the way of your grace.

How fortunate I am! I have just received you as the food of my soul. When I partake of food, I change it into my own body; but when you give yourself to me as food, you wish to transform me into yourself. I earnestly beg of you to do so through this holy Communion.

The characteristic of love is to transform the one who loves into the object of his love. How sincerely I want this to happen in my own soul. Make me a sharer of your thoughts and your sentiments. Communicate your virtues to me, but above all, enkindle in me the fire of love that you came to cast upon earth. *May the great power of the sacrament of the holy Eucharist work a change of myself into you by means of love.*

My beloved Savior, may your coming to me establish between your thoughts and mine, between your sentiments and mine, between your will and my will, such an exchange, such a oneness, that I may have no other thoughts, no other sentiments, no other desires than those of your Sacred Heart—and all this through love. May love yield my will to you, and through it, all my being, all my energies, and all that I am. This is what St. John meant when he wrote: "God is love, and he who abides in love abides in God, and God in him" (I John 4,16). And St. Paul expressed the same thought: "Have this mind in you which was also in Christ Jesus" (Phil. 2,5).

Jesus, now that you have united yourself with me in holy Communion, take possession of me and direct my whole life and reshape it on new lines, according to your great ideal. *Live in me by grace and your Holy Spirit.* Live in me in order to work through me, not only in church, but in the home, at work, at recreation, so that I may be Christlike in my thoughts, desires, words, and actions. Wherever I am, I am a member of your mystical body, a Christopher—a Christ-bearer. Continue your life on earth through me, for I earnestly want to represent your life in the world. Through me may your light shine, your example radiate, your life spread for the glory of God and the salvation of souls.

My Savior, through this holy Communion make me Christlike by giving me an increase of sanctifying grace and the actual graces I need to preserve your divine life in my soul. May your Holy Spirit purify, uplift, sanctify, and transform all my faculties of the power of His grace, so that I may love God with your heart, praise God with your life, and live by your life. Let your divine presence and your sanctifying virtue penetrate so intimately my whole being, both body and soul with all their powers, that I may become "Another Christ."

Friday : In Union With the Sacred Heart

BEFORE COMMUNION

Faith

Jesus, Incarnate Word, I believe that your Sacred Heart—which is a symbol of your undying love for mankind—is truly, really, and substantially present in the Blessed Sacrament, living and beating there with love of us.

With deep faith I look upon the Blessed Sacrament as the supreme gift of your Sacred Heart which has exhausted itself in loving us. Infinite wisdom could not devise and infinite power could not accomplish anything greater. Since love is the very soul of devotion to your Sacred Heart, and since it was the love of your Sacred Heart which prompted the institution of the Blessed Sacrament, may my love for your Sacred Heart be expressed by my love for the holy Eucharist, especially through frequent holy Communion.

Love

Jesus, as I kneel here before your altar where you dwell as a prisoner of love, my faith tells me that your Sacred Heart is inviting me to approach and receive this sacrament. "Come to me, all you who labor and are burdened, and I will give you rest" (Matt. 11,28). You want to enrich me, to sanctify me, to give me true peace and rest, to fulfill all the desires of my soul. You remain there on the altar pleading for the hearts of men, pleading for my love, pleading for my frequent communions with you. Surely the blessedness of heaven is better that the miseries of earth, and yet you love me so much that you desire to come down upon our altars at holy Mass to offer yourself as a sacrifice to your Father, to give yourself as food for our souls, to stay with us until the end of time. Love makes you do this: the burning, ceaseless, tender love of your Sacred Heart.

This morning, dearest Jesus, I desire to answer this invitation of your Sacred Heart and to receive you in holy Communion that I may in some way give you love for love. As I take you into the poor dwelling of my heart, how can I forget the tremendous love of your Sacred Heart? You lived, worked, prayed, suffered, and died for all of us. But not satisfied with this, your heart prompted you to do more: to institute the Blessed Sacrament, the everlasting miracle of love. Your heart so burned with love that it desired to live with men always and everywhere. It was love, pure and simple, that made you say that night of the Last Supper: "With desire I have desired to eat this Passover with you!" And St. John said of you: "Having loved His own who were in the world, He loved them to the end." That night as the eternal high priest, you offered the first holy Mass, gave the first holy Communion, ordained your first priests, and declared your last will: "Do this in remembrance of me."

All this was evidence of the burning love of your Sacred Heart. That same love makes you ardently desire to be united with my soul in my holy Communion today. In this sacrament of love I want to become one with you, and thereby begin on earth that union with you which you wish to continue through the endless ages of eternity. May my holy Communion be and act of gratitude for this devoted, beautiful love of your sacred Heart.

Longing

Jesus, I need your Sacred Heart. I acknowledge my helplessness, and, therefore, I come to you, the diving physician of my soul, that you may heal me. Who would know my needs so well as you who created and redeemed me? No one could desire my salvation and happiness more earnestly that you. Help me to realize that I can do nothing better for my own happiness and salvation, or that of my family and those I love, than to receive you in holy Communion as often as I can.

Sacred Heart of Jesus, I long for you in holy Communion as the food of my soul. You are the food of the Christian life. May my life always be a eucharistic life, till the veil that hides you from my vision will be withdrawn and I shall see you, no more with eyes of faith, but face to face, in the glory of your infinite beauty and loveliness.

> I need thee, loving Jesus,
>> Who art my manna here;
> Draw me to thine own Sacred Heart
>> And keep me ever near.

I need thy heart, dear Jesus,
    To make me more like thee;
Live in me through thy Eucharist,
    May I, too, live in thee.

I need thy blood, sweet Jesus,
    To wash each sinful stain:
To cleanse this sinful soul of mine,
    And make it pure again.

I need thee, dearest Jesus,
    Thou manna from above;
To nourish this poor soul of mine,
    With blessings of thy love.

AFTER COMMUNION

Love

Jesus, I have just now received you in the holy Eucharist. What wonderful consolation I find in the thought that your loving heart comes into my heart with all its love and tenderness. Never are friends so near as you are to me in this holy Communion. Dear Lord, welcome to my heart!

Sacred Heart of Jesus, now dwelling in my soul, I love you, and with the deepest humility I adore you. You are my Lord and my God. You are a burning furnace of love in this Blessed Sacrament. Help me to understand more and more the love that consumes your heart for my sake. O God made man, how can I love you enough? O furnace of love, inflame, possess, consume my heart, my soul, and my body in your divine flames of love.

O Jesus, open wide thy heart,
    And let me rest therein;
For weary is my stricken soul
    Of sorrow and of sin.
I've sought for rest and found it not
    In things of earthly mould;
One heart alone deserves my love,
    A heart that grows not cold.

O Jesus, Savior merciful,
    My soul to thee I turn;
Thou wilt not crush the reed that's bruis'd
    Nor sadden spirit spurn.
Then take me to thy Sacred Heart
    And seal the entrance o'er,
That from this home my wayward soul
    May never wander more.

B.32

> Yes, Jesus, take me to thyself,
>> I'm weary waiting here;
> I long to lean upon thy heart,
>> To see and feel thee near.
> O Mary, by the priceless love
>> Which Jesus' heart bore thee,
> Pray that my home in life and death
>> His loving heart may be.

Thanksgiving

Jesus, you are the greatest gift which a loving and merciful God has ever bestowed upon mankind, for you are God incarnate. The fact that you became man for me and died upon the cross to save my soul, is something infinitely great and truly divine. Yet that was not all. You wanted me to receive the abundant graces of redemption, not once only, but daily in the most holy Sacrament of the Altar. Because you loved me so much, you devised a means of giving yourself entirely to me and remaining with me always.

The Eucharist is this supreme gift of the love of your Sacred Heart. That love had at its service and infinite power, the omnipotence of God. During the holy sacrifice of the Mass this morning you came down from heaven to be offered for me as a victim to your heavenly Father, to become the spiritual nourishment of my soul, to abide on this altar, and to strengthen and console me by your presence. Stripping yourself of the splendor of the Godhead, you came to my heart under the lowly appearance of the eucharistic bread. After your abiding presence and constant sacrifice of yourself in the Mass, the last excess of your love in the holy Eucharist is the entire gift of yourself. You give yourself to me in holy Communion as if I were the only person on earth with all the love of your heart. I need not feel lost and forgotten in the vast number of human beings.

Dearest Jesus, I thank you for *the Eucharist,* the most precious gift of your Sacred Heart, the fruit of the love of your Sacred Heart. In this holy Communion I experience this love in my own behalf, for you have been so gracious as to visit my soul, to unite yourself most intimately with me, to pour upon my soul your richest graces that I may love you more and save my soul. I thank you for this love of your Sacred Heart.

Jesus, I thank you for the unspeakable love of your Sacred Heart which makes you dwell *a prisoner* for us in this sacrament day and night. There you reside as a good shepherd who wishes to remain with his flock; as a divine physician who desires ever to be at the bedside of the sick; as a father, full of tenderness, who will never leave his children; as a friend, tried and loving, who finds his delights in being with his dear ones.

I thank you for the love of your Sacred Heart which is ever occupied with our needs of soul and body, and ever bestows on us the *treasures of grace and holiness* which you acquired while on earth.

I thank you for the love of your Sacred Heart which employs your divine omnipotence in working *miracles* in this adorable sacrament, such as changing bread into your body, and wine into your blood in the holy sacrifice of the Mass.

I thank you for the love of your Sacred Heart that moves you *to sacrifice yourself* continually for us, a love which renews the bloody sacrifice of Calvary in an unbloody manner at holy Mass.

I thank you for the love of your Sacred Heart which enriches me not only with gifts and graces, but also *the gift of yourself,* whole and entire, in holy Communion. I thank you, my adorable Redeemer, for all that you give me this morning as an expression of the infinite love of your Sacred Heart: your divine person, your adorable body, your Precious Blood, your holy Soul, with all that you have and are.

Dearest Jesus, I thank you for the love of your Sacred Heart which you show to men as a proof of your goodness even though you receive from them nothing but coldness, indifference, and even hatred. I thank you *for being very patient*—especially with me. Forgive me for my base ingratitude. May this holy Communion be evidence of my sincerest gratitude and my good will to love you in return for your great love for me.

Offering

Dearest heart of Jesus, in return for this proof of you undying love you ask for my own generous whole-hearted love and the entire gift of myself. I offer you my heart, since you have given me yours. To give myself to you is for my own advantage; it is to find the priceless treasure of loving, faithful heart, such as I would wish my own to be. Thus I, who can give nothing, am always receiving.

Eucharistic heart of Jesus, I consecrate to you all the faculties of my soul, and all the powers of my body. I wish to endeavor to know and love you ever more and more, and to make you better known and loved by others. I wish to labor only for your glory and to do only that which your Father wills. I consecrate to you every moment of my life in a spirit of adoration before your divine presence: in thanksgiving for this precious gift; in preparation for my coldness and carelessness; and in unceasing petition, that my prayers offered to you and in you, may ascend, purified and fruitful, to the throne of God's mercy for His eternal glory.

Lord, my generosity is not like yours, but I love you. Be pleased to accept my poor heart, and although it is worth nothing, still it may become something by your grace. Since it loves you, keep it as your own.

Petition

Divine heart of Jesus, you have been so gracious as to come to my heart in holy Communion. What may I not expect from your kindness! You not only know all my wants, but you are also willing and able to relieve them. You have not only invited me, but even promised me your kind help.

I, therefore, present myself before you with that lively confidence which your infinite goodness inspires. I lay before you all my wants, my misery, and my weakness, and I confidently hope without the fear of being disappointed, that you will give me the graces I need for my salvation through this most Blessed Sacrament and through the mercy of your Sacred Heart. I also hope that you will give me the great grace of perseverance until death in your service.

Sweet heart of Jesus, since you delight in dwelling within my soul in the most intimate manner possible, may it be my most intense happiness to welcome you often. The Eucharist is a memorial of the love of your Sacred Heart for me. *By receiving this sacrament frequently, I desire to give you the best expression of my love and gratitude for your great gift of yourself to me.*

Make holy Communion affect me deeply. I believe it is as necessary for the life of my soul as the food I eat is for the life of my body and that there is no better way to remain good than to receive you frequently. May holy Communion be an effective remedy for my human weakness, and strong preventive against mortal sin, a powerful means of taking away my venial sins, and a most necessary nourishment for virtue. Holy Communion is truly the greatest gift you have given me to enable me to reach heaven and you. Dearest Sacred Heart, make these wonders take place in my soul through frequent holy Communion!

May your coming to me work a great change in my soul. May my soul be refreshed with this bread of angels to strengthen my faith, to support my hope, and to increase my love for God and my neighbor. Make my heart holy and good. Let me give you abundantly of my love. It is small return for all you give me. Help me to make good use of all opportunities to receive you into my heart. Let me never allow creatures to hold in my heart the place that should be reserved for you. Sacred Heart of Jesus, give me the grace to live and die for love of you.

Saturday: In Union With The Immaculate Heart of Mary

BEFORE COMMUNION

To Jesus

My Jesus, how utterly helpless am I to prepare a worthy dwelling for you in my soul. I cannot offer you the faith and humility, the love and ardent desires which you have a right to expect from me.

I renounce myself and all that is evil in me, and I am heartily sorry that I have ever offended you, my highest good. I take refuge in her whom you have always loved, Mary, your Mother, whom you have given me as my Mother also. In union with her I will receive you into my heart.

Jesus, Eternal Wisdom, splendor of the Father, you are the Word of God, by whom all things were created. I adore you. I earnestly beg you to come to me. Come to dwell in the place of your choice, the heart of Mary, the paradise of delights. She has adorned my soul with her virtues and her merits. I shall adore you as my beloved brother in the arms of your Mother. There I shall love you with all my heart.

> Savior God, possess my heart,
>> From it nevermore to part;
> Earthly pleasures make it chill,
>> Thou alone the void canst fill.

> Mary's voice pleads with my own;
>> Her fond love shall be thy throne.
> See her heart resplendent shine,
>> Canst thou such a plea decline?

> Well I know that Mary's name
>> All thy fondest love can claim.
> Come then, to my heart and reign;
>> Come, dear Savior, and remain.

> Jesus, Jesus, come to me,
>> All my longing is for thee,
> Of all friends the best thou art,
>> Make of me thy counterpart.

Dearest Lord, I live for thee,
    Son of God, I die for thee;
Jesus, I belong to thee,
    Now and all eternity.

Comfort my poor soul distressed,
    Come and dwell within my breast.
Oh, how oft I long for thee,
    Jesus, Jesus, come to me.

To Mary

Mary, my Mother, I am now about to become the sanctuary of Jesus. But what a poor dwelling I offer to the King of heaven! Receive Him in me and be to Him a dwelling-place. He finds His pleasure and delight wherever you are; even the stable of Bethlehem was delightful to Him because of your presence. He will be pleased to take up His abode in my soul, if He finds His dear Mother there.

Come, dearest Mother; give me your pure, loving heart in place of mine, so cold and guilty. Adorn me with your virtues and merits, and Jesus will find in my soul the perfect preparation which your soul offered Him at the moment of His Incarnation, and which He found there also after His Ascension, when you received Him in holy Communion. What happiness for me to be able to give you Jesus, the same gift the Heavenly Father gave you on the day of the Incarnation, and which He found there also after His Ascension, when you received Him in holy Communion.

Immaculate Heart of Mary, I offer you Jesus, your Son, the King of angels and of men. Through Jesus and in Jesus I wish to honor, love, and thank you worthily for the many graces and mercies you have shown me during life.

Mary, lend me your heart; help me to love my God. Help me to prepare my poor heart to receive Jesus.

Most chaste Virgin Mary, I beg you by that unspotted purity wherewith you have prepared for the Son of God a dwelling of delights in your virginal womb, that by your intercession I may be cleansed from every stain.

Most humble Virgin Mary, I beg you by that most profound humility whereby you merited to be raised high above all the choirs of angels and saints, that by your intercession all my negligences may be expiated.

Most amiable Virgin Mary, I beg you by that great love which united you so closely and inseparably to God, that by your intercession I may obtain an abundance of all merits.

Dearest Mother Mary, pray that my union with Jesus may daily grow more and more intimate. Spouse of the Holy Spirit, pray that the same Holy Spirit may be here on earth transform me in and through your Immaculate Heart into a living image of the Sacred Heart of Jesus. Amen.

To Our Lady of the Blessed Sacrament

O Virgin Mary, Our Lady of the most holy sacrament, glory of the Christian people, joy of the universal Church, SALVATION OF THE WORLD, pray for us and grant to all the faithful true devotion to the most holy Eucharist, that they may become worthy to receive it daily.

AFTER COMMUNION

To Jesus

My Jesus, God of my heart, you have now come to me in holy Communion with your divinity and humanity. You have lowered yourself to me. You are in me and I in you. I thank you for making this union of love and grace possible.

My dearest Jesus, I lead you into the sacred sanctuary of the most pure heart of Mary, your Mother and mine. Behold, this heart is open to receive you.

I give you to the Immaculate Heart of Mary: first and above all, for your greater honor and glory, and to please your loving heart; secondly, in order to thank this good Mother for all she has done for me, and to honor her as much as I can; thirdly, that you may remain in me, my Jesus, and that I may not lose you again by sin, but that, supported by Mary's love and grace, I may persevere in your love and friendship. In this manner my temporal and eternal union with you will be more easily secured.

What a privilege is mine. Jesus, you are in me and at the same time in Mary. You repose in me and at the same time in the heart of Mary, just as you repose after the consecration upon the altar.

Jesus, Son of the most blessed Virgin, I offer myself to you with all that I am and all that I have. I consecrate to you my body with all its senses, my soul with all its faculties, my heart with all its affections. As Mary, your glorious and virginal Mother, always acknowledged herself the humble handmaid of the Lord, so do I also wish to serve you, faithfully and joyfully, to the end of my life.

And that my consecration may be more pleasing to you, I unite it with the fidelity and willingness of her loving heart. Jesus, you humbled yourself to become our brother through Mary; through the effective intercession of your holy Mother grant that I may ever bear you, my God, in my heart. Amen.

Sacred Heart of Jesus, I give myself to you through Mary.

> Only a veil between me and thee,
> > Jesus, my Lord!
> A veil of bread it appears to me,
> Yet seemeth such that I may not see,
> > Jesus, my God!

> Lift not the veil between me and thee,
> > Jesus, my Lord!
> These eyes of earth can never see
> the glory of thy divinity,
> > Jesus, my God!

> Keep then the veil between me and thee,
> > Jesus, my Lord!
> Some day 'twill fall when my soul is free
> To gaze on thee for eternity,
> > Jesus, my God!

Till then may love keep me near to thee,
  Jesus, my Lord!
That day for day my own life may be
Thy Eucharist, pledge of love to me,
  Jesus, my God!

May that thin veil between me and thee,
  Jesus, my Lord!
Teach me to know of thy love for me,
And draw me close to be one with thee,
  Jesus, my God!

With Mother Mary I'll cling to thee,
  Jesus, my Lord!
With her devotion I'll learn to kneel
Before this veil and thy love to feel,
  Jesus, my God!

To Mary

Mary, my dearest mother, behold I have Him in my heart whom you have conceived of the Holy Spirit, whom you have brought forth and carried in your arms. He is my guest, my God, the life and bliss of my soul. From you, the most pure virgin, he assumed flesh and blood, that He might redeem me and become the food of my soul. You are truly Our Lady of the most Blessed Sacrament, because you have given me the eucharistic Christ. It is your Son who abides with me in the tabernacle as the best friend I have in this world, who offers Himself to the Father for me as the victim of Calvary at holy Mass, who gives Himself to me as food in holy Communion.

And now, most blessed Virgin Mary, perform your task for which I have given you Jesus in holy Communion. Praise, glorify, and thank Jesus for me. He is my supreme good in the Blessed Sacrament. Render Him adoration, such as all angels and men together are unable to render. Love him without measure; pay homage to Him, such as you alone are able to give. Meanwhile, I can do nothing better than withdraw myself into the abyss of my nothingness and love my God with the love of your own Immaculate Heart, as I repeat the beautiful hymn of thanksgiving which you uttered at your visit to Elizabeth.

"The Magnificat"

Our Lady's Hymn of Praise
  My soul magnifies the Lord, and my spirit rejoices in God my
   savior;
  Because he has regarded the lowliness of His handmaid; for
   behold, henceforth all generations shall call me blessed;
  Because He who is mighty has done great things for me, and
   holy is His Name;
  And His mercy is from generation to generation on those who
   fear Him.

He has shown might with His arm; He has scattered the proud in
the conceit of their heart.
He has put down the mighty from their thrones and has exalted
the lowly.
He has filled the hungry with good things, and the rich He has
sent away empty.
He has given help to Israel, His servant, mindful of His mercy—
Even as He spoke to our fathers, to Abraham and to His posterity
forever.
Glory be to the Father and to the Son and to the Holy Ghost,
As it was in the beginning, is now and ever shall be, world
without end. Amen.

Immaculate Heart of Mary, I believe that you are the shortest and surest way to the heart of the eucharistic Christ. Mary, my Mother, I beg you to lead me to my sacramental Jesus. Make me like Jesus through frequent holy Communion, because then only shall I resemble your own Immaculate Heart.

I come to you with childlike confidence and earnestly beg you to take me under your powerful protection. Grant me a place in your loving motherly heart. I place my immortal soul into your hands and give you my own poor heart.

Mary, show yourself my Mother; I desire to be your child and to serve you all my life. Look upon me with kind eyes when I waver; support me when I am about to fall; lead me when my steps falter; protect me when temptation approaches; and strengthen me when danger threatens my soul. You remained with your divine Son unto His death on the cross; remain also with me, your child, until death, that I may obtain the grace to behold, and eternally to praise you and your divine Son in heaven. Amen.

A Short Form of Devotion

BEFORE HOLY COMMUNION

Faith
Lord Jesus Christ, you have said, "My flesh is food indeed, and my blood is drink indeed." I firmly believe that you are present in this Blessed Sacrament as true God and true man, with your body and blood, soul and divinity. My Redeemer and my Judge, together with the angels and saints I adore your divine majesty. I believe, O Lord; increase my faith.

Hope
Good Jesus, in you alone I place all my hope. You are my salvation and my strength, the source of all good. Through your mercy and through your Passion and death, I hope to obtain the pardon of my sins, the grace of final perseverance, and a happy eternity.

Love
Jesus, my God, I love you with my whole heart and above all things, because you are the one supreme good and an infinitely perfect being. You have given your life for

me, a poor sinner, and in your mercy you have even offered yourself as food for my soul. My God, I love you. Inflame my heart so that I may love you more.

Contrition

O my Savior, I am truly sorry for having offended you because you are infinitely good and sin displeases you. Detesting all the sins of my life, I desire to atone for them. Through the merits of your precious blood, wash from my soul all stain of sin, so that, cleansed on body and soul, I may worthily approach the Most Holy Sacrament of the Altar.

Desire

Jesus, my God and my all, my soul longs for you. My heart yearns to receive you in holy Communion. Come, bread of heaven and food of angels, to nourish my soul and to rejoice my heart. Come, most lovable friend of my soul, to inflame me with such love that I may never again by separated from you.

Humility

"Lord, I am not worthy that you should enter under my roof." The thought of my unworthiness makes me cry out, "Depart from me, O Lord, for I am a sinner," but your kind invitation to approach your holy table encourages me and dispels all my fears. Come, take possession of a heart that wishes to belong to you alone. Jesus, Come!

AFTER HOLY COMMUNION

Faith

Jesus, I firmly believe that you are present within me as God and man, to enrich my soul with graces and to fill my heart with the happiness of the blessed. I believe that you are Christ, the Son of the living God!

Adoration

With deepest humility I adore you, my Lord and my God; you have made my soul your dwelling place. I adore you as my creator from whose hands I came and with whom I am to be happy forever.

Love

Dear Jesus, I love you with my whole heart, my whole soul, and with all my strength. May the love of your own Sacred Heart fill my soul and purify it so that I may die to the world for love of you, as you died on the cross for love of me. My God, you are all mine; grant that I may be all yours in time and in eternity.

Thanksgiving

From the depths of my heart I thank you, dear Lord, for your infinite kindness in coming to me. How good you are to me! With your most holy Mother and all the angels and saints, I praise your mercy and generosity towards me, a poor sinner. I thank you for nourishing my soul with your sacred body and precious blood. I will try to show my gratitude to you in the sacrament of your love, by obedience to your holy Commandments, by fidelity to my duties, by kindness to my neighbor, and by an earnest endeavor to become more like you in my daily conduct.

B.40

Offering

Jesus, since you have given yourself to me, let me give myself to you. I give you my body, that it may be chaste and pure. I give you my soul, that it may be free from sin. I give you my heart, that it may always love you. I give you every thought, word, and deed of my life, and I offer everything for your honor and glory.

Petitions

Jesus, since you have come to me to grant me graces, and since you have told me to ask with confidence, permit me to ask for some special favors.(Mention them.)

Give me also a full pardon and remission of the guilt of all my sins, which I once more detest with all my heart, and remit the temporal punishment which is due for them. Detach my heart from all created things, fashion it after your own most Sacred Heart, and unite it forever to yourself in the bonds of perfect love.

Jesus, help me in time of temptation. May I lead a good life and die a happy death. May I receive you before I die.

In Union with the Church Prayers After Holy Communion

Prayer Before a Crucifix

Look down upon me, good and gentle Jesus, while before your face I humbly kneel, and with burning soul pray and beseech you to fix deep in my heart lively sentiments of faith, hope, and charity, true contrition for my sins, and a firm purpose of amendment; while I contemplate with great love and tender pity your five wounds, pondering over them within me, calling to mind the words which David, your prophet, said of you, my good Jesus: "They have pierced my hands and my feet; they have numbered all my bones."

Prayer to Christ, the King

O Christ Jesus, I acknowledge you king of the universe. All that has been created has been made for you. Exercise upon me all your rights. I renew my baptismal promises, renouncing Satan and all his works and pomps. I promise to live a good Christian life and to do all in my power to procure the triumph of the rights of God and your Church.

Divine heart of Jesus, I offer you my poor actions in order to obtain that all hearts may acknowledge your sacred royalty, and that thus the reign of your peace may be established throughout the universe. Amen.

Anima Christi
    Soul of Christ, sanctify me
    Body of Christ, save me.
    Blood of Christ, inebriate me.
    Water from the side of Christ, wash me.
    Passion of Christ, strengthen me.
    O good Jesus, hear me.
    Within your wounds hide me.
    Suffer me not to be separated from you.
    From the malicious enemy defend me.
    In the hour of my death call me.
    And bid me come to you,

That with your saints I may praise you,
For ever and ever. Amen.

PART 2—NOVENA OF HOLY COMMUNIONS

HOW TO MAKE THE NOVENA

Since the sacraments are a God-given means of grace, and the holy Eucharist the greatest and holiest of the sacraments, no novena can be more fruitful than a novena of holy Communions. Holy Communion gives you the very author and source of all graces. Not only will you become holier and happier by receiving holy Communion often, but it is also a guarantee that your prayers will be heard, if it is God's will, for Jesus said, *"If you abide in me, and if my words abide in you, ask whatever you will and it shall be done to you" (John 15,7)*. Therefore, no prayer can be more effective than that said after holy Communion, when Jesus is present in your heart as God and man, as you best friend, ready to help you by means of the many graces He wishes to grant you.

Receive holy Communion on nine consecutive days of the week, that is, one after the other, or on nine Sundays IN PETITION for a special favor. Then make another novena of Communions immediately afterwards IN THANKSGIVING, even if you have not received the favor you prayed for. Your prayers at holy Communion were answered—perhaps not your way, but God's way; and He knows best!

If you are receiving holy Communion on nine Sundays, you need not go to confession before each holy Communion (though it is very good to do so), unless you are sure you have committed a mortal sin. Venial sins should not keep you from receiving, but make an act of perfect contrition and approach the holy table without fear. It is advisable, however, to go to confessions at least every two or three weeks.

Novena Prayer
(To be said each day of the Novena)

Jesus, my eucharistic Friend, accept this Novena of holy Communions which I am making in order to draw closer to your dear heart in sincerest love and to save my soul. If it should be your holy will, grant the special favor for which I am making this Novena. *(Mention you request)*

Jesus, you said, *"Ask, and it shall be given you; seek, and you shall find; knock, and it shall be opened to you"* (Matt. 7,7). Through the intercession of your most holy Mother, Our Lady of the most Blessed Sacrament, I ask, I seek, I knock. I beg of you to grant my request. Grant my prayer!

Jesus, you said *"If you ask the Father anything in my name, He will give it to you"* (John 16,23). Through the intercession of your most holy Mother, Our Lady of the most Blessed Sacrament, I ask the Father in your name to grant my prayer.

Jesus, you said, *"If you ask me anything in my name, I will do it"* (John 14,14). Through the intercession of your most holy Mother, Our Lady of the most Blessed Sacrament, I ask you in your name to grant my prayer.

Jesus, you said, *"If you abide in me, and if my words abide in you, ask whatever you will and it shall be done to you"* (John 15,7). Through the intercession of your most holy Mother, Our Lady of the most Blessed Sacrament, may my request be granted, for I wish to abide in you through frequent holy Communion.

Lord, I believe that I can do nothing better to obtain the favor I desire than to attend holy Mass and to unite myself most intimately with you, the source of all graces, in holy Communion. When you are really and truly present in my soul as God and man, my confidence is greatest, for you *want* to help me, because you are all-good; you *know how* to help me, because you are all-wise; you *can* help me, because you are all-powerful. Most Sacred Heart of Jesus, I believe in your love for me!

Jesus, as a proof of my sincerest gratitude, I promise to receive you in holy Communion as often as I am able to do so—at every holy Mass I attend, if possible. Help me to love you in the holy Eucharist as my greatest treasure upon earth. May the effects of frequent holy Communion help me to serve you faithfully, that I may save my soul and be with you forever in heaven. Amen.

FIRST DAY: CHRIST-LIKENESS

1. *Jesus, I believe that you make me Christlike by giving me in holy Communion and increase of sanctifying grace, the very life of my soul.* This grace makes me share in your own divine life, for you said: "He who eats my flesh, and drinks my blood, abides in me and I in him" (John 6,57). Just as the heavenly Father gives you His divinity, His power, His goodness, His life, from all eternity, so do you give me your divine life in holy Communion. As the stem and the branches of a vine are one and the same being, nourished and acting together, producing the same fruits because they are fed by the same sap, so too you circulate your divine life of grace in my soul through holy Communion in such a way that I live by your life and really become Christlike. "As the branch cannot bear fruit of itself unless it remain in the vine, so neither can you unless you abide in me" (John 15,4).

How marvelous is the fruit of sanctifying grace! It makes my soul holy, beautiful and pleasing to God, a sacred temple of the Holy Spirit. It not only makes me an adopted child of God, but also helps me to act as another Christ. It gives me the right to enter heaven, for without grace I can never see God.

Lord, help me to appreciate sanctifying grace. May it mean more to me than everything else on earth. People seek riches, honor, and beauty; but I know, dear Jesus, that there is nothing on earth that equal the riches of the sanctifying grace contained in one holy Communion; that there is nothing more beautiful than a soul adorned with grace. The more grace I have, the holier and happier I shall be in time and in eternity, for by grace I know you more clearly, I love you more sincerely, and I possess you more securely.

How precious is this union between my soul and you, my God and my all! This union is made possible by the love of your Sacred Heart and is effected by the grace I received at holy Communion. Let me hate and shun whatever may put me in danger of losing sanctifying grace through mortal sin.

2. *Jesus, I believe you make me Christlike not only by giving me sanctifying grace at holy Communion, but also by giving me actual graces*—helps from above—to preserve your divine life in my soul. Through these helps given me at holy Communion and in time of need, my mind receives the light to see and my will the strength to do what is right and avoid what is wrong.

Through frequent holy Communion help me to think and desire, speak and act like you. Make my thoughts upright, my desires pure, my words kind, my actions holy. As you are the image of the Eternal Father, let me try to be as closely as possible the image of you. Detach my heart from myself and from everything created, so that I may give myself to you with my whole heart as you give yourself to me. In this sacred union may your love and mine, your thoughts and mine, become one for the glory of God and the salvation of my soul. May your spirit rule me so completely that you alone may be the aim and the ideal of my life. Amen.

SECOND DAY: MARY-LIKENESS

1.   Jesus in the Sacrament of the Altar, you are the one source of my holiness; therefore, my aim should be to reach you. I am holy only in so far as I become like you and belong to you through perfect love. Of myself I am poor and helpless. For this reason you gave me, in your last moments on the cross, your own dear Mother so that she might be my very own.

No one ever belonged to you so completely as did your Mother. You spent the longest part of your life on earth in her company, but you lived in her by your love and grace more intimately than you do in all the angels and saints. I wish to imitate your example; I wish to belong entirely to your dear Mother, for this is your will. *I give everything I have to Mary, in order that through her hands I may give all to you for your greatest glory.*

2.   *Jesus, I wish to imitate your Mother especially in her devotion to you in the Blessed Sacrament of the Altar.* That devotion summarizes her last years on earth. How fervently she united herself with you as St. John daily offered the holy sacrifice of the Mass in his own home. She saw the sacrifice of Calvary repeated before her very eyes, though now in an unbloody manner. With what ardent love she received you into her heart daily in holy Communion! It was the same body she had conceived of the Holy Spirit at the Annunciation, the infant body she had carried in her arms at Bethlehem, the bleeding body she had seen hanging in torments upon the cross and Calvary, the glorified body which had ascended triumphantly into heaven. What emotion she must have felt as she knelt before the tabernacle and recalled all those happy and sorrowful events of her life with you! Her faith and love pierced the thin veil which separated her from you.

Help me to imitate Mary as Our Lady of the Blessed Sacrament, because she gave you to me. From her, the most pure virgin, you assumed flesh and blood so that you might redeem me and become the food of my soul in holy Communion.

Lord, at holy Communion I become your sanctuary, but what a poor dwelling I offer you, the king of heaven and earth! May you ever find your Mother Mary in my heart when I receive you! You find your delight wherever she is. She will adore and love you within me and offer her Immaculate Heart to be your dwelling place. Do not behold my wretched soul, but rather the virtues and merits of your dear Mother to whom I belong.

I realize that I cannot be a true child of Mary, nor can I be like Mary unless I have a very tender devotion to you in the Sacrament of the Altar. I can do nothing that would please you or her more than to be Mary-like in my devotion to the holy Eucharist, for Mary is the shortest and surest and easiest way to your eucharistic heart. May the holy Eucharist be my treasure as it was hers. May frequent holy Communion make me Mary-like in order that I may become more Christlike! Amen.

THIRD DAY: JOYFULNESS

1.   *Jesus, I believe that holy Communion is the surest way to true joy, because it*

unites me in divine love with you, my greatest and most lovable good. True joy springs from divine love. How earnestly you invite me to this banquet of divine love which you prepared for my soul that I might partake of your own body and blood! "Come to me, all you who labor and are burdened, and I will give you rest" (Matt. 11,28). As bread imparts to the body strength and a feeling of contentment, so does the bread of life bring peace and joy to my heart because of the wonderful fruits of grace which it produces in my soul. At holy Communion there is opened to me a world of life, light, and love, a gracious outpouring of the treasures of your Sacred Heart.

The moments of union with you in holy Communion are the happiest of my life. Holy Communion is the climax of your divine love for me, and it should, therefore, be the object of my fondest desires. You have made my heart for yourself. It yearns to be with you and to possess you even here on earth, so that it may prepare itself for an eternal union with you in heaven. At holy Communion I enjoy a foretaste of heaven, for I receive your glorified body and blood, your soul and divinity.

You have encouraged me to pray for this spiritual joy when you said: "Ask and you shall receive, that your joy may be full" (John 16,24). I pray for the grace to love holy Communion as the source of true happiness that your words to the apostles may be fulfilled in me through holy Communion: "You therefore have sorrow now; but I will see you again, and your heart shall rejoice, and your joy no one shall take from you" (John 16,22). In holy Communion I can see you with eyes of faith, and my heart will rejoice. This is the true and lasting joy which neither the world nor the powers of evil can take from me. Preserve my soul from sin, the cause of all unhappiness in this world, since it deprives souls of your friendship.

2. *Jesus, may frequent holy Communion fill my heart with joyfulness that will make serving you a pleasure even in the midst of the greatest sacrifices.* Suffering may be my portion in life, but holy Communion is my comfort. It is a fulfillment of your words: "Blessed are they who mourn, for they shall be comforted" (Matt. 5,5).

Holy Communion fills my soul with many graces which are the source of true joy. At this fount of joy I find the strength and courage to undertake great things for your glory and the welfare of my neighbor. Holy Communion is the foundation of my faith, the support of my hope, the nourishment of my charity, the best means I have of sanctifying and saving my soul. My heart is filled with heavenly bliss because you make it your little heaven of delights when you visit me in holy Communion. With your own dear Mother I thank you for this great treasure: "My soul magnifies the Lord, and my spirit rejoices in God my savior...because He who is mighty has done great things for me" (Luke 1,47). Amen.

FOURTH DAY: PRAYERFULNESS

1. Jesus, *you gave me prayer as an unfailing means of salvation and holiness, and you promised that my prayers would be heard.* "All things whatsoever you ask in prayer, believe that you shall receive, and they shall come to you" (Mark 11,24). But this will take place on the condition that I abide in you, for you also said, "If you abide in me, and if my words abide in you, ask whatever you will and it shall be done to you" (John 15,7).

"Abide in me, and I in you" was your farewell appeal for my love the night before you died. It is through love that we abide in each other. "As the Father has loved me, I also have loved you. Abide in my love" (John 15,9). In no other way can I be more intimately united with you in divine love than by the sacrament of your love. The special effect of holy Communion is that it makes me grow in my love for you by giving me an increase of sanctifying grace. Through love, you take possession of my whole being.

Lord, through holy Communion help me to love you, with my whole *heart*—with undivided love, so that I may love nothing created except for your sake.

Through holy Communion help me to love you with my whole *soul*—with all my inclinations. Make me hate sin above every other evil, for only then will my soul be well disposed and blessed with your peace.

Through holy Communion help me to love you with my whole *mind* so that I may value your good pleasure, your grace, your heaven, above everything else—above my convenience, above all earthly treasures, above all knowledge and friendship, above health and life.

Through holy Communion help me to love you with all my *strength* so that my body and soul may be consecrated to you and your service.

Lord, the Eucharist is the most wonderful work of your love. Out of infinite love you have given me not only what you have, but what you are. At holy Communion you give me your body, your blood, your soul, your divinity, your merits, and your graces. Nowhere do you bestow these graces more abundantly than in this sacrament. May such love awaken a return of love in my heart!

2. Jesus, I want to receive you in holy Communion more frequently *so that I may abide in you and you in me. Then will my prayers be truly powerful,* because they will come from a heart that is one with your own in deepest love and friendship, I shall pray to the Father in your name, and I shall be heard. "If you ask the Father anything in my name, He will give it to you" (John 16,23).

I can do nothing better than to present my prayers to you after holy Communion. These moments are most precious, because then you are with me as God and man for the very purpose of helping me and making me holy. You have promised to hear my prayer, "If you ask me anything in my name, I will do it" (John 14,14). You come to my soul to apply to me the merits of your most holy life, of your painful sufferings, of your most bitter death. You come to enrich me with your heavenly treasures, to make my body pure and my soul holy, and to help me live a life more like your own. May frequent holy Communion teach me prayerfulness and make me less unworthy of receiving your favors. Amen.

FIFTH DAY: KINDNESS

1. Jesus, when you were about to depart from this world, you said, "This is my commandment that you love one another as I have loved you" (John 15,12). You loved me even unto death: "Greater love than this no one has, that one lay down his life for his friends" (John 15,13). Help me to imitate your example by loving my neighbor with a love more like your own, for you said, "By this will all men know that you are my disciples if you have love for one another" (John 13,35).

I believe that holy Communion preserves and increases this love for my neighbor. It is a banquet of love which you have prepared for the children of God. Many grains of wheat are ground and mingled together to make one bread, and many grapes are crushed to fill the eucharistic chalice; in like manner you would have us become one through love and holy Communion. I believe that the Eucharist is the bond of charity that unites all Christians as members of one spiritual body, the Church, even as the soul gives life to each member of the human body.

2. *Jesus, through frequent holy Communion help me to carry out your great commandment of love for my neighbor and give me the grace to put away all unkindness.* I want to love my neighbor as myself for your sake. Let me respect and love him as God's image and likeness, as a child of our heavenly Father, as the temple of the Holy Spirit. You love him as you love me, and you give yourself to him in holy Communion as you give yourself to me. In fact, you identify yourself with him, for you said, "As long as you did it for one of these, the least of my brethren, you did if for me" (Matt. 25,40). How can I disrespect one whom you respect so highly? How can I be unkind and unforgiving to one for whom you offered your life on the cross? I cannot receive you into a heart that refuses to forgive. This would make me undeserving of your mercy, for you said, "Forgive and you shall be forgiven; give and it shall be given to you" (Luke 6,37).

Lord, give me the grace to partake of this banquet of love frequently so that the merciful love of your own heart may be enkindled in mine. I cannot love God truly unless I also love my neighbor, nor can I love my neighbor as I ought unless I truly love God. Increase both loves in my heart through holy Communion. May that divine charity be poured out upon your holy Church through the sacrament of your love so that your prayer at the Last Supper may be fulfilled: "That they may be one, even as we are one: I in them and thou in me; that they may be perfected in unity" (John 17,22). Amen.

SIXTH DAY: SINLESSNESS

1. Jesus, I believe that mortal sin is the greatest evil in the world because it turns me away from God, the source of all life, peace, and joy. Mortal sin causes spiritual death, and through it alone the devil can destroy your work of grace in my soul.

You teach me that *the main effect of holy Communion is to preserve and increase the life of sanctifying grace in my soul and to guard it against mortal sin.* "This is the bread that comes down from heaven, so that if anyone eat of it, he will not die" (John 6,50). Holy Communion also imparts *actual* graces which give light and strength: light to my mind that I may see the evil which I must shun, and strength to my will that I may fight against it.

Lord, I believe that after mortal sin nothing is more terrible than *venial sin.* It really offends your infinite majesty and brings me the punishments of purgatory. It banishes true joy from my heart because it draws me away from you, my highest good. Venial sin is an ugly stain which makes my soul displeasing in your sight. It hinders you from enriching me with so many more graces which could help me to love and serve you better.

I thank you for holy Communion, which washes away the stains of venial sin so long as I have no affection for it or desire to commit it in the future. Your coming to me awakens new love in my heart and encourages me to live in purity and sinlessness for your glory alone.

One holy Communion should be enough to make my soul holy and sinless, and yet, after so many Communions, I have not succeeded in correcting my faults. It is because I have not received holy Communion with greater fervor and more frequently, though you assure me that I cannot keep my soul alive—free from mortal sin—without holy Communion. "Unless you eat the flesh of the Son of Man, and drink His blood, you shall not have life in you" (John 6,54). Help me to receive your sacred flesh and blood in holy Communion often—at every Mass I attend, if possible—so that my soul may be sinless.

2. Jesus, *I beg you to cleanse and sanctify my body,* which is privileged to enshrine your own sacred body in holy Communion. Make it a fitting dwelling for the victim-body which was born of the Virgin Mary and sacrificed to atone for my sins.

With the poor leper I cry out to you, "Lord, if thou wilt, thou canst make me clean." Stretch forth your hand and touch me also in holy Communion and say, "I will; be thou made clean." (Matt. 8, 2–3).

Wash in your redeeming blood all the sinfulness of *my soul;* make it beautiful with the sinlessness of the angels. Sinlessness is a reflection of your own divine beauty. It draws your heart in loving friendship.

Lord, I beg you to remain close to me when I am tempted; do not permit any serious sin ever to separate me from you, or even lesser sins to weaken your friendship. Strengthen my soul by the power of your grace, that I may courageously resist all evil. I should fear nothing, for I am equipped with the strongest spiritual weapon, holy Communion. If you are with me, who can be against me?

Grant that my conscience may never be defiled by any evil thought, desire, word, or deed. Let me rather die than offend you by a willful mortal sin. Lamb of God, who takest away the sins of the world, have mercy on me! Through holy Communion make me sinless and pure of heart so that I may see God! Amen.

SEVENTH DAY: LOWLINESS

1. Jesus, you have always been my model and teacher of humility. You gave me many an example by word and deed during your earthly life. You said, "Take my yoke upon you, and learn from me, for I am meek and humble of heart; and you will find rest for your souls" (Matt. 11,29).

How great is your humility in this sacrament! Though you are the eternal and almighty God, you have lowered yourself, taking the form of man for love of me and for the sake of my salvation. Not only have you become my elder brother, a fellow-creature, but you have willed to be the very food of my soul in holy Communion. Once your human form covered your divinity, but now the appearances of bread hide even your humanity. I can see you only with the eyes of faith.

How humbly you obey your priests! One word from their lips and you come down upon the altar in holy Mass and renew the sacrifice of Calvary in an unbloody manner. You permit your priest to give you as the bread of life to those who come to the holy table; you do not shrink even from the unworthy. You allow yourself to be carried wherever your priests bear you. Heaven and earth are subject to you, O King of Glory, and yet you lower yourself before your sinful creatures—living with them in the sacred Host, offering yourself for them, coming to their hearts in holy Communion.

Lord, the greatest test of humility is the pain of not receiving love for love, and that, too, you bear. In this sacrament you live entirely for me. Your unbounded love urges you to unite yourself with me in holy Communion. You long to enrich me with your blessings and to gladden my soul. And yet what do I give you in return? What do so many of us Catholics do to return love for love? How many of us pay little attention to your invitation and fail to receive you in holy Communion frequently? Too often we are cold and ungrateful, unmindful of your love, halfhearted or even irreverent at Mass and holy Communion! You patiently bear with all this indifference. Despite our ingratitude you continue to grant us countless blessings, and thus teach us the noblest kind of humility: to love even when love is not returned and to embrace even humiliations.

2. Jesus, *behold how I am in need of lowliness!* I rely too much upon myself. I freely boast of the little good that is in me as if it were mine by personal merit; whereas, whatever good is in me really comes from you. I seek praise for myself, when I should refer it to you. My pride leads me into many daily faults: to sensitiveness, jealousy, rash judgment, uncharitableness, and anger.

The Eucharist is not only a school of humility, but the channel of graces which enable me to be humble. I wish to receive holy Communion often—at every holy Mass I attend, if possible—so that the power of your grace may conquer my pride. Only after I have become like a lowly child shall I enter your kingdom, for you have said: "Unless you turn and become like little children, you will not enter into the kingdom of heaven. Whoever, therefore, humbles himself as this little child, he is the greatest in the kingdom of heaven" (Matt. 18, 4) Amen.

EIGHTH DAY: UNSELFISHNESS

1. Jesus, you said, "If anyone wished to come after me, let him deny himself, and take up his cross daily and follow me" (Matt 16,24). Teach me to understand the value of suffering, and through holy Communion give me the help I need to bear it joyfully for your sake.

You came upon this earth to glorify your heavenly Father by your life and especially by your death. *I believe that your sacrifice of Calvary is renewed each day in an unbloody manner at holy Mass.* The separate consecration of the bread and wine reminds me of this: "This is my body which is being given for you" (Luke 22,19); "This is my blood which is being shed for many unto the forgiveness of sins" (Matt. 26,28).

You offer yourself to your Father now, though in an unbloody manner, just as you did on the cross. You offer yourself in the same spirit of love and resignation to His holy will, because you are present in the sacred Host as the victim of Calvary. That sacred Host is my food in holy Communion. It is the sacrificial banquet which completes the sacrifice of the Mass. By holy Communion I unite myself with you as you offer yourself again to your Father, and I become one sacrifice with you, for you have said, "He who eats my flesh and drinks my blood abides in me and I in him" (John 6, 57). May holy Communion give me the true spirit of Christlike unselfishness and sacrifice which I need throughout life in order to follow you!

2. Jesus, I believe that holy Communion opens the treasury of all the graces which you merited for me by your bloody death on the cross. Oh, may its richest grace be for

me a most intimate union with you, so *that I may become a living, holy victim, pleasing to God, and that all the actions, sufferings, tears, and disappointments of my life may be thus consecrated to you as a sacrifice for the glory of God.* Can I live for worldly comforts and pleasures after receiving you as the victim of Calvary, as one offered, as a slain, sacrificial lamb of God?

Divine victim of the altar, give me your spirit of unselfishness, for I want to live no more for myself, but for God. Give my heart sentiments like your own so that I may become a worthy co-victim with you through holy Communion. I promise to receive you often and fervently, that I may gradually die to my unworthy desires and inclinations and dedicate myself entirely to your holy service in the spirit in which you glorified God in life, and continue to glorify Him in the Mass.

May God's will always be my will. Thus may each holy Mass and holy Communion make me more and more a living image of you, so that the Heavenly Father, looking upon me, a co-victim with you in holy Communion, may say of me what He said of you, "This is my beloved Son, in whom I am well pleased" (Matt. 17, 5). Amen.

NINTH DAY: EUCHARIST-MINDEDNESS

1. Jesus, I believe that in holy Communion your divine life, which will make my soul live forever, is given to me. This divine bread is the spiritual food of my soul. As food strengthens my body, holy Communion nourishes and strengthens my soul by grace. It gives me the strength I need to overcome all the temptations of the world, the flesh, and the devil. It gives me the help I need to practice virtue.

Since holy Communion means so much for my soul, I can do nothing better than to receive it frequently. It is *your earnest wish* that I do so, because it is in this way that you can most surely save my soul. For this reason you made your apostles priests at the Last Supper and ordered them to offer up holy Mass in your name. Your words: "Take and eat; this is my body," were meant for me also. Since I offer the holy sacrifice together with the priest, I should also receive holy Communion as the priest does, for holy Communion is the sacred banquet to which we are invited that we may take part in this sacrifice. You are present in this sacrament not only to offer yourself *for* me, but also to offer yourself *to* me, to be the food of my soul.

Your holy Church—even as you do—wants me to receive you frequently. She urges me to receive your sacred body at every holy Mass I attend, and thus share most intimately in the divine sacrifice. This was the spirit of the first Christians, and Mother Church would have me imitate them. I, too, wish to be Eucharist-minded and make holy Mass and holy Communion my only treasure in this life.

2. *Jesus, nowhere is your love for me greater than in this sacrament.* Your gift of love to me is nothing less than yourself, whole and entire: your body, blood, soul, and divinity. You are generous, not for your own sake but for the sake of my salvation and happiness. Love for me urged you to leave with me the treasure of holy Communion as a parting gift the night before you died.

Help me to be generous in giving you love for love. My unworthiness and sinfulness should not keep me away for your holy table; rather, conscious of my shortcomings, I should come to you more frequently in order that my soul may be cleansed and sanctified. Only thus shall I become less unworthy of receiving you. Cure my blindness. Give me the grace to overcome my carelessness and lack of faith.

Lord, be my companion through life by frequent holy Communion, especially during the last painful struggle of death. Come in that hour to protect my soul which you bought with your own precious blood, and lead me safely into the home of your Father and mine. Help me to receive each holy Communion as if it were my last. May this be my great devotion in life and my consolation in the hour of death.

Apply the merits of your sacred Passion and death to my poor soul in holy Mass and Communion. I pledge myself to receive you as often as I can—at every Mass I attend, if possible. From now on I am resolved to be more Eucharist-minded. Oh, please give me that grace, for only then can I really become a saint! Amen.

APPENDIX

FROM THE DECREE OF HOLY MOTHER CHURCH ON FREQUENT HOLY COMMUNION

" 'The holy Synod would desire that at every Mass the faithful who are present should communicate not only spiritually, by a loving desire in their hearts, but sacramentally, by the actual reception of the Eucharist' (Coun. of Trent, Sess. 22, ch. 6).

"And this wish of the Council is in entire agreement with that desire wherewith Christ our Lord was inflamed when He instituted this divine sacrament. For He Himself, more than once and in no uncertain terms, pointed out the necessity of eating His flesh and drinking His blood, especially in these words: 'This is the bread that has come down from heaven; not as your fathers ate the manna, and died. He who eats this bread shall live forever' (John 6, 58). Now, from this comparison of the food of angels with bread and with the manna, it was easily to be understood by His disciples that, as the body is daily nourished with bread, and as the Hebrews were daily nourished with manna in the desert, so the Christian soul might daily partake of this heavenly bread and be refreshed by it. Moreover, whereas, in the Lord's Prayer we are urged to ask for 'our daily bread,' the holy fathers of the Church all but unanimously teach that by these words must be understood, not so much that material bread which is the nourishment of the body, as the eucharistic bread, which ought to be our daily food.

"Moreover, the desire of Jesus Christ and of the Church that all the faithful should daily approach the sacred banquet is directed chiefly to this end, that the faithful, being united to God by means of the sacrament, may derive from it strength to resist their sensual passions, to cleanse themselves from the stains of daily faults, and to avoid those graver sins which they may commit through human weakness; so that the main purpose of holy Communion is not that the honor and reverence due to Our Lord may be safeguarded, nor that the sacrament may serve as a reward of virtue bestowed of those who receive it... 'holy Communion is the remedy whereby we are delivered from daily faults, and preserved from mortal sins' (Sess. 13).

"This desire on the part of God (that the faithful should daily approach the sacred banquet) was so well understood by the first Christians, that they daily flocked to the holy table as to a source of life and strength. 'And they continued steadfastly in the teaching of the apostles and in the communion of the breaking of the bread and in the prayers' (Acts 2, 42). And that this practice was to continue into later ages, not without great fruit of holiness and perfection, the holy fathers and ecclesiastical writers bear witness...

"Frequent and daily Communion, as a thing most earnestly desired by Christ our Lord, and by the Catholic Church, should be open to all the faithful of whatever rank and condition of life; so that no one who is in the state of grace and who approaches the holy table with a right and devout intention, can lawfully be hindered.

"A right intention consists in this: that he who approaches the holy table should do so, not out of routine, or vainglory, or human respect, but for the purpose of pleasing God, of being more closely united with Him by love, and of seeking this divine remedy for his weaknesses and defects...

"Although it is more expedient that those who communicate frequently or daily should be free from venial sins, especially from such as are fully deliberate, and from any affection thereto, nevertheless it is sufficient that they be free from mortal sin with the purpose of never sinning mortally in future; and, if they have this sincere purpose, it is impossible that daily communicants should not gradually free themselves from even venial sins, and from all affection to them."

(Decree "Sacra Tridentina Synodus" of Pope Pius X, December 20, 1905.)

HOLY COMMUNION IS YOUR TREASURE

Consider what you lose when you miss one holy Communion:

1. You miss a personal visit with Jesus, the author of all spiritual energy and of all holiness.

2. You lose a special increase of sanctifying grace, that grace which makes your soul more pleasing to God.

3. You lose the sacramental grace which entitles you to special help in times of temptation and in the discharge of your duties.

4. You lose a precious opportunity of having all your venial sins wiped away.

5. You miss the special preserving influence which each holy Communion confers against the fires of passion.

6. You miss the opportunity of obtaining remission of a part or of all of the temporal punishment due to your sins.

7. You lose the spiritual joy, the sweetness, and the particular comfort that come from a fervent holy Communion.

8. You lose a greater degree of glory that would be yours in heaven for all eternity.

9. You may lose:
    a. Complete victory over some fault or passion.
    b. Some particular grace long prayed for.
    c. The conversion or salvation of some soul.
    d. The deliverance of a relative or friend from purgatory.
    e. Many graces for others, both the living and the dead.

Of what riches you deprive yourself daily by neglecting holy Mass! The Mass is the best preparation for holy Communion. At the hour of death your greatest consolation will be the Masses you have heard and the holy Communions you have received.

Pledge yourself to receive holy Communion at least once a week.

Authors by Location

Minnesota
Mallory Hoffman, *North Mankato,* 242
Mary Gigstad, *Sacred Heart,* 276
Tim A. Drake, *Saint Cloud,* 120

Missouri
Fr. Robert H. Blondell, *Macomb TWP,* 14
A. Ruth Talbott, *Springfield,* 66

Montana
Patricia G. Scown, *Butte,* 33
Tom & Lillian Byrne, *Denton,* 8

Nebraska
Annette M.Wurdeman, *Columbus,* 55

New Jersey
Sr. Agnes Valimont, OSC, *Columbus,* 307
Anne Cominskie, *Deptford,* 225
Deacon Bob Thomson, *Edgewater,* 148

New Mexico
Madeleine D. Fisher, *Carlsbad,* 105

New York
Anne M. Costa, *Baldwinsville,* 10
Deacon Robert Campbell, *East Rockaway,* 178
Deacon Rich La Rossa, *East Rockaway,* 227
Heidi J. Guevara, *Holtsville,* 269
Fr. John V. Ahern, *Liverpool,* 4, *237, 239*
Debbie M. Gerard, *Liverpool,* 36
Deacon Edward G. Beckendorf, *Mohegan Lake,* 71
Barbara A. Higgins, *New York,* 17
Robert J. Reddington, *North Bellmore,* 74

North Carolina
Loretta C. Wnetrzak, *Charlotte,* 248
Lynn Oeser, *Durham,* 22
Donna K. Hill, *Goldsboro,* 90

Ohio
Sister Mary Ishmael, CAC, *Canton,* 290
Fr. Nicholas Lohkamp, OFM, *Canton,* 106
Sr. Doris Gerke, OSC, *Cincinnati,* 283
Fr. Jeremy Harrington, OFM, *Cincinnati,* 225
Fr. Mark J. Hudak, OFM, *Cincinnati,* 253
Fr. Pat McCloskey, OFM, *Cincinnati,* 230
Fr. Jeffrey Scheeler, OFM, *Cincinnati,* 64

Sr. Marilyn Trowbridge, OSC, *Cincinnati,* 287
Fr. Jim Vanvurst, *Cincinnati,* 45, 134
Fr. Jack Wintz, OFM, *Cincinnati,* 85
Fr. Clyde Young, OFM, *Cincinnati,* 250
Mother Mary Jude, *Cleveland,* 306
Sr. Marie Christina LaDieu, P.C.C., *Cleveland,* 304
Sr. Marie Louise Pohlman, OSF, *Columbus,* 273
Fr. Norman Langenbrunner, *Fairfield,* 34
Molly N. O'Connell, *Mason,* 89
Maria de la Luz Lozano, M.D., *Olmsted Falls,* 138
Barbara L Barlow, *Reynoldsburg,* 138
Jeanne M. McCale, *Vermilion,* 181

Oklahoma
Coreen V. Marson, *Catoosa,* 25
Lawrence L. Chlebik, *McAlester,* 76
Kathleen M. Ellertson, *Moore,* 107, 209

Oregon
Deacon Francis Potts, MTS, NACC, *Portland,* 13
Joyce A. Iida, *Sixes,* 211
Maureen McNamara, *Tigard,* 177
Fr. Gary L. Zerr, *Tillamook,* 246

Pennsylvania
Shirley J. Bobek, *Fombell,* 114
Eileen Marie Glenn, *Havertown,* 3
Carol Ann Matz, *Hazleton,* 28, 179
Gloria J. Pinsker, *Horsham,* 1
Patricia E. Wolf, SFO, *Hummelstown,* 179
Marian K. Peck, *Lebanon,* 227
Edward M. Butler, *Minersville,* 19
Fr. Anthony Gargotta, *Natrona Heights,* 24, 118, 144, 242
Roberta H. Para-Sefchick, *Prompton,* 194
Jeanne M. Bechtel, *Reading,* 216
Teresa M. Pietruch, *Reading,* 198
Kathy Meyer, *St. Marys,* 96
Jeannie Paslawsky, *Willow Grove,* 275

Rhode Island
Madeleine R. Porter, *Cumberland,* 126
Lynn Y. Francis, *Providence,* 218

INDEX

COMING SOON…

101

Inspirational

Stories

of

Reconciliation